DANGEROUS
COMPANY

DANGEROUS COMPANY

The Consulting Powerhouses and the Businesses They Save and Ruin

JAMES O'SHEA
and
CHARLES MADIGAN

TIMES BUSINESS

RANDOM HOUSE

All rights reserved under International and Pan-American Copyright Conventions. Published in the United States by Times Books, a division of Random House, Inc., New York, and simultaneously in Canada by Random House of Canada Limited, Toronto.

Grateful acknowledgment is made to Michael Rothschild for permission to reprint an excerpt from "The Henderson Revolution" by Michael Rothschild (*Upside* magazine, December 1992). Reprinted by permission of the author.

O'Shea, James (James E.)
     Dangerous company : the secret story of the consulting powerhouses and the corporations they save and ruin / James O'Shea and Charles Madigan.—1st ed.
          p.   cm.
     Includes index.
     ISBN 0-8129-2634-X
     1. Business consultants. I. Madigan, Charles. II. Title.
     HD69.C6084   1997
     001—DC21   96-38019

Random House website address: http://www.randomhouse.com/

Printed in the United States of America on acid-free paper

9 8 7 6 5 4 3 2

First Edition

In memory of John O'Shea and Dorothy O'Shea Hanley
—James O'Shea

To my family
—Charles M. Madigan

CONTENTS

PREFACE

A secretive and elite army of management consultants is at work deep inside corporations everywhere, from the giants of the Fortune 500 to middle-sized and smaller companies. It is also expanding its influence all over the developing world, wherever economies are coming to life. And it has become partner to government, adviser to heads of state, and confidant to countless interests eager to exploit the promise of a growing world economy. It collects top dollar for its work, sometimes delivering all the sparkle and success it promises, and sometimes failing so remarkably that its clients seem more victim than customer. A relative newcomer to the world of business, management consulting has escaped all but the most cursory levels of scrutiny. It has only good things to say about itself. But there is a growing sense of unease about this exploding, and occasionally explosive, enterprise, a feeling that it is a palace built on a foundation of shifting sand. From a distance, it glistens like alabaster. Up close, a different image emerges. It centers on a key question: "Whose interest is being served?" All too often, the answer is that it is not the best interest of the client.

Dangerous Company is the first detailed examination of the business of management consulting, the closest look to date at what goes right, what goes wrong, who gets the benefits, and who pays the price. It presents a set of object lessons for every troubled employee who has seen his career end with a pink slip and an exit interview, every middle manager who has ever bristled at the arrogance of outsiders who move with a blind and sometimes fatal certainty. It is a book about wrongheaded conspiracies at the top, flubbed assumptions, brilliant performances, and many varieties of what businessmen of another era would have called "just plain foolishness." Most of all, *Dangerous Company* is a cautionary tale aimed at managers. Consultants invariably insist that their potential clients cannot live without their services. It is the most important part of the pitch and the glittering sharp end of the hook at the same time. "Do It My Way or Fail" might be the message reduced to its essence. The record presents a different reality. Crack the facade of management consulting and it becomes apparent that the growing suspicion and skepticism about this most aggressive of business services is warranted.

The decision to bring in management consultants is one that can place at stake the careers of the very people who hire them, the jobs of thousands of employees, millions upon millions of dollars invested by shareholders, and long-term relationships with customers. Indeed, the most valuable asset a corporation has, its reputation, can be put on the line. And all these risks are connected to the motivation of outsiders whose primary interest frequently is in fattening the treasuries of their consulting partnerships.

What separates the consulting success from the consulting disaster? That was one of the central questions posed during the two years of research that led to *Dangerous Company*. The answers are here, embodied in the stories of what has worked and what has not. At its heart, the dark side of consulting is about losing control and the bright side is about keeping close watch on what consultants are actually doing as opposed to what consultants say they do. That is the strongest message from managers who have used consultants well, and the most apparent message from those who have not.

Dangerous Company was never intended as an encyclopedic collection of all of consulting and what it has to offer. Instead, the authors looked for revealing situations, cases that present the realities that define the business. Some of the choices were obvious. McKinsey & Co., for example, has played such a central role in the development of the industry that inclusion in the research was mandatory. Andersen Consulting, because of its size and its connection to technology, seemed the perfect template for the accounting-giant-become-consulting-giant story. Because it reflected such a tale of disaster, the Figgie company's relationship with its consultants presented a strong cautionary tale. Sears, Roebuck & Co.'s sophisticated, limited, and surgical use of consultants presented the model of how the process can work to everyone's advantage. Gemini Consulting and its relationship with an insurance giant and a small hospital was a case study in a sweeping consulting philosophy that was hot in the marketplace for a brief time, but that cooled so much that Gemini found itself in deep trouble. Boston Consulting Group's health care initiative is the story of the growth of an idea, to the point at which it touches almost everyone. Bain & Co.'s troubles with Guinness show what can happen when a consultant gets too cozy with management.

Compelling characters seemed to command a place in *Dangerous Company*, with the brilliant James O. McKinsey and his tortured move into Marshall Field & Co. at the peak of the Great Depression presenting a revealing model of consulting engagements that would play out decades later.

There were literally hundreds of companies that simply didn't make the cut, in many cases because a review of the services they offered indicated there was a high risk of duplication. They would undoubtedly disagree with that assessment. But the truth is that many consulting companies embrace the same styles in vogue that year, then try to dress them up in more distinctive clothing. Calling a spade an entrenching device doesn't change its nature. These chapters are aimed at presenting situations that are indicative and relevant. They are intended for decision makers because they tell the stories of an industry that pushes itself deeply into people's lives, always at high expense and frequently at great cost.

—James O'Shea and Charles M. Madigan
Evanston, Illinois, April 1997

DANGEROUS COMPANY

I

The Price of Advice

WHAT DOES A HALF-BILLION DOLLARS OF CONSULTING BUY?

What is the value of advice?

This is more than a philosophical question. The simple answer is that good advice is priceless and bad advice can quickly lead a corporation into a threatening, expensive world of dangerous company. Trying to measure its value in dollar terms is a frustrating, almost hopeless enterprise. Advice is worth whatever an advice buyer is willing to pay for it.

For one of the stumbling giants of American business, AT&T, the price over a few years was very high, almost half a billion dollars by conservative estimate. That is what the nation's biggest telecommunications company paid its key management consultants between 1989 and 1994.* Throw in a few million more paid to lesser consulting lights and quite soon, it adds up to real money, a bite out of every long-distance telephone bill.

What is most amazing about the figure is not its size. AT&T is a huge company with an $8 billion annual cash flow, some $50 billion in assets, and a projected $51 billion in annual revenue, numbers that far exceed its consulting bills. What is amazing about the figure is the fact that AT&T seems as confused today, after half a billion dollars of con-

---

* These consulting fee tabulations are conservative numbers based on reports that AT&T was required to file with the Federal Communications Commission detailing how it spent every penny of its income. The requirement for filing ended in 1994, so figures for 1995 and 1996 are not available. However, we can assume that AT&T continued its vast consulting expenditures for the past two years.

sulting from firms that are undeniably the best in the business, as it did when the period began.

Time and time again, it wrote multimillion-dollar checks to find out what outsiders thought it should do to pull itself back on track in one of the most competitive businesses on earth. Over the past eight years, it spent $20 billion on new acquisitions and $19 billion on restructuring charges, two areas that are the traditional hunting grounds of investment bankers and management consulting companies.

But nothing seems to have worked. It has lurched and shifted from strategy to strategy, from consulting house to consulting house, all without landing on anything that seems to have provided much help with the challenge of finding a strategic resting place, a market position, a plan, that could give it some leadership and some stability during troubled times. It has made huge alliance decisions that have failed— the ill-fated takeover of NCR in another attempt to compete in computer manufacturing being only the latest—and it broke itself into three separate parts, only to find its long-distance flagship was still in trouble.

It has turned to a complete outsider who was on no one's shortlist, R. R. Donnelley's John R. Walter, to succeed longtime CEO Bob Allen, the complete insider, only to watch its stock price drop another notch as Wall Street collectively asked the question: John who?

It has nibbled at total quality management, business process reengineering, right-sizing, and a long menu of other favored management consulting philosophies and fads, only to find itself trying desperately to swat away its hungry, aggressive competitors and impose some sense of order and mission on its 125,000 employees. It has downsized to the point at which thousands upon thousands of longtime employees have been shown the door, tarnishing its own reputation and wrecking the morale of many of those who stayed behind.

In the wake of all of this, its many critics still describe AT&T as a concern desperately in need of a strategy that will carry it into the modern era.

As a company, AT&T is not representative of much of anything but AT&T. But as a consumer of management consulting expertise, it reflects a history all too common to big corporations. Even over the past few years, when corporate leaders and boards were growing skeptical about the huge fees paid to consultants, AT&T still gave some consult-

ing companies multimillion-dollar budgets and carte blanche to ramble where they wished. This violates the first and most important rule of all consulting engagements: Always know exactly what the goal is. Now the days of the rambling management consultant appear to be over at AT&T. In one of his first decisions, Walter concluded that the company was far too dependent on outside advice. A spokesman said Walter saw consulting bills as a ripe target for the cost savings he promised AT&T shareholders. Now there is a new rule: Mr. Walter will approve all consulting engagements. If you want to hire a management consultant, just call the boss and try to make your case. "It sends a pretty clear message to everyone," the spokesman said. What remains is an important historical question: Was the vast consulting bill worth it in the first place?

"I don't know," says one former AT&T insider who was close to the consulting process during his years there. "I know of various projects, but I don't really know. I have to make a judgment based on the level of performance of the corporation, and that is not impressive. AT&T has been losing market share. It has not made successes. You know, maybe much of the advice was never taken seriously, but you would think with consistent outlays of many millions of dollars, some of it must have been taken seriously. At the end of it all, what happened? Not much."

Then what did it mean?

"The one characteristic in all of these engagements is weak management," he said. "You don't go out and spend all that money if you are in a position of strength. To have a situation where there is a chronic dependence on consultants is an implicit admission of ineptitude in management. That is absolutely very worrisome. I don't think they have ever seen that. The other thing is that because of this mutual dependence [of] the consultant and the customer, it is often not to the consultant's advantage to come up with some delicate issues which should be addressed."

From his perspective, consultants should have been talking aggressively and AT&T should have been listening closely on a whole collection of important issues, the largest one being exactly what service AT&T would provide its customers, and the second largest being why it would want to be a computer company when its primary role was as a service company. He is not challenging the work of the consultants so much as he is challenging the way they moved inside of AT&T to a

tack the crucial questions. "Incredibly, over long periods of time it was not just NCR that was not profitable, but major parts of the AT&T system were not profitable, either," he said.

McKinsey & Co., the blue blood of American management advice and the partnership with the strongest reputation in the industry, collected $96,349,000 from AT&T over the period, with its fattest checks coming in 1992, when the company paid The Firm some $30,208,000 for its services. Monitor, Michael Porter's Harvard-connected consulting business, gathered up a total of $127 million from 1991 to 1994, collecting $58,817,000 of that amount in 1993 alone.

Andersen Consulting, the fastest-growing consultancy in the world with its computer whizzes, armies of business school grads, and business integration philosophies, collected $39,808,000 from AT&T in 1992 and $36,096,000 in 1993, billing a total of $87 million over four years.

Hundreds of smaller companies collected millions upon millions more as AT&T jumped from philosophy to philosophy and searched for big, medium, and small consulting engagements that pushed its consulting bill to $456,528,000 between 1989 and 1994. That might not seem like much to a company that spends $700 million a year on advertising alone, but it is a vast amount in the world of consulting. What did it get for all of that money?

In one of the built-in ironies in the industry, no one seems willing to say. McKinsey & Co. states that it never discusses client business. Monitor, McKinsey's big challenger in the 1980s and apparently the winner in the AT&T consulting bake-off, also says that ethical concerns prevent discussion of client business. Andersen Consulting says the money went for "systems integration." AT&T states generally that it has always purchased a lot of consulting advice and tries to spread its money around. Its spokesperson cannot say specifically what the half-billion dollars bought. But he notes that AT&T has been in search of its truest self for a long time, ever since it was broken into pieces following negotiations with the federal government over a decade ago. A lot of consulting money has been spent, he said, on trying to figure out what the new parts of the company should look like, and how and whether they should fit together.

What it was buying, in the most simple terms, was whatever the consulting houses were selling. Each of them has a fingerprint, a sign it

leaves behind of its engagement. Gemini Consulting collected $1 million from AT&T back when it was the king of business transformation, the elaborate reengineering product it was selling at the time. The Hay Group collected $2.8 million over three years. Compensation management and business process reengineering were Hay's speciality at the time. It also assesses the performance of executives to determine who can move up and who should move on. Delta Consulting Group, Inc., a small but very influential New York City strategy company, connected itself closely to AT&T and got $1,183,455 in fees for the relationship.

What about McKinsey & Co.'s $96 million? It costs about $250,000 a month to have one of McKinsey's consulting teams on-site. AT&T paid McKinsey just over $4 million in 1989, enough to keep a team and a half on board. In McKinsey's fattest recent year at AT&T, 1992, the check was for $30 million. That would pay for about a year's worth of ten McKinsey teams.

The same standard probably can be applied to Monitor's visit at AT&T. Although both companies would argue the point ad nauseam, Monitor and McKinsey have a lot in common, not only in structure and culture but also in the way they offer their services. Because it is competitive with McKinsey, assume the Monitor price tag was about the same. In its fattest year, 1993, Monitor collected $58 million from AT&T. That might cover the presence of about 20 consulting teams.

McKinsey's services range from very general overall surveys of companies to very specific types of strategic advice at the highest levels. But the rate increases quite rapidly when its teams of consultants are in place. The teams analyze specific areas in great depth, then report and recommend. Long-term relationships, personal contacts, and reputation are McKinsey's strengths, along with rigorous research and analysis. It has carefully avoided being attached to any particular trend.

Monitor is a guru-driven consulting company, with the intellectual Michael Porter being the guru at the top. Its sales pitch includes the note that most consulting interventions fail to achieve their goal and involve excessive promises, a reality, it argues, that has polluted the consulting process itself. Maximizing profit lines is one of Monitor's specialities. It is interested only in consulting engagements that "will engender action," it says. It loves creating long-term and trusting relationships that sound almost like marriages, obviously one of the goals at AT&T.

If all of this seems vague, that is part of the mystery of the industry. McKinsey and Monitor have both created cultures that make them more like law firms than consulting businesses, with secrecy and "client privilege" being dominant themes in both places. This has a legitimate purpose in that clients don't want their secrets discussed. But it also provides a perfect excuse for not talking about anything that might be uncomfortable.

There is another way to look at it.

Despite the expenditure, no one has been able to lead AT&T's management into the bright dawn of a profitable and certain future. At best, the consultants have been able to help it push through the murk created by the company's breakup over the past decade. At the same time, they have been having their own competition inside of the giant company.

Monitor's star has been rising at AT&T as McKinsey's has been falling. In the last year on record, McKinsey collected just $13 million from AT&T while Monitor got $50.6 million. Andersen's presence all but disappeared after 1993, with its AT&T revenues dropping from $36 million that year to a mere $700,000 or so a year later.

All of this raises an uncomfortable question: Did the consultants collect a lot of money for good advice that was never taken, or did AT&T closely follow what turned out to be a fortune in bad advice? "I doubt very much it was the latter," said the former insider. "I think more than likely it gave them good advice they did not or could not carry out. Or worse, the consultants were asked peripheral questions rather than core questions. . . . I cannot provide the answer. To me, it is amazing. It is just baffling. The only way I can speculate about it is the level of managerial ineptitude."

Or is it all just an example of what happens when a huge company buys into a whole gaggle of management consulting philosophies of the era? It is no secret that management consultants are sometimes called in to provide cover for executives who don't want to carry the weight of unsavory decisions. It is also easy to see how a company like AT&T would be swept away by the promising rhetoric and goal-oriented sales pitches of the modern consulting company. One outsider believes the AT&T experience reflects these larger realities in consulting engagements.

"My guess is that, from what I have seen from these many so-called experts and advisers is that they tell you what is the general thinking going on in the industry right now. It's mostly platitudes about synergy, or advice that computers are the way of the future. They hear that and they believe that and that is exactly what they are paying to hear," says longtime AT&T follower A. Michael Noll. A professor at the Annenberg School for Communications at the University of Southern California, Noll once worked at the company's Bell Labs. He is not meek in his criticism of consultant spending at AT&T. He thinks it is a waste of money and that the communications giant would do better to look to its own employees for advice.

"It is ass-covering. That is why these consultants are hired. You are afraid to stick your neck out in a big company like AT&T. You are punished if you are wrong, so you don't want to do that. You end up with consensus management. The net result of this is the fear of making a mistake. So bring in the consultants. . . . We are just doing what 'McKinsey' suggested. They are the world's best consultancy. No one has the sense to challenge that. How do you know if they are the world's best? What businesses have they managed? Look at the people they send, all under thirty and fresh out of business school, where they are mouthing whatever crazy ideas their professors threw at them in class."

In one quotation, Noll has summed up what amounts to the darker perception of this rapidly growing business. If the AT&T experience and numbers seem mind-boggling, multiply them times the Fortune 500, where management consultants do most of their most profitable work, to get some idea of what is at stake when outsiders with heads full of ideas come to call.

In its corporate heart, AT&T must indeed be asking: What is the value of advice? If it is impossible for this huge corporation to answer the question, it is not so difficult at another level. For the people on the other side of the contract, advice was just as good as gold. They made a fortune selling it, regardless of the outcome.

This is the story of the exploding business of management consulting, the clients who have helped create it, and the troubles and triumphs both sides have shared along the way. In some ways, it is a warning about what can develop when a corporation keeps dangerous company, full of object lessons about the nature of consulting and what happens when things go wrong.

Companies pay a high price when consulting engagements run out of control. The most obvious lesson is that ships that are not firmly directed often answer to the rocks, no matter how many consultants have joined the crew. But it is also an account that reflects the inherent brilliance that blossoms all across the industry, a brilliance that is apparent and central to both sides of the consulting contract. The differences that separate those extremes, great advice from dangerous company, play out in the stories created by this expanding industry:

- An Ohio company shoots the works on a whole collection of management consultants only to find itself collapsing under the weight of questionable advice and bad strategy decisions.
- McKinsey & Co., the consulting company with the most influence, one with all the attributes of a religious order, constructs a stunning old-boy network, builds on its own history, and becomes an international powerhouse, all the time wrestling with its own demons.
- Bain & Co., the most secretive of the management consulting firms, becomes ensnared in what amounts to an international thriller that underlines the dangers of conflicts of interest and ends up in a mammoth legal battle with the authorities.
- Andersen Consulting, a company that has turned its skill at technology into a fortune, stumbles over promises it has not been able to keep, a record proving with embarrassing clarity that the bottom line of management consulting in the slash-and-burn era of downsizing was money.
- Consulting moves into the living room. Boston Consulting Group, a company that once focused on boardroom issues, steps into health care in a big way, inventing strategies that affect millions of Americans and could ultimately change the way the nation goes to the doctor.
- Gemini Consulting, a relative newcomer to the field, invents an elegant, expensive, and complicated strategy, a case study in how ideas are marketed. But can business transformation work for a huge insurance company, a small hospital, and Gemini, too?
- Sears, Roebuck & Co., one of the nation's premier retailers, turns itself around under the guidance of an executive who believes that in the world of consulting, less is definitely more.

Management consulting has become one of the most successful businesses in history, with some $25 billion in annual revenues in the

United States alone, a figure that doubles when it is measured on the world scale.

Consultants are drawn to money the way hornets are drawn to ripe cantaloupes at a late-summer picnic. They are the modern-day variant of the old European traders, who followed business wherever it beckoned and reaped tremendous profits in the process. Because so many consultancies are partnerships, intense attention is paid to feeding the central treasury that determines everyone's annual income.

The record shows it can cost a fortune to hire a management consultant, and a look at how the companies bill their clients shows why. On average, according to a 1996 survey of consulting fees conducted by Kennedy Research Group, a partner at a big consulting company collects an hourly fee of $270. The highest hourly fee in the survey approached $700, although the authors independently unearthed some hourly fees double that. Nevertheless, assuming the "average" $270-an-hour partner works about 60 percent of the time during the year, his contribution to the partnership amounts to about $310,000.

Project managers, the next level down, spend more time on the job on average and collect $212 an hour for their efforts. Their contribution to the firm, then, is some $280,000 a year. Individual consultants, the third tier in the consulting structure, bill at $166 an hour on average. Because they are the workhorses of the industry, on the job 70 percent of the work year, their contribution to the firm totals some $232,000.

Entry-level associates bill at about $108 an hour, for an annual contribution to the company of $151,000.

But the arithmetic doesn't stop there.

Partners are golden. Few in number, they can't spend much time on the actual job. A big project might have one partner in charge, perhaps four project managers on site, along with sixteen consultants and as many associates. Stretch all of that out over a year's time and the "average" bill comes to $7,558,000. It helps explain why so many younger consultants and associates, fresh out of business school, frequently show up on projects. They are much cheaper to pay, but in their numbers, much more profitable to collect billings on.

The strategies of billing and personnel deployment are among the biggest secrets inside consulting companies. But one thing is apparent from even this oversimplified pricing scenario: The revenues generated by low-level consultants and associates fund the fat salaries garnered by those million-dollar-a-year partners.

It is in the interest of the consulting partnership, then, to send as many raw recruits to the scene as a client will accept. It makes more sense if one thinks of them as money mills.

Despite the price tag and growing resistance to high fees, the rate is expected to continue to grow by about 8 percent, the same as in 1996. The Kennedy survey pinpointed some curious developments, marketplace complaints about the fees charged for the youngest consultants being one of the most interesting.

Clients don't seem to mind paying more for veterans, but the complaints are a sign that the billing cat may well be out of the bag. Because of this problem, the big firms were said to be reconsidering their planning strategies.

And as big as the dollar amounts might sound, there are other problems. Consultants and associates suffer a high rate of burnout. That is no surprise given the fact they are on the job 70 percent of the available work year.

They can't be pushed much harder, but if their contribution falls below 60 percent, a partnership's profitability falls into jeopardy. There is not much margin for error, the Kennedy report concludes.

There has been a lot of talk in consulting over the past few years about shifting to a "value-based" method of billing, in which profits are determined by the economic benefits provided to a client. But the survey shows most of that is just hot talk. Only 3 percent of the respondents in the Kennedy survey actually used value-based methods.

By far the most frequently used billing method was project basis, because it is the easiest to budget for. Hourly billings were second most popular, with daily billings falling third, and monthly and time-and-materials billing coming in down at the bottom. For all this money, clients get consultants adept at adapting to the times.

In the late 1980s and early 1990s, when economic downturns and foreign competition threatened many a bottom line, consultants were the advocates of downsizing for corporations that had become so passionate about quarterly profits that they were willing to lop off their own arms and legs just to keep the money flowing.

Behind almost all of those surgeries were consultants advancing a ruthless version of efficiency that rumbled across corporate culture the way an earthquake rumbles up and down California. In their own defense, they noted that companies are run by executives who answer to boards and shareholders, not by consultants who are paid for advice and services. They pointed to the bottom line as the key measure of a company's success.

Midway through the 1990s, the philosophy of downsizing, with the tremors it sent across industry, began to change, and the agendas of consulting companies changed with it. Increasingly, CEOs began to realize that downsizing may not have been a panacea. It improved the bottom line, but it did nothing to increase revenues and grow businesses. If slash and burn was the previous theme, the new direction was to value employees and help them become more productive, a far cry from the mandate of a few years earlier to get rid of everything that didn't produce a profit.

Downsizing efforts may have brought corporations into the most dangerous company of all. The consulting companies were eager to tap the trend for all it was worth, and the executives they were dealing with were obviously not hard to convince, a formula that came in some cases with built-in blinders. Millions upon millions of dollars of investment in employees and their experiences over the years walked out the door in the bid to improve short-term gains by cutting overhead. But it was a devil's bargain, particularly for the businesses that found themselves unable to meet increasing demand from customers as the economy improved. The new message in corporate America is growing businesses. But it takes experienced, valued employees to do that.

Whatever the product—downsizing, growth, or something else—consultants need to sell ideas. The problem is that what consulting has to sell isn't always new, and certainly isn't always fresh. It is an unusual industry because it builds its knowledge base at the expense of its clients. From a more critical perspective, it is not much of a stretch to say that consulting companies make a lot of money collecting experience from their clients, which they turn around and sell in other forms, sometimes not very well disguised, to other clients.

New York–based Towers-Perrin consulting, for example, has built what it calls a diversity practice to help companies cope with the challenge of race and gender in the workplace. Its consulting engagements are involved processes that include hundreds of interviews, intensive

staff reviews, and rafts of recommendations (many of which the consulting company is willing to help carry out for a fee). But the company
faced a big embarrassment only a few months ago. Much of what it sold
as specific recommendations tailor-made for individual companies
amounted to generic, cookie-cutter stuff, hardly the individual service
the company promised in its contract bids.

Nissan USA was among the clients who were left unimpressed by
the Towers-Perrin experience. One of its executives said the Towers-
Perrin recommendations didn't seem particularly tailored to Nissan.
That was not surprising, according to one account, because the Nissan
report was quite similar to one the consultant sent on the same day to
Indianapolis-based Thomson Consumer Electronics Inc. Only the
names of the companies were changed. The recommendations for both
companies were identical. A review of eleven Towers-Perrin studies
over a two-year period revealed that the top-dollar consulting advice
provided to almost all of them was virtually the same.

The company, a $1-billion-a-year privately held concern, noted
that everything isn't always new and that diversity problems in the
workplace are so similar it is no surprise that the suggested solutions
would be the same.

But that begs some larger questions: Why do consultants continue
to promise unique, individual treatment on the selling end of the contract when so much of what they do is not individual at all? What would
happen if all purchasers of consulting services held a big convention just
to compare their consulting experiences? A conclusion might emerge
from that kind of session that Towers-Perrin was not out of line at all,
that it was merely a reflection of what the consulting business does to
make its money.

Consulting companies promise individualized versions of the bluest
of skies when they are looking for contracts, but what most of them actually have to offer is frequently more earthbound and amounts to variations on commonly accepted business practice.

That's not to say the ideas don't work and aren't valuable.

But "We'll do what works for everyone else!" is a very hard sell.

Imagine pitching a prospective client with the absolute truth: You
could probably do this yourself with some research because we aren't
creating cold fusion here. It just sounds as though we are.

At base, then, the Towers-Perrin story isn't really about selling the same recommendations over and over without even changing the words, it is about claiming up front that something special and unique would be happening when that simply wasn't the case, not an unusual situation in consulting.

Lawsuits have been filed over lesser disappointments.

The concerns raised by the Towers-Perrin story are far from academic, for the influences of today's management consultants reach far beyond the corporations that hire them.

Put a plastic card in a cash machine and you are participating in the financial markets component of consulting, a central force behind the modernization of banking around the world. Rent a car, and information technology, most likely perfected by consulting teams, quickly comes into play in setting prices and measuring whether the leasing company needs a fleet of Lincolns or little econo-boxes. Visit a supermarket and you will notice that the floor plan is a masterpiece of retailing architecture, the template for which rests somewhere in a consultant's computer.

Break a leg and visit the world of health care, a big target for modern-day consulting, and you will notice that you are no longer dealing with a doctor, but with a health maintenance system that has tapped the consulting data bank to become a lot more efficient, if a lot less user-friendly. It was a consultant who decided how many days your insurance company will fund for your particular ailment. Get a pink slip and wonder just why the people who head the corporation you work for decided you were no longer essential. Pick up a telephone and skate electronically across a system that consultants have helped reduce to a simple, vastly lucrative new telecommunications industry.

Nothing is too mundane for the business of consulting. In a little office at Andersen Consulting in downtown Chicago, for example, one of the technology group experts is working on a program that will analyze what might be causing french-fry profits to drop. Rough handling of frozen french fries in the storage process is a likely culprit, along with grease that isn't hot enough. Andersen has a computer plan that will identify the likely offenses and make daily recommendations to store managers on how to get back on the french-fry profits track. It sounds silly, but it most certainly is not. Anyone who visits a fast-food shop knows how important french fries are. Little changes that affect the volume of sales and inventory lead to huge profits over time.

The happy, intact french fry is a profitable french fry in the view of Andersen Consulting. But the significance goes far beyond potatoes. It is the use of technology that has won Andersen its fortunes, whether it is applied to potato coddling, complicated interoffice computing packages, or production line automation.

The influence of consulting is expanding as business is globalized. Nowhere is this expansion more evident than in developing countries such as China. The Chinese industrial landscape is fertile soil for consultants. Just outside Shanghai, rows of state-owned factories sit idle or underemployed, victims of poor planning by a moribund Communist government bureaucracy. The plants aren't dormant because China lacks money or workers. Government coffers bulge with capital, and cheap labor literally clogs the streets of Shanghai, a city that has one person for every six square meters. The problem is know-how. China desperately needs to learn how to utilize its capital and labor efficiently and make its factories hum profitably. Otherwise it risks upheaval among the millions of Chinese citizens trying to claw their way out of poverty. There was a time when the Chinese might have turned to industrial espionage for know-how. There's no longer any need for a cloak-and-dagger approach, though. Consultants traffic in such knowledge. The Chinese can merely hire a consultant to teach them what he learned while working for the competition.

There's no question that such a process is under way. Andersen Consulting has its sign out in Shanghai and other Chinese cities as does McKinsey, the Boston Consulting Group, A. T. Kearney, Bain, and many others. *Consultants News* now estimates that some of the top forty consulting firms generate anywhere from half to three quarters of their revenues from outside the United States. The trend isn't limited to China, either. Andersen now has 4,000 people in Asia. McKinsey's offices in India are growing faster than any others. Of the $600 million in revenue at BCG, a full $420 million came from overseas.

The industry's services have become more sophisticated, too. Always tightly pegged to the development of various lines of business and global growth, consultants have moved quickly into the world of finance and government, tapping fields like energy and telecommunications. Public-sector work used to be dismissed as quaint; now firms covet it. KPMG Peat Marwick earned $242 million from the public sector in 1995; Andersen, $224 million; and Coopers & Lybrand, $171 million. Not bad for government work. Not all of it comes from government clients in the developing world, either. McKinsey finances economic studies of nations such as France, Germany, Brazil, South Korea, and the Netherlands and then shares the results with the government as a way to get a foot in the door for future business. In Britain, consultants have reaped huge fees studying institutions such as the Department of Health and Social Security and the British Broadcasting Corporation.

Government isn't the only new turf. The industry has reached deeply into the workplace, too. As worker benefits grow more complicated and ingrained, whole arms of consulting companies dedicate themselves to human resources management, health care, pensions, and personnel. They have moved aggressively across the spectrum of the service industries, selling their business at every level. The big accounting companies have swelled the consulting ranks by moving aggressively into the business, to the point at which their consulting revenues now equal or surpass the money they collect from their accounting sides.

As consultants continue to expand across the globe, though, it is important to remember that their roots remain in the United States, where annual revenues of the entire industry now total $25 billion, or about half of the world take.

In one way, it is James O. McKinsey's legacy to the business he played such a huge role in creating so many years ago. He was a legend in his own time, probably the most brilliant business academic of his era, a University of Chicago professor who transformed his passion for accounting into a philosophy of management strategy. After World War I, during which he served as an officer rambling all over the United States in search of better ways to handle the U.S. Army's logistical supply nightmare, he decided to take all his experience and all his philosophy and wrap it into one very tightly controlled company. He called it McKinsey & Co.

Scratch a modern-day consultant deeply enough and down toward the center you will find a little bit of McKinsey, a man who was absolutely certain about what he was doing. He came from the dry world of numbers, but was obsessed with the idea of management.

Therein rests a lesson for the people who followed him down the course of management consulting history, and a lesson for everyone who would buy consulting services today. It is a story that began full of promise and carried this central figure in the world of management philosophy to the heart of a great corporation that desperately needed his help. It all ended very darkly.

The company still sits down on State Street in Chicago like a monument to American business, a department store so big and so steeped in the history of the nation's retail and wholesale trades that it is almost a shrine. For those who mix their nostalgia and materialism in equal measures in the twelfth month of the year, Marshall Field & Co.'s downtown Chicago store is Mecca. It is one of those places that makes its money at Christmas. It has always paid great homage to this fattest of sales seasons.

For countless thousands of Chicagoans, a Christmas cannot pass without a visit to Field's Walnut Room, where a gigantic Christmas tree stretches up three stories and a hot plate of potpie is as much a part of the season as a cup of cheer, some good cookies, and thoughts of presents under a tree.

Dig deep into Marshall Field & Co.'s history and there is a record of what it was like to build a store in a frontier boomtown. Long before Chicago burned to the ground in 1871, an event that saw Field's employees fighting a losing battle with the flames, Field's was a magnet for anyone who wanted anything of quality. It was so confident of itself that it constructed its own textile mills and sent its buyers all over the world to collect only the best. It had a vast wholesale business that was aimed at delivering that quality to small-town America, even as it catered to the new wealth of booming Chicago. Field's spent a fortune on its windows, which were thematic and expressed the latest in design and culture. It was a retail and wholesale formula that worked. Over the decades, Field's grew fat with profits and pretense, pushing itself to the forefront of American retailing by living up to its motto: "Give the Lady What She Wants!"

One important piece of Field's history is all but hidden under layer upon layer of Christmases past. There was a war six decades ago that pitted McKinsey against the traditionalists who ran the store. He was a brilliant outsider brought in to perform nothing short of a miracle. The survival of the business was in question. The themes that played out during the battle have their direct parallels in management consulting and business today.

He was the outsider with the golden reputation who first consulted, then moved inside, a path that remains quite common in businesses around the world. McKinsey was the advocate of scientific management and offered the latest in emerging business philosophy, another earmark of modern consulting. He was an aggressive advocate of downsizing long before it carried that name. He paid tribute to the bottom line. He could be as ruthless as he was engaging. He was absolutely certain at all points that he was right. And perhaps, most revealingly, he was not really as smart as he seemed.

Consulting was a new business then, so tiny that it escaped much of a measure of what it did and how it was growing. But what happened at Marshall Field & Co. back in the depression seems almost an augury of what the industry would become, with McKinsey, the key figure and a man whose performance and history have been all but lost, playing the prophet's role.

In his time, McKinsey had passed through all of the gateways required of the modern consultant, performing far beyond any competitor at every step. James Oscar McKinsey was the visionary of his era, brimming with ideas from the best business schools in America. Very little remains in the record about McKinsey. He is there in the yellowing pages of *Who Was Who in American History*, where he merited one paragraph. There is a tiny book about him, *Management and Consulting: An Introduction to James O. McKinsey*, written by William B. Wolf, a Cornell University professor, and published in 1978. In this book, McKinsey is treated as though he were the Moses of modern business, with his management plans serving as the Ten Commandments. It is not an easy book to find. Modern consultants glaze over when his name is mentioned, as though he were entombed in some distant place that holds the souls of significant business figures of the ancient past, somewhere down beneath the Carnegies and Rockefellers and Goulds and Stanfords who created the world into which he was born. They see little connection between what they do today and what McKinsey did so many years ago. But it is undeniable. Pull this business up by its roots and at the very bottom you will find the story of James O. McKinsey. What separates him from the consultant of today is mostly the passage of time. He was a workaholic before anyone even thought of labeling that particular obsession. His commitment to his clients was unquestioned, along with the value of the services he delivered. He made the practice of achieving profit his own religion. He believed that he could make things work, no matter what the demand and no matter what the cost.

At Marshall Field & Co., the challenge was vast. And, as it turned out for McKinsey, the cost was very high.

In the pits of the Great Depression, when the company's wholesale business was in such deep collapse that it seemed the institution might become one of the era's many victims, Field's abandoned its paternalistic culture and decided to reach outside for help. This was an unprecedented move for a company that took pride in pointing to a string of executives who had worked their way up from the lowest ranks. It was the kind of place where a diligent and aggressive office boy could end up in the hierarchy, making the climb the old-fashioned way through a long collection of sales and middle-management jobs. Sales was the pathway to power at Field's, mostly because all of its leaders had come from the sales staff. Turning to an outsider for help seemed the height of folly to the old-timers. They were determined to resist the effort at every turn, setting up obstacles that would have stopped almost anyone. But the depression had forced its way so deeply into the retailing formula that the company's tried-and-true method of increasing its profits, pushing the markup, would not work anymore.

The company was in big trouble. Field's president John McKinlay, who had been on board since 1888 and had started as a cash runner for $2.25 a week, had seen panics before. But nothing like this one. In 1931, the retail division had earned $1.6 million, but the losses in wholesaling were so huge that they wiped out that profit and added another $5 million in red ink. In 1932, the company paid no dividends for the first time in three decades. "We are like a ship," McKinlay told his employes. "And we are temporarily floundering. . . ." He tried everything to turn the company around. He spruced up the State Street store, investing $600,000 in escalators. He held his hope that Field's Merchandise Mart, a huge wholesale outlet, built at a gigantic cost overrun only a few years before the depression hit, would revive the collapsing wholesale division. But that didn't happen.

In 1934, wholesale division losses gobbled up retail division profits again. There was more bad financial news on the horizon. Field's was due to make payments on an $18 million loan it took out to build the Mart. Even without considering that obligation, it looked as though wholesale would lose $2 million in 1935.

In desperation, the executives turned to Marshall Field III to see what he thought. "Why don't we get an expert on corporate management in to look the company over?" he said. He had just the man for the job. He had served on a variety of boards in Chicago and had heard good reports about this college business teacher, James McKinsey, who had surveyed a number of companies and had become an expert at turning them around. The board grumbled for roughly an hour. Then the decision was made. McKinsey & Co. would take a close look at Marshall Field & Co. to see what might be done. In the darkness of winter and the depression, McKinsey and his brightest young men embarked on a three-month study of all of the Field's enterprises. It was an unusual choice.

McKinsey, the highest-paid consultant in the nation at $500 a day, believed that business was actually scientific and that the era of the clerk-to-mogul transformation was over. Businesses created track records that were apparent to anyone who knew how to read the numbers, he argued. And as an accounting genius, he knew how to read the numbers quite well. "The forceful personality, the man of action, who was great because he could make a decision on the spur of the moment, is giving way to a new type of leader," McKinsey said in a speech in 1925. "The scientific man, accustomed to research work and careful planning, is the one who is now chosen for the presidency of business concerns."

He was 44 years old, the recognized expert in just about everything connected to the business and science of management, when his company began studying Field's. He was one of the first great advocates of the business lunch and used it to achieve his goal of reaching anyone of any importance inside a company. His contemporaries recalled a man who never missed a chance to make a contact, never settled for being second best, and was so certain of his intellectual and personal skills that he carried his professorial demeanor everywhere he went.

He was the author of a whole collection of texts that were the basic handbooks of accounting. He wanted his students to think of themselves as managers, not bookkeepers. His goal was analytical thinking. Basically, he invented management by objective long before that became the rallying cry of an army of business consultants and gurus later in the century.

But he was not an easy man. He never spent much time around the house, a son recalled, and when he was home, his children were not allowed to make distracting noises while he was working. He almost always spent his Saturdays at the office and brought work home with him on Sundays. He wasn't much of a Santa. When his children asked for the trappings of childhood, McKinsey, who could well afford them, generally lectured them on the fact that they were lucky to live in a house that had servants. Toys and frivolous purchases were viewed as nonessential.

He was all business. And that was nowhere more apparent than at Field's.

To visit McKinsey's work at Field's in the 1930s is to get an early glimpse at the strategies and practices that would become common in modern management consulting. Even the scant record of his years at Field's reads today like an account of being present at the creation of consulting. He was so intent on carrying out his plan for Field's that he left his own company and moved inside of Field's to do it. His experience at Field's is both a template for the modern consultant and a warning, perhaps on the seductive and hidden dangers of hubris. Put yourself in the boardroom at Field's in June of 1935. Remember how dismal everything seemed. McKinsey and his men had completed their studies and were ready to report on them. It was the beginning of what became known in the Field's legend as "McKinsey's Purge."

"This was no meek, bespectacled professor who confronted the company heads. McKinsey was a robust six-footer, slightly stooped and balding, but loaded with self-assurance and facts. Speaking brusquely, he conceded that Field's was a splendid institution with a sound financial structure and well-managed retail divisions. But wholesale, said McKinsey, would have to be reorganized. Most of the textile manufacturing, converting and importing operations could be retained, with modifications, but domestic jobbing would have to go," says the Field's history.

McKinlay and his men couldn't believe it. Jobbing had been the heart of the wholesale division. Field's was the best in the nation at it. Their objections were strong. If the division were to be cut at all, it had to be cut slowly, they said. It had to be painless. It had to be done quietly. If word got out that Field's was abandoning its jobbing business, there would be hell to pay.

"Gentlemen," McKinsey said after he listened to their complaints. "I think you will accept my proposals."

Five months after the meeting, it was clear that McKinlay would not carry out McKinsey's recommendations. But McKinsey was not at rest during that period. The directors finally decided to make a point about where their loyalties were in this dispute. On October 9, 1935, James O. McKinsey was elected chairman of the company and given the title of chief executive officer. Everyone, including the president, was to report to him. The outsider had moved inside in a shift that stunned Field's 17,000 employees, rattling the company to its foundations.

"The way I started was not the way you'd plan to be popular," McKinsey said later. But popularity wasn't part of the agenda. You were either going to be on McKinsey's side or you were going to be out. It took six months, but the wholesale division all but disappeared. In the process, eight hundred people in wholesale and another four hundred in manufacturing lost their jobs. McKinsey received death threats. Those who survived his purge, the Field's history notes, would talk of this era "with a moan and a shudder" for years to come.

As part of this process, the very elements that were viewed as assets in McKinsey's biography became liabilities inside of the old Field's company. He lectured executives as though they were his old students at the University of Chicago. He was viewed as arrogant, self-important, and, worst of all, ignorant of the traditions of Field's and the ways of retail sales. An anecdote remains that highlights this problem. Talking with his silk buyers one afternoon, he advanced his belief that it would be smartest to buy silk when prices were low, and sell it when prices were high. The buyers had trouble deciding whether McKinsey was serious, or whether he was merely joking. And so they laughed.

It was the wrong choice. Red as a beet, he stalked from the room.

While all of this was happening, the ground was beginning to rumble under McKinsey. True enough, he had turned red ink into black ink, but he had made some big political and business mistakes along the way. He had tried to introduce cheaper grades of merchandise in the State Street store, which brought a strong, hostile response from a proud sales staff that would complain to anyone who would listen.

Against everyone's advice, he tried to buy a New England mill that produced a lower grade of hosiery, a scheme he was forced to abandon and one that put him on the wrong side of an important board member, Stanley Field. McKinlay, too, was growing tired of trying to work under McKinsey. He quit in 1936. The board flexed its muscle and sent a message, replacing him with Frederick D. Corley, another of the stockboy-to-boardroom veterans. It was a clear sign that scientific man had not yet arrived at Field's.

But it was the mistakes that caught up with McKinsey. Field's was not paying its bills on time, so its credit rating dropped. The board was upset that it didn't have the depth of financial information it wanted for its annual meeting. Even though McKinsey was able to announce in spring of 1937 a profit of some $3 million on sales of $104 million, there was trouble ahead. When McKinsey was pressed on the figures, it was revealed that the company had made heavy purchases of raw materials in the early part of the year, but the price had dropped. Silk that McKinsey had purchased for $2 a pound fell to $1.58. Wool went from $1.05 a pound to 81 cents. The price of cotton had dropped by half. He was stuck with huge inventories that were declining in value. He had moved deeply and aggressively into an area in which it was apparent he did not know what he was doing, the political kiss of death for businessman and consultant alike.

Early in November of 1937, McKinsey was called for a private interview with Marshall Field III and informed that, unless he changed his style of management, his resignation would be demanded by the end of the year. He had a cold at that point. Sapped by the pressures of his work, it developed into pneumonia. On the eve of the twelfth month of the year, just as Field's was getting ready to shift into high gear for the Christmas season, the front page of the *Chicago Daily Tribune* bannered the news: HEAD OF FIELDS STORE DIES. He was 47 years old. Inside the paper, commerce marched on. Shoppers were alerted that in this year of hard times, it was still crucial "to know how to say Merry Christmas."

In death, McKinsey was hailed by *American Business* magazine as a man who had faced "a tough assignment and one that called for a ruthless disregard of sentiment and a cold-blooded facing of facts. . . . He died, as so many businessmen have died, as sacrifice to a job that made impossible demands. . . ."

It didn't take Field's long to announce a change in direction. "Plans of the present management call for material changes from the program and organization conceived by Mr. McKinsey," said Corley, the new president.

Just how McKinsey felt about all of this went with him to the grave. But on the day before he died, the consultant legend shared an important final thought at Woodlawn Hospital with his friend and former client James Margeson. Making real decisions in a business is a lot harder than getting paid to advise people what to do, McKinsey said. It was a process, in retrospect, that carried everyone on both sides into quite dangerous company.

The Few, the Proud,
the Totally Insane

HOW CONSULTANTS RAN AMOK
AT FIGGIE INTERNATIONAL

James McKinsey paid a high price at Marshall Field & Co. during the Great Depression. Some 50 years later, Figgie International paid a high price for the kind of advice McKinsey pioneered. But the Ohio company did not get the stunning results it expected. It paid consultants more than $75 million to help make it a "world-class manufacturer." Instead, it became a world-class mess in a tale of consultants run amok.

Harry Figgie struck a tough but regal pose for the photographer from *Fortune* magazine. With a scowl on his leathery face, the chairman of Figgie International stood on the staircase at the company's headquarters, just high enough to tower over a bronze bust of Thomas Jefferson at the foot of the stairs. Figgie wore a dark suit and a conservative tie drawn so tightly that his collar seemed one size too small. His left hand was stuffed into his pocket, but his right hand clutched the polished wooden banister like an eagle's claw. His jaw was clenched, accentuating the lines that 65 years had etched into his rugged face. He stared at the camera and, when the shutter clicked, Harry was looking down at the photographer, a familiar pose according to those who knew him well.

To thousands of his employees at the Ohio conglomerate just west of Cleveland, Harry Figgie had earned his place in the February 1989 pages of *Fortune* for a piece on "America's Toughest Bosses." Over the prior two and one-half decades, Figgie had knocked heads together to build the company that bore his name into one of the largest corporations in America. He wasn't as notorious as some others on the Top 10 list, such as Frank Lorenzo, the union-busting chairman of Texas Air, or Richard Mahoney, the demanding boss at Monsanto. But the luster of his colleagues didn't diminish Figgie. As a boss, he made George Steinbrenner look like Mr. Rogers. Critics dubbed his management style "hire 'em, tire 'em, and fire 'em," a reflection of his tendency to sack hardworking employees if they didn't meet his bottom-line expectations. He was mercurial, blunt, brutal, and sometimes profane. "You don't build a company like this with lace on your underwear," he once barked at a reporter. And he left little doubt that he could manhandle executives and machinists alike: ". . . I won't deny it," he said, "I know how to chew ass."

The company he ran wasn't a corporate icon like General Electric or some of the other outfits run by the men in the *Fortune* story. But that didn't mean Americans hadn't seen Figgie's products. Starting in 1963, Figgie had acquired dozens of small companies and had merged them into Figgie International, the Ichabod Crane of American corporations. By 1989, it included 36 divisions with dozens of unrelated products, although most weren't publicly associated with the name Figgie. The company owned Rawlings Sporting Goods, the official supplier of major-league baseball and America's largest source of sports equipment for professional, college, and high school teams; Scott Aviation, manufacturer of emergency oxygen masks that dropped from the ceiling of an airplane when cabin pressure plunged; Sherwood Drolet, the world's leading producer of hockey sticks and the official supplier for the National Hockey League; a material handling division that made high-speed baggage handling systems used in the world's airports; American LaFrance, the nation's oldest manufacturer of fire engines; a power system division that made hydraulic and pneumatic cylinders and gears; George J. Meyer Co., a major producer of automated filling and packaging systems used by the soft drink, beer, wine, pharmaceutical, food, and cosmetic industries; plus numerous other divisions that made everything from missile parts for the defense industry to scissor lifts for construction crews and firefighters.

In the year Harry Figgie's picture graced the pages of *Fortune*, Figgie International climbed to number 286 on the Fortune 500, the magazine's infamous Who's Who of corporate America. Year-end revenues reached $1.31 billion. The company generated nearly $63 million in profits for its 10,887 shareholders and employed 17,000 people around the globe. Figgie recorded a stellar performance that year, and Harry Figgie knew it. But he also knew something that he didn't volunteer to *Fortune*'s readers: The glow of the company's earnings and its lofty perch in the corporate hierarchy overshadowed some serious problems festering in the company's far-flung divisions.

Some of the problems were acute. Figgie had made a string of bad acquisitions in recent years, particularly in the division that housed Figgie's insurance business, which lost $13.5 million between 1985 and 1988. But chronic problems plagued the manufacturing divisions, the core of Figgie International. Harry Figgie excelled when he acquired a company and strengthened its bottom line by wringing excess costs from its operations. He built Figgie from scratch after working as a management consultant in Booz Allen's Cleveland office, where he specialized in profit improvement and cost reduction. Repressing costs was a religion to Figgie. Controlling expenses, he would say, gave the bottom line much more adrenaline than efforts to increase revenues. Unfortunately, though, his tightfisted policies also applied to investment. He brutally scrutinized requests to spend money on things like new machinery and equipment, excoriating anyone who couldn't justify their plans with the hardest of numbers. So his managers often deferred investment to maintain their profits and stay on Harry's best side. The result: a company that generated short-term profits at the expense of long-term investment. Some Figgie divisions had relatively modern equipment, but many labored under outmoded business systems and aging equipment heavily reliant on high-priced labor.

By the time Figgie's picture appeared in *Fortune*, the days when manufacturers could ignore deficient plants had passed. Harry faced a dilemma: He knew he had to modernize his plants, but that required a huge investment—one that would hurt his bottom line at the very time the federal government had American capital markets in disarray with persistent federal budget deficits. Harry Figgie had talked for years about converting Figgie International into a "world-class" operation, a low-cost manufacturer that could capitalize on modern technology and equipment to slash its labor costs and compete on a global scale. Now was the time to act. But he didn't know exactly how to go about such a costly conversion, particularly on the scale that would be required of Figgie International. So he called upon his old profession, management consultants, to help Figgie International go "world class." And what he ended up with went beyond his wildest dreams.

Between 1989 and 1994, Figgie International would rack up more than $75 million in fees to some of America's most prestigious management consulting firms. He would hire so many consultants that one unit would run out of spaces in the parking lot. Figgie hired the best: Boston Consulting Group, the blue-chip Massachusetts consultant that created the term "cash cow"; Deloitte & Touche, the huge Big Six accounting firm that had a rapidly growing consulting arm; Andersen Consulting, the nation's premier information technology consultant; Price Waterhouse; and a band of others. The consultants produced high-priced studies and impressive reports about "world-class manufacturing," one of those buzzwords that captured corporate imaginations. Instead of a world-class operation, though, Figgie would get a world-class mess.

A lifetime of hard work would unravel before his eyes as the company Figgie cherished became a tale of consultants run amok. Eventually, Figgie International would flirt with bankruptcy, its workforce would plunge into chaos, and its balance sheet would drown in red ink. Thousands of Figgie employees would lose their jobs in a wrenching downsizing that would leave the company nearly prostrate. And the consultants would cringe at charges of incompetence, particularly Boston Consulting Group and Deloitte & Touche, two firms that faced the worst nightmare of all. Figgie filed suit against them, publicly airing charges of inept performance and poor advice. Figgie lawyers even accused Deloitte & Touche of padding already hefty bills with phantom hours and cash outlays for rendezvous in Dallas and New York stripper bars. Indeed, by the time the last consultant vacated the company's premises on a leafy estate just west of Cleveland, Figgie International's story would provide a rare glimpse into the inner workings of American consulting firms and become a case study of what happens when all of that high-priced advice just doesn't work.

The controversy involving Figgie and his company flared in public only recently. The lawsuits were filed in 1994 and were settled quietly out of court in 1995. But the litigation was only the latest chapter in the story of what actually happened at Figgie International. To truly understand how consultants helped wreck the company, it is necessary to go back many years, for the tale of Figgie International is hopelessly intertwined with the life and the ethos of the man who started it all, Harry Edward Figgie, Jr.

The House That Harry Built

Harry Figgie grew up in a comfortable middle-class suburb of Cleveland, where he excelled in school, saw his father die at a young age, and earned a baseball scholarship to college. He went off to fight in Europe during World War II and, once he returned to America, whizzed through engineering school in just five semesters. Eventually, he would also get a master's degree from the Harvard Business School and a law degree from John Marshall Law School. Ironically, his first major job would be in the industry that helped bring his company to the verge of bankruptcy: consulting. In 1953 he joined the Cleveland staff of Booz Allen & Hamilton, where he worked as a management consultant specializing in profit improvement, cost reduction, and corporate reorganizations and acquisitions. Like many others before and after him, though, Figgie's career at Booz Allen provided something besides the experience that comes with consulting. He also made some connections to the mother's milk of the business world: capital.

Harry Figgie remembers his first encounter with the core company in his Fortune 500 conglomerate the way some men remember falling in love. He had left Booz Allen in 1962 to take a job as a group vice president at A. O. Smith. "I let bankers around Cleveland know that I wanted to buy a company, preferably one with sales in the $20 million range. In early December 1963, I received a call from a Cleveland banker who had three companies to sell. One was a fastener manufacturer. I already knew that industry had experienced invasion by foreign producers. I never saw the third company data because as soon as I looked at the second company, I knew it was what I wanted."

Figgie's first love was Automatic Sprinkler Company, a Youngstown, Ohio, corporate basket case. Mired in debt, Automatic Sprinkler hadn't made a profit in five years. But Figgie sensed an opportunity, mainly because of its low price tag: $7.2 million, or about $1.4 million below its book value. He borrowed heavily to buy the company and set about to reverse its sagging fortunes. In one way or another, Automatic

Sprinkler became the template that Harry Figgie would use over the next three decades to build a Fortune 500 conglomerate with sales that would peak at $1.36 billion in 1990. Time and again he acquired a small, poorly run company in a leveraged transaction and wrenched excess costs from its financial statement through brutal yet efficient management. Despite the odds of failure at Automatic Sprinkler, Figgie turned the company around in just one year, posting an after-tax profit of $1.2 million on sales of $25 million just 12 months after he took over. The profits made Figgie so happy that he tried it again with another company and then another. "It wasn't unusual for us to look at as many as 50 companies a month. In one period of 25 days, we closed five deals," he said.

During his days at Booz Allen, Figgie had developed a "nucleus theory" that he used to build his conglomerate. He would buy a company like Automatic Sprinkler and use it as a nucleus around which he would buy other companies in the same general industry to form a group that was greater than the sum of its parts. Automatic Sprinkler, for example, became the nucleus of a Fire Protection/Safety/Security group that would eventually include other companies like Scott Aviation, which made "air-paks" that firefighters use to help breathe while in burning buildings, and American LaFrance, the nation's oldest manufacturer of custom and commercial fire engines, based in Virginia. Under Figgie's nucleus theory, each company in the group could share its expertise with other members, thereby allowing all to increase market penetration. Nowadays they call Figgie's idea "synergy," a fad pushed aggressively by the management consulting industry. To Harry, though, it was simply a good way to maximize profit while allowing Harry—and only Harry—to manage the far-flung enterprise. Figgie named a president for each company, who reported to a group president, who reported to Harry, who had a simple philosophy: Squeeze every last penny in excess cost out of the acquisition and operate with as little human labor as possible. Over nearly three decades, Figgie would acquire 86 companies and shoehorn them into five groups that would make everything from baseballs and security systems to industrial vacuum cleaners and high-speed labeling machinery. As long as Figgie could keep raising money for acquisitions and could keep squeezing costs, it worked.

In 1965, he took the company public, dramatically expanding its presence on the American business scene and increasing Figgie's personal wealth. A Figgie share that originally fetched $4 split and took off to reach $74, an astonishing 50 times the $1.48 per share it earned that year, and Harry and his family owned millions of them. The corporate perks started flowing. He bought airplanes, including a Gulfstream jet, and used his interests in companies like Rawlings Sporting Goods and Fred Perry Sportswear to curry favor with his sons' sports teams and coaches. He built a headquarters with three colonial buildings that looked like they belonged in Williamsburg, Virginia, rather than in Willoughby, Ohio, and filled them with millions of dollars' worth of art, rugs, and sculptures to his own taste. In later years, his tendency to use the public company's resources as if they were his own would get him into trouble. But in the early years, no one questioned Harry but Harry. Company wags called the headquarters "The House That Harry Built."

As the company grew, Harry ruled over it with an iron fist and a streak of midwestern independence. A maverick in every sense of the word, he joined few boards, helped few local charities, belonged to few clubs, prohibited his executives from engaging in civic activities, and was not popular with Cleveland's business establishment. Word had it that his shoot-from-the-hip style earned him a blackball at Cleveland's Union Club, a pillar of the local establishment, but Harry said he pulled his application first. In a snit with local officials, Figgie once moved his entire corporate headquarters to a 1,200-acre site near Richmond, Virginia, only to move it back to Willoughby a few years later, reportedly because of the cool reception he got in the South. The moves cost the company an estimated $70 million.

Autocratic, mercurial, and opinionated, Figgie relied on his brains, guts, and instincts to run the company. By all accounts, he demanded a lot from his managers and tolerated few mistakes. "We bought small companies with no management depth. There's no room for error," he would say. If a manager didn't measure up to his standards, he'd be sacked. Someone at corporate headquarters once did a study of the average tenure for 26 of Figgie's division presidents. It was less than three years. But Figgie also awarded successful managers with good salaries, and many of his managers respected his skills as a businessman and leader.

"He had these amazing instincts," said Richard DeLisle, who worked with Figgie in several capacities, including as director of operations at Scott Aviation. "His office at Willoughby looked out over the parking lot. One day he looked out and saw that all the parking spaces were full. So he came into my office and said, 'When we moved here, I told them to build a parking lot larger than the one we had [at the old headquarters] in Richmond [Virginia]. Look at that lot out there. It is full. Somebody must have hired additional people. I want you to go out there and count the parking places and then find out how many parking places we had in Richmond. If there are more, find out why. If there are more people, I want to know why. Report back to me.' So I went out and counted the parking places and then I called someone down in Richmond and told them to go out and count the parking places and don't ask why. When they called back, there were more spaces in our new lot. And you know what, he was right. We had hired 15 additional people and I had to go and find out why. But that was how he was."

Each year Figgie displayed his unparalleled knowledge of the company for a wider audience at "Hard Core," annual sessions in which he summoned division presidents to corporate headquarters to present their five-year plans, even though most of them wouldn't be around that long. Figgie folklore flowed from the sessions like lava. "You'd show up at your appointed hour and be ushered into the boardroom," one former executive said. "It was intimidating as hell." No official seating chart existed, but everyone knew his place. Figgie sat at the head of a long, elegant, antique wooden table and his staff, the CFO, and others lined one side. Each had a chair with a former board member's name on a plaque attached to the back. Hard Core was no shirtsleeve session. Figgie usually dressed in a suit, and his tie was secured to his white shirt with a tie clasp that had a small music box attached to it. Jim Anderson, Figgie's longtime confidant and the head of human relations, sat at the far end of the table, and the victim—the division president—had to take a seat on the other side of the table near Mr. Figgie, in a chair bearing the nameplate of former director Hans Rinderknecht. On cue, the executive would present his five-year plan while Figgie looked at the written document.

"Harry was incredibly thin-skinned," said one former Figgie executive who attended the sessions. "All you had to do was say the wrong thing, and he'd fire you. . . . If you went in there and said something like, 'Now, Mr. Figgie, you have to understand,' you'd be gone. He'd say something like, 'Are you talking down to me? I think you are talking down to me.' And that would be it. . . . After the session, he'd say to Anderson, 'Jim, can I have a moment of your time?' And then Anderson, who was known around corporate [headquarters] as 'Dr. Death,' would come out and tell you the bad news. I used to take people over there and I would have to coach them on what to say. There were certain things you just couldn't do, like challenge him. If you did, you were history." Even if the executive gave a faultless presentation, Figgie displayed an astonishing knowledge of the conglomerate's business. A former executive described the scene: "He'd sit there listening to you and skimming through your five-year plan. He wouldn't even have to read the whole thing. After about five minutes, he would close the book and say, 'I see the profit projected in the third quarter of the fourth year in your plan is far below the profit in the third quarter of this year. Why is that?' Or he'd say, 'You project a 30 percent increase in revenues over the next three years without adding any new products or new people. How are you going to do that?' And you'd better have an answer or he would rip you apart. You had to justify everything, down to the last penny."

If Figgie didn't like the presentation, he'd let the division president know before he (and it was always a "he") even finished. If a manager said something during the presentation that Figgie thought was stupid, Harry would enter the statement in a book he called the "Hall of Shame." Sometimes, midway through the presentation, Figgie would finger his tie clasp and click on the music box attached to it. A light melody would resonate through the boardroom like a requiem as Harry's staff sat silently looking at the executive. The "tie music" meant Harry didn't like the plan. If he was lucky, the division manager would be sent back with a deadline for a new plan. Harry decided to sack more than one executive on the spot. Anyone who tried to mislead Harry Figgie would be fired immediately. Attempts to snow him didn't fare much better. Sometimes, a former Figgie executive said, Figgie would talk to his staff about the plan as if the division president weren't in the room. "He'd turn to someone and say, 'What do you think of this, Jim? It sounds like cow shit from Cairo to me.' He would talk like the poor guy wasn't even there. And if he didn't get an answer that he liked, he'd say, 'Sounds like it's time for a little tie music to me.' "

Figgie's board gave Harry great latitude in his stewardship of the company, mainly because he stacked it with his pals and business associates. He could hire major executives on a whim or a feeling in his gut that the guy was right for the job. Recalling when Figgie hired him to run the conglomerate's manufacturing operations, Larry Schwartz said Figgie told him: "I think you have a rocket up your ass and I want to point it in the right direction." Figgie treated company property as if it were his own, too. A lawsuit filed against Figgie by a company insider said he used the company's $26 million jet to fly toys to his grandchildren, ferry a favorite landscaper from Richmond, Virginia, to Ohio, and for things like hunting trips, tennis matches, and vacations in Florida. Harry's transgressions raised some eyebrows among the staff, but there wasn't much anyone could do about it.

Like many postwar business leaders, Figgie's tight grip on the conglomerate served him well during the 1960s and 1970s. Even as other conglomerates encountered troubles during the 1980s and sold off everything but the best stuff, Figgie kept at it, tenaciously building a company that bucked all trends. By the late 1980s, though, two things happened that would thrust Figgie International into the arms of the consulting industry and set the stage for a world-class debacle. One was Figgie's growing concern about the future of the company, and the other was Wall Street's rising concern about Harry.

Is There a Doctor in the House?

Figgie's concerns about the future had been festering for some time. As Figgie International's equipment aged, labor grew more expensive and the world became more competitive. The federal government continued to ravage the economy with deficits, angering Harry. But no one had ever publicly raised questions about Harry until *Forbes* magazine ran a biting piece about the company in October of 1988.

The story focused on a stock buyback maneuver that Harry had engineered. It diluted the power of the average shareholder by replacing one class of Figgie stock with another that had less voting power. The move bolstered Figgie's already considerable control over the company and incensed Wall Street analysts, who accused Harry of boosting his fortunes at the expense of shareholders. But *Forbes* saved its best shot for last when discussing why anyone should continue holding the stock. "The hitch here," the magazine said, "is that when you buy Figgie International, you are basically buying Harry Figgie, Jr., a man who believes he is rarely wrong. And though he does not seem to be contemplating retirement anytime soon, he has also, it seems, never bothered to groom a successor. Figgie himself is what keeps it all together. Shareholders have to bet he will continue to do so, or that when he steps down or out, the conglomerate's parts will prove to be more valuable than the whole."

Although Figgie probably would never admit it, *Forbes* had hit a bull's-eye. Harry Figgie had few business confidants. He relied mainly on himself and his family. He had a reputation as a solid family man. You wouldn't find him lingering around clubs or cocktail parties after business hours with buddies and hangers-on. He would go home. He involved almost all family members in the business, with the exception of a son who was an orthopedic surgeon in New York City. Figgie's wife became a vice president for facilities planning, a fancy title for a corporate decorating consultant who made somewhere between $30,000 and $50,000 a year. The youngest son, Matthew, became director of mergers and acquisitions at age 27. Figgie's third and oldest son, Harry III, joined the board and often dabbled in the company's affairs on special assignment, even though he was an orthopedic surgeon, too. But Harry had no well-publicized succession plan.

The *Forbes* article touched a sensitive nerve. Within 18 months of its publication, Harry Figgie acted on his concerns and those raised in the article. His response to anxiety about the company's future? A modernization plan that would stun almost everyone. Figgie created a new hierarchy at the company—the Office of the Chairman. It would be a triumvirate, with Figgie at the top as chairman and chief executive officer; Vince Chiarucci, who would remain in his job as president of the conglomerate; and a new position, vice chairman—technology and strategic planning. He named his son, Harry III, to the job. Executives around Figgie gagged at the appointment. Figgie had just created an heir apparent and had placed an orthopedic surgeon in charge of the company's modernization drive.

The main problem on the staff's mind involved Harry III's experience, or more precisely, his lack of it. He had no operating experience at a Fortune 500 conglomerate. Harry III had been named to the board at Figgie in 1985, when he was 31, or 19 years younger than the next youngest director. He was president of Clark Reliance Corp., a family-owned privately held manufacturing company a fraction of the size of Figgie International. What's more, Harry III had been named president of Clark Reliance when he was also developing a practice as an orthopedic surgeon. One couldn't help but wonder just how much experience he really had. If that weren't enough, his rocky and relatively brief career in medicine raised even more questions about the appointment.

After graduating from medical school in 1979 and serving his residency, Harry III started practicing as an orthopedic surgeon specializing in prosthetic joint replacements and degenerative diseases at Cleveland's University Hospitals. At first, he prospered as a physician. In the late 1980s, though, a jury awarded one of his patients $6.2 million in a medical malpractice suit in which he was also cited for altering medical records to conceal his mistake. Harry III then changed careers; his father hired him in a job that shortly thereafter would pay him nearly $1 million a year.

No one should have been too surprised by the appointment. Harry Figgie had a lot of confidence in his son, who was known around the company as "the doctor," and Harry III knew it. At 36, he looked a bit like Rush Limbaugh. He came off as supremely self-confident, and had a physician's penchant for being slow to admit a mistake. During the medical malpractice suit, he refused to even consider a settlement of the case, even though an arbitration panel had recommended that the charges be dropped against all defendants in the case except Figgie. Arrogant to a fault, he dismissed questions about how he could run the family's manufacturing business while practicing medicine full-time. He said he ran Clark Reliance on slow afternoons and on weekends. He fancied himself an expert in manufacturing modernization schemes. In 1985 he told an interviewer: "We can walk through a plant in ten minutes and tell if we can automate it."

In many respects, Harry III resembled his dad. He was smart, competitive, and aggressive. But Harry III differed from his father in key respects, too. A formal man, the elder Figgie came to the office in suit and tie, often wearing long-sleeved dress shirts with a pin through the collar. At company business retreats on Michigan's Mackinaw Island, guests could always spot the guys from Figgie, thanks to Harry's unofficial dress code. They all walked around in suit and tie. In contrast, Harry III would show up at Clark Reliance in his hospital scrubs. Shorter than Harry and weighing in at around 200 pounds, Harry III had a receding hairline and sometimes walked around the office in his stocking feet. He plastered Rambo and Grateful Dead posters on his office walls and seemed to get off on Arnold Schwarzenegger movies. One former company officer said his office looked like a teenager's room. His outside interests included tennis, tae kwon do, and swimming. He would boast that his swim coach used to say he could beat Mark Spitz. During Hard Core sessions, he would howl like a baying dog if he didn't like a presentation and give people the high five when he approved of something. When it came to office gossip, the elder Figgie was a prude. Even a hint of an office romance would be dealt with severely. Close relationships between the sexes were taboo. But appearances weren't as important to the doctor, who grew up as the boss's son. Harry III raised eyebrows when he hired his former nurse at University Hospitals to be a consultant to the company on workers' compensation and wellness programs.

The biggest difference between the two involved their respective strengths as executive and leaders. Decades of experience made Harry Figgie a disciplined businessman. He carefully planned everything. No one spent a penny at Figgie International until the old man rigorously assessed its impact on the bottom line. He made everyone prove their case and, although he wasn't liked, he was respected. Harry III was more of a visionary, blinded to practicality by illusions of grandeur. Many longtime Figgie executives grew to dislike him and they had no respect for his skills, although they would readily admit he was smart. He didn't fear spending money, either. He acquired huge pieces of machinery without even talking to the managers who would use them. At one point, he stopped by the 1990 international machine tool show in Chicago with another Figgie executive and ordered $40 million worth of state-of-the art machinery for the company.

Here Comes Valdez

It didn't take long for Figgie employees to notice the change at the top. Soon after he took over, the younger Figgie summoned some of his key people to a meeting at corporate headquarters. Paul Kearney, then Figgie's director of purchasing, remembered getting a call while at a Figgie facility in Chicago. "It was a Friday afternoon and I got this phone call from Dr. Figgie. He told me to be in Willoughby the next morning at eight A.M. for a meeting." The next day Kearney drove up the long, winding driveway leading to Figgie's headquarters on the old Sherwin-Williams estate about an hour west of Cleveland. As Kearney and a dozen other Figgie executives entered one of the company's many meeting rooms, they discovered Dr. Figgie had some company—two consultants from the Cleveland office of Deloitte & Touche, the big accounting firm that also had a consulting arm.

The men gathered around represented decades of manufacturing experience. They had manhandled lathes, grinders, and mills that could bend, cut, or bore through thick steel bars like they were bratwurst. Brawny machinists succumbed to their orders. They could turn large gray machines and screeching grinders under their control into a commercial symphony that crescendoed into an aria of finished goods. Over meetings for the next few days, they listened intently as Dr. Figgie explained that he would launch a massive modernization drive in his new capacity as vice chairman. Some like Kearney were excited at the prospect: He knew Figgie's old business systems and computers needed updating. Some were concerned: Harry III's plan seemed terribly ambitious. Most were simply astonished at the doctor.

After introducing Thomas Lawson and Craig Giffi, the Deloitte & Touche consultants in the room, Dr. Figgie told everyone about a movie he had seen recently called *Valdez Is Coming*. Made in 1971, it starred Burt Lancaster as Bob Valdez, a Mexican constable who kills a man by mistake and spends the rest of the movie trying to extract a $100 donation for the widow from a gang of bad guys who were really responsible for the victim's death. Valdez, Dr. Figgie told the group, was a determined man. Armed with a sawed-off shotgun, an elephant gun, a rifle, and a pistol, he kept chasing the bad guys, seeking the money for the widow. At one point he killed a bad guy and sent the body back to the gang with a note attached that said, "Valdez is coming." He never gave up until he got the job done, mowing down anyone who stood in his way. The men in the room soon learned that Dr. Figgie had recruited them to be on his Valdez Team, a no-nonsense, take-no-prisoners group of Figgie executives, management consultants, and representatives of equipment makers that would modernize Figgie's divisions or else. Soon Dr. Figgie would spread the message "Valdez is coming" to divisions near and far, and anyone who stood in the way of his modernization drive would be mowed down just like the bad guys.

As the key man in charge of the Valdez team, Thomas C. Lawson hardly resembled a gunslinger. Described as a big, affable guy who looked as if he had just walked off a football field, he'd been a management consultant for just under 10 years before he corralled what would become the one of the largest and most controversial consulting engagements in Deloitte & Touche's history. He first met Dr. Figgie at University Orthopedic Associates in 1989, about a year before the doctor would go to work full-time at Figgie International. A Deloitte & Touche CPA had audited books for the Figgie family for years, and when the doctor's medical practice needed a consultant for an operations review, Lawson made the proposal for Deloitte & Touche. UOA didn't really want much. Lawson prepared a report suggesting improvements in the practice's billing procedures. Dr. Figgie was one of three physicians on the committee that selected Deloitte to implement Lawson's recommendations.

At first, Lawson viewed the engagement as routine. He'd done a lot of health care work since he got his MBA from Vanderbilt in 1979. His first job was with a small Atlanta, Georgia, consulting firm that specialized exclusively in health care. Two years later, he landed a job at one of the firm's clients, a hospital in Mullens, West Virginia. After 10 to 12 months on the job, though, Lawson was fired. He'd had a disagreement with the owner. Then, in 1982, he signed on as an associate consultant in the Cleveland office of Touche Ross, one of two accounting firms that would be merged into Deloitte & Touche seven years later. And he'd been there ever since, mainly doing health care work.

By most yardsticks, the UOA engagement was small stuff. But Lawson also learned that there was potential for other business. Soon after the engagement began, Lawson hung around to talk with Dr. Figgie in his office one night and learned that Harry III was a real Renaissance man. Not only did he run a thriving medical practice, he ran a small family-owned manufacturing firm on the side. What's more, his family controlled a Fortune 500 conglomerate, and Dr. Figgie had some ideas about how it should be run. As the weeks went by, Lawson and Dr. Figgie talked regularly about the manufacturing business. This doctor was one smart fellow. He knew more about manufacturing than Lawson. In fact, Lawson had never worked in the manufacturing industry. As a consultant, he had completed only two manufacturing engagements in his career and he couldn't even remember the names of them. But the doctor could talk extensively about modernization concepts, using buzzwords like "world-class manufacturing," "just-in-time inventory" and "kanban." After a decade as a management consultant, Lawson may not have known much about the buzzwords, but he knew marketing. When Figgie invited him to take a look at Clark Reliance Corp., the small manufacturing company that Dr. Figgie ran on the side, Lawson jumped at the opportunity. Giffi, a thin, mustached man with dark brown eyes and a professorial air, also joined the tour.

As Lawson and Giffi would soon learn, Clark Reliance had a strange, symbiotic relationship with Figgie International. The similarities between the two companies made corporate incest almost inevitable. The Figgie family owned Clark Reliance, a manufacturer of steam traps, valves, and gauges for various industrial applications. Based in Strongsville, Ohio, the company had no public shareholders and few outsiders on its board. Harry Figgie, Jr., held the chairman's title, the doctor was president, and everyone referred to Clark Reliance as "the family company." In terms of size, Clark Reliance paled in comparison to the Willoughby-based Figgie International, a $1 billion conglomerate whose stock traded on NASDAQ. Nevertheless the Figgie family also controlled the conglomerate, which was known as "the big company." Although Figgie International had more than 10,000 shareholders, the Figgie family controlled the largest block of voting stock. Harry Figgie, Jr., also chaired the big company, and his son was in the wings.

The two companies had differences, too, but they were equally problematic. Because Clark Reliance was solely owned by the Figgies, Harry and the doctor could do as they pleased. If they wanted to launch a modernization drive, they simply came up with the cash and ordered it done. There were few questions asked. Figgie International, on the other hand, was a much more cumbersome outfit. It had public stockholders, and disclosed its profits and affairs under the public reporting requirements of the nation's securities laws. Stock analysts scrutinized it for clients and it had an independent board with outsiders, although most were appointed by Figgie. Implementing sweeping change at the big company was a far more difficult proposition. In fact, the place seemed organized to thwart change. To maximize profit and control,

Harry Figgie had set up the divisions like independent businesses, each with its own president and its own profit and loss statement. Targets set during Hard Core determined bonuses, raises, and promotions. They were chiseled into five-year plans by the same hard-nosed corporate staff that would hatch modernization schemes. The thinking among division presidents was: Miss your Hard Core targets and Harry would have your head. Past efforts at changing production techniques at Figgie had often failed, primarily because of opposition within the divisions. Managers resisted change if it extended to the color of the ink on their bottom lines. Figgie's head of manufacturing, Larry Schwartz, had attempted to implement some world-class manufacturing techniques at Figgie a few years before and had failed miserably, primarily because of opposition within the divisions. "The corporate staff was not viewed as one that was welcome in the divisions," he said. "There was this old cliché, yeah. 'The corporate guys come down here, they fly in like seagulls and shit on our heads and leave.' With a mentality like that, it's pretty difficult to go into an environment and think that you can be productive."

Lawson and Giffi also learned that winning the Clark Reliance business wouldn't be easy. Although the doctor was friendly, he viewed consultants skeptically. So did Schwartz, the Figgie International executive brought in on the discussions. He thought consultants were people who never got their hands dirty and loved to crank out costly, ponderous reports. He'd tell how Booz Allen, where Harry Figgie used to work, came into Rawlings Sporting Goods and did a great analysis, concluding that Rawlings made 13,600 different products but fewer than 1,000 of them accounted for 80 percent of the business. Schwartz didn't see anyone "putting his flesh to the task," though, or actually showing up at the plant to resolve the problems. Instead, they handed Figgie officials an elaborate report and an even more elaborate bill—$890,000. For his part, Dr. Figgie didn't want to hire anyone who wouldn't give him access to the top. He told Lawson how frustrated he'd become with his inability to speak to the top people at Arthur Andersen, Figgie's accountant.

The two consultants had a powerful organization and a lot of resources behind them, though. The product of a recent merger between two accounting firms, Deloitte & Touche had amassed vast resources when two hard-charging chairmen decided to join Deloitte Haskins &

Sells, a onetime staid, traditional accounting firm and Touche Ross, a relatively young, irreverent firm with an independent streak. Mike Cook, the leader of Deloitte, and Ed Kangas, of Touche Ross, both wanted to market their consulting services to accounting clients. In fact, Cook had restructured Deloitte's compensation plan to make accountants less like auditors and more like business advisors. Ed Kangas had made a name for himself by taking Touche Ross's management advisory fees from $28 million to $100 million. By the time Tom Lawson and Craig Giffi walked onto the floor of Clark Reliance for their tour, Cook and Kangas had engineered a difficult merger that created a new "professional services" firm with nearly $2 billion in revenue from a global network of 60,000 people and offices in more than 100 countries.

Most of the money flowed in from Deloitte & Touche's audit and tax clients, such as tire maker Bridgestone Firestone, and Merion Merrell Dow, a worldwide pharmaceutical firm. But a growing management consulting arm accounted for 20 percent of the firm's revenues. The company billed itself as one of the world's leading management consultants with strength in both general business consulting and specialized information technology. Clients included Armco Steel, which had hired it to help restructure its carbon steel operations in the Midwest; The Home Depot, which had commissioned it to develop software for its information systems; and Cornell's North Shore University Hospital, which had hired it to cut costs and reshape the hospital's patient care delivery system. On paper at least, it appeared well qualified to help Figgie.

The plant tour taught Lawson and Giffi about the problems at the family-owned company, but they learned a lot more about Clark Reliance and Figgie International in talks with Dr. Figgie over the next several months about the modernization drive. Before long, they eroded the initial skepticism of Schwartz and Dr. Figgie about consultants. Lawson and Giffi both had come out of the newly merged company's Touche Ross culture, which tended to be more hip than most accounting firms but also had been plagued by a schlocky reputation. Although Lawson had little experience in manufacturing engagements, Giffi, who had been with Touche Ross since 1983, was the firm's associate national director of manufacturing consulting. Neither Lawson or Giffi was a CPA. Both had MBAs and had risen through the ranks in the consulting divisions. Both men impressed Schwartz. They had a hands-on approach; they didn't fear rolling up their sleeves and getting their hands dirty.

By mid-1990, a proposed game plan for Clark Reliance and Figgie International had emerged, and Lawson had dealt with the concerns voiced by Dr. Figgie. First he took care of Harry III's worries about lack of access to the top brass at Deloitte & Touche. The firm would make Figgie an "Office of the Chairman client." This was one of those hand-holding deals for big clients with big egos. A Deloitte vice chairman would be assigned to monitor the account, and every once in a while Cook himself would drop by for a visit. Lawson dealt with the inevitable worries about cost, too. Deloitte would bill Clark Reliance at 70 percent of its standard rates—a discount as large as any that the firm provided. Deloitte considered the engagement a foundation for a long-term relationship with Dr. Figgie, who had just been named vice chairman of Figgie International. If Figgie liked Deloitte as a consultant, the firm might be able to lure Figgie's auditing business, too. It was worth about $1 million a year to Arthur Andersen. Lawson also committed Deloitte to limiting the number of hours billed each week to 50 per consultant, even though his team members would probably work longer hours.

By October, they had a deal that set the stage for the initial meeting in which Paul Kearney and his colleagues from Figgie International learned they would be on the Valdez team. Lawson spelled out the details of the deal in a letter to Schwartz at Figgie International: For $375,000, Deloitte & Touche would help Clark Reliance become a laboratory for world-class manufacturing by early January 1991. Aided by the consultants, the Valdez team would sweep into the family company, reorganize it, and convert it into a true world-class manufacturer. Some eyebrows might be raised because resources, personnel, and equipment at Figgie International, a stockholder-owned company, would be used to modernize the privately owned Clark Reliance, which had already dabbled unsuccessfully in world-class conversions. It could appear that Dr. Figgie wanted to enrich the family company at the expense of Figgie stockholders. But the doctor ordered a cost-, revenue-, and technology-sharing agreement with Figgie International to cover such concerns. Indeed, Clark Reliance would become an R&D project for Figgie International. The new equipment and business systems installed at Clark Reliance would make it a prototype for world-class manufacturing. Figgie International, or "the big company," could then use Clark Reliance as a showpiece to demonstrate the benefits of modernization to those recalcitrant division managers. In fact, they would call the operation "Project Showpiece." Division managers could be summoned to Clark Reliance to see firsthand how good things could be if they modernized their operations, too. Eventually members of the Valdez team—Figgie executives, people from the equipment manufacturers, consultants and employees of systems people like IBM—would descend upon Figgie International divisions and make them like Clark Reliance. "He told us that we had three months to make it work at Clark Reliance," recalled Kearney. "And then we were going to do the same thing in Buffalo. You know how hard it is to motivate people under those conditions. You tell them you are going to have to work day and night and put this system in by January and if you do it, your reward will be you get to move in the middle of the winter to Buffalo and do the same thing there."

"The Few, the Proud, the Totally Insane"

The consultants had their work cut out for them. No one outside of the Figgie family knew much about Clark Reliance. On the surface, it appeared successful, and Harry always bragged about the company and Harry III's tenure as its leader. Prior to Showpiece, though, things were rocky. With his father's blessing and encouragement, Dr. Figgie had embarked upon a world-class manufacturing effort at Clark Reliance in 1989 and 1990, acquiring $8.5 million worth of numerically controlled machines, which he then tried to blend into a computerized integrated manufacturing project. The project flopped. Company personnel never successfully developed a manufacturing process that used the machinery efficiently. Instead of declining, inventories rose. The flow of material was highly inefficient, and by mid-1990 Clark Reliance officials had to contact major customers and reassure them concerning the future production capability of the company. Harry didn't blame the doctor for the problems. He thought the trouble was in the difficulty of what the company wanted to do. No company had ever implemented world-class manufacturing in a production environment like Clark Reliance's. Crucial elements, such as the necessary computer software, didn't even exist. Clark Reliance officials figured they would have to develop their own strategic business information system. Each time the company tried something new, though, new problems surfaced. Instead of cutting back, Dr. Figgie and his dad decided to plunge ahead. Figgie let Harry III try the same thing with the big company's money.

The ink was hardly dry on the Showpiece agreement when Lawson and Giffi charged ahead. Schwartz couldn't believe it. Clark Reliance's parking lot soon overflowed with the cars of Deloitte & Touche consultants, IBM employees, equipment makers, and Figgie executives. Schwartz spent most of his time there. So did the doctor. The team swept into Clark Reliance intent on turning the place into a world-class manufacturer in 10 to 12 weeks. It was unprecedented, probably impossible. But that didn't stop them. Within weeks, the factory floor had been reorganized six to eight times, straining the company's capacity for change as team members tried to wring inefficiency out of every element of the manufacturing process. Lawson, Giffi, and the Deloitte consultants led the way. "Tom Lawson and Craig Giffi and the staff that reported to them, that was their home, too. They were there all the time, I mean we couldn't find any room in the parking lot," Schwartz later recalled. "It was hard to tell them from the employees. . . . There were no ties and white shirts. I mean this was roll it up, get it down. When I would leave the plants [at night], there were more people employed by Deloitte & Touche there than people employed by the divisions." IBM employees were there to ensure a smooth implementation of the IBM hardware and software going into the plant. Equipment makers were there in force, too, from Mazak, Tsugami, Maho, Weldon, Trumpf, Royal Machine, ASEA, and GMF Robotics, all of which had or would have equipment installed for Showpiece.

Although Dr. Figgie and Schwartz approved everything, Deloitte consultants ran the show. They controlled the information and by doing so made key decisions, such as recommending the shop floor control systems that helped managers reconcile available resources with scheduled completion dates on the production line. They worked on slashing inventories; improving "throughput," or the time it takes to move a product through the plant; installing inventory control systems; reducing "head count," or replacing humans with machines; and cutting the space in the plant devoted to manufacturing while increasing output. They wanted to create a "lights out" manufacturing process that would operate with "minimal human effort." In other words, they wanted to replace people with machines, create the ideal Figgie company, one with as few human employees as possible.

The consultants got right into the spirit of the Valdez team. Soon Lawson, whose nickname was "Bubba," would be firing off memos he called "Bubba Dumps" extolling the merits of the team's efforts. He encouraged others not to let problems diminish their enthusiasm. At one point he told Giffi "not to let the turkeys get him down" and he embraced the spirit of the Valdez team, playing up the "go get the bad guys" metaphor to the hilt. He closed one letter to Dr. Figgie with the inscription:

> The Few!
> The Proud!
> The Totally Insane!
> The Valdez Team!

Within weeks of their arrival at Clark Reliance, the consultants and the corporate brass reported progress. Word went out that the Valdez Team had made tremendous strides at Clark Reliance, thanks in no small part to the leadership of the doctor, whom Harry Jr. started referring to as Figgie's "world-renowned expert on world-class manufacturing." The official story was that Clark Reliance inventories dropped; products moved through the plant faster; head count fell, eventually by 44 percent; the pace of inventory turns quickened, freeing up cash for other operations; and, perhaps most visible of all, Clark Reliance used half the shop floor space to manufacture more. The work was far from done, but Dr. Figgie nonetheless summoned division presidents to Clark Reliance to see his plan in action. Stock analysts came, too, so they could see the doctor's genius at work. Some of the division heads raised questions about how all of this would work in their plants. But they simply didn't know about the cutting edge. Change always exposed backward-thinking Luddites. So what if the research cost alone was running $3 million a year? It would be worth it. Naysayers would just have to wait and see.

Actually, Dr. Figgie and his team had made some strides. They went into Figgie's divisions and cherry-picked Figgie products and parts that were easiest to make profitably. They then transferred production of these items to Clark Reliance, bought new, efficient machinery, and sold off the less efficient old stuff, sometimes to other Figgie divisions. Thanks to the wizardry of modern creative accounting, they were able to minimize reported expenses and create profits. By early 1991, the doctor and his dad figured it was time for the board of directors to see the Clark Reliance miracle. After all, the big company was paying for most of this. Under the cost-sharing arrangement, Clark Reliance, which had encountered severe problems just months before, paid only 6 to 7 percent of Operation Showpiece's research costs, and shareholder-owned Figgie International paid the rest. What's more, the board members soon would be asked to formally approve the Valdez Project, the dramatic expansion of Showpiece designed to upgrade all Figgie divisions to world class. The board's stamp of approval would be a snap. Figgie's board was no different than most in America. It was loaded with old pals like Dale Coenan, who had helped Harry get his start, and business associates such as Fred Brinkman, a Clark Reliance director and former partner in Arthur Andersen & Co. A lot of the directors had a stake in keeping Harry happy. Vince Chiarucci, Figgie's president, pulled down nearly $650,000 in annual salary and bonuses; Harrison Nesbit II, an insurance broker, earned nearly $75,000 a year in commissions from sales of insurance to Figgie International. Most were friends of Harry's and each of the nonmanagement types got $20,000 a year plus $1,000 for each board committee membership. All directors received options to buy the company's stock. With all those perks it was a good bet they would go along with the plan. Giving them a tour first was good form, though.

The directors showed up at a Strongsville restaurant for dinner in the spring of 1991. Soon Harry Jr. got up. It was like a family sing-along. He introduced Dr. Figgie, who got up and called upon young Matthew Figgie, a Clark Reliance employee about to head off to the Harvard Business School, to give an overview of the Valdez program. Pretty soon the board members were deep into a presentation of the magic of world-class manufacturing at Clark Reliance. Lawson gave a presentation, too, as did Giffi. They told the directors how the savings from Valdez would more than pay for the consulting fees they would charge, particularly once the project was expanded to the big company. The consultants projected the Valdez reforms would increase the market value of Figgie International by $350 to $800 million, and they outlined what the directors would see on their tour of Clark Reliance's shop floor. Larry Schwartz had slides that showed the normal flow of material and how the Valdez team had rearranged it to push components through the plant in record time.

Construction was just getting under way at Clark Reliance for another promising feature—a 5,000-square-foot Tech Center, where the Valdez Team could test alternative manufacturing processes and machinery for other Figgie divisions. Schwartz saw it as a place to test new equipment and personnel: "It was a separate area in the [Clark Reliance] manufacturing building. . . . [Eventually we] would bring equipment into that facility, develop the processes that we normally would have expected our division to develop. . . . And once we reached the point where the machine was performing to our expectations, [we would require the] division [to] send their personnel down for training, and that would be their first [exposure to] what we were going to deliver to them. . . . It was a development, prove-out process and a sign-off of the whole cell. We'd [then] pack [the machine] up and ship it to them and install it, and, hopefully in a short period of time they'd be producing the products as we did at the Tech Center."

Soon vans pulled up and whisked the whole entourage to Clark Reliance for the tour. Everyone was impressed. This was cutting edge. Clusters of directors wearing headphones moved from workstation to workstation where select employees would step up to a microphone and tell of the magic spell created by the Valdez team. At the end of the tour, Harrison Nesbit, walking with a cane, asked when this would be done throughout Figgie. The answer: soon. Harry Figgie, Jr., got into his limo, looked at Schwartz, and said, "You really did it." He was proud. So was the board. Everyone was proud. Over the next several months, bankers, analysts, division presidents, and even the dean of the Harvard Business School would troop through Clark Reliance on similar tours. Dr. Figgie was proudest of all. Now it was time to roll out the project to the rest of Figgie's sprawling plants. Valdez indeed was coming.

World Class? What's That?

Lawson liked the Valdez business; it was good for his career. He'd been named a partner just about the time he landed the Figgie account. By early 1991, though, he realized that the Figgie engagement would generate a lot more income than he had originally thought. Winning the initial contract with Clark Reliance would generate $375,000 or more for his employer. No one sneezed at a onetime fee like that. It soon became clear that Clark Reliance would require more work, though. Lawson and Giffi, who hadn't made partner yet, also looked around at Figgie International and noticed many other problems that could use some consulting. They passed on their observations to Dr. Figgie and Schwartz, and in no time Lawson projected getting $5 to $6 million in additional business from Figgie. His bosses were obviously thrilled. So was Giffi, who would soon be promoted to partner, too. Deloitte & Touche wanted to increase its profits by a whopping 40 percent in the first year after the merger. A big increase in billable hours from Figgie would help, particularly since the firm was about to boost its hourly rates for consultants like Lawson by 25 to 45 percent. There was some competition. Both Booz Allen and Andersen Consulting angled for a slice of the Figgie business. But Lawson had a good relationship with Dr. Figgie and he had a good inside source at the company. Schwartz kept Lawson informed. He knew what the competition was up to. As a result, Deloitte & Touche would get most of the business.

As the total billings rose, Lawson's burden and problems increased, too. Although he got along well with almost everyone, Lawson had to walk a fine line, particularly with Dr. Figgie. Both Lawson and Giffi admired the guy for his brains and ambition. He could consume and spit out information like an IBM mainframe. But the doctor's ability to go ballistic rivaled his dad's. He could react to bad news temperamentally and respond to challenges with excess enthusiasm. His timetables for Showpiece and Valdez were way too aggressive, and Lawson knew it. There was no way the rest of the conglomerate could swallow the Valdez initiatives as quickly as Dr. Figgie had suggested to the board. The corporation would gag. The numbers were all off. When the doctor asked Lawson and Giffi to help sell the plan to the board, both made presentations but neither volunteered their doubts about the game plan. Anyone who spent any time at Figgie knew you didn't cross or embarrass a Figgie. Besides, Deloitte & Touche hadn't done any studies to determine if the Valdez program made economic sense for Figgie. The consultants had no data backing up their claims that the savings from Valdez would more than pay for the consulting fees and add $350 to $800 million to the market value of Figgie International. Lawson and Giffi sort of made up the rules as they went along. They didn't guarantee success, either. No consultant ever did that.

Indeed, when Lawson was asked to define a "world-class manufacturer" years later, he couldn't even say what the term actually meant. He said he'd read a couple of books about it. But as far as he could determine, there wasn't really a precise definition or any way to tell if a company ever achieved world class. Giffi, who had helped write a book on world-class manufacturing, agreed. His book, funded by the National Center for Manufacturing Science, a Michigan-based nonprofit outfit that got most of its money from the federal government, didn't exactly run off the bookshelves. Published in 1990 by Dow Jones Irwin, *Competing in World-Class Manufacturing* drew a narrow audience and few reviews. Deloitte purchased a bunch of copies, though, and handed them out to clients, including the people at Figgie. It was a great marketing gimmick for the firm. Nevertheless, even as a coauthor, Giffi couldn't come up with a simple definition for "world-class manufacturing."

"The definition of world-class manufacturing includes a very wide variety of topics and techniques," Giffi would later say, "[but] there was no standard definition. . . . Coming up with an exact definition of world class and, therefore, ascertaining a status against some absolute standard was in our opinion extremely difficult if not impossible." In fact, Lawson and Giffi spent a lot of time with the Dr. Figgie and Larry Schwartz in early and mid-1990 trying to figure out what *they* meant by the term, and came away with a general feeling that the company wanted to do more with less.

By early 1992, though, they had a lot more to worry about than definitions and ambitious timetables. Thanks to the consultants' previous work and presentations to the board, Figgie's directors had authorized the Valdez team to invade the rest of the corporation. Under the original timetable, Deloitte & Touche and other consultants would convert the company into a world-class operation by 1995 at a cost of millions of dollars in consulting fees. But computer problems had surfaced in the IBM software system that Dr. Figgie and Schwartz had bought before the expanded mission had even started. Called MAPICS, the software was supposed to integrate the financial reporting and manufacturing systems at Clark Reliance. Initial reports suggested it wasn't as good as the system it replaced, though. Lawson thought the MAPICS performance was spotty. That wasn't a good sign; the system was a key element of the prototype plant. Lawson had never installed a MAPICS before. For all he knew, no one else at Deloitte & Touche had, either. They would have to look for some enhancements to make the system work properly. But before he could resolve that problem, others surfaced.

By now Lawson was working full-time on Figgie business trying to manage 50-plus people. Giffi worked like a dog, too, but he was out of his league. He had more experience working for manufacturers than Lawson, who later admitted he wasn't the best Deloitte & Touche partner to take charge of the Figgie engagement. Even with the research he did for his book on world-class manufacturing, Giffi had never been involved in anything quite as complex and sweeping as Figgie. Neither had Deloitte & Touche. It would help to go slower. But instead of slowing things down, Dr. Figgie kept speeding things up. Once the Figgie board approved the expansion of Showpiece, the doctor started this "Valdez is coming" business. The original Valdez team split up and fanned out into Figgie's far-flung network of plants. Division presidents honored by a visit from Valdez got the word: Cooperate with the consultants, equipment makers, computer geeks, and other Valdez team members or else. Deloitte & Touche retained overall responsibility for managing the engagement and focused on manufacturing and operational issues. Both Lawson and Giffi also took on specific projects at numerous Figgie divisions. Other consulting firms got a piece of the action, too. Andersen Consulting went to Scott Aviation. Boston Consulting Group, the prestigious Massachusetts firm, landed a huge strategy engagement designed to develop opportunities for Figgie within products and markets, assessing where Figgie should concentrate its efforts once it achieved world class.

As things got more complex, though, a mini-rebellion stirred within the ranks. Not all division presidents liked what they saw. These guys lived and died by the targets carved in stone during Hard Core. People like Glen Lindemann, the president of Scott Aviation, complained that the goals of Valdez clashed with those of Hard Core. At one meeting of division presidents, Lindemann and others questioned the doctor's timetable, peppering Lawson and others at the five-day meeting with questions: Where would the divisions get the people required? How were they expected to pay for all of this? Lawson had some answers. He projected that Figgie International would save $50 to $100 million over three to five years by applying Valdez throughout the company. Those savings would help the divisions pay for modernization. Moreover, the company's workforce would plummet from 17,000 to 11,000 to 7,000 employees; 25 of Figgie's 40 major manufacturing plants would be shuttered. And that didn't count the $50 to $100 million that would be saved by the improved working capital program designed by Deloitte & Touche. The division presidents viewed Lawson's estimates of future savings as fool's gold, though. Indeed under Hard Core guidelines set up by Harry Figgie, Jr., they couldn't even use the projections offered by Lawson in their presentations to the old man. Their projections were far too flimsy for Hard Core. The presidents left the meeting on Valdez in 1991, frustrated by a lack of satisfactory answers. A few of the division chiefs risked their jobs by flatly refusing to sign appropriation requests from corporate headquarters. They doubted the integrity of the projections prepared by Lawson and Giffi.

But things had changed. The division presidents no longer were dealing with the clods from corporate headquarters. Their opposition made them bad guys facing the feared Bob Valdez. At Dr. Figgie's request, Deloitte & Touche had started grading the division managers. Coincidentally, most managers who opposed the Valdez team got low grades and were candidates for termination. Those who embraced Valdez reforms made the honor roll. Larry Schwartz explained that the Valdez project was uniquely designed to wipe out opposition in the divisions via the shop floor: "If you can't get the organization to change, then maybe you can change something about what [people] do that forces them to change. And if you think about the shop floor, it is the driving force. If we want to make the upper echelon change, you might find you could do that by implementing new manufacturing technology and tools that would physically force people to do things differently." For the most part, the intent was to drive it from the shop floor back up through the organization, protests be damned.

Consultants Run Amok

The strategy might have sounded good to Schwartz, who'd been frustrated by resistance in the divisions. But it proved devastating at places like Scott Aviation, where people like Dick DeLisle worked. By the time Valdez arrived there, DeLisle had been named director of operations at Scott near Buffalo. A tall, balding physicist turned corporate quality control expert, he'd worked for Figgie since the mid-1980s. When Harry Figgie needed someone to set up a training center in Virginia, he called on DeLisle. He'd been transferred to Scott in 1988 to run the manufacturing plants. His first brush with Valdez came when he glanced out the window of his second-floor office in 1991 and saw a flatbed truck pull into the lot near Scott's machine shop carrying a huge machining center half the size of a Denny's restaurant. It must have cost a fortune. DeLisle knew no one could order equipment like that without Harry Figgie's okay. Yet DeLisle didn't know a thing about the machine, even though he was responsible for Scott's output.

At first he figured the driver had made a wrong turn; no one would have ordered anything like this without telling him. When he went downstairs and checked the driver's papers, though, the packing slip read: DELIVER TO SCOTT'S MACHINE SHOP. There was no doubt about that. DeLisle got on the phone to Willoughby and tried to reach Dr. Figgie. As usual, the doctor was unavailable. Larry Schwartz took the call instead and confirmed that the machining center belonged to Scott. The doctor had acquired it, Schwartz said. Although DeLisle didn't know it yet, Dr. Figgie had big plans for Scott Aviation.

DeLisle was dumbstruck. He'd been frustrated enough in recent months with all of the consultants running around Scott. He had six different consulting firms working on 10 different projects at Scott. These guys made pit bulls look like poodles. They attacked problems real and imagined. Sometimes it seemed he couldn't turn around without bumping into another consultant. "They always wanted to meet with you and ask questions. I'd walk through the plant and see them sitting there looking at a computer screen. They didn't seem to know what to do and they always wanted to meet with me. I'd go see them and they'd ask me, 'What do you think we should do?' "

As the executive responsible for the output at one of Figgie's best divisions, DeLisle didn't have time for all of this. "I was working seven days a week, coming in on Sundays because I couldn't get my work done with all of these meetings," he recalled. Now Dr. Figgie had come along with this huge machine that would take weeks to install and would disrupt his operations. DeLisle felt the least he could have done was consult him before buying the thing.

DeLisle would soon learn that the surprise delivery was part of a massive plant consolidation the doctor had launched. Over the next several months, Figgie would close old plants and shift their production to company facilities with cheaper labor and new, efficient equipment. For its part, Scott would be converted into Figgie's "center of excellence" for machining parts. Gone were the days when Figgie divisions would machine their own parts or farm out the business to small job shops. The divisions would now send their orders to Scott, where they would be filled at the "center of excellence." Indeed, the machining center parked in the lot was only the start of something big. Scott would get 20 to 25 more new sophisticated machines the doctor and Schwartz had ordered. With the new equipment, managers such as DeLisle would have no choice but to modernize. They would have to conform to the demands of their equipment. Pretty soon other trucks would show up at DeLisle's shop with more new machines and orders to pick up the old gear that DeLisle used 24 hours a day to make things like valves for Scott's Air-Paks, oxygen units that firefighters carry on their backs so they can breathe when they enter burning buildings.

Had anyone consulted DeLisle, they might have had second thoughts. The multimillion-dollar machining center would take about six weeks to program, debug, level, tool, and install properly. What's more, an initial inspection suggested the new machine couldn't be programmed to make some key valves that Scott needed. DeLisle needed valves about the size of a coffee mug for his Air-Paks. The smallest one that could be machined on the new equipment was about the size of a coffeepot.

Timing was a problem, too. Ideally, DeLisle would have phased out his old machines as the new ones came on-line, particularly since Scott would soon inherit about 90,000 hours' worth of new work from other Figgie operations, thanks to the doctor's "center of excellence." Dr. Figgie had ordered the old machines removed before he could bring the new ones on-line, though, so DeLisle would have to improvise. He had to get his Air-Pak valves machined at a shop outside the company.

To DeLisle, the whole scheme seemed crazy. Fire departments and municipalities got touchy about the quality of their Air-Paks. Firemen, after all, used them for breathing while in burning buildings. Going to a costly outside supplier risked quality control problems, even though DeLisle knew of a good machine shop in town. He tried to explain his position to Schwartz. But his objections made him a bad guy. Dr. Figgie and Schwartz didn't want to hear why things couldn't be done. They'd heard enough of that in the past. The Valdez team treated anyone who spoke out as a doubting Thomas opposed to change. "It was almost like they were saying, 'I'm sorry but we had to hire these consultants to take care of this because guys like you don't know what in the hell you are doing,' " said DeLisle.

The consultants were no better. DeLisle said they were intelligent. But it was clear they had never met a production schedule or machined a valve. They requested meetings constantly. "If I would resist a meeting or tell them I didn't have the time, they'd say, 'Well, Dr. Figgie ordered us in here to modernize this plant and we don't want to go back and tell him that you didn't have time to meet with us.' "

So he installed the huge machine, despite his doubts. Sure enough, it was a waste of time. Instead of becoming the pulse of a "center of excellence," the machine was like a cadaver. Scott Aviation used it about an hour a week. It became the butt of jokes on the shop floor. Meanwhile, the Valdez team and platoons of other consultants kept coming. At one point, Andersen Consulting had three teams working on plant consolidations. Boston Consulting Group was there developing an air-purifying product strategy; Deloitte & Touche had three projects— just-in-time manufacturing, world-class distribution, and world-class manufacturing. Price Waterhouse had activity-based costing, which involved figuring out the cost of each phase of production. Interaction Associates was there for strategic planning, and Pritsker for automated scheduling. DeLisle sat down and made a list of all projects under way. It included 20 different undertakings, ranging from a working capital reduction program to the installation of a computer-aided design system for engineering. Any one of these things involved a major project. But 20 of them—simultaneously? It was unbelievable! Chaos reigned. One consultant's goal often clashed with another's.

It was clear the consultants hadn't done their homework. They needed help from guys like DeLisle, who resented them because they abused his time, bullied his people, acted like they didn't have to deal with anyone except at the top, and didn't seem to know what they were doing. A team from Scott had to assume the leadership of the strategic planning process because Interaction Associates was moving too slowly. Scott officials also had to hold a meeting to give some direction to Andersen and to help set a timetable for Boston Consulting Group, which billed Figgie up to $1,300 an hour for its efforts.

DeLisle would go home shaking his head. He'd put in 12-to-14-hour days, seven days a week. Yet no one seemed to see the big picture. The consultants created as many problems as they solved. One of Deloitte & Touche's goals was to cut inventories. So they came up with a just-in-time inventory reduction plan. The result: a huge problem. Scott made a lot of money on the airline industry, which had a rule known as "airplane on the ground." Everyone at Scott knew it: Keep an airplane on the ground because you can't supply a needed part within 24 hours and you lose the contract. The just-in-time program removed excess parts from Scott's inventory, though, jeopardizing its ability to deliver within 24 hours. DeLisle challenged the logic of the directives and asked some tough questions, but it didn't do any good. Questions made the "bad guy" worse—a target for Valdez and his big guns. On October 30, 1991, Valdez got his man. Larry Schwartz and Dr. Figgie called DeLisle's foreman, Warren Boneburg, and told him to stop taking orders from DeLisle. Instead, they hired Boneberg as a part-time consultant for corporate headquarters, from which he would get his orders from now on. DeLisle resigned the next day.

"Bankruptcy 1995"

DeLisle was not alone; many Figgie veteran executives quit or got fired. That didn't seem to bother the doctor or his dad, though. Harry Figgie, in fact, was quite worried about the inflation wracking the nation's economy. He was thinking about writing a book to warn America that the nation faced bankruptcy by 1995 unless someone did something soon. Ironically, he had a problem with inflation of a different sort closer to home. By 1992, Figgie International's tab at Deloitte & Touche had soared thanks to the Valdez team; going world class cost a lot. Figgie projects that had sounded simple on paper had become complex in practice, adding hours and costs to the bill. At one point, the Valdez team decided to develop a standard tooling process for Figgie. If team members could develop technologies that minimized the number of times a machinist had to change the tools in his machine, they could minimize the time that the machine was idle. That sounded simple enough. Actually, it wasn't. Team members first had to define all components made by the machine, and then develop new tools that could make a wide range of parts required by the Figgie manufacturing process, which was characterized by numerous batches of small orders for different components. The Valdez team spent hours changing components or developing novel programming and machining techniques, and time was expensive when you had consultants from Deloitte & Touche charging $300 to $400 per hour. Special tooling had to be developed, designed, and acquired, too, because commercially available tooling couldn't process the range of parts being made at Figgie's plants. In some cases, two or three efforts with several vendors would be required. Similar programs were under way throughout Figgie.

At the offices of Deloitte & Touche, Lawson was like the guy who rode into town on a white horse. He started out with this one small engagement and before long Deloitte had 60 or 70 separate engagements at Figgie. Eventually some 250 Deloitte consultants would stalk Figgie plants, charging anywhere from $70 an hour to Lawson's $420 an hour. The consulting side of the business loved it. Few clients generated such fees, and even fewer had the potential to generate so much more. But there was a wrinkle: Figgie hadn't paid all of its bills. By year-end 1991, Figgie had paid Deloitte & Touche about $7 million. But it owed the firm another $9.3 million in outstanding fees and expenses, and the tab was rising. Lawson and Giffi soon got a call from Dr. Figgie and Schwartz. Figgie, they said, had cash flow restraints. The company intended to pay its bill. It just needed some time and a reasonable payment plan. In a later meeting at Figgie headquarters, Lawson told Dr. Figgie to come up with a number—an amount of money that Figgie could afford to pay each month. Any billings in excess of the monthly payment would be added to the total and paid off in time. The doctor suggested $750,000 a month. Deloitte & Touche top guns went along with the deal. Figgie, after all, was an "Office of the Chairman" client. And the meter kept running.

Other troubles quickly overshadowed the cash flow problems for Larry Schwartz. Driving the modernization by forcing change on the shop floor proved far more tricky that anyone had imagined. Schwartz had helped the doctor make major investments in capital equipment and ship the gear to many Figgie units. Outsiders might think the divisions would be happy to get this shiny new stuff. They weren't. A prime example was Scott Aviation. To get maximum utilization of the new machinery, Scott would have to run Saturday and Sunday shifts. But Scott's unions balked at weekend hours. Schwartz got tough; he moved Scott's entire health, safety, and machining operation to another location. It was an expensive and risky proposition. But he did it and then shut down the New York facility, which got the attention of others at Scott.

The trouble was that new problems surfaced faster than the old ones disappeared, and some were insoluble. Figgie had invested a lot of money and new world-class equipment in two plants in Swainsboro, Georgia, that made parts for other Figgie operations. Once the equipment was installed, though, machine downtime surged, just as it had at DeLisle's operations at Scott. Soon other plants complained of tardy parts deliveries from Georgia, and Schwartz swung into action. He remembered his visit to the Swainsboro plant vividly: "I was watching an individual have a difficult time producing a part, and I asked him a question about the gear range he was using. He says, 'I'm not sure.' And I said, 'Well, you get the manual and I want to go through it with you,' and he pulled the manual out and he handed it to me. And I said, 'No, [you] find it. I want to know that you know how to use this tool.' And he said, 'I can't read,' and this was the foreman! The corporation sent down a team of people from human relations and we had the entire plant tested. And if I recall right, the reading level was third or fourth grade. That also was the same in the plant next door. And on the basis of that . . . a decision was made. . . . We can't make this work . . . pack [the plant] up and move it."

If the rank and file wasn't the problem, the managers were. Division chiefs complained about the choice of equipment that Dr. Figgie and Schwartz had ordered. Either it didn't work well, or it conflicted with their Hard Core obligations. Executives like Rick Barkley detected an early and genuine concern on the shop floor at Figgie's Closetech packaging operation about a decision to move the bulk of the company's machining operations to New York and Georgia. Barkley's men feared taking precision parts made by experienced handcraftsmen and moving them to shops characterized by little experience and sophisticated machinery that no one seemed to understand. Schwartz showed them. He and Dr. Figgie showed up and conducted a public auction at Closetech, which made equipment used to fill and close containers like cans. The doctor and Schwartz sold the machining equipment right out from under them. Barkley was told he could get his parts from another modernized Figgie unit—Consolidated Packaging and Machinery Co. in New York. Barkley switched to Consolidated, but soon had trouble getting his parts. So he called to find out what was wrong. As it turned out, Consolidated had new equipment, too, and couldn't achieve the tolerances for many of the parts that had been made by the Closetech Equipment that Schwartz and Dr. Figgie had sold. Compounding the problem was Consolidated's inability to meet the specs on the parts it delivered. Barkley complained to Harry Figgie, Jr. The doctor and Schwartz then sent in a team to resolve the parts transition problems. The team was from Deloitte & Touche; Barkley recalled the scene: "They seemed to be the ones organizing the work, they seemed to be the people taking responsibility for scheduling and the throughput and the machinery that was in there, and the floor layout and the—just the whole project management activities of the transition."

It never worked, though. It was like the rest of the world-class conversion; no one could figure out exactly what was going on. "I think as a general statement about the whole process, and Deloitte & Touche's role in the whole world-class [initiative], I was never sure who was responsible for what and who had initiated action. The thing obviously was not going well," said Barkley. The problems with the machines continued, costing Barclay frustration and lost sales: "I can't necessarily blame Deloitte & Touche for everything, but my view of it was [once they came in] we went backwards, we got less and less product out," Barkley said.

Others in Figgie shared Barkley's sentiments. Just after the company's spring 1992 board meeting, Deloitte lost a big chunk of business at Snorkel Economy, a Figgie unit that made aerial platforms and scissor lifts. Lawson questioned the wisdom of the move, particularly since his consultants were about to put together an important report for Rick Solon, Snorkel's president. Lawson fired off a memo to Schwartz, questioning the capability of Snorkel's management team to avoid deterioration if Deloitte & Touche left the operation. He was careful. He asked Schwartz to keep the memo from Solon, a capable guy whom Harry

Figgie admired but also no fan of the world-class initiative. Solon obviously wouldn't like Deloitte & Touche criticizing his executives behind his back. But the board's action on Snorkel raised broader questions. What was going on here? Lawson knew there were problems. But Figgie had embarked on a massive transformation. Now the company was sending mixed signals. Even as it cut back at Snorkel, Figgie asked Deloitte & Touche to launch an inventory reduction program at 10 to 15 other divisions. No one seemed angry, either. Lawson got along great with Schwartz. He gave the guy's son, David, a summer job with Deloitte & Touche, on a Figgie project at that. He only billed $70 an hour for the kid. And things seemed even better with Dr. Figgie. He was talking to Lawson about a big job—director of operations. Not bad for a guy who had never worked for a manufacturer. In fact, Lawson angered the doctor when Lawson declined the offer because he wanted more money and a vice president's title. And there were those evenings on the town while visiting Figgie plants. Lawson picked up the tab for Schwartz and the other Figgie guys in topless bars in Dallas and New York, although he insisted that he didn't expense all of the fun money to Figgie's account. The cash he passed out to everyone for their use during an evening at a New York City stripper bar came from his own pocket. To lose some business in such an atmosphere didn't seem to make sense.

Lawson didn't get much time to dwell on the problems, though. As he pondered his fate at Figgie, Harry dropped a bombshell. The first hint of trouble came when the consultants learned that Harry was sick with pneumonia. It knocked him flat on his back and left Dr. Figgie solely in charge. The pneumonia kept Figgie out of his office for some 15 months. That didn't stop him from publishing his book. *Bankruptcy 1995*, a scary tome that warned America of a fiscal Armageddon, came out in the fall of 1992. In the introduction, Harry compared himself to Paul Revere riding through the countryside warning the citizens. About the same time, Figgie decided his company faced a dire future, too, unless it could implement world-class manufacturing soon. Waiting until 1995, the original target, was too long. The country might be bankrupt by then. Figgie International would have to complete the drive to world class within 18 months.

The Big Chill

The news stunned Larry Schwartz. Dr. Figgie had issued the order: Complete world class in 18 months! The chairman's orders! The very idea took Schwartz's breath away. It was hard enough to convert this corporate misfit into a modern corporation. To do it within 18 months was absurd. Figgie would have to add employees precisely at a time when they were pressing for head-count reductions through Hard Core! Lawson had a similar reaction. Schwartz understood the consultants' concerns; the timetable would give the organization a hernia. The doctor said he understood, too. This was a risky proposition. In the end, though, Lawson bowed to the inevitable. Harry Figgie had made a decision, and Deloitte & Touche would live by it, despite any reservations. Once Lawson left his office, the doctor set his sympathies aside. Actually he was confident the decision from Dad was right. The timetable was slower than the one he wanted, but faster than the one sought by Deloitte & Touche and Schwartz. That made it just about right.

The decision worried Lawson more than he let on during his meeting with Figgie. Somebody had to inject some reality into the situation, and Lawson soon talked to Giffi about approaching the doctor with some straight talk. This was touchy. Dr. Figgie was volatile. He didn't like to hear bad news. Sometimes he reacted okay, but often he took off like a rocket. The list of canned Figgie executives was as long as Figgie's driveway, and most of them had gotten axed for being frank. Charlie Miner, a smart and savvy group vice president, had stood up to the old man. Harry wanted to junk the union contract at Automatic Sprinkler Co. and go nonunion. Miner, a guy with a lot of integrity, thought that was a dumb idea and told Figgie. Miner compared the transition from a union to a nonunion contract to a sex-change operation. "You wouldn't like the outcome," he told Harry. Instead, Harry didn't like the answer. Miner was transferred and eventually dismissed. The trouble was, Figgie International didn't have the "bull pen" to keep firing people, particularly able executives. Already Dr. Figgie was asking Lawson and Giffi to cut the number of consultants in Figgie plants and transfer their work to Figgie employees. Too much was going on simultaneously. Deloitte & Touche's billable hours at Figgie had soared. In the 19 months since the $750,000 payment plan had started, Figgie

International's outstanding tab at Deloitte & Touche had reached $25 million and was still growing.

One reason the bill soared involved the Figgies; tightfisted Harry wasn't minding the store—the doctor was—and the doctor didn't pay too much attention to such details. Another problem was the padded bills submitted by Deloitte & Touche. Lawyers for Figgie would later confront Giffi with invoices on which he billed Figgie for 42 hours at $275 an hour for a project when his time sheet to Deloitte & Touche suggested that he had worked only 26 hours. A similar pattern existed in invoices for numerous other consultants, but Giffi said the lawyers took the records out of context. The main reason for the huge bill, though, was that Deloitte & Touche consultants continued to do a lot of work for the conglomerate.

Figgie's workforce kept shrinking as it consolidated plants and shuttered warehouses. Meanwhile, the wrenching downsizing increased pressure on the consultants to do more. Problems were as common as pumps at places like Figgie Power Systems, a recently launched plant consolidation. The Tech Center at Clark Reliance was losing money big time, too. Lawson and Giffi had supported Figgie as much as they could despite the rising stock of unpaid Deloitte & Touche invoices. At one point Lawson short-circuited a Deloitte & Touche report on activity-based costing that challenged some of the company's ideas. Had that thing landed in Figgie's corporate suites, he had written to his consulting colleagues, he'd have gotten "his ass cooked in oil." But he and Giffi also knew something had to be done. Figgie's executive corps simply wasn't up to the job, and someone had to tell the doctor. Giffi got the job.

It was a cold winter day when Giffi met with Joe Skadra in Willoughby. Skadra knew the score. As Figgie's top financial officer, he knew the soaring consulting fees threatened his financial statements. So far they had not dragged down earnings. Figgie had capitalized a lot of the fees, sinking them in the financial statements like a submarine. Arthur Andersen, Figgie's outside auditors, had bought the argument that the consulting fees were like assets that would produce income over time. The money had been dumped into projects that would eventually benefit Figgie's bottom line. But that was a bit of financial subterfuge. Skadra saw the tab rising, while benefits from world class

remained marginal at best. If they didn't start producing smashing results soon, Skadra would be forced to convert the fees into expenses that
would erode Figgie's bottom line. The submarine cruising around in his
financial statements would fire a torpedo, and it would score a direct
hit, particularly if he also had to account for the unused inventories hidden in places like that old dairy building. And now he had Giffi in his
office telling him that world-class manufacturing might not work at
Figgie! The consultant was diplomatic enough. There was a lot of
mumbo jumbo about the need to "bolster competencies of some of
their human resources, particularly their executives in a number of the
key divisions," or else they "were going to have difficulty achieving the
level of success in the times frames they had desired." What Skadra
really heard, though, was that after spending $25 million plus on
consulting fees and $100 million on new equipment, this guy was say-
ing world-class manufacturing was never going to work at Figgie.
Skadra asked Giffi if he would care to deliver the same news to Dr. Figgie. The answer: Only if Giffi got some assurances that the doctor
wouldn't blow up.

Giffi and Lawson had always liked Dr. Figgie. They talked about
how smart he was—his genius. Sure, his people skills weren't that great.
He was a good man with numbers, though. He consumed information
like Bill Clinton ate junk food. The doctor liked these guys, too, especially Lawson. But his warm feeling cooled to a big chill when Giffi
showed up and told him Deloitte & Touche couldn't get the job done
with Figgie's existing executive corps. The doctor didn't like that news.
He'd authorized $25 million, $30 million, even more in consulting fees,
acquired all of that equipment. He couldn't also replace all of Figgie's
management! Giffi sized up the situation right away. The doctor didn't
blow up, but he was "visibly agitated." Giffi couldn't tell why. Either he
was angry about the news itself or he was furious that Giffi had told
Skadra first. Either way, there was no question he was upset, and Giffi
kept talking. The big chill turned to ice before Dr. Figgie started to
warm again to the consultants. He knew how persistently his executives
opposed change. He actually authorized Deloitte & Touche to give him
a formal evaluation of division personnel and to prepare a "management guide." They'd do a book that outlined what various departments
and personnel should be doing on a daily, monthly, quarterly, and annual basis.

Figgie International decided to stop paying Deloitte & Touche any money less than a year later, though. Larry Schwartz didn't necessarily agree with the decision made after a meeting at Willoughby. Vince Chiarucci first suggested suspending the $750,000 monthly payment. Figgie had already paid Deloitte & Touche $20 million or so, and it still owed the firm more than $29 million in outstanding invoices. But concerns about the quality of the consulting firm's work had multiplied. There were complaints about Figgie Power, Figgie Fire, and Meyers-Mojoiner in Charleston. Many divisions complained about the MAPICS computer software program. When MAPICS emerged from the Clark Reliance test facility with changes engineered by Deloitte & Touche consultants, several divisions reported troubles. Skadra was unhappy with Deloitte's work on the inventory reduction project.

Schwartz really didn't agree with the decision to suspend payment. People weren't thrilled with the Boston Consulting Group's work on the markets Figgie should enter. Charlie Miner said it was terrible. "They come in and they tell you they want to make you number one in a market. Let's say it's the wallpaper market. Then they say, 'No, we're going to make you number one in the brown wallpaper market.' Then they say, 'No, we are going to make you number one in the brown wallpaper with red borders market.' Then they'd say, 'No, we are going to make you number one in the brown prepasted wallpaper with red borders market.' . . . They'll eventually make you number one in a market, but the market will be so narrow that there won't be anyone to buy anything." Despite such hostility, Figgie didn't stop paying BCG, even though its hourly rates dwarfed Deloitte & Touche's. Eventually Figgie would pay BCG about $18 million for consulting services. Schwartz thought suspending payment on work currently under way was one thing. But the $29 million owed to Deloitte & Touche was for work previously done. Schwartz couldn't very well oppose the decision, though, for the doctor wasn't happy. In fact, he told Schwartz to investigate the quality complaints about Deloitte & Touche and report back to corporate headquarters. He then summoned Lawson and Giffi to Willoughby again.

It was winter 1993. Harry Figgie had returned to his office after months of suffering from bacterial pneumonia. By then, his book was a smashing success, occupying a spot on *The New York Times* best-seller list for months. He was soon firing off memos to division chiefs just like the old Harry. Tom Lawson hadn't been around Willoughby for months. Ever since Giffi had given Dr. Figgie the bad news, the two consultants had had "limited reasons to appear at Figgie's headquarters." Meanwhile, Figgie continued to hold up payment on its bill, and Lawson felt the chill in the atmosphere when he entered the room. Dr. Figgie avoided eye contact, and Schwartz went over several points. His comments weren't friendly: "Pissed away a lot of money and what did we get for it"; "Charleston facility, Deloitte [& Touche] consultant running the place"; "inventory reduction a complete failure"; "MAPICS at Figgie Packaging—failure."

These guys were using words like "malpractice." Well, they owed Deloitte & Touche $30 million, and Lawson's bosses wanted it paid. Besides, the meter was still running; Deloitte & Touche consultants still worked in Figgie plants. Lawson said his firm could be reasonable. Deloitte & Touche would offer some reductions off the invoices or some additional consulting time free if Figgie could reach a fair decision on the outstanding fees. The meeting ended with an agreement to meet again. As Lawson and Giffi drove down the long, winding driveway at Willoughby, though, it was clear that the chill in the air would last beyond winter.

The Inquisition

A month later, Figgie's first losses surfaced publicly. Harry Figgie, Jr., went to Wall Street to tell the company's story. The stock analysts in the room at the Park Lane Hotel in New York City watched him walk to the microphone. The session was called Lehman Brothers Eleventh Annual Diversified Companies Seminar. It was more like Judgment Day for Harry Figgie. He had to tell them Figgie International would report a whopping loss in its third quarter, the first in 25 years.

Harry talked about "strategic vision"; the precarious global situation; the latest technology and the havoc wreaked on the economy and businessmen by a profligate federal government bent on debt and tax increases. He told them how Figgie International had cut its divisions from 43 to 27; had slashed employment by 25 percent (he expected future cuts of another 24 percent); had shuttered 47 plants and had dropped the number of machine tools it needed from 3,300 to 225. Dr.

Figgie took over and gave a slide show on Figgie's "world-class conversion." He talked of significant increases in market share, significant marketing advantages, depth of customer penetration, and global expansion. But the hard numbers on the bottom line told a different story. Only six of Figgie's 27 divisions were on budget for the year, the worst performance Harry Figgie, Jr., had ever seen. Three of its largest divisions would lose big money during the year, and the rest couldn't make up for it. Midwestern floods had decimated a fourth large division, racking up $20 million in cleanup costs for Figgie. The company would report a third-quarter loss and have a bad 1993, the Figgies said. Dividends would be cut from 12.5 cents per share to 6 cents. But 1994 would be different. Figgie's troubles were behind it. Dr. Figgie's conversion into a world-class corporation would be completed in 18 months, a job that Harry originally had figured would take five years. The presentation went well. There were questions, including some tough ones about Figgie's total debt, which would grow to more than $400 million, and its cash reserves, depleted when the accountants translated the company's financial sleight of hand into hard numbers But Harry Figgie fired back that the company could handle the situation. He wasn't a tough boss and a best-selling critic of government debt for nothing. Indeed, by the time he and his son left Wall Street to return to the industrial prairies of the Midwest, the company's stock price had dipped only marginally. Hard-charging Harry Figgie was back, and no one was the wiser for his absence.

Figgie's plane had barely touched down when the lawsuit was filed. Charlie Miner, the guy Harry had fired in 1992, hit the Figgies with a class-action suit in early December. Harry, Dr. Figgie, and the board were defendants. It took guts to file suit against the Figgies. They were powerful people in Cleveland. Figgie had fired dozens of executives, but no one had pulled anything like this. Miner raised some tough and touchy issues in the suit, too. He and his lawyer, Dennis Murray, a class-action litigator from Sandusky, Ohio, portrayed the Figgie board as a collection of Harry's cronies and pals all lining up at the trough of a stockholder-owned company for their perks and pay. Miner leveled charges of flagrant nepotism—Nancy as the corporate decorator; young Matthew, director of mergers and acquisitions flying around Europe on the company plane; Dr. Figgie as the incompetent heir to the throne; Clark Reliance, the family company, a corporate leech sucking cash out of the publicly held Figgie; and the imperial Harry, who ran the place like a personal fiefdom. The suit said the family had modernized Clark Reliance at the expense of Figgie stockholders, played games with Figgie's financial statements, and diverted corporate property to their personal use; the suit even took a shot at the Norman Rockwell family portrait paid for by the big company. Miner's lawyer had imagination; the suit called the company planes Figgie's Air Force. The Figgies denied the charges.

The suit didn't have half the impact of the losses, though. The company floated hints in January that things were worse than initially expected: Figgie would report a loss for the fourth quarter of 1993, too, leading to a full year in the red for the first time in the company's history. But there were no specific numbers. They didn't come until the March board meeting, and they stunned those savvy Wall Street "analysts." Figgie International lost $179 million on sales of $768 million during 1993, partially because Figgie International's creative accounting finally caught up with it. Harry was not happy. The losses amounted to more than $10 a share and he owned a lot of Figgie stock. Bad publicity followed. Pretty soon there were headlines in newspapers and magazines. *Business Week* wondered: "Does the House of Figgie Need Cleaning?" Then the board got worried. Things started spinning out of the Figgies' control. Board members, acting as if they didn't know the score, started questioning everything. They hired accountants and consultants to look at what consultants and accountants had done to the company. Ernst & Young started a sweeping audit. Then came Jay Alix and Associates, a consulting firm that specialized in turnarounds. Pretty soon the whole place was under scrutiny.

By springtime 1994, an inquisition had started. Walter Vannoy, the retired vice chairman of McDermott International, the corporate parent of Babcock & Wilcox, and a Figgie board member, had taken over as temporary head of Figgie. He had called a meeting to discuss Deloitte & Touche's unpaid bills, and Larry Schwartz could see that Tom Lawson wasn't happy. Lawson didn't say much; he didn't have to. His body language told Schwartz that Lawson found the tone of the conversation offensive. Ted Stenger from Jay Alix and Associates took the lead in the discussion. Stenger didn't mince words. He'd already stunned those young guys from Boston Consulting by telling them he would no longer pay for their work. Now he talked bluntly to Lawson and other Deloitte & Touche officials: Everyone was concerned about the condition of Figgie International, Stenger said, with respect to world class and Deloitte & Touche's involvement. A lot of money had poured into the project and there had been no improvements to speak of. He made sure that Lawson and Deloitte & Touche knew of Figgie International's anger, and that payment of Deloitte & Touche's invoices would not be forthcoming. Schwartz had tangled with Stenger before. Not long ago, they had been in Vannoy's office and Stenger had taken off on the world-class effort at Figgie Power. He said it was hard to believe that Figgie officials could have committed that kind of money to a division that looked as though it had only $15 to $18 million in sales. Schwartz got mad and told Stenger he didn't know what in the hell he was talking about. Vannoy finally had to tell him to calm down. Now Stenger was doing the same thing to Lawson. Al Fisher, a senior Deloitte & Touche official, was there, too. There was a long pause once Stenger quit talking, as when someone has an outburst and no one knows quite what to say. The room was quiet. Figgie wanted Deloitte & Touche to make some sort of settlement offer on the bill. Otherwise they would pay nothing. But Lawson didn't say much. Neither did Fisher. Incredibly, Deloitte & Touche, at the time, was still consulting for Figgie. The ink was barely dry on the May letter Deloitte & Touche had sent Figgie promising to correct the MAPICS problem at Figgie Fire. Deloitte & Touche had actually assigned more personnel to the project. In light of the frosty relations, the letter, which also evaluated some key Figgie Fire purchasing and planning employees, seemed surreal. The consultants had graded the executives—three got Fs and one got a D, grades that would earn the employees a recommendation to be axed. The other six got Bs and Cs. There were no As. The meeting adjourned without any agreements.

It was July 1994, and a lot had happened at Figgie. Schwartz was at Akron Packaging when he got the news about Dr. Figgie. Someone called and said the doctor had resigned. Schwartz phoned the doctor and it was pretty clear from the conversation what had happened. The doctor told the board that world class was the company's only hope and that he was the driving force behind it. But the board still wanted his resignation. Dr. Figgie told Schwartz that he'd just have to see "how it all fell out." Next Schwartz went to see Harry Figgie, Jr. It was an emotional meeting, sitting in Harry's cluttered office talking about the state of the corporation and Schwartz's concerns about the future. Schwartz felt a personal investment in the millions of dollars that had been poured into world class. It seemed as though he were watching a slow death. Day after day another machine would be idled. Pretty soon the vultures would start selling them. He couldn't deal with it, and he confessed his fears to Harry. "And he said to me, 'Larry, if you don't stay here and help us finish this, I don't know who's going to be able to finish this, because I'm not so sure who understands where we are in this program.' And he shared with me, he said he plans to be here, and as long as he's here, he hopes I'm there. . . . And we shook hands and I made a gentleman's agreement." Shortly afterward, Harry Figgie, Jr., resigned. Schwartz left, too. He got another job with Okuma Machinery, but was also available for consulting work at Figgie for $1,000 a day.

By August 1995, the guard booth at the entrance to "the house that Harry built" was empty. The gardens at the old Sherwin-Williams estate were in full bloom, although the fountain in front of Figgie's Willoughby headquarters had ceased shooting water high into the air. An oil portrait of Harry Figgie, Jr., still hung in the entry to Figgie International as Ira Gamm came down the steps and noted how the place had changed. "A lot of the artwork's been sold," he said. Figgie International had changed a lot. Despite spending more than $75 million for advice, it had barely escaped bankruptcy in 1994. Sales of $1.3 billion in 1989 had plunged to $319 million by 1994; profits of $63 million had turned into losses of $166 million. Instead of 17,000 employees, Figgie's workforce had plummeted to just 6,000. It had sold seven divisions in 1994. Fifteen more divisions and more employees would go by the end of 1995, all to raise money to pay off its debt. The old cafeteria for employees was filled with artwork about to go on the block. The headquarters was for sale, too. A Deloitte & Touche official had talked to Dr. Figgie a few months back, and the doctor had blamed the whole catastrophe on the board. They had abandoned world class and doomed the company to failure, he said. Vannoy had commissioned a Figgie employee to scrutinize the consulting fees and he was furious at the results. Boston Consulting Group had charged anywhere from $400 to $1,300 per hour, the highest fees that Vannoy had ever seen in his business career. BCG said its top fee was not that high. Nevertheless, Figgie officials said they were not happy with the results at any price, even though they have already paid most of the bill. After paying BCG $17.4 million in fees and expenses, Figgie refused to pay any more. It still owed BCG more than $1 million in additional fees. Instead, it filed suit, alleging that BCG had provided flawed market studies and strategies. Figgie had paid Deloitte & Touche about $22 million and still owed more than $30 million. Vannoy refused to pay Deloitte & Touche any more, either, and filed suit against the firm. Allegations of fraud and incompetence flew. No one was really happy with the consultants who were not named in the suits, either, but there was no other litigation. Eventually the suits involving the consultants were settled out of court, and the resolutions remained secret. Boston Consulting Group said it had made no mistakes and that its work at Figgie was solid. Deloitte & Touche officials defended their consultants' work, too, and said the firm's strategy had fallen victim to a change in Figgie's management. "We were not found guilty of doing lousy consulting work," said John Fox, a partner in Deloitte & Touche's Chicago office. "We didn't have to pay any penalty, we just took a haircut on our fees." Harry Figgie retreated to his family and the family company. Neither he nor Dr. Figgie would comment publicly on the problems. The Figgie family settled the Miner suit, too, agreeing to pay more than $3 million in legal fees and compensation to Miner and other plaintiffs. As part of the settlement, Harry Figgie, Jr., also gave up millions of dollars in back pay, benefits, and bonuses. Figgie and his son remain in the Cleveland area, working at "the family company" and scrutinizing the new management at Figgie International as sizable shareholders of the company's stock.

Although the Figgies remain mum about their downfall, there are some lessons to be learned from their sad story. Beware of consultants marketing buzzwords like "world-class manufacturing." They are usually peddling vague concepts that can't be measured or judged. As a later chapter on Sears, Roebuck & Co. will demonstrate, it is best to hire consultants for a specific task and avoid carte blanche engagements like Figgie. A consultant can't bail you out of trouble, either. Consulting firms are no substitute for vision and good management. Harry Figgie had moments as a good manager, and his misguided son at least had some vision. The consultants had neither. Check out the backgrounds of the consultants. Lawson clearly never should have been given such a large engagement, and the "Office of the Chairman" program was a joke. All too often the big guns land the contract and then send in the guys with the peashooters. Watch the billings carefully. And always remember that the greatest attribute of the American management consulting industry is its ability to market itself. Deloitte & Touche was just doing what most others do every day: selling themselves. But Figgie's experience makes it pretty clear that consultants often tell you what they think you want to hear and not what you should see. Perhaps the most important lesson is to listen to your own employees. More often than not, they know as much as or more than a bunch of people who make their money peddling change. Had Harry Figgie or the doctor listened to people like Charles Miner or Dick DeLisle, everyone would have been better off. In fact, the new management at Figgie recently rehired DeLisle. Lastly, keep in mind that the consultants often have little to lose. If things work out, they claim credit. If not, they blame employees or changes in management or a host of other problems.

The experience at Figgie didn't hurt Deloitte & Touche. It remains one of America's most successful management consulting firms. There was precious little publicity about its spat with Figgie, and most of the damaging court papers remain sealed from public view in boxes stored in the corner of a courthouse in Cleveland. Tom Lawson's career wasn't hurt; he went on to become a partner in charge of the company's Mexico City office. After Dr. Figgie resigned from Figgie International, he even suggested he and Lawson might do some consulting together. Giffi remains in Ohio. Actually, the one who seemed hurt the most by the experience was Harry Figgie. His gloomy predictions that things would go to hell in 1995 came true. Ironically, the victim was Harry Figgie and not America. Gamm recalled the last time he saw him:

"It was really sad. Here he is, you'd think he'd be walking out of here honored as a captain of industry who built all of this. I saw him, he was walking down that hallway out there late in the afternoon. The sun was setting and he was all alone. I looked out the door of my office and watched him walking down the hall with his back to me. He was carrying a box under his arm. He had just cleaned out his desk."

3

The Jobs Elimination Festival

HOW ANDERSEN CONSULTING
MOVED INTO THE BIG LEAGUES

If the story of Figgie International is one of consultants run amok, the story of Andersen Consulting is one of consultants multiplying like field mice. Very early on, Andersen recognized that technology would be dictating the course of the business future. That is what gave it its edge, and what keeps it growing so quickly today. But it's not just about computers anymore. Part of the lesson is that consultants make their money by doing what their clients want.

Buried in a court file in Jefferson County, Alabama, is a copy of a contract that helps answer a small part of the question "How is it that you become the biggest consulting company in the world?" In great detail, it explains exactly what Andersen Consulting would do over time for O'Neal Steel Co., how the consulting engagement would play out, and what would be achieved. Andersen's plan was to take O'Neal's operating structure, particularly its customer service department, superimpose the latest in technology, and bring it all up to twenty-first-century standards. But it was a consulting marriage that did not work. Instead of landing in the scrapbook of successful cases, which almost all consulting companies are eager to present, it landed in court, a staging area for a catalog of charges and countercharges. Computers didn't work as expected, rollouts didn't occur on time, defects were abundant. It was the basic consultant-client nightmare. These things happen.

But down in "Count I—Breach of Contract," paragraph 24, items "h" and "i," sits the framework for a broader discussion about the consulting business and what it does to make its money, and perhaps for some thoughts about what is right and what is wrong in the marketplace. Andersen Consulting is accused in those paragraphs of "h. failure to improve overall operating efficiency so that O'Neal could achieve substantial reductions in personnel; i. failure to achieve operating efficiencies which would eliminate the need for at least 100 employee positions, as well as other intended benefits such as improved customer service, increased sales and improved pricing. . . ." Behind that claim is an agreement between Andersen and O'Neal that would have seen the consulting company reap a small fortune based on the number of positions it could cut, or lose money should it be unable to cut any jobs. The incentive on both sides is clear: The more positions you shed, the bigger your check; the fewer, the bigger your penalty. It is both uncomfortable to read and uncomfortable to think about

"Andersen Consulting and O'Neal agree that the economics of the Customer Service System are based on improved operating efficiencies intended to eliminate the need for at least 100 employee positions, as well as other intended benefits such as improved customer service, increased sales and improved pricing. Andersen Consulting is committed to working with O'Neal to ensure that this system is capable of enabling O'Neal to achieve these benefits. To this end, the following schedule reflecting how Andersen Consulting and O'Neal share in the risk and rewards of the project shall apply," the explanation of the agreement states. It goes on to say that:

- Andersen would pay a penalty of up to $550,000 should it fail to cut any positions.
- At the 100 jobs cut point, it would break even.
- At a cut of 150 jobs to 174 jobs, its bonus would be $184,000.
- From 175 jobs to 199 jobs, its bonus would be $257,000.
- From 200 jobs to 224 jobs, the bonus would be $334,000.
- From 225 jobs to 249 jobs, the bonus would be $409,000.
- From 250 jobs to 274 jobs, it would be $484,000.
- From 275 jobs to 299 jobs, it would be $559,000.
- From 300 jobs to 324 jobs, it would be $634,000.
- From 325 jobs on up, it would be $709,000.

And that, unfortunately, is one of the more simple answers to the question "How is it that you become the biggest consulting company in the world?" You do it by tapping the spirit of the moment—the computers and technology that would lift Andersen early in its history from the bowels of an accounting firm into its own strong position, the downsizing virus that swept through American businesses in the case of O'Neal Steel and countless hundreds of other companies only a few years ago—and by agreeing to do whatever a client wants. It provides the perfect "technology-made-me-do-it" cover for the executive who argues it was all just a move to stay competitive and the ideal "I-was-only-responding-to-client-commands" rationale for the consultant. True to that construct, Andersen says it does not include these kinds of job elimination incentives in its standard contracts, and that this was a special case negotiated with the individual client. But the reality of the arrangement is apparent.

On September 14, 1992, the date on "Exhibit A" in the O'Neal Steel lawsuit against Andersen Consulting, it was all about money.

The O'Neal case will eventually work its way through the courts, and the issue of the downsizing agreement is unlikely to play much of a role. The case is about the claim that Andersen wasn't able to do much at all, despite its promises. The job elimination festival as depicted in the contract never got to happen. The balls-out era of downsizing has become tainted of late, and the new focus in consulting seems to be on the need to empower employees and make them feel wanted. If that gets enough of an audience, undoubtedly Andersen and its peers in the business will embrace it with as much fervor as they embraced job cutting.

That is how you become big and profitable in the world of consulting. In the world of consulting, no one is bigger than Andersen Consulting. And it has the profits to match its size.

The story of Andersen is a story of astute decision making and aggressiveness in an era of unprecedented change. It is also the story of how a collection of accounting companies used technology to move quite aggressively into the world of management consulting, sweeping past their more conservative, blue-blood competitors.

Remarkable Growth

Only a few decades ago, the thought that Andersen and its management advisers could challenge a McKinsey & Co. or any of the other top strategy houses would have drawn a resounding collection of snorts and rebuttals from any collection of business analysts. But it has become remarkably successful in a short period of time. Just as it embraced downsizing in Alabama, it smelled computers as a moneymaker even before IBM realized they would be so profitable. It recognized the change in business culture that would transform publicly held companies into bottom-line profit machines. It knew before anyone else that the world of business would view technology as the key to productivity. It understood what was meant when futurists said that international borders have disappeared and the economy has become world driven and world scale.

Andersen's story is both the measure of those developments and a revealing account of the kinds of pressures that rippled through accounting firms as management consulting was growing in importance. It also tracks, from the very beginning, the development of computer science as a lucrative target for consultants, although one that has always been full of risks because of the nature of technology, its sophistication, and the fact that it is sold on a collection of bright promises that don't always come true.

The seeds of the world's biggest consulting business were there even a quarter of a century ago, when Andersen Consulting was a small collection of management consultants who found themselves growing far beyond the confines of their conservative world. Arthur Andersen & Co. was founded by accountants, run by accountants, and, most importantly for Andersen Consulting, wedded to the idea that there could be room for only one kind of culture, the culture of accounting. There were so many signs of trouble over the years that it is remarkable all of the accounting houses didn't conclude early on that the accountants and consultants were the oil and water of business services.

Today, Andersen is the strongest example of the arrival on the management consulting scene of the big accounting firms, which field thousands upon thousands of consultants all over the world. They compete for business and for staff with all the strategy and aggressiveness of armies on the battlefield. There is a reason for that. The accounting business was basically constructed on the assumption that there would always be a dependable pool of clients who needed the numbers to add up the right way at least several times a year, to the point at which fees were almost viewed as annuities.

That was before management consulting started growing with all the persistence and eagerness of a healthy baby. Its revenues, pegged to the very expensive services it offered, started playing a bigger and bigger role in the financial health of the accounting companies. If the pool of potential big-time accounting clients was essentially stagnant, along with the kind of services offered by accounting companies, now mature businesses, management consulting was a field with almost unlimited potential and an endless array of clients.

No one seemed to know what to make of management consulting inside of Arthur Andersen, except for the fact that it had found a way to turn the business world's emerging passion for computers and its thirst for advice into a proven moneymaker. Technology is one of the important subtexts that runs along beneath the story of Andersen's growth. As time passed, computers became less and less the scary machines humming away down in a well-cooled data processing room and more and more components of how businesses actually ran. This trend would reach its zenith in the mid- to late 1980s and come to fruition in the era of business process reengineering that began with an article in *Harvard Business Review* in 1990 and exploded in popularity a year later with the publication of a book about reengineering.

Technology plays such a big part in reengineering efforts that it is generally impossible to separate the two. And business processing reengineering, an idea so heavily hyped it seemed every company was off on a reengineering romp in the early 1990s, has been a bonanza for the technology consultants. Andersen says about a quarter of its 1994 revenues—almost a billion dollars—came from business process reengineering.

Consulting Splits Off

Andersen Consulting was born in 1989 in a split from the accounting company and has grown at a remarkable rate. It is on the prowl in a major way. In fiscal 1994, in the United States, it hired 1,778 brand-new consultants off campus and added 684 veterans to its ranks. It planned to add another 2,700 off campus in fiscal 1995, along with 700 to 800 experienced consultants. In 1996, it was counting on continuing its phenomenal growth and planning to add an estimated 8,700 more professionals at a variety of levels in offices all over the world. Today, with an international staff of nearly 40,000 consultants, Andersen is a giant that dwarfs all but a few of its competitors. It is so big that it has its own universities to train consultants by the thousands. Its revenues hit $3.3 billion a year in 1994, jumped to $4.2 billion in 1995, and were expected to continue growing at 20 percent plus over the next few years. It also has an ambitious plan for the consulting future that is aimed at finding ways to erase the lines that separate traditional strategic management consulting from information technology.

But more than size separates Andersen Consulting from its competitors and the other big consulting houses. While McKinsey & Co. and the Boston Consulting Group tend to search for their candidates among the graduates of the best of business schools, Andersen hunts a bit there, but searches far afield for its consultants. It needs its share of MBAs, but there may not be enough MBAs in the whole world to meet its needs. It looks for strong graduates of colleges that are not primarily known for their business education, finding its candidates at Notre Dame, for example, or at big state-supported universities. Its emphasis remains on teaching the new consultants the Andersen way of doing business, which carries them early on to Saint Charles, Illinois, where Andersen has transformed a former girls' school into a state-of-the-art Consulting College. One of Andersen's bosses remarked that a gold-plated business degree won't carry anyone far at Andersen Consulting, where the weight is placed more on performance and growing experience on the job than on academic credentials.

While this has the advantage of immersing everyone in the Andersen culture, it also has some drawbacks. Early in the 1990s, Andersen started hearing complaints that it was sending too many raw recruits into the field. The average age of Andersen consultants at that point was 27. The companies paying for consulting services didn't want to view themselves as training programs, one of the reasons why Andersen reached out to hire hundreds of veterans over the past few years and wanted to add some 3,500 more to its collection in 1996.

A Beer and a Career

Even going back to the days when Andersen was controlled by its accounting parent, it was creative in its collecting of consultants. Terry Neill has been with Andersen for a quarter of a century. At age 50, he now heads the company's change management division. But he recalls when and why he was first drawn to the company. The place was Dublin. He had just graduated from Trinity College with degrees in physics and mathematics, and Andersen was among the army of corporate recruiters searching among Ireland's literate and dependable graduates for future employees. Freed of the weighty demands of academe, Neill was testing the marketplace and thinking about his future when Andersen came along with the siren call no young Irishman could readily ignore: beer. It would be wrong to imply the Irish are hopelessly drawn to free drink. But young men are young men everywhere, a free beer is a free beer, and Arthur Andersen & Co. had put together the recruiting event that had that crucial difference.

"We got a wonderful presentation, forty Andersen people who were working in Ireland from all over Europe, they had worked in England, America, Germany. I suddenly got a sense of this extraordinary organization that I had never heard of before. So I decided at that point to go to business school, and after that, I went to Andersen. It is truly terrifying how happenstance comes along in your career," Neill said.

Keeping talented people on board has never been easy at Andersen. An attrition rate that has sometimes approached 25 percent a year and has settled in now at 16 percent is a problem. Andersen's successful young consultants are ripe candidates for recruitment elsewhere, either at other consulting houses or at businesses that are constantly searching for experienced managers. In an ongoing bid to keep its staff, the company has tried to change some of the work conditions that may have led its most valued young consultants to jump ship. The "up or out" philosophy that leads to so many departures from McKinsey before the fifth year, for example, is no longer part of the package at Andersen. At one of its training sessions at Saint Charles last year, a new collection of managers said they no longer felt so pressured to advance or depart. There was a sense, they said, that Andersen recognized that some of its young employees, particularly those with families, were more interested in staying in one place and doing one kind of job than rambling all over the world and collecting an encyclopedia of consulting experiences.

Carol Meyer is in charge of personnel at Andersen. She has seen the company shift its hiring policies to the point at which it now bases its decisions on the results of "critical behavior interviewing." If the old model was to collect up all the brilliant, high-grade business school grads a consulting company could find, Andersen is much more interested these days in taking a close look at the behaviors that might put a candidate on the track to a partnership, at best, or at least to a very successful consulting career. "We found," she said, "that over a twenty-five-year career, it is not necessarily Scholastic Aptitude Test scores that made them become partners at Andersen. It was much more the kind of behaviors that they were able to parlay into that kind of success." The ability to juggle the complexities of life, even the nascent life of a college senior, plays a big role in Andersen's hiring decisions.

"I am looking for good people at good schools with good academic records, along with what I would describe as a robust résumé filled with lots of interesting things. We eventually ask our people to do a lot of juggling, client work, the demands of travel, mixing personal life with professional life. What they are juggling is a little less important to me. If the summer job is at a grocery store and the fact is they are juggling that along with everything else, then that is more important than whether they worked at a Wall Street firm. We are looking at their critical behaviors. How they solve problems. How they manage multiple tasks. Are they easy to work with or hard to work with? I can see those behaviors and try to understand their success at that, no matter what environment they are in," said Meyer.

To find those kinds of candidates, Andersen returns every year to a collection of favored schools: Cornell, Stanford University, and the University of Chicago, among them. It might hire up to 40 graduates from each school each year, building a long-term relationship it can depend on. If Andersen knows what kind of student it wants, the universities know, too. Once it has tapped the candidates it is interested in, Andersen will put them through a series of hypothetical situations to see how well they think on their feet. They will schmooze with Andersen partners and visit Andersen offices to get a look at how consulting actually works. Partners and associate partners at Andersen will be watching this process and will make the decisions on hiring recommendations. If the job offer comes, the money attached will depend on where the candidate is headed.

Andersen says its starting salaries for strategy consultants are in the same league as McKinsey & Co.'s and Boston Consulting Group's, in the $100,000-a-year range. Because the market is different, there is a different salary schedule for those new hires who will head into technology. The money there is more in line with the salaries at CSC Index or IBM, two companies that have also moved aggressively into the technology business. Because of this process, its selection of candidates is much broader than at companies that focus their recruiting on business schools. While this kind of hiring is relatively new for Andersen, it need only look to its own executives to measure the weight the company has put on diverse educational experiences.

If Neill with his science background represented one class of Andersen hires almost three decades ago, George Shaheen, the company's managing partner, who has been with Andersen since 1967, represents another. He holds bachelor's and master's degrees from Bradley University in Peoria. London-based Keith Burgess, who heads business integration, holds a bachelor's degree and a doctorate in solid-state physics from Bristol University. Steve Johnson, managing partner in Andersen's consumer products practice, has a bachelor's degree in chemistry from Wabash College, and a master's degree in industrial engineering from Purdue. Pete Peterson, the partner who heads the products industry section, has degrees in engineering and business administration from University of Illinois.

The science backgrounds might seem somehow appropriate for a company that has put so much emphasis on technology over the years, but the Andersen Consulting of the 1990s is trying to move away from the computer consultant label as quickly as it can. To be sure, technology is still at the heart of what it has to offer, but because the nature of consulting has changed so much over the past few decades, Andersen has been eager to find some way to expand what it is selling. IT, as it is called, may have been the ticket for the past. These days, Andersen's principals reject the argument that it is essentially an information technology company. While that change has its basis in Andersen's emerging and evolving philosophy of management consulting, it is also market driven. Information technology has become somewhat tainted over the past decade, failing in some cases to live up to its promises.

Reengineering wasn't the magic bullet that its advocates had promised, and it left something of a blind bitterness in its path that encompasses everything from technology to implementation.

Some of Andersen's own IT people concede privately that the nation's businesses are far too obsessed with equipment and have not yet clearly understood that the goal is what it can do, not whether it runs on the latest operating system. There remains a computer nerd attitude that has executives pointing to the flashiness of their systems, a short-term pride that runs sour rapidly, particularly when the expensive systems don't produce what was promised. Besides, computer equipment has the shelf life of unrefrigerated butter in August. Today's speedy, gleaming marvel is tomorrow's collection of slow, outmoded junk. The objective is finding out what role it can play in the structure of a business, and Andersen's top tier argues that that is a question that is as much strategy as it is information technology.

Because of that, thinking about Andersen as a more modern variation of its own roots isn't quite accurate. It is not just about computers anymore. They are still very important to the company's fortunes because they are very important to businesses everywhere, but in its most recent incarnation, more because they are an integral part to achieving an end, not the end itself. This reality tracks the evolution of computers in the workplace. Once the stomping ground of mysterious technocrats who spoke their own strange computer language, computers have moved directly into the work space and have become a part of everyone's business. Training at Saint Charles still focuses heavily on what big computers can do and the weird languages that drive them, but the context has changed. The goal now is to make the whole process seamless, friendly, and rational.

With the addition of hundreds of veterans from the world of strategy, Andersen wants to become a top-down model of big-time management consulting in the future. There will always be boutique consulting companies that do specific things, and strategy houses that focus on the upper echelons of business. But Andersen has the muscle to take note of and create its own versions of the best of its competitors' ideas, invent its own, and form industrial and business partnerships aimed at carrying the company well into the next century. It has an array of computer software programs that perform various business services. They are constructed on the basis of Andersen's experiences with its clients.

Find something that works well, reproduce it, and sell it is the simple way of viewing this component of Andersen's consulting. Frequently, the client that initially helped develop the product will share in its long-term profits as it is sold by Andersen to other industries. This part of the business is so important to Andersen that it has a managing partner heading a worldwide division called Industry Markets and Packaged Knowledge.

Andersen also completed the formation of its own Foundation Software Organization at the end of 1995. The organization is the Andersen response to a big shift in the business of computers from mainframes to something called client/server systems, basically the vehicle that puts computers on everyone's desktop and gives them some measure of control over what they do. FSO is aimed at providing worldwide technical support for any Andersen client. Its field of expertise—and this is an oversimplification—is whatever computer process or program Andersen uses, anywhere and for anything. The company has its own string of programming products and is said to be expanding the mix available to clients through its relationships with a whole collection of computer and programming giants and industry leaders.

Andersen's Foundation products are already widely used by hundreds of its customers. Generally, they provide the computer programming base companies need to develop their own tailor-made client/server applications. Andersen software has been the source of some controversy over the past few years, with Andersen fending off reports it is interested in leaving the software business and shifting to market-tested software products available from other companies. It has reorganized the division, which brings in some $48 million a year, recognizing that specialty software hasn't been the magnet to clients that Andersen hoped it would be. The software shift sent rumbles through Andersen's client base, much of which has come to depend on its products. If anything, this shift is another measure of how sensitive consulting companies are to pressures in the marketplace. Growing threats of liability for products that don't work as expected probably also play a role in this rethinking, according to analysts. Andersen has faced a collection of lawsuits over the years from clients who were not pleased with the results of their consulting engagements.

Aggressive Marketing

Andersen is one of the most aggressive marketers of consulting services in the world, eager to tell its story to potential clients in everything from sophisticated television campaigns to traditional ads in business magazines. It holds whopping big media and analyst seminars at very good hotels. These information fests seem to leave everyone fat and exhausted, but frequently lead to glowing assessments of where Andersen stands in the world of consulting. This, too, separates it from the strategy houses like McKinsey & Co. and Bain & Co., which seem to have a particularly old-fashioned attitude toward the dissemination of information. For many of them, the less said is viewed literally as the better option. But Andersen isn't like that. It has a very snappy media and public relations division headed by a pro who is as comfortable discussing politics as he is discussing the complexities of Andersen Consulting. To its credit, it answers almost all questions, sometimes in exhaustive, almost overwhelming detail. (One question it won't answer: How much does everyone make?)

When Andersen was looking around for ways to spread its world image, for example, it settled on a $10 million campaign that included sponsorship of a huge, worldwide sporting event. This being a consulting company and the target being business, the sporting event was that businessperson's obsession, golf. The Andersen Consulting World Championship of Golf started in Japan as 1995 dawned and stretched all over the world before it was completed on New Year's Day of 1996. Just to get everyone's attention, it attached the fattest purse in golf history to the event, a total of $3.65 million. British golfer Barry Lane won and walked away with $1 million, noting in his victory statement that $400,000 of it will be collected by the tax man, but that it was still a good day's work. Andersen also spent quite some time wrestling with one of those strange challenges of the modern, televised world. The name of the event was just too long, and it would take quite a big hat to carry the description "The Andersen Consulting World Championship of Golf." But the real problem was television, which always wants to boil everything down to its commercial and visual essence. The event was broadcast in 80 countries. All over the world, golf addicts were able to see the important abbreviation "Andersen Consulting" on signs around tees, fences near greens, and flags. Andersen also sponsors the

Melbourne Cup horse race in Australia, and backs opera and theater all over Europe.

Despite all this sophistication in technology and imagery, Andersen suffers from the same plague that seems to afflict all of modern consulting: It is very difficult to say exactly what an Andersen consultant does. Abstraction is the best friend and worst enemy of all of the consulting houses. It allows consultants to lift off into flights of business fantasy, complete with charts and graphs. It all really does look good on paper. After one 90-minute session at Andersen, which involved a particularly complicated diagram, the question was asked: "Why do you draw so many charts?" After a moment of thought, the reply came, "I don't know. Everyone here does." There are no brief conversations with consulting company executives. They are marathons full of the special language and the philosophy of the particular company involved. Ask a key consultant to tell consulting stories, and he or she is likely to puzzle a bit and then say, "What exactly do you mean?" Or they will fall back on the rhetoric of the business, which at Andersen boils down to: "Helping our clients be more successful." Or they will draw a chart. Hence, if one asks, "What did you do today?" the response will be crafted in such a way that "Helping our clients be more successful" becomes integral to the explanation.

Ask Rudy Puryear, Andersen's managing partner for the Americas, about technology, for example. Then stand back. Information technology and strategy are his strong points, and asking questions about them is akin to asking a priest about redemption. He knows all about it, having spent 25 years in information systems and 15 years consulting to various companies about information technology strategy and planning. Based in Chicago, he became an Andersen partner in 1991. Dig into his background and you find the résumé of a modern Andersen executive. There is no Harvard Business School here. His degrees in computer science, a B.S. and an M.S., are from North Carolina State University at Raleigh.

If the operating image of technology types is that they carry their pens in pocket protectors, talk in DOS, and look like people who never quite got around to dating, Rudy Puryear shatters the cliché. He is as sharp as a well-honed Wüsthof-Trident chef's knife, crisp from his white shirt to the tips of his shoes, a handsome character who is as comfortable in a room full of industry analysts, explaining gigantic charts on an overhead projector, as he is at the table in his spartan office. On average, he conducts a conference talk or a client session on information technology about once a week.

"What is this technology stuff all about?" Unfortunately, there is no shorthand way to record the response. What it amounts to is a business school–level class on the future, according to Andersen, with due reference to how things worked structurally in the worlds of management and technology in the past and how they have to change to accommodate a complicated and demanding future. Keep in mind that this is what consulting is all about in the abstract world where technology and business strategy meet.

"When I use the word technology, I clearly mean broader than just information technology, which a lot of times is being relegated to just business computing. But I don't mean it so broadly as to include biotechnology. But I do mean it more broadly than just classical business computing.

"I am going to draw an overly simplistic diagram," he says. He talks and draws at the same time. At the top of his chart are the words "business strategy," and at the bottom, "technology." Down the left-hand side is a curving line called "driving," and down the right-hand side is another labeled "enabling." It all forms a loop. In the old days, he says, pointing to the top of the chart, business strategy drove technology. Decisions would be made at the top of the loop and then passed down to the people below, who would try to carry them out, assuming they understood them. The two key groups in this drawing would know very little about one another, and in fact would probably view one another with some suspicion, if not hostility. He adds some more words to the chart: "Align. Link. Reactive. Responsive. Implementation." Then he draws another graph in which strategy, people, technology, and procurement are basically connected. It does not seem simple on paper and it is not simple in practice. Puryear broke from the task at hand to discuss consulting. At the moment, he was preparing a mammoth presentation that included 51 slides describing what he and Andersen Consulting view as the challenge of the twenty-first century. It is called "Competing with IT Enabled Business Strategies" and it covers everything from philosophy to practical examples of the strategy at work. It is aimed at shattering the old assumptions reflected in the strategy/ technology chart he has sketched.

A lot of what has happened in the worlds of strategy and technology over the years has been almost coincidental, he says. The people at the top of the loop come up with their plan and pass it along to the technology sections, and then, perhaps with the help of Andersen or another consulting company, something happens. Puryear notes that once in a while, maybe in 5 percent of the cases, there will be a technological success that enables fundamental strategy. That, he argues, has to change. But the gap between the two groups is natural and growing. Technology people want to know all about the latest operating systems and the tiny chips that speed them along, how they function, what to do when something goes wrong. They delight in scratching their heads and solving problems, bringing those little babies humming back to operating life with a few simple adjustments a couple of thousand lines into a program.

The last thing a big-time executive needs, on the other hand, is a computer that tells him something has gone fatally wrong with his autoexec.bat file and he better do something complicated about it right now or his entire effort will go straight to computer hell. They do not want to know, or need to know, any more about what goes on inside computers than they need to know what goes on inside the engine of their car. In both cases, the tool just has to get them where they want to go, and without trouble.

"What I am submitting to clients around the world is that one of the keys is going to be making this thing very predictable and systematic. Think of it as a systematic way to understand the implications of technology without understanding the technology itself. I am talking about the business executive understanding the implications of it all without having to know the raw technology," Puryear says. That hasn't happened up to this point, he says, because the world of strategy and the world of technology speak different languages. There is indeed a big gap between the top and the bottom of his little chart.

"It is almost like taking executives into a room and giving them a technology fair, showing them the difference between Windows and Lotus, or some Newtons and showing them some wireless communications, and then expect that next week, when they start their business strategy process, those strategies will become technology enlightened. It will just not happen. There has to be some kind of language that allows you to span this gap," says Puryear.

Then he shifts to another chart. This one is more simple, tracking the frequency of change and the certainty of change. The importance of this drawing, he says, is that it shows that change is coming more quickly and more unpredictably than ever. A business run out of someone's vest pocket, with traditional structures and traditional systems of dealing with strategy and technology, simply won't work in this new world. The mean time between surprises is getting very short, he says. Smart companies must be aware of the implications of technology, infusing it at the very top, then driving it back down through the organization. That will take more than the kind of scant knowledge picked up at technology fairs.

"I would argue that in strategic consulting, we have moved from systems integration to business integration, where we integrate and optimize components of businesses. If you read our mission statement, our goal is to 'help our clients be more successful.' [There's that phrase again.] I would argue that in the future, a significant chunk of change is going to need to be technology enlightened at a minimum, possibly technology enabled or even technology driven. Therefore if you think of Andersen capitalizing off its historical strength in technology to move into technologically enlightened business change, it begins to draw strategy and technology together."

That ends the class. But what does that mean in the real world?

Hog Heaven

Welcome to Harley-Davidson, motorcycle maker without compare and a strong business success story for Andersen. Andersen has been on board at Harley since 1981, a long-term relationship that has seen the motorcycle company through bad times and good. There is no one "thing" Andersen has done at Harley that could be viewed as an indication of what Andersen actually does. Instead, there are dozens of small to middle-sized efforts, all of which marched in lockstep with Harley's own struggle to shift from years of decline through a difficult transition and into an era of blue skies, profitability, and, finally, beloved motorcycles that don't leak fluid all over the place.

Harley had been around since the turn of the century, and by the late 1970s was one of the few survivors among what had once been a robust American industry. The Japanese were moving rapidly into the American market, first with some little motorcycles that were no threat to Harley's road monsters, and then with some bigger, more muscular (and at that point, more dependable) bikes that were gobbling up market share. The Yamahas and Suzukis and Kawasakis were a lot cheaper, didn't leave an oil slick, and did not require a master mechanic for continued operation. Harleys at that point were for specialists or for those who were so enamored of the name and image that they didn't mind that the machine's reputation had plummeted after the company was bought by American Machine and Foundry (AMF) in 1969.

Production was so bad that more than half of the bikes failed inspection after they left the line, and had to be set aside in factory "hospitals" until they could be repaired. Sometimes it took days. There were mountains of outdated spare parts that would not fit or that had deteriorated in storage. Only 5 percent of Japanese bikes failed inspection off the line. Adding to all of those problems was a decades-long image assault sparked by the 1954 movie *The Wild Ones*, in which Marlon Brando and a gang of bikers terrorized a small town. In one of those ironies that must drive marketers mad, he wasn't even riding a Harley in the movie, but the link between Harley cycles and very bad dudes had been forged and was all but impossible to break.

By 1973, AMF put out the word that Harley could be bought. Thirteen of Harley's managers cobbled together some bank loans, crafted a leveraged buyout, and purchased Harley for some $80 million. Some hard times ensued, along with some hard thinking and some hard work. Andersen Consulting came in to help with a parts-numbering scheme. It was developing some expertise in the motorcycle business because Yamaha had hired Andersen to help import some American business practices. Andersen's people in Japan watched closely and learned all about just-in-time manufacturing and a host of other innovations the Japanese had instituted. Enthused by what it had seen in Japan, Andersen put together a seminar on Japanese manufacturing practices.

One of the companies that attended was Harley-Davidson.

It is a classic of consulting: Tap into what works elsewhere, learn from it, and market it. The Japanese had worked out a lot of the kinds of problems that had been plaguing Harley forever. And Andersen was in a position to help bring some of those lessons home. Andersen consultant Tom Arenberg is the contact point with Harley-Davidson today, a man so happy in his work that he gushes praise about Harley with no prompting. He is so enthusiastic about what has happened at the motorcycle company over the years that, at age 43, he now has his own burgundy Harley-Davidson Sportster in the garage, has taken lessons on how to ride it safely, and is eager to go blasting down Route 66 as soon as possible, bugs on his grinning teeth and the wind rushing through his helmet.

"Right about the time of the leveraged buyout Harley came to us and said we need to do some of this stuff, but our suppliers don't get it. Come in and help us," Arenberg said. "In 1981, right in the valley of despair, we did a pilot just-in-time project. . . . We did some internal improvements and instituted a supplier program that enabled them to talk to their suppliers. They executed those plans pretty much on their own for the next three years. That was when they focused on quality, cost improvement, and partnering with their suppliers. . . . In 1986, they started growing again and they needed help in manufacturing planning. That is when they brought us back in. We have been involved ever since then."

Both Arenberg and Harley-Davidson eagerly point out that Andersen is not laying claim to saving Harley-Davidson. That is something the company did on its own. Through it all, Arenberg said, what has been apparent is that there is a connection between Andersen and Harley that goes beyond motorcycles and addresses an area that is much less tangible: philosophy. One of Arenberg's favorite trinkets is a little laminated company values card that includes some shared Andersen–Harley standards. Under "Values," the card says, "Tell the truth. Be fair. Keep your promises. Respect the individual. Encourage intellectual curiosity." Under "Issues," the card says, "Quality. Participation. Productivity. Efficiency. Flexibility."

The relationship has evolved. From initial nuts-and-bolts kinds of efforts, Andersen now helps Harley-Davidson with strategy issues. The consulting company has scrupulously avoided taking credit or, one of the biggest criticisms of outside consultants, taking charge. "If I had to characterize the working relationship, all of the teams are joint teams. It is never six Andersen consultants and one Harley worker. There is always a Harley person who is going to own the project when it is done. The second thing is that the more successful projects have very, very active executive sponsorship and intimate involvement in the effort," says

Arenberg. "They are the fire and the effort that moves it ahead. The Harley culture is unique and the Andersen culture works as a hidden strength. Harley is the one place where I have seen a culture that is as deep and as rich as ours. They think internal teams and internal empowerment, and it is really rare to run into this kind of thing."

For Andersen Consulting, the Harley connection is what every consulting company wants, a long-term relationship with a client that is skilled at carrying out innovation. And while Harley doesn't have much to say at all about Andersen (strangely, its public relations division says it is only interested in commenting on its own terms on motorcycle issues that "add value" to the company), the relationship has lasted for a long time. Consultants who don't please their clients are shown the door with an almost blistering sense of immediacy. It is clear from Andersen's long list of Harley projects that it has advised and implemented in just about every corner of the company. That has included everything from a "strategic information plan" for the whole company in 1988 through a "product development tools selection and integration design" in 1990 and a full-scale client-server computer system just last year. It also helped Harley develop its retail store strategy. The Harley name is golden, and clothing that carries it sells at a premium, but only through Harley-Davidson. One of the company's big struggles was to get control again over exactly how its name is used. It was showing up on everything from underwear to cigarettes. That is under control now and working under a "kiosk" program Andersen helped implement.

"The theme through all of these projects is that Harley is very, very good at executing," said Arenberg. "This is the only client I have ever had who has taken a plan, a four-year plan to fix manufacturing facilities for example, and executed it in three years. Ninety five percent of clients take four to five years to do that."

It will be interesting to watch over time how Andersen implements the lessons it has learned at Harley. It is clear that with every successful consulting engagement, Andersen climbs a little higher up the learning curve and finds another collection of ideas and practices it can market to other clients. If making money from helping to manage change is what consulting is all about, Andersen clearly has found a profitable and productive formula.

As with Harley-Davidson, where Andersen played an important role in long-term thinking for a company that was all too accustomed to putting out brush fires and managing crises, Andersen obviously wants to sell its clients on long-term strategies that will ensure its own growing role in consulting. Future thinking, then, has become as salable a commodity for Andersen as computer programs and technology were early on and as downsizing was over the past decade. What is likely to happen to stores in the twenty-first century?

Shifting back into the world of the abstract, Puryear says managers must be aware of what technology is going to do to what he calls the "in-store buying paradigm." What is the point of signing 20-year leases if technology means most of one's business is going to shift, quite dramatically, to computerized shopping? If a retailer can construct a virtual retail world that a wired nation visits for many of its consumer purchases, the idea of a store as a place might not disappear, but it could be radically altered. Of course the world is not yet completely wired, and this kind of talk frequently falls on deaf ears, particularly on the deaf ears of those who are not astute about technology. There may well come a time when everyone shops through holograms in the quality living quadrant of their very own technologically enhanced space, but reality commands that at this point, everyone recognizes that most people are not computerized, that many of those who are have become completely baffled about what to do with computers, and that the "in-store buying paradigm" is still very much intact. It is why malls are so popular.

But this is probably a caveat that Puryear and other consultants who are involved in long-term strategy cannot afford to embrace. What kind of client would Harley-Davidson have been if it had not bought into Andersen's vision of change? And what company is going to pay a fortune to have Andersen report: "Don't change a thing and beware all of this mysterious technology talk." Given the assumption that everything changes as much as profitability can justify, it pays for consultants to think of and advance high-tech visions.

Where does it lead?

A Different Formula

"A result of a lot of the change to date has been downsizing, reengineering, slashing and burning, layoffs," Puryear said. "But what you are going to see is a profound shift from technology as the eliminator to technology as the creator. And there are many new roles that you are going to see all around that creation, new freedoms, new creativity. Change is always disturbing to people, but that is partly because a lot of the change we have been associated with in the past ten years is in terms of cutting, slashing, downsizing. My sense is that you are going to see an awful lot of change coming that is associated with creation. New jobs. New careers. New freedoms." That may ultimately be true, but it hasn't happened yet. And it raises an important question: Will business invest in technology that creates as many jobs as it replaces?

The classical structure of business consulting, Puryear says, required the consultant and management team to look at observable facts and arrive at a set of shared assumptions about the future. Then the challenge was to design a strategy to achieve a goal. The McKinsey and Boston Consulting Group teams would argue that the first task was to get the strategy right, "then throw it all open to the technology guys." What that did was reinforce the initial diagram Puryear sketched out, with decisions made at the top and implementation carried out at the bottom. But Andersen's process, business integration, argues that there is heavy interdependence among the various components of a business, and that technology-blind strategies passed down from on high are things of the past. Strategy, people, technology, and processes all play important, interlocking roles in the Andersen philosophy.

For a business culture in which hierarchies are still the operative model, this kind of philosophy is right on the cutting edge. But that is obviously where Andersen wants to be. There is a good measure of how astute consultants can be in Puryear's comments about the era of downsizing and reengineering. His argument that business is on the verge of a new era in which technology will create jobs and freedoms fits handily with the growing sense in corporate America that the formulas of the 1980s simply won't work well in the 1990s and beyond.

Puryear and a whole school of other consultants are now arguing that the pathway to profits has changed, that growing the business is probably going to be much more critical over the long term than cutting costs on the inside. But that is a lot more difficult than improving the numbers by cutting costs. It will take some time for businesses, still eager to find the quickest path to immediate improvements, to catch up to this change. In the interim, companies like O'Neal Steel will have no problem finding any number of consulting companies eager to assist in the deep pruning of employee numbers.

Just as downsizing and reengineering were the clarion calls in the most recent era, using technology to expand business opportunities will be the theme in the next century. And as all of that develops, Andersen is likely to be in an even stronger position to ride the technology wave. But the company's business won't become any more simple to describe or to understand, which is why Andersen is one of the biggest advocates in consulting of the equivalent of elementary school "show-and-tell," reflected in a collection of business centers it has constructed around the country. The Retail Place in Chicago was one of its first, filling a few floors in what was once a Sears warehouse on Chicago's near west side. It is a very old building, and Andersen went to lengths to make it comfortable. From the outside, it doesn't look at all state of the art, and inside, the thick oak beams and supports that hold the building together have been lovingly preserved and restored. They sit up there like solid monuments to the past, almost oxymoronic amid the space-age lighting, wiring, and colorful heating ducts that were added to bring the place up to code and standards.

The connection to the past ends with the architecture. Inside, Andersen has constructed a series of idealized work spaces, one of which mimics the retail sales outlet of the future, full of sports equipment and little computerized recording devices that track sales and inventories. Another area on another floor reflects Andersen's idea of what manufacturing headquarters might someday become. Still another area is aimed at supermarket and food sales. It is fully stocked with an eternally ripe collection of plastic groceries, along with a comfortable kitchen with a huge table, just for gathering to talk.

These places are not what they seem. It only looks as though Andersen is considering opening its own supermarket, or operating a Harley-Davidson store where a customer can draw up the particulars of his own hog on a computer. They are designed to carry executives away from their own surroundings and give them an atmosphere in which they can think and have some sense of what technology can actually accomplish.

If Andersen's goal is ultimately to erase the lines between technology and strategy, then this is one of the places where the consulting company can show its clients how that happens and talk with them about the attitudes they need to develop to make the transition. There are only a few computers visible in the whole place, and they are only terminals set up to show what communications can do in the design process. This is video-linked state-of-the-art equipment aimed at eliminating distance as a component in business strategy formulas. There is no need to fly an engineer to Paris, for example, when she and a partner can work on their terminals in real time to solve design problems.

In the supermarket section of the building, Andersen has constructed a computer model of shipping patterns for the distribution of groceries, an object lesson in how complicated everything can become when businesses simply decide to add another layer to the shipping structure. The program superimposes a spiderweb of shipping routes across Chicago and its suburbs. The visual impact of the display is enough to spawn a whole series of questions: Why would a supermarket in the distant western suburbs want to collect its supplies from a warehouse near Lake Michigan? What is the point of sending huge trucks past long strings of stores without stopping to deliver supplies? What does efficiency mean in the delivery of huge quantities of foodstuffs? How can stores more efficiently connect buying patterns with wholesale deliveries? What happens when the store as a place is transformed into the store as a collection of questions on a computer about what a person might want to buy?

It is not intended to provide answers so much as it is to spawn some thought and discussion. The same process occurs in the industrial and retailing sections of the building, all of which is set up so that it can be changed almost overnight to meet the needs of clients. If Puryear's discussion of the melding of strategy and technology is abstract, this is the place where it all becomes concrete. Making the rounds of the displays in the industrial exhibit, for example, carries an executive all the way from the manufacturing process through distribution. Along the way, there are big doses of user-friendly technology and exhibits that underline the global nature of modern industry.

Andersen runs facilities like these in Europe and Asia, too. In Atlanta, it has a virtual environment called Logistics 20-20, which is aimed at showing customers how they might lower costs and improve logistical networks. It is all very impressive, but almost pales beside Andersen's latest effort, its DAVINCI Virtual Corp. projects in Palo Alto and in Sophia-Antipolis, France, which opened at the end of 1995.

They reflect a considerable leap for Andersen, because they carry the world of make-believe way past the consulting company and into partnerships with a range of very high-class, high-tech talent. Intel, AT&T GIS, Bay Networks, Compaq, Hewlett-Packard, Intergraph, MCI, SAP, and Sequent Computer Systems have all contributed to the DAVINCI project.

This is Andersen's philosophy come to life, a virtual corporation in which strategy no longer drives technology, but works in lockstep with it. The goal, Andersen says, is to challenge everyone's assumptions and look for new business capabilities that can be ready to go on-line as soon as possible. The format plays out on a world scale, putting executives into a global business plan in which a city of 50,000 residents is to be constructed from the ground up, even as rich gold and copper deposits are tapped and money is flowing into the local economy.

The consultants have created an interesting world, where "electronic collaboration support tools" come to the rescue of a "smart" industrial pump in Indonesia, "electronic distribution channels" help a family move to Indonesia, a collection of venture partners decides to build a hotel, and an alliance is formed between a hotel chain and a mining company, with information technology smoothing out the bumps and clearing the way for a good partnership.

A Consulting Fantasyland?

It looks, smells, and acts like it is real, but it isn't.

Spending too much time around any of it conveys the impression that the world actually works like this, that brilliant consultants with the best of intentions and best of equipment are out there helping the captains of industry meet the challenges of the future, assisting them so they can "be more successful." It is sleek and neat, moves with the speed of light, and, most of all, seems wonderfully friendly.

But all of it is to reality as the cushy, sparkling hoopla of Disneyland is to reality, a collection of ideals carefully programmed and wired together to present an impression of something that has never really existed. It is important in this comparison to remember that Mickey and Minnie were actually rodents, which in real life spend much of their time copulating, that dogs generally poop on the lawn and don't wear pants, that there is a magic dust that makes everyone feel better, but it doesn't come from Tinkerbell and will ultimately dominate and then try to ruin your life, and that nothing actually works the way it works in Disneyland.

And, complicating everything, in real life there are lawyers!

To make its spunky versions of the high-tech world more authentic, Andersen Consulting would have to program in some genuine disasters. To enhance that verisimilitude, a most important component would be some deeply peeved businesspeople backed by teams of hungry and aggressive lawyers. The case study would involve a big consulting company, self-assured of its standing as the premier information technology consultant in all the world, a very complicated business challenge involving millions upon millions of dollars in potential riches, all constructed on the assumption that a stunning transition can be made from the old ways to the new ways. Then there would be a set of promises of what could be achieved and when it could be achieved.

Then none of that would happen as planned, bitterness would ensue, and the lawyers would be called upon to set their case out in the almost Victorian hyperbole of the modern lawsuit. "They smote us mightily, delivering not on their promise, whence great sums were lost that we want to squeeze from their being" is probably how it would go. And where might all of that be found?

In Stamford, Connecticut, in Superior Court, a company called UOP of Des Plaines, Illinois, has cast a completely different picture of Andersen Consulting and how it does what it does. There are echoes of the O'Neal Steel complaint in this suit in that it, too, is about something complicated that just didn't work out at all. UOP is a conservative company that makes its money in the delicate but fast-moving world of chemical and petrochemical engineering. You want to build a petrochemical plant? UOP can design it, no small feat in a world of technology that is inherently frightening to ignorant outsiders, one that involves cooking oil and chemicals and the like. It has a fairly high kaboom component if things aren't exactly right. Technology makes it all relatively safe, if abysmally complicated. UOP hired Andersen to modernize and computerize complicated bidding procedures.

The suit was filed in March of 1995. It asks at least $100 million in damages, alleging misconduct, fraud, incompetence, neglect, and wrongdoing. It is a bitter account, packed full of steaming claims. To be certain, it is a charge with which Andersen strongly disagrees. But first, a digression.

Andersen Consulting has many satisfied clients. They range in stature from the British government, which hired Andersen to computerize its social security program, to a whole range of big, successful companies around the world that have turned to its consultants again and again. They are not little contracts. Sun Refining & Marketing, for example, is on board for $200 million over 10 years. Voluntary Hospitals of America, $50 million over 10 years. The Workers' Compensation Board of Alberta, Canada, $50 million for five years. British Petroleum Exploration Europe, $89 million over five years. One simply does not become this huge in the world of consulting without establishing a formidable track record, despite the problems alleged by UOP and other plaintiffs in suits against Andersen. It can present chapter and verse of its success stories and draw in dozens of clients to confirm that it did, indeed, deliver on its promises.

There is also a "dark side of the moon" component to measuring anything on the basis of lawsuits or completed contracts, because such a process overlooks disappointments and failures that are negotiated and resolved before anyone takes a dispute to court. And there may also be some reluctance on the part of a client to sue a consulting company that has had access to its highest executives and its innermost secrets, sometimes at great depth and for years. But the suits are certainly signs that even in the sparkling world of high-class, high-tech consulting, there is a substantial kaboom factor at work, too.

The courts will ultimately decide the fate of the UOP suit. In the interim, it is clear that Andersen has one enormously angry former client on hand, mightily upset about what it perceives to be unfulfilled promises. There are so many issues connected to the UOP suit that it bears some examination for what it says about consulting in general and for what it alleges about the way consultants drum up business.

The information technology business is fraught with peril on many levels. Many a CEO can tell stories about computer systems that were supposed to be the vanguard of a new era, but that failed to live up to their promise. They are, after all, computers, beloved by computer people and viewed with no small amount of anxiety and hesitation by everyone else. There is a dichotomy at work in information technology that separates its advocates, its believers, from the rest of the world. This is the wellspring of many a problem. "You said it would do this, but it doesn't. You said it would make it all easier, but it hasn't."

It is a question of where one's interests sit. The advocate might argue that the stumbling system will, indeed, work as planned in due time given enough attention and adjustment and reeducation of its newly confused operators. It is, after all, technology. There is an almost religious conviction about this among technology people, who wouldn't have much to believe in at all if they started out assuming their systems simply weren't going to work. And Andersen is fairly loaded with technology people.

But this means nothing to the distraught client, who sees only big bills and lost opportunities. The argument that something will just take more time translates into nightmarish visions of a giant taxi meter, its increments measured in thousand-dollar chunks. Generally as long as the consultants are on the scene, this meter is running. The client has heard all the sermons and promises of the glory of technology. He is ready to believe, has already bought into the contract and, most of all, awaits some results. All it takes is a brief brush with a system that doesn't work, or doesn't work as well as promised, to understand why there is such resistance to the very idea of information technology. It cannot be pleasant in these situations to hear that an Andersen needs another 18 months to determine whether something will actually work. What is a client to do in these situations, shut it all down, kiss the millions of dollars in consulting fees good-bye, and try again with someone else? Or does he just bite hard on the bullet, dig a little deeper in the well, and come forth with more money and more patience?

A Troubling Lawsuit

All of those things seem to be at work in *UOP v. Andersen Consulting*, a lawsuit that is being closely watched by the consulting industry and many clients of consultants. On the very surface, the case has drawn questions about how far consulting companies should go in promising results in attempting to win contracts. Andersen, it appears, was fairly bold in presenting its claims. *Consultants News*, in its brief review of the case, concluded the company had presented a "Litany of Language to Avoid in Proposals."

Wise consultants, it has been noted many times, never really promise a client much of anything other than objective advice and proposed solutions that clients can accept or reject. The buck might well speed on its way to the pocket of the consulting company, but it never stops there. Still, competition is competition, and the temptation is always there to put as much brass into a proposal as it will hold. As *Consultants News* pointed out, "We've never seen a winning proposal that says 'maybe we can solve your problem.' How much is too much?"

In light of that, the newsletter's editors read the UOP complaint and came up with a list of things consultants should probably never say directly.

"Here's some of what could get you in trouble: . . . we continually deliver success . . . we are able to respond to customer needs up to 50 percent faster . . . we know how to manage risk . . . we are prepared to assume responsibility for the price and quality of the solution . . . we can create an environment in which all team members work cooperatively . . . we deliver on scope, schedule, quality and cost commitments . . . our project manager will have ultimate responsibility for ensuring successful development . . . our philosophy is to get the job done, not excusing the responsibilities . . ."

The suit against Andersen alleges none of that happened as promised or implied, and notes that the strong language in Andersen's proposals was what induced UOP to award the contract in the first place. The buyer's best friend, *caveat emptor,* apparently fled in the face of this hot high-tech sales rhetoric. That is why this suit is destined to be followed closely in the consulting community. Competition is turning up the heat under proposals, and consulting companies are generally becoming more and more sensitive to their clients' interests in having some assurance that big projects will go as planned. On Andersen's part, the consultant notes that UOP discontinued the project after two prototypes were completed, paid in full for the work, and waited a full 16 months to file its suit, which, Andersen says, is "completely without merit."

One component or another of Andersen was at UOP from 1991 until January of 1994, when UOP said it had had enough. It began with UOP's decision to seek bids to automate and computerize the engineering specifications and documents its clients need to build new refineries and petrochemical and chemical-processing plants. This apparently is a paperwork nightmare that sometimes takes teams of engineers thousands of pages to complete. UOP already was using computers to do much of the work. But the idea was to use state-of-the-art technology to cut the time needed to present those detailed estimates for customers, centralize the process, and integrate the computers. That part was to be called the "Computer Assisted Schedule A" system, CASA for short. UOP knew it was going to be very complicated and very expensive, but the cost benefits were worth the investment.

It also wanted to make a similar change in its cost estimate procedure, another demanding task, so complicated, in fact, that it limited the number of proposals UOP could make to prospective clients. It wanted its engineers to use a computer-generated form to save time and costs in preparing the estimates. This project was called CECE, for Computer Enhanced Cost Estimating. In 1991, Andersen got the nod to develop a software prototype for the cost-estimating project. That also put it on the shortlist for the CASA system, according to the suit. Ultimately, it was chosen to do both systems.

The suit asks the court to accept its contention that the promises Andersen made and its descriptions of its technical expertise at systems development should actually be viewed as part of the contract. It referred to 54 points at which Andersen makes claims, including its statement that it is the largest and most successful information consulting business in the world. It seems from reading the complaint that Andersen promised just about everything anyone could want, from risk sharing down to project management and on to implementation, a huge catalog of can-do's constructed on the conclusion that UOP was dealing with a company that could design this mammoth thing and make it dance an amazing technical ballet that would pirouette UOP right into the twenty-first century.

The cracks that would ultimately end this marriage started showing up in December 1992, in UOP's version of the story, when the original completion date for phase one of CASA came and went. The other system missed its deadline, too. UOP says it pressed Andersen for an estimate on when all of this could be completed, but found the consultant strangely reluctant. This was when the process that might be called "The Great Swelling of Hours" began. First, UOP alleges, Andersen increased its time estimate from 55,000 hours to 58,900 hours. In July 1993, Andersen revised its hourly estimate on the second program from

58,900 to 68,500, and then from 68,500 to 75,600. Then the numbers went from 75,600 to 86,000, and from 86,000 to 88,700. These were all "ominous signs of more serious things to come," UOP said. "Indeed, as Andersen began delivering component parts of the CASA and CECE systems, it soon became evident to UOP that Andersen had grossly misrepresented its abilities and had falsely promised that the CASA and CECE systems would have qualities and performance characteristics which, as delivered by Andersen, they lacked."

In brief, the systems were "materially defective, failed to comport with Andersen's prior representations and promises, greatly exceeded budgeted costs, and were delivered far beyond original target dates and in violation of project schedules." There were 21 specific shortcomings in the one system and five with the other. Then there were problems common to both systems, 15 of them by UOP's count.

UOP confronted Andersen with its complaints. Andersen, UOP alleges, didn't deny any of them and admitted responsibility for many of the problems. It recognized "the need for substantive changes in how the projects are managed and executed in pursuit of the overall goal. . . . We do not have answers at this time to a number of these issues—most importantly, whether the overall goal can be achieved." Then there were some confessionals. Andersen, UOP said, admitted, "The current project team obviously failed to provide early warning of significant changes in CECE's schedule, cost and scope. . . ." It also admitted making "errors in assessing the real status of the work, and in communicating the importance of unresolved issues and their impact on project progress." If there was a final explosion in this collection of complaints, it came with this portion of a letter given to UOP on December 3, 1993:

"We have candidly discussed with you our disappointment with the substantial escalation of estimates to complete CECE and with the length of time that elapsed before the magnitude of this problem was recognized. . . . We also understand and agree with your need for an answer to the basic question: How can CECE and CASA be completed within the remaining budget? We are unable to answer this question now since parts of the selective scope are not yet supported by formal, agreed-upon requirements definitions."

That did it. UOP had a letter of its own, dated December 22, 1993: "In accordance with the provisions of the Systems Integration Agreement dated May 1, 1992, between UOP and Andersen Consulting, UOP wishes to inform Andersen of our intent to reduce your work under this Agreement to zero." Then it asked Andersen to complete the work for nothing. There was some more hot mail and, eventually, the lawsuit.

By its tabulation, obviously one sympathetic to its case, UOP claims it spent $8 million on direct systems development costs, lost $3.5 million in interest on that money, must spend at least $21 million to get the system up and operating, and has lost $50 million in potential business because it lost "competitive and strategic advantages" that were aimed at increasing its revenues. It also claims it lost something called "engineering productivity" to the tune of $36 million.

All of this involves allegations of breach of contract and express and implied warranties and a big collection of other legal rhetoric that basically spells trouble should judge and jury agree. The lawyers did their dance at the initiation of the case, with Andersen moving to dismiss and then slicing the original complaint into so many little pieces that it was withdrawn and refiled, just to eliminate any technical problems. Then the whole package went under its docket number into the Superior Court files and awaits either an out-of-court settlement or some Solomonic pie-slicing by the state court.

In the past, consulting companies have moved quickly to resolve these kinds of disputes because of the embarrassment attached to having disagreements hashed out in public. Some have gone to lengths to seal court files and keep everything as quiet as possible, an impossibility in the UOP case because the engineering company has been gabbing to the media about its complaints against Andersen.

At the very least, the allegations should give everyone pause about promises tendered and received from consulting companies, particularly on big technological projects. Beyond that, other consultants say UOP might have made a crucial mistake early in the process in assuming Andersen could move ahead alone to attack such a big challenge. At base, from this perspective, the business always remains the responsibility of the people who run it. If Andersen did, indeed, move way off track with its effort, part of the blame should rest with UOP, which should have followed the engagement more closely. For its part, UOP said Andersen's consultants were insular and didn't share information with UOP engineers, and that a mood developed around the project that helped keep UOP's specialists at arm's length. If that is true, it also flies in the face of Andersen's commitment to keep the client fully engaged and informed about the progress and the problems that pop up along the way.

There is also a component in the consulting business that believes this kind of problem could happen to anyone and that with a company as big as Andersen, it is inevitable that some clients will be miffed or that projects will fail. There are so many variables in consulting, on both sides of the contract, that the potential for trouble is quite strong. Some say it all comes down to the quality of the team the consultant sends. A bad mix with too many inexperienced youngsters running about is one sign of trouble. Too much talk, too many flowcharts, and too little action is another.

To be sure, conversations with corporate executives about consulting sometimes lead to the "they'll-never-work-in-this-building-again" kind of reaction that signals an engagement gone wrong. This is by no means limited to Andersen Consulting. McKinsey & Co., Deloitte & Touche, Boston Consulting Group, indeed, all the big houses, have experiences they would rather not discuss. Gemini Consulting has teams that are ready to sweep in and solve problems when they bubble to the surface.

Lawsuit as Learning Experience

Regardless of the outcome of the UOP suit, it is likely Andersen will process the details, analyze them to find the points at which problems occurred, and try to find some way to avoid this level of explosion in the future. It seems to place a high value on learning experiences, to the point at which its veterans can talk at length about how projects work, what can go wrong, where the surprises are, and how they should be handled. It is clear from these conversations that there is room for blame everywhere in the client-consultant relationship. Some consultants are simply incompetent and some clients simply won't play along, pay no attention to top-dollar advice, and persist in building small fires around their own feet no matter how determined the consulting advice against that practice.

There is also that immeasurable component that sometimes helps define the nature of an engagement, an inherent craziness in some situations that waves a red flag. What consultants want as much as money is a good reputation, because that, too, is marketable. Taking on a client that is too much of a challenge can cause big problems.

Andersen's Keith Burgess recalls meeting with officials of the Russian Oil and Gas Ministry a few years ago. Communism had collapsed, and they were concerned about collecting billions of dollars in back payments from former Soviet republics that had walked on their energy bills. To this day, he believes the Russians were only joking when they asked for his advice on whether military action would be appropriate, sort of an Armageddon of debt collecting, but he is still not sure. "That is slightly beyond the area of Andersen's competence," Burgess told the Russians.

Eager to get in on the ground floor with an important component of the Russian economy, Burgess said, Andersen lowballed a bid, $100,000 to set up a system that would help the Russian energy people keep track of bills. It was a $200,000 job at least, but oil and gas was 30 percent of the emerging Russian gross national product and it would have been nice for Andersen to get a piece of that action. It had such an old and well-established track record with utilities that it made good sense. The gas and oil people wanted lots of help and liked this idea. Then they asked Burgess whether Andersen could go to the World Bank or someplace to get the money to pay for the engagement, because they were broke. They wanted not only good advice, they wanted Andersen to find the money to pay for it.

"At that point, we just parted company. If it was so important and so key that they couldn't come up with $100,000, just forget it. There was no point in pursuing it," he recalls. Even now, the whole story still ends with a pause and a smile, as though Burgess were pondering what might have become of this strange, lost opportunity.

One of the Irishman Neill's own stories about client wackiness goes back to an engagement years ago at a hospital in Cork, where Andersen had been called in to help develop some efficiencies and make the place run more smoothly. It was something of a baptism of fire in that Neill went into the place believing firmly that logic and reason would always win the day, and came away with some experiences that put a particularly human face on what happens in the consulting businesses. There was trouble right out of the gate, when he was invited to deliver his presentation on technology and efficiency to the medical staff.

"It was the first major health care assignment I had sold," he said, "and I put a lot of work into crafting the rationality. The administrator arranged for me to make the presentation of a superbly crafted and logical program of change and new technology for the medical staff. I waited outside the room while they covered their other agenda items. I made a wonderful presentation. Then I was savaged by the entire group, particularly the head of the neurological-surgical department."

He was practically knocked off his feet by this experience and wondered just what he had done wrong. Was it his personality, his presentation, his information? Had he made a mistake all those years ago in taking that free beer and deciding to sign on with Andersen? Clearly the doctors wanted to unsheathe their scalpels and rearrange his paradigm right on the spot.

"It was only after my presentation that I learned that the agenda item before I appeared was all of the budget cuts they were going to apply to the various departments. I was next up as the expensive consultant who was going to come in and spend a lot of money. I had no idea of the emotional context that was created before I came on. Logic had long since gone out of the window," Neill said. Being a consultant and never one to be shy about taking advantage, Neill said, the attack actually created some sympathy for him. The most aggressive of the neuro-surgeons ultimately became an ally, "one of our best friends and supporters and in fact, a key player in moving it all forward."

It didn't stop there. He remembers the morning he was called in by an administrator who had a very delicate problem in the radiation lab he didn't quite know how to handle. It was discovered that some doctors were using the equipment to X-ray dead pheasants. Was it a sensitive research project? Something aimed at determining the effect of ballistics on targets? That might have some benefit in Ireland, what with the troubles up north. But that wasn't it at all, Neill learned after a brief investigation.

"The reason was that they had been out shooting and there was some dispute as to whose gun had killed three of the pheasants. So they were X-raying the pheasants to determine the caliber of the shots. Now, this wasn't the biggest problem at the hospital, but it was an interesting symptom."

The mysteries of technology created a good anecdote, too, about computers that don't work as planned. "I was doing a quality assurance review of a big on-line system and I said I wanted to see what we had designed in terms of security procedures to make certain that only authorized people could have access," he said. "As an afterthought, I decided to try to get access. The system asked me for a password, so I typed in just any old word. The screen came up that I had typed in the wrong password. Then it said, 'The correct password is . . .' and then it gave me the password. Somewhere down in the bowels of this thing we had a very user-friendly programmer. You have really got to check these things to make sure they are actually working as expected." Indeed.

That has been the challenge for Andersen, to make certain everything is working just as expected. It wants to hold the O'Neal Steel and UOP suits to a minimum. It has done well enough at this to maintain a hold on the leader's position in the world of technology consulting, and its strong move into strategic consulting will be closely watched. There were concerns among analysts in 1994 that this shift would dilute Andersen's strength as a technology leader, but Andersen's partners are betting that the melding of technology and strategy will be viewed as the kind of marriage that separates it from its many growing competitors on the IT scene. If it is a weakness, it has not shown up on the balance sheet. And Andersen's sophisticated move into the world of virtual consulting, with its fancy showpieces and strong emphasis on the belief that technology and strategy must march hand in hand, could be the ideal consulting ticket for businesses that have been shy about bridging the gap between their executives and their technicians.

Perhaps a better measure of the move is that some consulting houses that once based their billings almost solely on strategy advice are moving much more deeply into the world of information technology as quickly as they can. Either they absorb or are absorbed by technology specialists—the EDS–A. T. Kearney merger, for example—or they reach out to connect with technology-based companies when necessary.

Beyond all of that, Andersen has the bigness it needs to be present almost everywhere. Even its big golf outing was a world-scale production. Inside the company, it is pushing hard on the fact that its consultants are now connected all over the world through something called the Knowledge Xchange, a sophisticated computer communications system aimed at tapping Andersen's many layers of experience. It is also in position to leap into whatever is ultimately created by the convergence of computers, telephone systems, cable, television, education, and entertainment. No one knows yet what this market will be or how it will be shaped, but as surely as it awaited the arrival of computers, tapped into the era of changing business culture, and has shifted into strategy, it is getting ready.

The assumption is that it will be big and profitable and present a whole collection of challenges and opportunities, all centered around the changes it brings. True to Andersen's history, it has invented a word to cover it. It calls the emerging mishmash of information technology components the "Infocosm," a word that has already seeped deeply into Andersen's corporate rhetoric, even though no one really knows what it is yet.

4

Taming "The Monster of the Midway"

THE RISE, FALL, AND RISE AGAIN OF SEARS

Andersen Consulting's challenge is to marry the mysteries of technology and strategy. At Sears, Roebuck & Co., CEO Arthur Martinez faced the challenge of making one of the most dramatic turnarounds in American corporate history, a story that shows how, over time, consultants have been used to hurt or help a great American corporation.

When the invitation from Arthur C. Martinez arrived in the mail, waves of anticipation rippled through Sears headquarters. Direct and simple in tone, it said: "Please join me and other managers of Sears in Phoenix, Arizona, May 23 through May 26, 1993, to discuss the opportunities and challenges ahead of us." For the 75 to 80 top executives whom Martinez graciously summoned to Phoenix, the gesture was unprecedented. Sears bosses of old—the tall, gray-haired midwesterners with their dark Sears suits and Norman Rockwell miens—didn't do such things. It simply wasn't Sears. But in the ten months since the stylish, blue-eyed outsider from New York had been named chairman and CEO of the Sears Merchandising Group, Searsmen had discovered he was indeed cut from a different cloth; he bought his suits at Paul Stuart or Neiman-Marcus, not Sears. During his first six months on the job, Martinez canned 50,000 people, closed more than 100 unprofitable stores, and killed the most sacred of Sears cows—the famed Big Book, the semiannual, money-losing catalog, a dinosaur long protected as the heart and soul of the renowned retailer. And now he was doing something even more revolutionary: seeking the views of the people who worked there about the fate of the company. The site of the three-day meeting was The Pointe, a posh Phoenix resort also known as Tapatio Cliffs, and the challenge was to come up with a strategy that would rescue the giant retailer from a looming financial disaster.

Years later, sitting in a small, well-appointed conference room adjacent to his office at Sears headquarters in suburban Chicago, Martinez would call the 1993 meeting in Phoenix a "seminal" event in one of the most dramatic turnarounds in the annals of American business. It was no accident that he chose Phoenix as the meeting's site. From that day forward, Sears, a troubled retailer, would rise from its ashes and soar across a corporate landscape littered with other fallen merchandisers. Within three years, he would also prove wrong those who had dismissed Sears as an endangered species. Sales, which had been anemic, would soar, earnings would nearly triple, and Martinez would become a story unto himself. His picture would grace the cover of *Business Week*; *Financial World* magazine would name him its twenty-second CEO of the year; and he would become the first outsider to assume the chairmanship of Sears in 110 years when Edward A. Brennan, a 39-year company veteran, stepped down. But there is more to the reversal of fortunes at Sears than a story about a kid from blue-collar Brooklyn who made it big. Also embedded in the details of how Martinez revived a major American corporation is an object lesson in the effective use of consultants. Arthur Martinez had a lot of help at Sears—mainly from his management team and from his employees. But consultants had a hand in the turnaround, too, and the rifle-shot approach that Martinez took is a case study of how to hire a consultant so things work out.

In days past, Sears had taken an approach all too familiar to many American corporations: It hired consultants with marquee names, firms like McKinsey & Co. or Monitor Co., and authorized carte blanche engagements that gave the consultants wide sway within the company. McKinsey was the top of the line, the blue blood of strategy consulting, and Monitor the fresh, brilliant young product of Michael Porter, one of the smartest professors at Harvard, the nation's most prestigious business school. The strategies these firms produced sounded good on paper, and the bills reached into the stratosphere. In some cases, though, the results left much to be desired. Martinez viewed such broad-based assignments as a big mistake, an abdication of authority by a CEO. He and his executive team would set the strategy and put the consultants to work on targeted, tightly focused assignments where they could be integrated into a company team. And that went along with an emerging trend among big companies that hire outsiders: Define the objective, never lose control, and watch the outsiders like hawks because faulty advice can generate losses that dwarf the profits spawned by good counsel. In short, Martinez believed in controlling the consultants, not in letting the consultants control him, and the results would speak for themselves.

To appreciate how far Martinez has come and how far he still has to go, it's crucial to understand the magnitude of the challenge he assumed when he left Saks Fifth Avenue in New York in 1992 and headed for the Great Plains and Chicago. Before he fired the first employee, closed the first store, or hired the first consultant, he had to study and comprehend the nature and the culture of Sears Roebuck & Co., the huge retailer whose fate was now in his hands. It was no small task, and Martinez soon realized that Sears' strong and proud tradition played a prominent role in the troubles he faced.

A War Is Born

In many respects, the story of Sears is the story of America. The idea of the company sprang to life during the 1880s in the mind of Richard Sears, a handsome young spellbinder and salesman who hit upon a way to sell gold-filled pocket watches to farmers who told time by looking at the sun. Sears quickly became a parable of Yankee ingenuity, the entrepreneurial spirit that turned fledgling young companies into the powerful American corporations that would dominate the nation's economy for much of the twentieth century. Its history is a chronicle of power struggles, money, barter, booze, and, above all else, people—people like General Robert E. Wood, an eccentric but brilliant merchandiser who dominated the company from 1922 until his death in 1969.

Operating out of the company's headquarters on the west side of Chicago, Wood would have the greatest impact on Sears in its first century. Soon after taking charge as chairman, Wood lauched a blistering pace of growth, etching Sears and its stores into America's expanding commercial landscape. He became known across America as "the General." He also made Sears an American icon. It became a company at which employees never suffered layoffs, a place steeped in the General's values, which included a distinct distrust of New York, bankers, and Harvard, not necessarily in that order. Publicists referred to it as "the Monster of the Midway." By the mid-1960s, Sears employed some 300,000 people and one in five Americans shopped there. Later in the decade, *Fortune* magazine called the General's company "the paragon of retailing" and noted that it was bigger than the entire tobacco or furniture industry.

In his quest to make Sears an American icon, though, the General also created an unwieldy corporate structure that would electrify and plague the company for decades. Sears' powerful cadre of buyers and executive corps had the General's ear at company headquarters in Chicago. But Wood also created independent regional headquarters led by highly autonomous executives in the field to represent the sales forces in the stores. In good times and bad, competition between the "parent" in Chicago and the "warlords" in the regions was stiff. When sales started to slow in the early 1970s, though, the rivalry intensified as each side jockeyed to gain a competitive advantage or to shift blame for slumping sales. As the decade matured, the competition endured, resisting recession, hard times, corporate reorganizations, and the best efforts of the three chairmen who succeeded Wood, each of whom seemed to make the situation that Martinez would inherit worse.

Home Rule Is Where Ed Lives

Edward Riggs Telling learned that he would be chairman of Sears on a crisp fall day in 1978 at the reading room of the Chicago Club, a gathering spot for Chicago's business elite. He got the word from the current chairman, Arthur Wood. (Wood wasn't related to the General, but, in a sign of the General's lasting influence, he had anointed Arthur Wood to succeed Gordon Metcalf in 1972, even though the General had died in 1969. Wood was the son of one of the General's friends.) Like most Sears executives, Telling and Wood were tall and white. But that's where the similarities ended. A lawyer by training and an aristocrat by inclination, Wood, in the words of Donald Katz, author of *The Big Store*, a book about Sears, "looked and talked like an Englishman, wore funny-looking prep school suits and was always talking about someone 'having his innings.' " Telling exuded midwestern reticence. Tall, plainspoken, and quiet, he was an enigma, an introverted man who laced his sparse conversation with country-boy sayings like "There's no need to beat a horse that can't pull." Both men had an enormous influence on the situation that Martinez would face years later, though.

Wood's main contribution was his choice of Telling for the top job. The decision wasn't as easy as it might sound. Wood actually broke tradition in the late 1970s when he passed over Dean Swift, then president of Sears, a position that was always occupied by the heir apparent. But, late in his tenure, Wood feared for Sears' future. By the early 1970s, too many Americans had already bought their first Kenmore washer or Craftsman power drill from more than 800 Sears stores spread across America. The market was saturated. Competition had intensified, too. Montgomery Ward, JCPenney, and an outfit named Kresge, which would later become Kmart, had set up shop in America's malls and suburbs. When oil prices quadrupled in 1973, Wood saw Sears' profits drop by $170 million. He responded with the unthinkable—he ordered some layoffs. A year later, profits dropped again by 58 percent and Sears stock tumbled from around $90 a share to under $60. War soon broke out over the slumping sales between the powerful factions within Sears. On one side were the sellers—407,958 workers divided among the five territories. On the other side were the buyers and the corporate staff, some 9,500 strategically placed employees operating out of Chicago. Both sides blamed the other for Sears' problems, and nothing seemed to move up, down, or even sideways within Sears without a fight between the home office and the powerful, autonomous territories.

At first, Wood turned to outside help, becoming the first chairman to bring consultants in to Sears. In early 1975, he commissioned Hay Associates of Philadelphia to assess the climate within Sears. Later in the year, though, he realized that the General's decentralized system would not change on its own, and he hired McKinsey & Co. to study the structure of Sears and suggest what could be done. To win the contract, McKinsey promised the full attention of its Chicago office to the retailer for the two months the company estimated its study would take.

McKinsey committed half the time of its number-two man in the firm, Jack Caldwell, and all of the time of Phillip Purcell, a young hotshot who, at 27, had become the youngest principal director in the firm's history. Actually, McKinsey & Co.'s study of Sears would take a year and a half. Purcell would travel to the far corners of the empire, to the territories and to Sears corridors where the General's ghost still roamed. He found the company fascinating and cherished the old Searsmen who regaled him with colorful stories, like the yarn about the Las Vegas manager who sold bedding to the ladies of a red-light district and chalked up the huge profits to "sporting goods." In Purcell's mind, Sears was America, a place where smart, savvy hustlers could get ahead regardless of their pedigree. In the end, though, Caldwell and Purcell would both come to the same conclusion. The revival of Sears' fortunes, they told Wood, depended on the next chairman's ability to dramatically change the status quo within Sears. And the right man for that job, both agreed, was Ed Telling, the chairman who would play a big role in creating the mess that Martinez would inherit.

At first, Telling's ascension to power didn't seem too out of character. When he ran Sears' East Coast territory, Telling seemed like any other territorial warlord. He had risen within the ranks, bought all of his clothes from Sears (with the exception of his 13-A shoes), ignored orders from Chicago, and routinely left the office early, defiantly instructing his administrative assistant to tell anyone who called that he was home raking leaves, including Sears Chairman Gordon Metcalf, whom he derisively referred to as "the Superchairman." Judging from his actions, Telling seem to share Searsmen's suspicions about strong centralized home offices. But the rank and file would soon learn differently. Purcell and others who got to know Telling (as well as anyone could know the taciturn midwesterner) discovered that he opposed a centralized corporate structure only when it applied to people above him. "Ed Telling believes in home rule," his aides used to say, "and home is wherever Ed happens to live." Actually Telling loathed the Balkanization of the company. He dreamed of unifying Sears—top to bottom, coast to coast, "field" to "parent"—into one, efficient, centrally governed organization, and he got his chance when Wood took McKinsey's advice and named him chairman in late 1978.

Telling didn't even wait to be officially sworn in before he lashed out at the power of the territories. As Searsmen gossiped about the new boss, he boarded a Sears Falcon jet and flew to a small airport near Pueblo, Colorado, where he informed John Lowe, the king of the Western Territory, that he was out. The move stunned Lowe; such things simply weren't done at Sears. But it sent a strong message resonating throughout Sears. An era was about to end; Ed Telling intended to shake things up. Telling didn't disappoint, either. The next thing he did was a first, too. McKinsey had recommended that the company centralize its decision-making process to promote greater responsiveness to the company's strategies. Telling agreed. So he hired an outsider as the vice president for planning, a job that had been recommended by McKinsey. His name was Phil Purcell, formerly of McKinsey & Co., the firm that had been brought in to another old-line Chicago retailer, Marshall Field & Co., years before.

From his first day in office, Telling would wrestle with problems that would reverberate within Sears until Martinez's day. He assumed the chairmanship at a time of slumping profits. A severe recession loomed on the nation's horizon, and interest rates had started to soar. Sears' stock price tumbled below $20 per share, and Telling's campaign against the autonomy of the territorial bosses merely intensified the turmoil already raging within Sears. At times, it seemed like every step Telling took created more problems than it solved.

He installed Purcell in executive offices and gave him a staff of planners that Searsmen soon dubbed "the kids in 702-P" (702 was the account for "executives' offices" and contained the shortest list in Sears' 200-page phone book—Ed Telling and two secretaries). But Purcell and his corporate planners confronted the skeptics with a "decision tree matrix" designed to define a chain of command within Sears and force some hard decisions. Most Searsmen viewed the matrix as a joke, a tool straight out of the elitist Harvard Business School, the nation's Ivy League factory for snot-nosed MBAs. Soon, though, the skeptics learned better. "The kids in 702-P" flooded Sears with planning matrix forms modeled on the Boston Consulting Group's infamous portfolio product matrix. They ordered buyers to rank each of the 800 lines of merchandise available through Sears according to their long-range profit potential, ranging from invest and grow (the best lines in the upper left-hand corner of the matrix) to harvest and abandon (the lower right-hand corner of the chart). When the paperwork came back to 702-P, the kids discovered that it would take more than a matrix to change the Sears the General had built. Only one buyer in Sears concluded that he had bought a product that should be milked and forgotten. The buyer with the largest and most profitable item at Sears—washing machines—wouldn't accept that his market might be "mature." It was a $600-million-a-year business, something that he wouldn't call bad in writing.

One bad thing just seemed to lead to another, and after a year or more on the job, Telling had little to show for his stewardship. In fact, when Sears' first-quarter earnings for 1980 came out, things looked bad; the company had lost $432 million in the quarter compared to a $67 million profit in the first three months of 1979. Morale plunged along with the stock price (it fell to $15.25). Rumors swirled through the company that some board members wanted Telling's scalp.

But the tall, withdrawn chairman had more on his mind than a few bad quarters in the Merchandising Group. Ever since he'd hired Purcell, Telling and the boy wonder from McKinsey had been working on a secret plan to move the company in an entirely new direction. From the General's day forward, Sears had known only one way to grow—expansion. When the company wanted to increase revenues, it simply built more stores and priced its merchandise better, often ignoring the state of the American economy. During good times, and even during some of the slack, the formula had worked fine. But that was the 1950s and 1960s. The 1970s were different. Sears' costs and competition had increased dramatically, and the economy had slumped. Telling figured that the company could never retain its premier status simply by trying to sell more stuff to Americans. The margins simply weren't there, for Sears or for other retailers. Telling also thought new family formation would decline in the 1990s, intensifying the glut of retail capacity already evident. Sears, he and Purcell had concluded, would be better off diversifying, particularly considering the size of the company and its market. Despite its recent troubles, Sears still had billions of dollars in resources. It had started a well-known insurance company called Allstate; polls showed it to be one of the most trusted of American corporations; more than 8 of 10 Americans had a favorable opinion of the company; and its credit card reached into the homes of more than 70 percent of Americans with incomes of more than $36,000. If Sears could use its resources to acquire new businesses, it could capitalize on the trust and access to the massive pool of Americans that the Sears merchandisers had attracted.

Telling didn't ignore the problems festering in the Merchandising Group. He couldn't. In early 1980, he gave it a new boss, Edward A. Brennan, a young hotshot and career Searsman who had vastly improved results in the Southern Territory through aggressive merchandising and equally aggressive cost cutting. Brennan's appointment was just a stopgap, though. Eight months later, Telling took a far more significant step that addressed the real problems: He announced a massive reorganization that went hand in glove with the spirit of the earlier McKinsey study spearheaded by Purcell. McKinsey had recommended an organization that would centralize decision making. Under Telling's plan, Sears would become a holding company led by a small corporate office headed by Telling. The chairman would preside over three distinct businesses—the small Searco Real Estate Group, the Allstate Insurance Group, and the Sears Merchandising Group. All would have a chairman and CEO who would report to Telling. The reorganization was much more than a bureaucratic reshuffling. It meant that the chairman of Sears would no longer run the merchandising company, and the merchandisers would no longer run Sears. Indeed, Telling had built the corporate shell for the new kind of Sears he and Purcell envisioned. They called it "The Great American Company."

The Supermarket Where Sears Starved

At first, Telling didn't have much luck finding suitable acquisitions for The Great American Company. He wanted to acquire a company like Sears—one with solid American values and a balance sheet as strong as an eagle's claw. He and Purcell looked at AT&T, Walt Disney Productions, IBM, Standard Oil of California, and Deere & Co., the nation's premier supplier of farm equipment in Illinois. Telling liked the idea of Deere or even Disney. Both ideas were dropped, though; Deere said it wasn't interested, and Purcell decided Disney wasn't on Sears' wavelength after a visit to Hollywood. The former McKinsey consultant then told his planning team to revert to an earlier idea: Identify a venture that could "leverage off the existing strengths of the company." In other words, find a company or industry that could capitalize on Sears' customer base. Several weeks later, the team told Purcell that Sears could best exploit its customer base and trust quotient by entering the business of caring for and keeping other people's money. The idea wasn't really that revolutionary. Richard Sears had established a banking department within Sears in 1899 but abandoned it four years later when he discovered customers were more interested in Sears as a retailer. Nevertheless, Purcell took the idea to Telling, a banker's son from Danville, Illinois. Suddenly, Telling knew what to do.

The idea of Sears as a "financial supermarket" sounded great on paper. By some estimates, Sears, in one way or another, reached into nine of ten American households. That figure probably was exaggerated. But in the early 1980s, Sears could show that 20 million Americans held insurance through the company; 36 million families shopped there; its credit card reached into three of four American homes with incomes of $36,000 or more; and millions more contracted for the range of services it offered, like installation of appliances and auto care. Why not tap into that huge customer base and see if Sears could lend its customers money or keep it in interest-bearing savings accounts?

Congress already was at work stripping the financial services industry of restrictive regulations that protected the industry from outsiders. Customers trusted Sears, too. The company could enter the financial services industry on its own, or it could use its vast resources to buy a brokerage firm, one that already was offering clients money market funds that paid savers interest rates far in excess of those available at banks or savings and loans. By offering a full range of financial services, Sears could offer the ultimate in one-stop shopping. Creditworthy Sears customers could enter a store, put their money in a bank, borrow funds to buy a house (through a Sears real estate broker, of course), furnish the place with Sears furniture and appliances, insure it with Allstate, buy the tools, paint, and equipment to fix it up, have Sears mechanics install their windows and air conditioners, and, if needed, buy a new set of tires for the car in the driveway. For someone like Telling, whose father had been demoted and humiliated when hard times hit the local bank in Danville, the temptation was irresistible. It would all work, assuming customers would continue to flow through the doors of Sears retail stores. That was the problem, though: Telling had assumed too much.

Ed Brennan, the homegrown Searsman who would hire Arthur Martinez, had been given the unenviable job of keeping the customers flowing into Sears in 1980. Handsome, aggressive, and smart, Brennan had grown up poor, Catholic, and Irish on Chicago's West Side. He had retailing in his blood, though. His grandfather had worked beside Richard Sears and his father; two uncles and a brother had all worked as Sears buyers. Even when he went off to Marquette University in Milwaukee, Brennan worked in the retail business, and he went to work at Sears not long after he graduated. He had a broad Irish face that wore a smile as natural as the wave in his hair. He smoked big cigars and talked of retailing the way a pastor of the local church talks of the priesthood—it was a calling, not an occupation. Brennan was known to personally fit every new board member with a custom-made Sears suit.

At first, Telling named Brennan president of Sears, a job that put him in charge of the Merchandising Group and also made him heir apparent. All that changed with the reorganization, though, and Brennan's job was "restructured down" so he could focus his energy on merchandising. Energetic and decisive, Brennan took to the challenge with relish, despite internal reports that showed a shrinking customer base in 1980 and a severe recession that plagued the nation's economy. Strong competition from discounters such as Kmart had hurt Sears, and morale within the company had plummeted with each sorry report on earnings. Brennan fought back with cost controls, consolidations, "head-count reductions" or layoffs, and sales promotions. He authorized a widespread study of individual stores and product lines to determine their strengths and weaknesses and conducted intensive customer surveys to assess customer happiness with stores and their displays. Armed with knowledge from his surveys, he soon unveiled an aggressive $1.7 billion "Store of the Future" program designed to upgrade 600 dark, dingy Sears stores into clean, uniform retail outlets with something new—brand-name products, such as Levi's jeans. He attacked Sears' legendary high costs with several reorganizations. By the mid-1980s, the number of officers and managers at Sears had fallen by nearly 40 percent from the levels that had prevailed in 1978. Initially, things went well, particularly as the nation's economy shrugged off the recession. By early 1984, the Merchandising Group reported that profits had nearly tripled since Brennan had taken over, despite many new and untried managers, a wrenching consolidation that had uprooted thousands of employees, and a sick international division.

On the surface, Telling and Brennan appeared to be quite a team. Telling was the big thinker who had built a financial supermarket. Freed from the direct responsibility of the Merchandising Group, he had acquired Coldwell Banker, a real estate broker, and Dean Witter, a huge stockbrokerage firm, for a total of about $800 million in 1981. A year later, he started Sears World Trade, a trading company based in Washington, D.C. Sears launched the Discover credit card in 1985 and dabbled in the banking industry with Sears Savings Bank, which basically came and went. By the time Telling was done, Sears had 852 stores and 2,388 catalog outlets in American cities and small towns to help sell the real investment, insurance, and real estate products of 324 Dean Witter, 3,000 Allstate, and 400 Coldwell Banker offices. The company was not only America's largest retailer, it was also the nation's second largest property and casualty insurance company, the thirteenth largest life insurance company, the largest residential and commercial real estate broker, the largest institutional shopping center developer, and the seventh largest securities brokerage firm. The same critics who'd called for Telling's scalp now considered him a hero, Sears' first national figure since the General, a man who had made Sears a force to be reckoned with in the financial services industry. "I said 10 years ago that Sears would be our principal competition in the 1980s," said Citicorp's Walter Wriston, "and no one would listen to me then. Now they're listening."

Meanwhile, Brennan, the merchandiser, had kept customers flowing through Sears' doors. Not only were sales up at the retailer, profits also started to gush in from Telling's investment in financial services. During some quarters, the company's profits leaped more than 100 percent. Telling was so happy that he named Brennan president and CEO of Sears in August 1984. Two years later, Telling retired and Brennan inherited the job he had always coveted—chairman of the board of Sears, Roebuck & Co. Unfortunately, though, he would soon learn that the Sears he'd inherited from Telling was no longer "the Monster of the Midway." It was a monster of a different sort.

It is hard to pin blame on one person for what would happen to Sears over the next six years. Telling obviously pushed the idea to make Sears a financial supermarket. He deserves the credit and blame for the ill-fated scheme. He had a lot of help, though, from Purcell, who is a great example of how McKinsey & Co.'s influence can extend beyond its direct role with a client. Once on board at Sears, Purcell hired McKinsey for some select assignments but never for any other company-wide engagements. It was not McKinsey but Purcell's planning department that came up with the idea of a financial supermarket. But by riding the pipeline that flows from McKinsey to the upper reaches of corporate America, Purcell brought McKinsey's philosophy and values with him when he joined Sears, where he became a highly influential alter ego to Telling. It is hard to overstate the effect such positions and philosophies can have. Casting blame for the troubles that would ensue isn't crucial, though. The important thing is that the strategy of making Sears a financial supermarket didn't work.

The megacorporation that Telling created caused problems on many fronts. One didn't even seem like a problem at the time. Off and on, Sears' financial services generated profits—enough of them to offset and overshadow the poor performance of the Sears Merchandising Group, which struggled throughout the 1980s. But the profits from financial services also eased the pressure on Sears to solve its merchandising troubles, which were the fundamental problem that Sears faced even when Martinez took over. The company also had increased its debt, giving it less competitive flexibility. But the most significant problems were created by the capital demands the financial supermarket placed on Sears. Both sides of the business devoured huge amounts of capital. If Brennan decided to devote too much capital to resolving the Merchandising Group's problems, financial services would suffer. But the financial services side of the business had a voracious appetite for funds that Brennan couldn't ignore, either. Regulators set the capital requirements for financial services. Moreover, Allstate and Dean Witter, which were paying internal dividends to their parent company, needed capital to expand. Indeed, one yardstick of the demand—the receivable that had to be financed for the Discover credit card—soared from $3.8 billion in 1987 to $14.7 billion in 1991. Martinez would later put his finger on the problem:

> What was wrong was that too much of the strategic focus, management energy and financial capital [had gone] to building the financial supermarket side of the business and no attention, or let's

say insufficient attention, was paid to the retail side, which was the mother lode of the whole thing. If you didn't have customers coming into your store, happy with their relationship with the store, they weren't necessarily going to be interested in anything else you had to offer. Strategically, the idea [of the financial supermarket] was sound. The problem was, while they were building another floor on the house, the foundation was rotting.

Enter Monitor and Martinez

It wasn't as if Brennan, who had retailing in his blood, ignored the problem. He made several efforts to fix things. He launched reorganizations, laid off thousands of employees, revamped stores, and brought in new merchandise. But he also pulled his punches. He budgeted $1.7 billion for his Store of the Future "upgrade," but spent only $1.2 billion as the economy slogged out of its recession. Meanwhile, a glut of stores in the retail industry, as well as high costs, persisted. Problems new and old continued to dog the company, too. At one point, Brennan named Michael Bozic, a young Sears executive who had turned around Sears Canada, as head of the retail group. Bozic almost immediately fell victim to the warring factions within the company, though. He tried to create "neighborhood stores," strategically placed outlets that would include only "soft goods," items such as apparel and home furnishings, both high-margin categories. But Sears executives from the "hard lines"—appliances, electronics, and home improvement products—argued they couldn't be left out of the stores. No one could resolve what Bozic termed a "creative confrontation," and the stores never opened. It was hard to even find out what was going on in the stores thanks to Sears' decentralized accounting methods, a legacy of the General. Buyers in Chicago couldn't find out how screwdrivers were selling in Albuquerque. As a result, no one had information to work with, and Sears found it hard to react to its own sales patterns.

But Sears' most devastating mistake occurred after it hired one of America's most influential consultants to help the ailing retail arm at Sears devise a strategy to deal with its persistent problems. It is hard to underestimate the importance of Michael E. Porter and Monitor Company, the Cambridge-based consulting firm that the Harvard Business School professor cofounded in 1983. "Measuring Michael's impact on the [rest of the] consulting industry," said Liam Fahey, a consultant and former Boston University professor, "is like comparing the [101-story] Sears Tower to the Tribune Tower," a 24-story Gothic landmark that is home to the *Chicago Tribune*. Porter's book *Competitive Strategy*, published in 1980, and later tomes, *Competitive Advantage* and *The Competitive Advantage of Nations*, are considered bibles of strategic thought among businessmen and students, and Porter remains one of the nation's most highly paid academic consultants. From his perch at Monitor, which was founded to put his ideas into practice, Porter was a pioneer in applying traditional economic theory to management problems. He argued that competitive forces in the marketplace shape corporate strategy rather than the interplay of marketing, production, and other functions. Brennan hired Porter's Monitor Company in the late 1980s after hearing the Harvard professor speak at a business gathering, and gave the firm wide sway within Sears.

Monitor talked a good game. A relatively small firm often referred to as a "boutique," Monitor's sales pitch plays off the failures of other consultants. "Most consulting interventions ultimately fail to achieve the ends intended," the firm says in a description it passes out to potential clients. The company doesn't blame the consultant, though. "[The] purchasing process . . . calls for the consultant to make highly subjective judgments about the complexity of the problem to be addressed before actually studying the problem itself." The process often encourages the consultant to make "excessive promises," Monitor says, and "pollutes" the consulting process. To overcome such obstacles, Monitor advocates a strong dialogue between the consultant and the client and stresses that it goes beyond the mere recitation of competitive circumstances to create the convictions that managers need for a correct course of action and change. "Ultimately, we believe that institutions should view the cost of consulting as an investment rather than a period expense," the firm says. "We believe strongly that firms should maintain long-term relationships with their consultants" so the advisor can "gain sufficient familiarity with each client, [its] industry, current strategies, and history to allow us to make a significant contribution."

Brennan said Porter himself came to Sears and made a presentation to the board. That was the last Sears saw of him, though. His clones at Monitor soon showed up and stayed for about two years. At the time, Sears was organized along geographic lines with the various regions compiling geographic profit and loss statements. "The big thing that Monitor did was to get us to start thinking about competition by industry and business rather than profitability by geographic market," said Al Stewart, who ran the Sears planning department at the time. That sounds simple enough, but what grew out of Monitor's work at Sears is a good example of the profound impact a seemingly innocuous consulting engagement can have.

A by-product of Monitor's work was a disastrous policy Sears embraced called "everyday low pricing." Prior to the Monitor engagement, Sears used the tried-and-true techniques that most retailers employed to get customers in the door; it marked up merchandise for a while and then advertised a big sale in which prices were slashed to lure bargain hunters into Sears stores. A $15.99 hammer, for example, would go on sale twice a year for $10.99, and that's when Sears would sell most of them (55 percent of its goods were sold at reduced prices). Under "everyday low pricing," Sears changed dramatically to compete along industry and business lines. It cut prices sharply and permanently on most items, eliminating the deep-discount sales. The hammer would sell year-round for $11.73. Had the policy worked, Sears would have increased its margins. It didn't work for two reasons, though. One: Sears had conditioned its customers to expect deep-discount sales. After an initial burst of enthusiasm, customers sat back and waited for Sears to cut its "everyday low prices" in one of its traditional sales. Two: Discounters like Wal-Mart had used "everyday low pricing" so successfully that Sam Walton's stores had eclipsed Sears as the nation's largest retailer. But Wal-Mart was a low-cost operation. Sears, by contrast, was one of the highest-cost operations around. For Sears, the policy was a disaster.

To this day, there is a lot of finger-pointing about what went wrong, which is typical when things go awry. At one time, Monitor had 40 to 50 consultants in Sears charging up to $2,000 to $2,500 a day per person. One knowledgeable executive estimated the bill ran $15 to $20 million a year. No one wants to admit to mistakes when the cost is so high. Under Brennan's account, the idea of everyday low pricing was a by-product of Monitor's work at Sears. "It grew out of the work that they did," he said. Other former executives at Sears say Brennan deserves the blame for what went wrong, though. He ignored the advice of several of his top merchandisers, who thought the "everyday low pricing" scheme was ill conceived. Monitor consultants opposed the timing of Brennan's decision to implement the scheme, under these accounts, but not necessarily the policy itself. Stewart said Monitor's consultants merely advanced "a view of the world" or a policy that Sears managers failed to execute properly. Regardless of who is right, the bottom line soon became clear: "Everyday low pricing" cost Sears dearly. Sears spent $200 million on an ad blitz promoting the scheme, but in the final analysis, Brennan had to cancel the policy soon after it was implemented. The skeptics within Sears proved right. The Merchandising Group's earnings plunged, and Brennan dumped Bozic, who was widely perceived as the "fall guy" for the whole fiasco. "Yes there was some resistance to the idea [everyday low pricing] at the time," Brennan said. "But you have to bear in mind that I wasn't running the Merchandise Group. . . . Mike Bozic was." Brennan declined to comment on whether he thought Monitor's performance was good. "They had some very bright people on their staff," he said. "But I don't think they had ever taken on anything so massive as reorganizing the entire merchandising operation of the nation's second largest retailer." Another former executive with a direct role in the fiasco said it would be unfair to blame everyday low pricing on Monitor, but he, too, said the company's work left a lot to be desired, particularly given the price tag. "I would have to say that, at that time, Monitor was smaller than it is now. I don't think they had the breadth of talent to deal with a huge business like Sears, particularly in the areas of the company that were run by people who had less than a global perspective on the business, which is how we referred to the manager who couldn't see the forest for the trees. Some of these people I don't think challenged Monitor consultants and they let them make many of the decisions. I don't think much good came out of the time they were here."

As the 1990s approached, Monitor disappeared from the scene at Sears, and Brennan himself came under severe pressure. Although Sears revenues and profits had bobbed up and down from one quarter to the next, investors zeroed in on the long term and the picture wasn't pretty. Revenues had creaked upward at a compounded rate of only 2.9 percent during the five years ending in 1989, but expenses had remained high. Indeed, the retail group's profits had tumbled an average 7.7 percent over the five-year stretch. Meanwhile, prices at Sears floated as much as 50 percent higher than other retailers' and its share of general merchandise in the United States dropped from 18 to 13 percent, a loss of $8.4 billion in sales to competitors. Sears stock price had slid 40 percent since Brennan had become CEO. *Fortune* magazine soon ran a piece calling Sears "a century-old, muscle-bound behemoth crushed by its lumbering corporate culture, needing new strategy and probably new management." Many of the company's investors agreed. At one point, Brennan invited 15 of the largest institutional shareholders to breakfast at the Sears Tower to give them an update on the company. When he started to give his upbeat appraisal of Sears, though, the investors lashed out, even suggesting that Brennan's job was on the line. "It was like nothing I've ever seen," one participant said.

Adding to the pressure on Brennan was a 1987 study by Goldman Sachs that said Sears was vulnerable to one of the corporate raiders so prevalent in the 1980s. A raider with designs on acquiring the company, breaking it up, and selling the pieces could pay a 37 to 69 percent premium over Sears' market value and still make a killing. By contrast, a restructuring scheme Brennan had hatched would yield only a premium of 23 to 38 percent for shareholders. When Brennan opted for the restructuring scheme in 1988, shareholders had revolted.

By the early 1990s, Brennan had not only slapped a FOR SALE sign on the company's signature Sears Tower, he had also come under intense pressure to take more drastic steps. Angry shareholders and investors had increased the pressure to break up Sears, by either spinning off the retail arm or selling its financial services. He had also done something unthinkable at Sears. Ed Brennan, a man who had once said, "Running [Sears] is a calling, and no outsider . . . could come in from the cold and try to run it," launched a search for an outsider. It would end just over a year later at a cabin in Maine owned by man who would have made the General's skin crawl—a Harvard-trained New Yorker.

Arthur C. Martinez

Arthur Martinez had been vice chairman of Saks Fifth Avenue for three years when his secretary told him that Herb Mines, a friend of 15 years and a well-known New York headhunter, was on the phone. It was the summer of 1992, and the retail industry was a mess. Plagued by the excesses of the 1980s, the industry had too many stores and too many retailers. Bankruptcy loomed for some of the best-known names in the trade. P. A. Bergner, the company that owned Carson Pirie Scott department stores in Chicago, wanted to hire Martinez to lead it out of Chapter 11 bankruptcy. Martinez recalled that negotiations for the new job were under way when he took the call from Mines: "[Herb] said, 'I hear that you are talking to Bergner. Have you done anything that legally binds or commits you to go to them?' I told him I hadn't but that we were still talking, and that we were at a fairly advanced stage. And he said, 'Well, I think I have something that could really top that opportunity for you. Sears has made the determination that it needs outside leadership to take over the merchandising side of its business and I think you would be perfect for it. I'd love it if you could give it some consideration.' "

Although Martinez didn't know it at the time, the Sears board was only weeks away from assembling at Chicago's Park Hyatt Hotel, where board members would vote to break up the $56 billion financial supermarket by selling or spinning off Dean Witter and Coldwell Banker. Facing a severe cash crunch, the board realized it couldn't supply its retail and financial services arms with the capital both needed. Already the rating services had downgraded the ratings on the company's debt. Eventually Allstate Insurance and everything but the retailing arm of the company would go in transactions that would raise billions of dollars, help Sears cut its debt, and raise the money it needed to modernize its stores. Sears investors loved the breakup.

Martinez wasn't paying much attention to the doings at Sears, though, and he didn't think Mines's inquiry would go too far: "I said, 'Wow, that's a big company and big problems. I hadn't spent a lot of time studying them,' and I said, 'Frankly, Herb, given what I do know about the company, I don't think they could move fast enough. I'm going to be forced to make some decisions about this [Bergner] opportunity within a couple of weeks and nobody could possibly come to a decision about me in that situation that fast. Besides, I'm leaving on vacation in two days.' He said, 'That's my problem. If you are interested in talking and free to talk, let's see if I can get a conversation started.' Two days later I went to my vacation house in Maine." A few days later, Ed Brennan showed up.

Martinez found Brennan to be an agreeable sort when the Sears chairman hopped off the plane for a chat with the vice chairman of

Saks. "We talked for two or three hours," Martinez said. "I found him a very pleasant guy who clearly needed a lot of help, and the thought of being responsible for, hopefully turning around, an institution like Sears Roebuck & Co. was pretty heady stuff. It was clear to me that he was open to bringing in new outside leadership. My question continued to be was the board behind him on this and can it happen as quickly as it needs to. We went back to the headhunter. Ed felt good about things and I felt good enough to take the next step." For Martinez, the next step was a visit to some Sears stores, both in Maine and in Westchester, his New York home. For his part, Brennan flew back to Chicago and arranged for outside directors to sit down with Martinez and give him their views of the company. "I was trying to determine the real appetite for change," Martinez recalled, "because, at the margin, Sears had been guilty of modest, incremental change, and there had to be a real openness for a little bit of revolution here. You know, was I going to have the freedom [I needed]—with reasonable oversight, of course? And, having gone out and looked at some stores, was the capital going to be available to do what I knew had to be done to make the stores competitive?"

Martinez's wife, Liz, was skeptical: "She told me, 'I have all the confidence in the world in you, but do you think Sears is too far gone for anything to happen? Is this a crusade that can't be won?'" Moreover, Martinez's job negotiations with the owners of Carson's were a lot further along that he lets on. He had flown to Switzerland to iron out details of an employment agreement with Bertrand Maus, the chairman of P. A. Bergner & Co. He had also informed Saks that he would be leaving to take the CEO job with Bergner, and the Bergner board had approved his appointment to the top job at the ailing retailer at a salary of $1 million a year plus a $1 million nonrefundable sign-on bonus. Indeed, approval of the Bankruptcy Court was all that was needed to make it official. But the opportunity to revive an American institution proved too enticing. After two weeks of talks, Martinez took the job with Sears. He informed the Bergner organization on August 10, one day before a Bankruptcy Court hearing scheduled to approve his appointment as CEO of P. A. Bergner & Co. He was surprised that Sears could act as quickly as it did. But he also knew that he faced a daunting task: "Somebody recently reminded me that I said to them after I took the job, 'Well, this is going to be a clear win or lose. Either I'm going to be a hero, or I'm going to be a bum. There is no middle ground . . . no shades of gray on this one.' " Regardless of the outcome, Martinez would be a rich hero or bum, though. His salary and bonus at Sears would total about $2 million a year.

Arthur Martinez contrasted sharply with the men who had run Sears Merchandising before him. The only son of a fish wholesaler and an Irish woman who came to America from County Rosscommon, Martinez grew up in the Park Slope area of Brooklyn, a blue-collar enclave that didn't even have a Sears store. His father's side of the family came from Spain, but he doesn't use the Spanish pronunciation (MartinEZ, he says, is the way it has been pronounced for generations). Ed Brennan may have been reared in Sears outfits, but Martinez didn't even enter a Sears store until he was an adult. Sears had a store in Flatbush, which was a subway ride away from Park Slope, but it might as well have been in Montana for young Arthur.

After graduating from Harvard in 1965 with an MBA, Martinez moved up the corporate ladder quickly in a variety of diverse jobs at big corporations, mainly on the finance side. By 1970, he was a vice president in the financial arm of RCA Corp., and he went to Saks in 1973 as a senior vice president and CFO. Within a few years, he was vice chairman of Saks, the tony, upscale retailer. Martinez developed an eclectic management style that made him seem as comfortable closing an unprofitable store as giving a customer directions to the bathroom. He possessed a healthy skepticism about how much outside help he would need from consultants and others and a leadership style that Searsmen would find unique. "I don't have a single source of inspiration," he said. "I try to watch what others do but I try not to copy [them]. My style is a unique one and it comes from looking at the best that's out there and taking the best of the best and putting it together. Early on . . . I worked for a guy named Dave Thomas. This was pre retailing, when I was working for Exxon in the chemicals business. Dave was an important thinker for me on two dimensions: One, the primacy of the customer and two, the importance of being fact-driven in my decision making. He was a good thinker, a very good thinker." By the time he walked into Sears headquarters to meet the staff in September of 1992, Martinez knew from his experience that things would get worse before they got better.

"My first set of actions was to meet the management team that was in place, see what was on their minds, the kinds of issues they were facing," he said. "It was very clear to me that they were looking to me to provide some focus to the business. We were a very unfocused organization at the time. A lot of initiatives had gone nowhere; some had failed miserably, like everyday low pricing, which was a major catastrophe for our company. There were operations that were bleeding dollars, like the catalog, and there were very direct questions at me about what are you going to do about that. [People said] we need to invest in our stores but we don't have the cash because the catalog business is losing a lot of money. They were very direct in their challenge to me about when we were going to get on with things. I knew that I didn't have a year or even six months because the business was in such . . . disarray . . . is perhaps the kindest word to use. The organization was very impatient for some direction. You really couldn't tell people, 'Well, just keep doing your job for a while and when I get a new direction, I'll let you know. . . .' I really thought that speed was of the essence—an imperative driven by a deteriorating financial performance and by my sense of an organization that was very impatient for direction and leadership."

Sears had just lost nearly $3 billion, the largest bath the company had ever taken. Sales continued to lag in the industry, margins were weak, inventories were bulging, the net worth of the company had taken a steep drop, and analysts talked of Sears as if it were lumbering toward bankruptcy. "Bankruptcy was too strong a word," Martinez said in describing the Sears he had agreed to join. "[We'd had] a steady erosion of profitability in the [retail] business beginning basically in 1984. [We were] getting in that dreaded position where you're in that dreaded loop where you are not generating enough profitability and cash to invest in the business and keep yourself competitive and that's the way you fall further and further behind."

A Men's Room in the Lingerie

Some of the problems Martinez faced sounded familiar. "Sears [had been] busy building the Discover [credit] card, which was on a very aggressive growth path and . . . was sucking up all of the capital. You know, capital was going to where the best returns were and the best returns at that point were in the financial services business. So the [retail] problem was exacerbated by this. It was also very apparent to me . . . in a couple of so-called planning sessions [that] there was very much a lack of alignment [among senior managers] inside the company on what direction we ought to take. The people who were here at that time were talking past each other and they weren't very clear on a common direction."

Consultants love the kind of predicament that faced Martinez at Sears. A new CEO at a huge, financially lethargic company manned by dispirited executives and dazed workers usually is an equation for consulting fees that can make the Sears Tower look like a grain elevator. But Martinez doesn't believe in broad-brush strategy engagements like the one that gave Sears "everyday low pricing" and Michael Porter: "I have to be very careful about my words here, because I don't want to indict any prior administration or anything. But it was very clear that the people who had been in the company most recently was Porter's group, Monitor, and they had been given a sort of unlimited mandate. That's just not the way I like to operate. It's an abdication, frankly. The Monitor organization was given carte blanche to look at this company, and I just don't like unfocused assignments like that. I think the missions and objectives . . . and the output [should be] clear. I don't like to use consultants to provide broad diagnostics. I think that is what I'm paid to do, and that's what my senior management team is paid to do. . . . If the person at the top of the organization can't create a clear line of sight as to where they want to go, then he or she is a little bankrupt personally, I think. Consultants can be helpful facilitators, but they can't substitute for clarity or purpose or vision at the top of the house. The guy or gal who gets in the chair and says to McKinsey or Coopers & Lybrand 'Come help me figure out what I should do with this company,' I think is just a little bit bankrupt."

So he started assessing the situation himself and put off the use of consultants for another day. Instead, he relied on his gut instincts, his experience, and existing Sears staffers like Jane Thompson, who had been a McKinsey consultant, and Russ David, his chief financial officer, to help him develop a broad strategy. From the outset, Martinez knew that time was his enemy. He didn't have a year, or even six months. He stated publicly he would come up with a plan by Christmas, a mere 100 days away, and he started studying the company. He already knew he would have to cut Sears' costs; they were the highest in the industry (selling, general, and administrative expenses totaled 23 percent of revenue in 1992 compared to 14.9 percent at Wal-Mart). But a couple of incidents also convinced him that deep personnel and cultural changes would be needed at Sears: "I went out to visit some stores and I walked into one in Omaha that had been remodeled according to the view of remodeling then, and something struck me visually that showed we were so disconnected from our customer. The men's room was right in the middle of the intimate apparel department. It showed the most fundamental lack of understanding of who the customer was in the store, just a total lack of fingertip sensitivity toward the business of retailing and how you present a store to the customer." He also commissioned some research to learn about customer perceptions of Sears. "I remember one of the first focus groups I sat through when I came to the company," he said. "I forget how the question was phrased, but I'll never forget the answer one woman gave. She said, 'What I think about Sears is that it is a bunch of old, gray-haired men in dark suits sitting in a boardroom choosing bad merchandise.' "

After 100 days, Martinez said he knew what he would have to do: "What I truly saw was a great American name that has lost its direction, didn't know who it was, didn't know who its customer was, a very insular organization that I knew, from absolutely day one, needed significant infusions of new talent, not that employees weren't working as hard as they could work, it was just that they didn't know how to work, they didn't know what others were doing and how they were winning. We had to get a more outwardly focused organization that knew who its customer was, knew the basis upon which it had to compete to win." He came up with a battle plan and presented it to the board headed by Brennan. It called for some sweeping changes to cut costs, a new emphasis on women customers, and a huge infusion of capital to improve the merchandising operation, which he had identified as the mother lode of Sears. Martinez's plan was approved by the board in December 1992.

Martinez started slashing costs almost immediately. The 101-year-old catalog was the first thing to go, despite an internal effort to reverse the book's fortunes and make it something Sears could be proud of again. "There was a team of guys, many of them new to the company, who were running the catalog at that point who had worked very hard at creating a turnaround plan for the business [which was losing $1.5

billion a year]," Martinez said, "and it was a plan that I thought had a lot of credibility. It had many of the right elements . . . but it was going to take them three years to implement, it would be cash flow negative for the entire period and there was significant risk in getting it done when they said it would be done. At the end of the day, we had to focus on the most important piece of our business—the stores' business. The judgment was, could we simultaneously manage two turnarounds—the catalog and the stores. The decision I made is that we couldn't. We had to get very focused on getting our stores [straightened out] right away. . . . It [the catalog] was the soul of the company—its roots. It was like telling your grandmother you don't want her around anymore. That is difficult on an emotional level. On a rational level it was easy."

Just as swift was his decision to shutter other Sears properties that were beyond repair—113 unprofitable stores and the Pinstripes Petites chain. He offered a generous early retirement program to approximately 4,000 Sears executives, consolidated regional support services, and implemented several other changes to correct problems he'd detected. "One thing I think is interesting," he said, "is that in that hundred-day period of time, when we were trying to figure out how to restructure, we didn't use consultants," despite corporate America's tendency to use them to deflect responsibility for unpopular decisions. Overall, some 50,000 people lost their full- and part-time jobs, and Martinez took sole responsibility for the layoffs as he whittled away at Sears' cumbersome bureaucracy in the largest retailing restructuring ever. Overall the cuts would save the company $300 million a year and put new managers, including many from the outside, into half the company's stores.

"Everyone knew something dramatic had to be done," he said. "There was a very brief period of mourning for the catalog; a longer period of sorrow for the people involved. But there was no lingering period of affection for the businesses. The sad part is, it [wasn't] the people's fault. They were working as hard and as diligently as they could given the direction they were getting. It wasn't as if they had screwed up, and that's what made the decision harder. They were doing the best they knew how and it came to an unhappy end and that was unhappy for me. One of the emotions that goes through your mind at that point in time is that you don't want to be someone who destroys things, you want to be someone who builds things or fixes things. So there was a strong tug to try to fix it, but in the cold light of day, we just couldn't take it all on."

Just as the shock from his initial steps started to wear off, Martinez mailed his invitations to senior executives for the May 1993 "seminal" meeting in Phoenix. The proposition that they all assemble at The Pointe may have caused anticipation in the ranks, but Martinez viewed the meeting as a crucial challenge: "I think one of the most important aspects of that for the organization and for me was to demonstrate that I was, in fact, going to be the hands-on leader of this company, and I personally facilitated the entire two and a half days of meetings, which was a breakthrough in terms of the way that the organization had perceived the role of the CEO as Sears before, which was too ceremonial, too remote, too uninvolved in the details of the business. What I wanted to demonstrate to the organization is that I was going to be on the ground with them. I wasn't just going to be sitting in the corner office raising issues, criticizing, issuing proclamations. I was going to be on the ground with them involved in the steps we had to take to get this business put back together. . . . The other thing that was important was, I *really* wanted to hear what they had to say about things. Sears had a deserved reputation for waiting for instructions from the top before [employees] set out in a given direction. But there was no way I . . . could have all the answers. Their input and constructive thinking processes were critical to get us moving again."

Consultants, Not Generals, in Arthur's Revolution

Since the Sears board had just voted to dissolve the financial supermarket, Martinez knew the pressure on his executive team would increase. The company's sole business soon would be retailing, and the focus of employees, customers, and investors would intensify as eyes turned to see how well they managed Sears' basic business—selling merchandise to millions of customers.

Martinez's looks can be deceiving. Sears employees almost immediately found him quite approachable, a quality not in vogue among his predecessors. But his stylish wardrobe and calm demeanor obscured an intensely competitive and driven man. By the time he joined Sears, he'd already run the New York City Marathon four times. Employees soon found that his young face and intense blue eyes reinforced his hard questions as well as enhanced his quick smile. He wasted no time making decisions. When he arrived at Sears, the stores seemed organized for the white men who ran the company. The women's departments looked like something out of the TV sitcom *Roseanne*. But Martinez's scrutiny of the customer base showed that the typical Sears shopper was a woman from 35 to 64 years old with an annual household income of $33,000. Within months he increased floor space devoted to women's apparel by 20 percent, mainly by moving Sears furniture to a new chain of shops called Homelife, and added new brand-name clothes to take advantage of the high profit margins they generated. (Clothing had accounted for only 26 percent of the prior year's sales, but had generated 64 percent of its operating profit.) He accelerated a $4 billion store renovation effort and initiated the "Softer Side of Sears" ad campaign designed to attract female shoppers to Sears' more fashionable selections.

The most important thing he did in those early months, though, grew out of the three-day meeting in Phoenix. He reached down into the ranks to devise a corporate strategy that had a clear goal. From that day forward, the company and its executive team would use its talent and resources to make Sears a compelling place to work, a compelling place to shop, and a compelling place to invest, a goal that he called the "3 Cs." Participants in the Phoenix meeting would form teams of Sears executives and employees who would fan out across the country and come up with specific ways to make Sears a better place to work, shop, and invest. He restructured his executive team to make it reflect Sears' customer base: "We had a very diverse customer base, so why should our management team be so homogeneous? We said the woman in the family was our target customer. So I thought it was only right to have more women in our senior management team. Sears for generations was a company run by tall white guys." Martinez soon changed that. He turned to consultants for help after—and only after—he established his initial internal team that would manage a massive turnaround that is still under way.

Martinez's philosophy regarding consultants is just as eclectic as his management style. "Most [consulting firms] will tell you they are full-service consulting organizations," he said, "but they all have a dominant strain, something that has caused them to be successful. . . . I don't place much stock in the journals they publish or the conferences they run. It's having experience with them or knowing someone who has had experience that is most helpful. We have not done a lot of beauty shows, or bake-offs, either, where you bring in four or five firms and ask them to all present on the same subject and pick the winner. I much prefer to go from judgment, references, and experience with the organization that I think can get the job done. . . . The bad thing about consultants is, they think they have all of the answers. The good thing is, sometimes they have some of the answers."

Martinez kept three factors uppermost in his mind when he considered which consultants to hire at Sears. First, the consultant had to have a demonstrated set of skills in the area under scrutiny. "Price Waterhouse Management Horizons has a well-developed practice in retail management information systems consulting," said Martinez. "I know they've been there; I know they've done it; I've seen their work; and I know they can do the job. . . . I turned to [them] to come in and give me an assessment of what our needs were and what we had to do in terms of a planning process. . . . In that case, it was a specific individual that I wanted to work on the question with me because I've worked with him before." Second, he demanded a commitment from the senior-level members of the firm to actively work on the engagement: "I want the people who come to present [their plans] to me to be the people who actually do the work. I don't want the new business pitch from the new business guy and then some other team comes in and takes over." Last, he weighed the all-important "intangible" factor—the fingertip feeling that he felt good about the person who would do the job. Martinez became personally involved in the hiring of all major consultants at Sears because "you are renting a partner for a period of time and . . . you just have to have them pass your judgment test. . . . Do they strike me as being able to behave in a way so that the organization will respond favorably to their skills? It's a pure judgment call about their ability to succeed in our environment." They would become captains—not generals—in Martinez's revolution at Sears.

One of the first consultants he hired involved an engagement designed to help him and some of his new managers out of a dilemma. To make Sears a compelling place to invest, he'd already cut costs. But he couldn't also make Sears a compelling place to work if his cost-cutting drives simply generated consolidations and layoffs similar to the 50,000 jobs that had gone with the catalog. "I was sitting with Russ Davis, my

CFO at the time," he recalled, "and we were talking about where we would take the next big chunks out of this company for cost improvement, productivity improvement and discussing this dilemma we had. We just kept coming back to this same old well, cut benefits, cut people, do this, do that. But you just can't do too much of that; you'll end up with a really dispirited organization. So we looked at where the dollars went out of this building. They go out in payroll checks but they also go out in merchandise checks to people who provide goods and services we use in the operation of this business. And when we added up the dollars going out of this building, that's where the beef was. We said, why don't we take as rigorous an approach to those costs as we did our labor, personnel, and organization costs."

Martinez knew he lacked the internal expertise to determine things like whether suppliers were using the best manufacturing processes. He thought he could use a consultant, but he didn't know whom to hire. "I looked around for examples of some companies going through fairly serious restructuring and one where I happened to know somebody was American Express. John Lennon, the vice chairman, and I were reasonably good acquaintances and [I] called him and asked him how they were doing it and if he knew of anyone useful. I got a good reference on A. T. Kearney . . . which had helped them on some productivity programs involving third parties, not just internal stuff. So I invited Kearney in here to talk to us about it."

A Chicago-based consulting firm founded when Andrew Thomas Kearney split from McKinsey & Co. in 1936, Kearney is known for its operational expertise, basically the roll-up-your-sleeves, results-oriented approach to consulting popularized by William Bain and Bain & Co. A rapidly growing outfit, Kearney, since 1980, had nearly doubled in size three times before it merged in 1995 with Electronic Data Systems, the Plano, Texas–based company once owned by Ross Perot. The merger hadn't occurred, though, when the Kearney team showed up at Sears and impressed Martinez: "They brought a very powerful array of very operationally focused people to the table. What I liked about them is, they had some dirt under their fingernails from being out in the field. . . . I didn't see a lot of twenty-eight-year-old MBAs in the presentation group. I saw some people with gray hair sitting around the table and we decided to charter them to start helping us."

Martinez had already heard through the grapevine about Sears' reputation as a buyer. Most vendors thought that the famed purchasing operation that dated back to the General's day had lost its edge: "There were people in the industry just sort of talking about how Sears still existed in the sixties the way they approached their vendors, you know, 'They think they are buying smart, but they are not buying smart; they are not working partnerships the way the Wal-Marts of the world [had] vendor partnerships.' " Martinez had talked to his executive vice president, Anthony J. Rucci, another outsider whom he had brought in from Baxter International, the big drug company in Deerfield, Illinois, and Rucci agreed that outside help was needed. "The nature of the historic relationship between Sears and its vendors in specific cases had probably gotten to the point where we weren't pushing them and they weren't pushing us," Rucci said. "We had gotten so collegial that, frankly, maybe there wasn't enough tension in the relationship. Many of the Sears suppliers didn't feel compelled to bring us their best ideas first because it was Sears and 'We have done business with these guys for years.' As a result, I think we lost out, because suppliers who had great new ideas didn't think of Sears first. So we brought Kearney in."

From the outset, Sears took a rifle-shot approach: "You don't abdicate responsibility to a consulting firm," Rucci emphasized. "You bring them in for targeted assignments as opposed to an open retainer. . . . You have to control them; they can't control you. . . . What we did [with Kearney] was say, 'Look, we have to redefine the terms of Sears' relationships with its key suppliers, its vendors, and that doesn't mean bang on them to get price concessions. That means let's take the entire pipeline from raw materials to the consumer who walks out the door with it, maybe the warranty on it after they walked out the door, and how can you and me, Mr. Supplier, how can we jointly improve quality, take cost out of the system? We are willing to share the savings in doing that, so what kind of joint process improvements can we make?' "

The Hired Guns from A. T. Kearney

Paul Baffico had been recently hired to run Sears' automotive group, which had been engulfed in a scandal involving charges that it had sold customers unneeded auto repairs. During an executive committee meeting, Baffico volunteered to go first in the vendor review. "He said he'd like to take a look at the battery business to get this started," Martinez recalled. Sears spends millions on batteries, and the relationship with its supplier, he said, "hadn't changed in a long, long time and he was new in his job and was open to change. So we started down the path with Kearney and our automotive team."

Johnson Controls, Inc., a Milwaukee-based company that had developed the DieHard battery for Sears, had been selling it to the Chicago retailer for more than 25 years. The Sears business had helped Johnson Controls post 19 consecutive increases in its annual dividend, which meant about $137 million in sales. The Sears team of purchasers and consultants that showed up in late 1993 differed vastly from the old days, though.

"Kearney . . . has manufacturing and engineering expertise in their firm that allows them to go into a supplier's manufacturing operations and assess how close to best practices they are in the manufacturing process," said Rucci. "The Kearney folks go through a supplier's plant. They look at the state-of-the-art practices, the state-of-the-art robotics, those kind of things. They come back and give us an assessment, to the plant as well as to us. Frankly, Kearney is very tough-minded in these circumstances, because, very often . . . there can be some posturing on the part of one or both of the parties. Kearney just does not back down. They are confident enough of their skills and their assessment that they will not back down. The other thing I like about them is that they are not bashful about coming in and telling us when we are the problem, and that is a very valuable characteristic in a consulting organization."

Kearney's assessment concluded that Sears could save more than 20 percent in the costs of batteries by looking at alternate sources. "The magnitude of the savings shocked everyone; it was really staggering," said Martinez. "We found that there were alternative suppliers in the market who could provide the quality that we wanted in a product with improved features and benefits for less money than we were paying Johnson Controls. A lot of the long-term people around here were surprised, but it was such a demonstrable difference . . . that it was kind of a slam-dunk decision. Johnson Controls was given full opportunity to become competitive; we weren't trying to disadvantage it. We just wanted the best answer for us and our customers. They [Johnson Controls] chose not to believe we were a credible threat and that we would, in fact, take the business away. They had been here for 26 years and they couldn't imagine it. Well, we took the business away.

"The process for making this decision was put in the hands of Sears people. Kearney was there to provide the support, the knowledge, the skill base and, from time to time, the backbone to push a little harder. But it wasn't Kearney negotiating with the battery supplier for Sears. It was our battery-buying team negotiating on behalf of Sears with the support of the Kearney organization and its resources."

Battery sales accounted for only 11 percent of Johnson Control's revenues, but Sears accounted for 25 percent of those sales, and the decision hurt the company. James Keyes, Johnson's CEO, said he met with Sears officials before they announced their decision and he still didn't know any one reason why Johnson lost the contract. The company's employees paid the price for his confusion. After Johnson Controls lost the Sears business, it eliminated 180 salaried jobs in the company's battery division, including 120 executives, engineers, and secretaries at the company's headquarters. Two months later, the company also disclosed plans to shut two of its 13 battery plants in Dallas, Texas, and Owosso, Michigan. From then on, the AC-Delco division of General Motors Corp. and Exide Corp. of Reading, Pennsylvania, supplied Sears with batteries and the retailer benefited in more ways than one.

Kearney would go on to look at dozens of other situations involving vendors. Over the next two and a half years, Kearney would have a team of consultants in Sears, about as long as Monitor had. "In most of these situations, and maybe it was because of what happened with Johnson Controls, we have on very few occasions changed vendors," Martinez said. "What we have been able to do is strengthen the partnership with vendors, get a better answer for Sears shareholders and customers. So it doesn't always result in a loss of business. It's not like what [corporate officials] did at General Motors, where everybody was told to take a 6 to 8 percent cut [regardless of] the consequences. It was intended to be a very focused but deep understanding of each of the categories we went after."

Either the cost savings went to Sears' bottom line, or the proceeds were reinvested in more features or better pricing of the product. Rucci said the vendors often benefited from the process, too: "Over the years, [Kearney] has developed extraordinary benchmark data. They can go to a supplier and they can tell instantaneously whether that supplier is low cost in the industry and whether it has state-of-the-art manufacturing practices and if not, why not. And that would allow us to go to those suppliers and say, 'Gee, if you switched to this kind of process, you could take 500 basis points out of your internal cost of operation and wouldn't it be great if we could split that 500 basis points?' . . . a lot of vendors who initially were skeptical came back to us and said, 'By the way, we are hiring Kearney, too, because these guys helped us think about the best way of doing things. They gave us ideas we didn't know about.' "

Although the success of the cost-cutting campaign put Sears on the road to recovery, Martinez recognized that more was needed. "[Cutting] costs is important, but you can't build a long-term successful business strategy on cost alone. The real enduring success in this business has to do with revenue growth and market share growth." He didn't need outside help with that; his gut instincts as a retailer would do. By modernizing the stores and using floor space better, Martinez soon saw Sears' sales per square foot grow. They climbed from $289 per square foot at the end of 1992 to $346 in 1994 and $365 by late in 1995, a good advance but one that still lags behind Wal-Mart. The company enjoyed its first billion-dollar week in December 1995, and by early in 1996, Martinez, who had been named CEO of the entire company, was a hero—indeed, almost a cult figure—at Sears, except, perhaps, to the employees who were no longer there. Since he had taken over Sears' merchandising in 1992, sales had jumped 13 percent to $35 billion despite some of the most difficult years in retailing history. Earnings almost tripled to $1.25 billion. Same-store sales, a standard industry yardstick for success, rose 6.8 percent, head and shoulders above the competition; operating profit margins nearly quadrupled; while expenses fell from 23 percent of revenues to 21.7 percent. The company's stock? It went from $15 a share to $46.50, not counting the gains that investors enjoyed in the various spin-offs.

Now Comes the Hard Part

Relaxing in the spacious Sears Gulfstream jet roaring across the skies of the Great Plains, Martinez says his job is far from done: "It's trite to say that you'll never be there. But the turnaround aspect of this is about two-thirds complete. . . . The challenge is to ensure that we stay focused; that we are continuing to take market share from our competition. The weaker competitors are falling by the wayside. So those that remain are tougher. So our challenge is to be better and better against the people who are better than the people who went before them. That is challenge number one. Challenge number two is to convince people around here that we don't have all the answers and that we haven't gotten everything fixed. There is a tendency to want to believe all of the nice press clippings . . . and relax and say the job is done; we've won the war and now we can relax. . . . But we also [must] talk about transformation, really transforming the company into a nimble, agile growth retailer."

There is no end to consultants with "cultural transformation" programs. In fact it is one of the latest buzzwords in the consulting business. But once again, Martinez isn't buying—at least not yet. "I know all of the people out there today who are selling consulting services, cultural transformation, reengineering," said Rucci. "With an isolated exception, we [are] not using consultants on that. The reason is . . . cultural transformation is something very personal, another word for culture is the soul of an organization and that is a very personal thing. One of the things I said to Arthur is, 'You know what, we have got to do this ourselves because at the end of the day, the people who have to define what world class is and the changes necessary to get there have got to be our own people.' "

Rucci's "isolated exception" is David Ulrich, a University of Michigan business school professor whom Martinez and Rucci consulted on how to transform the Sears culture. As head of the school's executive education program, Ulrich is a strong advocate of a brand of corporate reorganization that goes far beyond moving people around or changing organization charts. "Most people think of changing an organization as changing how the company is structured—who reports to whom, what three people should we get rid of, or what box goes here on the chart, that kind of thing," Ulrich said. "My idea of change is transformation; you look at the organization and ask, what capabilities do we need to serve the customer better. That is what we did at Sears. Better customer service was the goal, and we looked at the organization and asked, how do we transform it, what capabilities do we need to do that."

At Sears, for example, Ulrich said he met with Rucci and Martinez and they decided that Sears could improve customer service if the company's 300,000-plus employees understood the economics of Sears' business better. "That was a capability. So we constructed learning maps [or graphic devices designed to educate employees on Sears' finances and operations] to improve the economic literacy of Sears sales associates." Another capability Sears tackled was to help employees understand why customers shopped at Wal-Mart or another retailer instead of Sears. Sears hired Ulrich to address such subjects at periodic management meetings or to conduct educational sessions at the company. But Ulrich said the major responsibility for transformation rests with the managers. "I think a lot of what most consultants do is sell consulting," Ulrich said. "My business is helping the managers better manage themselves." Martinez, for instance, reinforces the drive to improve Sears' capability to understand the competition better during his frequent visits to Sears stores. He quizzes sales associates on their knowledge of competitors' stores—asking about things like how competitors display their merchandise and what kind of goods are on sale at the store down the street or mall.

But both Martinez and Rucci say Ulrich's advice on transformation was worth far more than the cost of the engagement. "David . . . is a bit of a maverick," said Rucci. "He is willing to tell CEOs what he thinks. He has consulted with most major corporations in the country. I have been in the room when David has looked at people who are not the nicest guys in the world. . . . He has looked these guys in the eye and said, 'You are kidding yourself. If you believe that, this company is in big trouble.' He has gotten his head handed to him a couple of times . . . but that is the beauty of this guy. He doesn't tell you what you want to hear. We have brought him in selectively. . . . He and I and Arthur went to dinner and we just said, 'David, talk out loud. What are the five things that Arthur as a CEO needs to do to . . . make all of this cultural transformation work?' David wasn't in here with hordes of associates running the meetings and facilitating and designing. . . . We probably paid for—I am guessing—maximum ten billing days over the last two years, but boy, did we get our money's worth. This guy is the clearest thinker on organizational management practices today."

Martinez agreed. He described Ulrich as an advisor rather than as a consultant. "We didn't need a consulting organization to provide some sort of a blanket solution," Martinez said. "We needed someone who has seen lots of practical applications and who has seen some of the academic work on motivation. With a consultant, I am asking him to propose a solution. With an advisor, I am testing solutions that we are inventing."

Sears has made other sweeping changes since Martinez arrived. Store managers now spend 80 percent of their time on the sales floor and 20 percent in the back office instead of vice versa as it was in the old days. Nearly half of his executive team is new—outsiders like Rucci. Martinez junked the old Sears manual of rules and procedures, which was 29,000 pages long. He's replaced it with a slim folder containing a one-page letter from him, a one-page list of shared beliefs, a 16-page segment that outlines leadership principles, and a 17-page code of conduct. It uses outside consultants like McKinsey on some projects, and relies on its own staff in other instances. In all cases, though, the consultant is part of a process that is run and managed by Sears employees. "When we have updates," Martinez said, "they are not one-on-one updates where [consultants] function as snitches. There's always a cross-functional team that will be responsible for the project. . . . It isn't anyone coming to me and saying, 'Joe is doing a lousy job down here and you ought to do something about it.' The broader-gauge involvement of the senior team avoids that."

Sears still has problems. It still has unhappy customers, and Martinez and his eclectic management team still make eclectic mistakes. Recently, for example, a federal judge in Boston slammed Sears for hounding bankrupt customers for debts owed to the retailer. The legal problems also focused attention on the growing share of Sears profits that flows from its credit card operations rather than merchandise, a factor that could make the company more vulnerable in an economic downturn. Martinez said the company's policy regarding bankrupt customers was wrong, and it will probably cost Sears upwards of $100 million to buy its way out of the problem. It has other challenges aplenty, too. "One challenge is, how do we find sources of growth that support our financial objectives," Martinez says, "because just running stores better isn't going to get the kind of growth in earnings that we are actively seeking. This whole notion of focus is so critical to me . . . what Sears is and what Sears stands for. Retailers have a personality, and if you deviate from it, your customers get a little jittery. . . . So we have to be consistent with our image. We want to take Sears to more customers. . . . This whole home services thing is big for us. Think of the range of things that happen inside your home that are provided by service providers . . . everything from home improvement projects to appliance repair, installation and delivery of merchandise, maintenance around the home, home security. When you look at our name, and what we stand for, when you look at the whole area of integrity and trust that the customer grants us, who better could be the premier provider of services for the American home than Sears? Today we have a $3 billion business in that area. It is a $180 billion industry. At $3 billion we are the leaders. We just see a tremendous opportunity to grow a large business there and fairly quickly."

But the company also has something going for it now that no consulting firm can supply, regardless of its reputation or skills. It has a CEO who reaches down into the organization to involve employees, who listens, who shows up at Saturday-morning store openings, who quizzes department managers on their needs and then takes notes, and who really does give customers directions to the bathroom.

5

"A Medicine Man in a Room Full of Funeral Directors"

HOW BOSTON CONSULTING GROUP PACKAGES AND PEDDLES IDEAS

Arthur C. Martinez's limited use of consultants reflects one new strategy inside a company. Boston Consulting Group personifies the growing influence of consultants in the living room. The most innovative of the major consulting firms, BCG is a case study in how consultants package and peddle ideas involving health care reform and other issues that affect a broad range of Americans.

Kim Wellman remembers the first moment she suspected her daughter, Jody, had chronic asthma. The hacking, wheezing gasps of a three-year-old child struggling to breathe startled her from sleep just as the sun crept above the horizon, bathing the black earth of the corn and bean fields surrounding her home with the first light of dawn. Over the next few years, the guttural cough of asthma would become as familiar in Kim Wellman's home as the brown lamps in her living room: "It would always start early in the morning and she wouldn't stop for about the next two days. I kept taking her to the emergency room. I'd tell the doctor, 'I think this kid has asthma.' But he'd say, 'That's not what's wrong with her.'"

In the early 1990s, though, the Wellmans unwittingly got a break when a wave of politically inspired health care reform swept the nation. Gregg Wellman's employer, Deere & Co., the Moline, Illinois, farm implement maker, offered employees several options for health insurance, including the John Deere Health Care HMO, a wholly owned Deere subsidiary and one of the best health maintenance organizations in the nation. A machinist who makes bolts on a Deere production line, Wellman joined the John Deere HMO, and the choice proved a godsend for Jody.

"I had taken her to regular doctors and my mother-in-law's allergy specialist and didn't get many answers," Kim Wellman recalled. After they joined the Deere HMO, she heard about asthma information classes for members. "I took Jody with me and we went to the class. While we were there Jody started coughing and the doctor teaching the class said, 'That kid's having an asthma attack. She needs to be on a nebulizer [a device that helps the user receive a medicated spray that alleviates the symptoms of asthma].' He put her on it and she's been using it and [the drugs he prescribed] for the last two years and she's a lot better."

Just a decade ago, the Wellman family probably would not have received the care that has made their little girl's prospects so much better. Jody, who is now nine, probably would have been consigned to a life of inhalers, emergency room traumas, frustration, expense, and fights with insurance companies. But that was before organizations such as the John Deere HMO tried "disease management," a pioneering approach to health care that borrows the principles of total quality management from the business world to devise cost-effective strategies to combat diseases like asthma.

In coming years, patients of all types are likely to hear more about disease management, for it is one of the hottest topics in health care today. What makes disease management even more unique, though, is that it is not an idea that emanated from the nation's medical schools, research labs, or other traditional fonts of original thinking in medicine. Disease management is an idea that was developed and sold by a management consulting firm, the Boston Consulting Group, one of the most influential and innovative consulting firms in the world.

On one level, the story of how the Boston Consulting Group created and pushed the idea of disease management is the story of BCG and what makes it so unique to the consulting industry. Management consultants like to portray themselves as anonymous aides-de-camp devising winning strategies for the generals of free enterprise in the war of the bottom line. Actually, they're smart salesmen who peddle ideas.

They wrap their products in elegant brochures, erudite book jackets, or the colorless pages of the *Harvard Business Review*. But strip away the pontificating prose and ubiquitous graphics and a simple formula for the successful consultant remains: Devise an idea, repackage it, give it a catchy name, and then sell the same thing in a new wrapper to another client. Few would like to admit it, but that is what the consulting business is all about, and few are better at devising and selling innovative ideas than the Boston Consulting Group. How the firm sold and spread the idea of disease management is a primer on how innovation can lead to good management consulting and good results.

On another level, though, the story of BCG's role in disease management also is a dramatic example of the growing influence of consultants on the jobs and lives of ordinary people around the world. The John Deere Health Care HMO is no anomaly. Management consultants often work in shadows, cloaking their missions and client lists in secrecy. But their influence is spreading rapidly and widely as they grapple with social problems that emanate in the workplace. The industry's revenues are one yardstick; they are now estimated at $50 billion worldwide. But more important is the range of clients now using consultants. Corporations still use consultants for traditional jobs, such as advising them on plant conversions and that sort of thing. Dig behind the headlines announcing any corporate downsizing or restructuring and chances are you will find a management consultant telling the boss who should stay and who should go. But consultants also are moving into equally controversial areas where they have a much wider impact on the average American. BCG's globe-trotting consultants helped NYNEX, the New York telephone company, devise a plan to eliminate more than 16,000 jobs in an effort to improve phone service in New England. BCG advised the Times Mirror Company when it shut down the New York edition of *Newsday*. When the Corporation for Public Broadcasting wanted an outsider to study its sources and use of revenue, it hired BCG, which recommended that public television stations across the country ax their local programs and devote their limited resources to national shows. When Russia decided it needed to reorganize its international oil industry, it hired BCG.

Nowhere is the potential for rising influence greater than in the field of health care, though. BCG and other consultants are becoming a major force in health care, helping to bring order—and sometimes chaos—to a fragmented industry that constitutes about 15 percent of the nation's economy. If the innovative reforms pushed by BCG were replicated beyond the firm's list of clients, the entire health care system probably would benefit. But to really understand BCG's role in helping the Jody Wellmans of the world, one has to go back to the 1960s and Bruce Henderson, BCG's legendary founder, for the story of disease management really is a tale about innovative consultants who brought a breath of fresh air to an insular industry. And Henderson is the one who breathed the fresh air into BCG.

"He Had Enough Huckster in Him"

The son of a Tennessee Bible publisher and an engineer educated at Vanderbilt University, Bruce Henderson launched his career from the purchasing department of Westinghouse. He'd joined the company after a stint at the Harvard Business School and shortly became Westinghouse's youngest vice president in five decades at age 37. But Henderson was far more interested in how corporations made decisions than in climbing a bureaucratic ladder. So he left corporate management in 1959 and took his first job as a consultant, joining the Boston-based staff of Arthur D. Little & Co. At Arthur Little, Henderson advised corporate giants such as Shell Oil and United Fruit Co. But he soon found out that his zeal for the cutting-edge ideas was a little too racy for ADL. He'd done some consulting for the Boston Safe Deposit and Trust Co., Henderson told an interviewer a few years ago, and when the bankers learned of his frustrations, "they said, 'Look, if they don't want you working for them, come on up here and set up a consulting department for us.' Well, with four kids . . . it looked pretty good to me. We worked out an arrangement where I could pay my taxes and keep the kids fed. So I started out in a department of a bank. Can you think of any less likely place as a seedbed for a consulting company than the trust department of a bank?"

Henderson had a big problem from the day that he started his one-man department: He had few clients. Years later people like James Kennedy, the editor and publisher of *Consultants News*, would praise Henderson, who died in 1992, as a genius in the industry. "I'd classify him as an innovative giant in the management consulting world," said

Kennedy, who never hesitates to skewer his subjects. "He spawned a whole genre of focused consulting firms. He gave new meaning to the term 'strategy.'" But Kennedy also suggested how Henderson overcame his problem. "He had enough huckster in him to sell [his ideas] to some of the most prestigious business giants." Henderson's initial strategy was so simple it seems audacious today. "If you don't have any history, how do you get clients?" he asked an interviewer. "I got this idea of [condensing] articles sort of like the *Reader's Digest.* I'd take an article [from a business or other publication] that was interesting and condense it down. I accumulated them. We designed a mailing list." Henderson called the articles he sent to his growing list of clients a "Perspective."

Over the next three decades, Henderson would use his Perspectives to establish a close relationship with his clients and potential clients. They were short, personal essays on the hot business topics of the day that would arrive in the mail ten times a year. The exclusive nature of his mailing list made a Perspective seem like a short, thoughtful personal letter written exclusively for a client. In a classic demonstration of his chutzpah as a salesman, Henderson even addressed some Perspectives as open letters to people like President Richard Nixon or President Jimmy Carter. They may have missed his messages, but corporate America didn't. BCG's mailing list would reach the top brass of America's biggest and most important corporations. Eventually, Henderson and his growing team of consultants would become advisors to much of the Fortune 500. What attracted these corporate titans to this fledgling firm in Boston? A unique brand of strategic thinking that revolutionized the American business world.

On the surface, Bruce Henderson didn't look like some latter-day Patrick Henry of the consulting business. It would be easy to mistake him for a small-town banker or someone's grandfather. He was tall and lanky, wore wire-rimmed glasses, hardly ever raised his voice, and spoke with a self-deprecating southern drawl and a mischievous twinkle in his eye. But his looks were deceiving. In his world, Henderson was a revolutionary, a pinstriped bomb thrower in a world full of CPAs and starched shirts. He combined his skills as an original thinker with his ability to sell something ephemeral. "He reveled in the role of the revolutionary," said Kennedy of *Consultants News.* "He was like a medicine man in a room full of funeral directors. Here were all these consultants in their three-piece pin-striped suits and here was Bruce with his smile, his flash, his bottle, and his snake oil."

When Henderson founded BCG, corporate brass hired consultants to study operational problems, specific issues that affected their operations, such as overdue invoices, or whether a company or group of companies was properly organized. Consultants would descend on a business, study the problem, submit a pricey report, and be on their way. Corporate strategy, or making decisions about a company's long-term future, was a seat-of-the-pants sort of thing. Senior executives and board members would sit around corporate offices and brainstorm. Gut instincts drove bet-the-store decisions such as launching a new product, acquiring a competitor, or shutting down a factory. A vacuum of strategic theory and quantifiable numbers made rigorous analytical approaches impossible. Companies depended on a growing economy to improve their fortunes, a rising-tide-will-lift-all-boats philosophy. They hired consultants to make sure the companies were properly organized to ride the rising tide.

Henderson changed all that. He didn't think companies could rely on economic growth and gut instincts alone to increase profits and keep their assembly lines humming. He felt corporations needed a long-term strategy to sustain that growth, particularly as growth started to taper off, as it did in the late 1950s. That's where the consultant came in. "Bruce's real insight was, he looked at all the other consulting firms and said that everybody was inwardly focused," said Sandra Moose, a BCG vice president whom Henderson hired as an economics Ph.D. fresh out of Harvard. "They all were focused on how clients could do things better. McKinsey, how can we organize better; Booz Allen, how do we operate more efficiently or how do we compensate better; Arthur Little, how do we forecast better, how do we lay out our plant better. Bruce said, that's all inwardly focused, all management techniques that anybody can quickly copy. Growth had started to slow and you were starting to get imports in the U.S. for the first time. The people in the [U.S.] steel industry were crying about imports, and Bruce said, you can't be inwardly focused. You've got to do something unique and you've got to pay attention to your competitors. So his was an external perspective. And it focused on [developing a strategy], looking at the company as a whole instead of [as] individual business units. And he defined success as having a relative economic competitive advantage that was sustainable."

Henderson's Hotbed

Under Henderson's logic, developing such a strategy required analysis of the company, its competitors, and the economic structure of the firm's industry. He reinforced his strategic theory with tools that led to groundbreaking insights about the nature of profitability and competition in the business world. Ever since he'd headed Westinghouse's purchasing operations, Henderson had wondered why competitors with virtually identical manufacturing plants would submit wildly different bids when trying to win the company's contracts. At the time, conventional economic theory said that wouldn't happen. Producers with similar plants were supposed to have similar unit costs and offer products at roughly the same prices. Henderson didn't know why economic theory was wrong, but he had asked a crucial question. The answer, which came in a study he did for a client, was simple yet profound: A manufacturer and its workers became more productive as they gained experience. BCG started applying similar thinking to clients like Texas Instruments, an electronics firm that hired BCG in the late 1960s to study its production costs. The consultants plotted costs against production experience and soon learned that Texas Instruments' costs fell predictably as its semiconductor division gained production experience. Indeed, every time Texas Instruments doubled its production experience with a particular part, its costs fell, on average, about 20 percent. BCG didn't exactly invent the phenomenon, which became known the "experience curve," but Henderson played a key role in marketing it to American business.

Knowledge like that might seem "old hat" to today's savvy managers, but it was a revolutionary insight at the time. If Texas Instruments or any other business could predict its production costs with such precision, it could take risks that would scare the pants off its competitors. The company soon slashed the prices of its products to stimulate demand. As customers snapped up Texas Instruments' products, managers accelerated the pace of its production lines, and costs fell, giving the company economies of scale that made further price cuts and higher profits possible. Armed with this competitive tool, Texas Instruments ignited fierce competitive wars in the handheld calculator and digital watch markets, which were soon characterized by rapidly declining prices at sales counters. Overreliance on this insight eventually hurt Texas Instruments, but the idea of the experience curve caught on elsewhere. Michael Rothschild, author of *Bionomics: Economy as Ecosystem* and a former BCG consultant, explained how the curve could be used in a strategy:

> Once the experience curve was understood, the importance of being the first one to enter a new market became clear. Properly executed, the preemptive strike could mean long-term market leadership and long-term profits. Similarly, the experience curve explained why defending market share mattered. Raising prices to boost short-term profits sold off market share, slowed experience growth, and often handed over low-cost leadership to an aggressive competitor. It's a scenario that has been played out hundreds of times as "experience conscious" Japanese competitors have overtaken their profit-conscious rivals. Armed with the experience curve, Bruce Henderson was the first one to explain—and warn against—this suicidal corporate strategy (selling off market share to shore up short-term profits). Without him, many more American firms would have been overwhelmed. Simply put, Bruce Henderson's experience curve explained how an industry's past shapes its future. Where conventional economics had banished history by blithely assuming that technology holds constant, Henderson used the experience curve to show how new insights generated by practical experience were translated into higher productivity and lower costs. Where conventional economics taught the law of diminishing returns, Bruce Henderson taught the law of increasing returns.

The experience curve was just the start of things to come. Before the company's path would lead to disease management and Jody Wellman's door in Moline, Illinois, BCG would convert dozens of other theories into tools and hard realities that Henderson could use to extract money from clients. In fact, under Henderson's leadership, BCG would become a hotbed of radical thinking in the world of business and finance. As his client list grew, Henderson invaded the nation's best business schools, the Harvards and Stanfords of the world. He eclipsed McKinsey as the top recruiter at Harvard, aggressively wooing its best students with high salaries and the chance to make a difference in a cutting-edge firm. He encouraged the brilliant young minds he hired to come up with innovative ideas that would dazzle hardened corporate veterans. Sometime he seemed dazzled himself by the success of the whole business. "Consulting is the most improbable business on earth," he would say. "Can you think of anything less improbable than taking the world's most successful firms, leaders in their businesses, and hiring people just fresh out of school and telling them how to run their businesses and they are willing to pay millions of dollars for this advice?"

Henderson had egalitarian instincts. He revered young people as visionaries willing to roll the dice and bet on change. Ira Magaziner walked into Henderson's offices in dungarees during the early 1970s. A disheveled Brown University graduate, Magaziner had made national news in a speech to Brown's 1969 graduating class by exhorting graduates to protest the Vietnam War by turning their backs on Secretary of State Henry Kissinger, who was there to get an honorary degree. Most did. Magaziner told Henderson that he didn't care about money; he just wanted to learn how the business system worked to do good in the public sector. Henderson took him at his word. He hired Magaziner for less than half the going rate for MBAs. His instincts were right, though. Magaziner cut an odd figure at BCG with his rumpled clothes and decidedly absent mind. He once showed up at a client's offices without shoelaces. But he proved himself with his capacity for long hours and his analytic mind. Assigned early on to a client that owned an expansion-minded steel company, Magaziner traveled the world measuring new steelmaking capacity. He calculated how quickly it would come online and shattered widely held industry assumptions by predicting a glut in capacity. He was right. The steelmaker dropped its plans, saving its parent millions.

Magaziner's fate at BCG would prove prophetic for the young consultant, who went on to design the Clinton administration's abortive effort at health care reform. In Magaziner's tenure, BCG specialized in corporate strategy and, like most consulting firms, preferred to work in obscurity. When the government of Sweden commissioned BCG to study its economy in the late 1970s, though, Magaziner convinced Henderson to give him a shot at the engagement. His answer to Sweden's economic problems? A sweeping industrial policy that ignited a national debate. BCG pooh-bahs cringed when Magaziner appeared on Swedish TV and in newsmagazines spelling out the policy, which called for an active government hand in the nation's economy. "We had to run around Europe for six months reassuring clients that we hadn't gone Communist," said one insider. "Half the partners wanted to execute Ira on the spot." Expenses for the project soared as Magaziner went all out. BCG even feared the engagement would erode that year's profit until the Swedes agreed to pay double the original $300,000 fee.

Some of the strategic tools and theories hatched by BCG's growing cadre of bright young consultants were flashes in the pan. Sweden tried a few of Magaziner's proposals with mixed results. But others would have a widespread and lasting impact. Indeed, BCG's most famous tool, the product portfolio matrix, would put Henderson and BCG on the map, would give the world terms like "cash cow," and would set the stage for the firm's foray into health care.

Cash Cows and Stars

Before the 1960s, the business world had never heard of anything like a portfolio matrix. McKinsey & Co. dominated the consulting world with its breakthrough theories about how corporations should be organized. A wave of conglomeration had swept through the American economy, and BCG had many clients that wanted to become conglomerates— huge holding companies that owned a wide range of unrelated businesses. The idea was to acquire many different companies and organize them into profit centers to be managed from headquarters as individual ventures. Management would set performance goals for each business and allocate capital according to the profits they generated. Earnings per share dominated the thinking on Wall Street. "We had a lot of clients in those days looking at how to become conglomerates," said Moose.

But Henderson found fault with the management of these huge organizations and challenged the conventional wisdom, searing into BCG's culture an iconoclastic philosophy that would last for decades. "In large scale, diversified multi-product companies," Henderson wrote, "it was impractical for central management to be familiar in depth with each business, each product, each competitive segment and each unit's implied strategy." Under Henderson's thinking, managers who let each business fend for itself allowed short-term thinking and a fixation on earnings per share to dominate their decisions. In fact, a high-growth company with potential couldn't get the capital it needed to sustain growth in such an environment. Corporate managers simply couldn't justify giving them any spare cash based upon the earnings they generated. Conversely, a slow-growth property with more cash than it needed would consume the excess capital simply because managers could justify the investment. "There was little real management judgment possible at the corporate level," Henderson said.

Instead of viewing their properties as profit centers, BCG advised conglomerates and would-be conglomerates to consider their business units as a portfolio of companies, each with a different potential to generate cash and each with different strategic objectives. Success, Henderson said, should not be measured by the then-popular earnings per share but by market share, or the percentage of the total sales in a given market that a particular company garnered. Managers could take cash from mature businesses with strong competitive positions and give it to rapidly growing subsidiaries that needed the cash to gain market share from competitors. Under BCG's portfolio theory, the ideal conglomerate would contain a mix—some stable properties, some high-growth, high-risk properties, and some that should be disposed of when opportunity knocked. BCG's rule of thumb said that a company with twice the market share of its largest competitor should have lower costs and therefore higher profits. "We needed to show them that it was cash that counted, not earnings per share," said Moose.

To visualize the idea, BCG created a matrix or a chart that looked like four squares on a checkerboard. By plotting their businesses on the chart according to their ability to generate cash and gain market share, conglomerate managers could more easily make decisions about where to invest their capital. Businesses that fell into the lower-left square or quadrant of the chart were "cash cows"—slow-growth outfits that nevertheless generated a lot of cash because they dominated their markets. Companies that fell into the lower-right quadrant were "dogs"—low-growth firms that were corporate basket cases. Those in the upper-right quadrant were "question marks," or firms in fast-growing markets that had not yet achieved a competitive advantage. They needed capital to enhance their ability to move into the upper-left quadrant, the home of "stars," or high-growth companies and competitive leaders that generated most if not all of the cash they needed. The trick was to have a portfolio rich with cash cows, question marks, and stars. Managers could then milk their cash cows and use the excess capital to feed their question marks and convert them into stars. The infusion of cash would keep the stars shining until they saturated their markets and became cash cows. If a cash cow dried up and became a dog, it would be sold off or otherwise discarded.

The idea got rave reviews in the business world. Soon phrases like "cash cow" and "dog" would become as familiar in the business lexicon as "bottom line" or "red ink."

With its catchy labels and visual simplicity, the matrix gave corporate headquarters a tool that any dumb cluck could understand. "CEOs loved it," said Moose. "For a CEO of a conglomerate that had hundreds of businesses, this gave him a way to get a picture of everything on one slide. . . . CEOs and CFOs also are always looking for a way to say 'no' to those out in the divisions. . . . This gave the CEO a rationale to say 'no,' and it didn't take a lot of explanation." If a manager of a cash cow wanted a new plant or an expensive piece of machinery, the CEO could justify rejecting the request, particularly if he ran a cash cow with cash that was needed elsewhere. "It became a nonemotive way to have a productive confrontation between corporate, the CEO and the CFO who controlled the purse strings, and the business unit managers who wanted to spend the money," said Moose. ". . . The CFO could say, I don't believe your plan because you are not going to have the kind of growth and profit [you project] because you don't have a competitive advantage. . . . It became a very objective framework for the allocation of resources that could be explained and everybody could understand." The concept also had an enormous impact on BCG. "That was the thing that put them on the map," said Kennedy of *Consultants News.* "That and Bruce's decision to expand their offices from the one office in Boston is what accounted for their rapid growth."

Henderson characterized the matrix as the single chart sufficient to tell a company's profitability five years out. "The payoff for leadership [in market share] is very high indeed, if it is achieved early and maintained until growth slows," Henderson wrote to clients in a Perspective. "Investment in market share during the growth phase can be very attractive, if you have the cash. Growth in market is compounded by growth in share. Increases in share increases the [profit] margin. High margins permit higher leverage with equal safety. The resulting profitability permits higher payment of earnings after financing normal growth. The return on investment is enormous." In other words, an increased share of the market boosts profits sharply and allows a company to take on debt more aggressively, which is exactly what many firms started to do in the 1970s and even into the 1980s.

Knowledge of the matrix spread rapidly. CEOs invited to BCG's conferences spread the word. Henderson's Perspective on the matrix helped. Articles on the portfolio matrix, including some written by BCG consultants, appeared in august journals such as the *Harvard Business Review* or popular magazines such as *Fortune*. The BCG matrix soon became standard fare in business textbooks, too. By the 1980s it would become the most widely used portfolio method in U.S. firms.

Was the Matrix a Dog?

Despite its notoriety, the matrix, like a lot of ideas hatched by management consultants, didn't receive much scrutiny from skeptics during its heyday. Evidence later surfaced that Henderson's matrix wasn't all that it was cracked up to be. Two university professors investigated the use of the index and, in 1992, nearly two decades after Henderson invented it, suggested the BCG matrix had some real problems. "Despite the continuing use of portfolio methods," said J. Scott Armstrong, a professor at the University of Pennsylvania's Wharton School, and Roderick Brodie, a New Zealand professor, "we have been unable to find any empirical evidence to support their use. We were able to find only one empirical study on the value of the BCG matrix. This was a field study [in 1987]. It found that firms using the BCG matrix methods reported a *lower* return on capital than those not using them."

The problem seemed to be more with the application of the matrix than with the chart itself. Over a five-year period, Armstrong and Brodie created a hypothetical investment decision for 1,015 students in management programs at universities in New Zealand, America, Malaysia, Argentina, Canada, and West Germany. Some of the students were undergraduates, but nearly half were MBAs with at least two years' business experience. The professors asked the students to select one of two different investment opportunities—one firm that was obviously profitable and one that was not. Only they labeled the profitable firm a "dog" and the unprofitable choice a "star." "The description contained sufficient information so that the profit maximizing decision [was] obvious," they wrote. "The issue was would the subjects apply the BCG matrix blindly." The answer? Many did.

In fact, depending on whether they were in a control group or not, between 45 and 87 percent of the students selected the unprofitable choice that had been labeled a star. "Our study provides empirical evidence that the BCG matrix interferes with profit maximizing. Results were obtained in a test of extremes: a choice between an investment that allowed the company to double its investment, and one where half the investment was lost. Despite being faced with what we thought to be an obvious decision, subjects who were provided with information about the BCG matrix were easily misled." Only 13 percent of those who used the BCG matrix in their analysis invested in the more profitable project.

Nevertheless, the professors found the matrix had been widely adopted by many firms around the world with little discussion that it might produce poorer results. It probably helped that CEOs could use the matrix to justify steps they wanted to take anyway. But the matrix received an equal lack of scrutiny in the boot camps for budding executives—the world's business schools. Armstrong and Brodie unearthed one 1991 survey of 34 business schools in the United Kingdom: "The BCG matrix is taught at all schools and warnings are seldom discussed." Armstrong and Brodie concluded that the matrix, with its catchy labels, was more powerful as a communication tool: "Because labels are intuitively appealing and easy to use, they may lead decision makers to overlook profit maximization. . . . We speculate that decision makers use the BCG matrix because it legitimizes an intuition that many people have about business decisions. Simply stated, people believe that you should 'stick with your winners.' "

One executive who has used the matrix suggests that the two professors are only half right. "I found it [the BCG matrix] to be useful," said Stuart Early, an Amoco human relations executive who used the BCG matrix when he worked as a corporate planner at Westinghouse and FMC Corp. in the late 1970s and early 1980s. "It was helpful in forcing you to define your market. It put the burden on you. If you were classified as a dog, the more sophisticated users would go back and re-examine the market to look for other opportunities." But Early also said one can't rely too heavily on the matrix; gut instincts and judgment are equally important to good decisions. "It [the matrix] wasn't something that could replace judgment," he said. "If you came up with something that didn't seem to jibe with the realities of the marketplace, then you would go back and look again to determine why. You couldn't rely on it [the matrix alone]. You had to have a mixture of it [the matrix] and your own judgment. Trying to apply it without using your own judgment was like trying to drive a nail with a screwdriver."

Even today, business school professors and executives argue about the utility of BCG's matrix, but there is no dispute about Bruce Henderson's influence on the advice business. He started a new branch of consulting that made strategic thinking as much a part of corporate America as a boardroom. Over the next two decades, consultants emulating Henderson's approach would give American business ideas that would create thousands of new jobs, new products, new factories, new industries, and new wealth. But strategy consultants would become the Darth Vadars of downsizing, too. They would advocate ideas that left millions of Americans jobless. Their intellectual products would make shuttered factories a part of the American landscape, and they would create havoc in struggling communities across the land. Seeing BCG's success, new strategy consulting firms soon surfaced. Many key firms, such as Bain and Co., had their roots at BCG.

BCG's First Step into Disease Management: Diabetes

David Matheson was one of those bright young men BCG recruited from Harvard. A lawyer by training but a visionary by inclination, his career at BCG would show how Henderson's troops took his initial ideas and ran with them, expanding BCG's access and injecting its consultants into policies that would reach from global corporate boardrooms to the families of farm implement workers in rural Illinois. From the day he walked into the corridors at BCG, Matheson could see the firm he had joined was different from its competitors. Even today, BCG's more open and accepting atmosphere reflects partners and consultants who tend to be more creative and innovative than McKinsey, which has a reputation for arrogance, or Bain, which is viewed as a more secretive, insular place. Matheson said he selected BCG because he liked the people.

"The mean at BCG is really, really higher," said Robert Frisch, a vice president at Gemini Consulting, who used to work at BCG. "You are talking about guys who are way, way off the chart in a particular kind of intelligence. I was pretty close to the top of the class in terms of the 'keeping clients happy' quotient. But that is only one way of keeping score at BCG. There is also a whole separate thing. Are you doing work that makes people's heads spin because it is just analytically gorgeous? There, on a personal basis, I was clearly below the mean; I was an exceller, but again, the mean there is unbelievable. Their people are unbelievably smart—really, really smart. . . . I call it pure mental horsepower."

Matheson fit right in. A native of Scotland and the son of a Presbyterian minister, he had impeccable academic credentials—an M.A. with first-class honors from Saint Andrews Presbyterian College, where he majored in logic and metaphysics; a law degree from Harvard Law, where he also served as an editor of the *Harvard Law Review;* and an MBA from the Harvard Business School, where he graduated with distinction. He also knew a good deal when he saw one. By and large, consultants are people who got straight A's in school and want someone to pay for it once they graduate. Henderson had set up a company designed to do just that. By the time Matheson signed on, BCG already was a money machine. In less than two decades, it had grown from a one-man operation in the Boston Safe Deposit & Trust Co. to a firm with seven offices on three continents, more than $35 million in revenue, and over 200 professional consultants. In 1975, just two years after William Bain defected to set up his own firm, Henderson helped acquire the Boston bank's stock in BCG and created one of the nation's first Employee Stock Ownership Plans (ESOP), making the employees owners of the firm. By any measure, consulting is an incredibly profitable business. Unlike companies that actually make things, firms like BCG have little or no raw material costs, no inventory to finance or huge, expensive plants to maintain. They have rent to pay, travel expenses, and that sort of thing. But most of the money paid to BCG flows right through to stockholders and employees. And thanks to the ESOP, most of BCG's employees are stockholders. Indeed, by the time

Matheson survived his apprenticeship and joined the firm's permanent staff, BCG was taking in nearly $49 million in annual revenue. Of that, $37 million flowed through the company's income statement to employees in the form of salaries and wages, profit sharing, and deferred compensation. A starting consultant like Matheson could become a manager within 2 years, assuming he or she did well, and a vice president within 5 to 10 years. Annual salaries and bonuses for a BCG consultant with 5 to 10 years' experience in the early 1980s could easily exceed $250,000.

At first, Matheson drew the usual assignments that firms use to test a novice consultant's mettle—strategy assignments at a paper company, a clinical lab, and a plastics firm. Before long, though, he would plunge into the world of health care consulting on a BCG engagement for a Dutch pharmaceutical giant with questions about a struggling product line. He would emerge from the experience with a deeper knowledge of diabetes and a model for disease management that would be widely replicated in clinics, American drug companies, and HMOs like the one at John Deere.

Boehringer Mannheim Group had been founded in 1859 as a classical pharmaceutical company. During its first 100 years, the company focused on Europe, selling drugs in Germany and other European nations. By the 1980s, though, the company had started using its skills to detect glucose, cholesterol, and enzymes released into the blood by a damaged liver. Diabetics were an ideal market for the company's thrust. At the time, diabetes patients, particularly those with severe strains of the disease, had miserable lives. They spent much of their time in hospitals, a lab, or in a doctor's office getting glucose tests and insulin to manage their disease, racking up huge costs for which they would seek reimbursement from insurers. "Our idea was, why don't we move the lab to the patient," said Jerry Moller, the president and CEO. "Really diseased patients had to tend to themselves ten times a day to measure their blood sugar. [We decided] to build a small product that would enable patients to do these kinds of tests themselves at home or wherever they were—at work, in the hotel, on vacation, in the restaurant." Boehringer Mannheim called the test strip it developed "dry chemistry." Simultaneously, insulin companies developed insulin that could be applied by patients. It was a marriage made in marketing heaven. Diabetes patients could prick their finger with a small pin and put a drop of blood on a test strip. The strip, which cost about 40 cents, could then be inserted into a small meter that would tell them their glucose level and how much insulin they needed. The meter cost about $200 to $300 at the time, although the cost now has slipped below $100. "We also had to prove that the capillary blood was as good as the blood that the labs took from the vein," said Moller. Obstacles soon surfaced, though.

"Typically these kind of things are good in theory but you have to overcome the established system," said Moller. "In those days the doctors would not just do the job, they would also make money on it. And the hospitals would also make money by having the patients come to their labs as outpatients. And despite all of the ethical orientation of the medical societies, money was an issue. So we worked with this idea in several European countries, especially Sweden. You know the Scandinavians are quite innovative when it comes to new kinds of health care services. Their professionals are less financially motivated; they don't make so much money because of socialized medicine. The same applies to the U.K. So there were several doctors who felt this was an absolutely outstanding idea and that they should support it, and they did. It started to develop slowly in the U.K. and in Scandinavia and to a certain extent in Germany. And the question then became how to develop this in the largest market in the world—the United States." That is where BCG and David Matheson came in.

Moller said BCG's reputation for innovative strategic thought and its international experience drew Boehringer Mannheim to the consultant's doors. Boehringer Mannheim faced a complex situation. It needed help on at least two fronts. Even if the company had the greatest product in the world, it wouldn't do much good if patients couldn't get reimbursed for their outlays by American insurance companies operating under government health insurance guidelines. That had to change. But the second problem was even more sensitive.

"In the U.S., we [Boehringer Mannheim] were a classical laboratory diagnostic company," Moller said. "So we had customers also in the U.S. labs where they did the analysis work." By introducing a home test, Boehringer Mannheim would start competing with its existing customers in its lab business, which, at the time, was Boehringer Mannheim's bread and butter in America. Making matters worse, prevailing market conditions had drained the company of spare cash.

"There was no excess money to do this pioneering work. No market existed. We would have to hire [about 100] sales reps that would go after this new business. That was the question we put to BCG and Dave Matheson: Should we go after this new business or should we sell this to another company?" Matheson managed the BCG team that showed up in Boehringer Mannheim's offices and soon saw that "the client really was disposed to sell the business."

But the BCG consultant and his team took a hard look at the situation. "We spent a lot of time talking to people in the diabetes field and how the product could help them," he said. As Matheson and his team would discover, diabetes is a deadly and debilitating disease. A new case strikes an American every 52 seconds; an estimated 100 million citizens worldwide suffer its effects, which can range from blindness to heart disease and early death. It strikes when the pancreas, an irregular-shaped gland behind the stomach, fails to produce insulin in amounts necessary to efficiently use blood glucose, or the blood sugar that is released by the liver and is the fuel that runs the brain and the cells of the human body. Too little glucose can trigger a coma and death. Too much can damage the eyes, nerves, and blood vessels.

The BCG consultants found diabetes to be horrifically expensive. By one estimate, the health care system spends about $102.5 billion caring for people with diabetes, or one seventh of total health care outlays. That translates into about $9,500 for each of the 13 to 14 million Americans with the disease compared to $2,600 spent on patients that aren't diabetics. Matheson and his team dug into the data they collected and drew an economic profile of diabetes, determining exactly how much was spent during treatment on hospitals, doctors, drugs, diagnostics, and other factors like administration. Understanding the economics of the disease was just the first step. BCG also classified patients according to clinical attributes, treatment needs, and economics. Less than 10 percent of diabetics, for example, suffer from juvenile or type 1 diabetes, which occurs when the body produces no—or very little—insulin on its own, requiring daily injections to regulate blood sugar. Yet type 1 diabetes accounts for more than 20 percent of the cost of the disease, primarily because it requires a higher frequency of treatment. It costs less per patient to treat the more prevalent adult-onset, or type 2, diabetes, which occurs when the body produces some insulin but not enough to prevent glucose from building up in the blood and causing damage. Yet type 2 diabetes often triggers far more serious diseases, such as heart failure, hypertension, and other problems. Indeed, the economic cost of treating diabetes is so high because it includes outlays for treating the disease plus the cost of care for complications like end-stage renal disease, premature vascular disease, blindness, amputations, and other collateral problems.

Matheson and his consultants pored over the data looking for insights that they could use to determine if Boehringer Mannheim's self-monitoring kits could lower the overall costs of treating diabetes and improve patient care. They drafted treatment flows, or maps of how care was being provided. "We were looking for critical junctures," Matheson said, "points at which things go awry and costs escalate, points where intervention in the process could lead to significant cost savings." Once they isolated the "critical junctures," Matheson and his team applied the principles of systems analysis and total quality management—concepts usually reserved for the business world—to health care practices, assessing how the medical industry could promote quality treatment and lower costs simultaneously. By the time they finished their research, the BCG consultants concluded that Boehringer Mannheim would be foolish to sell its glucose-monitoring business. "They said, 'Jesus Christ, if you don't develop this or if you sell it, you will miss a real opportunity,'" said Moller. "They were really insistent. It was more than advice. BCG insisted that Boehringer Mannheim enter this business. They said if you don't, we will never help you again. . . . It was really interesting how quickly they understood the logic and how quickly they also contributed to analyzing what had to be done."

Boehringer Mannheim obviously took the advice. It invested around $10 million to hire 100 salespeople to learn about—and market—the product, which is now called the Accucheck, a meter and glucose strip system that gives diabetics a digital readout of their blood sugar. BCG designed a cogent economic argument and strategy that Boehringer Mannheim could take to the American Diabetes Association and other patient groups that would help them in the drive to get reimbursement from insurers and acceptance in the medical field, where such a product would affect physician, hospital, and laboratory incomes. "BCG helped us with the economic value calculation. These guys are very, very sophisticated in their tools. They know how to make the obvious really objectively obvious. They are great guys in these strategies. They developed the economic structure of the disease. They were more than just a sounding board."

Moller said Boehringer Mannheim benefited greatly from the advice. It went from a company with a toehold in Europe to a leader in a worldwide market that could soon reach $1 billion a year thanks to BCG's analysis and influence. Sales of the company's glucose-monitoring kit now are second only to those of Abbott Laboratories, the giant drug company in suburban Chicago. Moller said that patients and the health care system benefited, too: "We were now able to help patients better manage their diseases. By doing so, the health care system, the insurers, benefited, because there were fewer complications by diabetics who would run into really severe health problems that would cost a lot of money when they would end up in the intensive care unit or the emergency room. It was the first example of disease management that was driven by the medical need and the medical understanding of how that disease could be managed. Diabetics could almost live a normal life. If they could properly test themselves and apply the insulin accordingly, they could eat almost anything they wanted or go hiking or whatever whenever they wanted. They just had to check to see that they were in the range they should be in, where healthy people were."

From Diabetes to Asthma: A Lucrative Path

The patients, the company, and the health care system weren't the only ones to benefit. BCG did, too. The obvious benefits, like the fees generated by Boehringer Mannheim, were welcome. More important, the success of the initial engagement led to more business for BCG and a long-term relationship. The revenues that the Boehringer Mannheim engagement generated paled in comparison to the main benefit that BCG got from its business with the Dutch company, though—the experience it gained.

One of the nice things about being a consultant is that you can make a lot of money selling the experience you gain from one client to another eager to find out what you know, particularly if you helped a foreign competitor invade the home turf. BCG had mastered the process with its fabled CEO conferences. At a time when Marriott lobbies are clogged with confabs on everything from astrological financial planning to 45 new ways to liposuction, it's hard to believe that hardly anyone used conferences as a marketing tool until Bruce Henderson came along. "That may sound unusual," said BCG's Sandra Moose. "But nobody was doing it. . . . Hardly anyone had focused on conferences talking about strategy and targeted to the CEO and the CFO." Over the years, Henderson raised the conference technique to an art form. "I used to organize those things," said one former BCG employee. "Once a year for three days, we would host a conference at a nice hotel, usually a Ritz-Carlton, in a nice place, like Florida, during the winter. We would start with a mailing of 400 or 500 invitations, mainly to CEOs who were clients or CEOs who we wanted as clients. We spent a lot of time on who to invite, you know, discussing whether this guy was a BCG kind of CEO. . . . We'd usually get about 150 responses to the mailing. About 50 would show up. One partner was assigned to every CEO. Over the three days there'd be some golf, a little outing. But most of it was salesmanship. It was our take on our experiences with our clients in the market."

In between golf outings, oysters Rockefeller, and chardonnay, the CEOs would attend panels where BCG consultants and officers would showcase their cutting-edge ideas and experiences implementing change in plants and offices around the world. Consultants don't like to view conferences such as those organized by BCG as hucksterism. The sessions usually feature scholarly handouts of articles written by consultants as if the whole thing were a seminar at Oxford. But conferences luring the corporate brass to the consultant's lair are a sophisticated marketing tool for the industry. At BCG, the sales pitch features programs like "Time-Based Competition" (TBC), an approach designed to show CEOs how to gain a competitive advantage by bringing products to market faster. The presentations, of course, are limited to success stories. Like any consulting firm, BCG has its dogs. The firm, in fact, played a big role at Figgie International, the Cleveland diversified manufacturer that nearly went broke following the advice of consultants like BCG (see Chapter 2). Indeed, the company's patriarch, Harry Figgie, attended several CEO conferences and eventually hired BCG, even though several partners wondered whether the mercurial and independent Figgie was a "BCG type of guy." They got their answer in 1994: After months of following the advice of BCG's consultants, Figgie International sued the firm, alleging that the advice and programs it had paid for, including time-based competition, were egregiously flawed and had cost Figgie millions in lost sales and profits. BCG countered that Figgie had been satisfied enough to fork over a whopping $17.4 million in consulting fees for its services. The litigation eventually was settled quietly out of court. But no one volunteers information about situations like Figgie at the CEO conferences. BCG features its happy customers, and the firm has plenty of them. "We'd spend $500,000 to $1 million on a conference," said the former BCG staffer. "All [the CEOs] had to do was get there and the rest was on us. It [the cost] might sound like a lot. But it's not much if you think of it [the conference] as R&D [and a way to market services plus secure future revenues]."

The Boehringer Mannheim experience would become part of the BCG lore communicated to health care executives invited to conferences later on in the 1980s. By then, BCG could talk about a lot more than diabetes, for the company's experience with the Dutch pharmaceutical firm put BCG on the cutting edge of health care reform, which started sweeping through the nation in the 1980s. Indeed, just as the firm rode the wave of conglomeration with its portfolio matrix, BCG would ride the wave of health care reform with disease management— "an approach to patient care that coordinates resources across the entire health care delivery system and throughout the life cycle of a disease."

After BCG's experience with diabetes at Boehringer Mannheim, Matheson and his team of consultants felt quite good about their work, and justifiably so. BCG consultants had not only helped a client make more money, they had also made a significant contribution to the nation's health care system. Viewed as an industry, medicine is a fragmented network of mom-and-pop physician shops scattered throughout America. Treatments for diseases such as diabetes range widely from highly effective techniques at state-of-the-art hospitals to shocking ignorance of the best practices elsewhere. There are few guidelines identifying the best practices, and doctors often learn of the latest advances in technology from salesmen pushing medical equipment or drugs. In short, patients are at the mercy of their doctors, who can either be informed or ignorant of the latest advances. In the Boehringer Mannheim situation, Matheson and his team were able to step in and help bring order out of chaos in the way diabetes was treated, which was no small accomplishment, particularly given the opposition physicians usually mount to anyone trying to give them advice.

As word of BCG's approach spread in the health care industry, the firm started getting other health care inquiries and more business. "We got a call from a small 150-bed hospital in Denver that was doing some interesting work in asthma," Matheson said. Soon BCG consultants showed up at the National Jewish Hospital in Denver. "They came to us along with a number of other specialty hospitals," said Matheson. "In the early 1980s, there was a big rush of HMO formations, and each of these specialty hospitals [was] very worried that they would lose a lot of their business because they were hospitals that [specialized in certain diseases nationwide] and HMOs were clearly locally focused. Let's say there was a physician in the Chicago market who might have thought about sending an asthma patient to National Jewish Hospital. If that patient was in an HMO, he wouldn't be sent to National Jewish [because a local hospital would be selected]. So the problem they were trying to solve was, how could they market a highly specialized capability in an HMO deep environment?"

Matheson and his team went to work constructing an economic profile of asthma. "A hospital can gather data for itself," Matheson said, "but it is hard to get it from other sources because the medical industry is so fragmented." Thanks to its experience with diabetes, BCG knew where to collect or buy good medical data. Working with its Denver client, BCG learned of asthma's unique economic structure. Like diabetes, it could be costly to treat—about $10 billion a year. The average cost of treatment in the United States is about $600, but extreme cases could cost $13,500. The big cost driver—600,000 annual hospitalizations that cost about $7 billion a year—was due to lack of patient compliance and misuse of medicines, mainly steroids. Overall, 5 percent of asthmatics accounted for 70 percent of the costs associated with treatment of the disease. Emergency room visits like those that Kim Wellman used to experience with her daughter Jody in Moline, Illinois, accounted for one fourth of the total system costs. If hospitals could come up with a better drug protocol and insurance companies would encourage patient education through their reimbursement policies, the patient, the insurer, and the employer would all be better off. "We put together argumentation that pulled together the case that National Jewish Hospital could make that for a certain proportion of the asthma population, National Jewish would be [a] highly cost-effective [option]." The idea was to convince HMOs to make an exception to their rules and allow severe asthma patients to be sent to National Jewish Hospital in Denver rather than to a local institution. BCG not only made its case for the client, but once again, it added to the body of knowledge about asthma and identified the best practices for treatment. It also added asthma as another element to BCG's growing practice in disease management it could offer to clients such as John Deere.

Cutting to the Quick in Moline

BCG gets most of its business—about 80 percent—from new engagements at existing clients and about 20 percent from new clients. The combination drove BCG deeper into the health care consulting business as new and existing clients hired the firm for health care engagements. As BCG analyzed different companies, hospitals, and diseases, Matheson and BCG consultants learned that diabetes and asthma epitomized more widespread problems in the nation's health care system. As pressure to control costs intensified in the 1980s, American health care managers relied on something called component management to battle the relentless growth in health care outlays. In other words, they focused on individual health care transactions—a doctor's visit, a specific procedure or a test—as the target for cost control. Health care managers established statistical norms for the cost of each component—so much money allotted for a doctor's visit, so much for an injection of insulin, and so on. They then established incentives or penalties for compliance with the norms. The idea was twofold: Adopt a confrontational approach to physicians and hospitals to discourage nonessential operations, excessive tests, and too many drugs; and drive the cost of each component as low as possible through aggressive contracting, case management, and other cost-control techniques. But true to Henderson's legacy, BCG consultants challenged the conventional thinking. They noted that component management had its limitations: It assumed that the overall direction of health care was correct and that the mix of individual elements of care merely needed adjustment. Component managers would target the aggregate cost of drugs or specialist consultations for an asthma patient, BCG consultants said, but they would ignore other crucial considerations. A higher investment in drugs and a specialist for a severely ill asthma patient might cost more initially, they said, but the higher up-front costs could be offset by much larger savings downstream from fewer overall emergency room and hospital visits.

BCG argued that a new approach was needed: "disease management." Using blood glucose monitoring for diabetics and a better drug protocol for asthmatics as examples, Matheson and BCG colleague Craig Wheeler argued for application of a systems-oriented approach to health care to better manage disease. Coining a phrase like "disease management" didn't have as big an impact as the theme that Matheson and Wheeler struck, though. They targeted drug companies and said pharmaceutical manufacturers could apply the systemwide economic models of disease management to promote their products to cost-conscious hospitals and third-party payers in a newly integrated health care system. "I'm not saying that we went out and shouted from the rooftops this is the way to do it," Matheson said, "but I do think we had a pretty significant role in the development of disease management."

The drug industry got the message. Within a few years, a coalition of 20 major drug companies, including Bristol-Myers Squibb, Johnson & Johnson, Pfizer Inc., and the Upjohn Company, would hire BCG to document the pharmaceutical industry's historic contribution to the nation's health care system. Under attack in Congress and in the press for high profits at a time of soaring health care outlays, the drug industry needed all the help it could get. Bill Clinton had made health care a major issue in his 1992 campaign for the White House. The industry took bids from about 15 to 20 consulting firms, and BCG won the engagement. "It was the kind of study that as a firm you just love to do. It gives you so much perspective over the whole history of the industry," Matheson said. BCG capitalized on its experience to devise an answer for the drugmakers. BCG suggested that drugmakers adopt disease management as a strategy and jump on the health care reform bandwagon, promoting drugs to managed care companies as a cost-effective way to supplant other more costly medical treatments. BCG not only proposed that drugmakers capitalize on disease management to promote their products as cost-effective medical treatments, they also noted that drugmakers had huge databases that were invaluable to HMOs and hospitals trying to implement disease management strategies on their own.

The result? Today most major pharmaceutical companies have some kind of disease management effort under way or planned.

BCG's promotion of the idea wasn't limited to new clients. Old clients were interested, too. BCG had been advising Deere & Co., the Moline, Illinois, farm implement maker, for 20 years. "One day [in the late 1980s or early 1990s]," said Matheson, "the CEO of Deere approached one of our partners who was out there in another meeting of some sort and said, 'Look, we have some internal problems with our health care costs. They are ballooning out of control.' " So Matheson went to Moline, Illinois, to talk to Hans W. Becherer, Deere's chairman and CEO. It would prove to be a rewarding trip in more ways than one.

Deere & Co. operates from the heart of the Great Plains. Its modern, sleek headquarters building near Moline contrasts sharply with its surroundings in an area known as the Quad Cities, which is like the farm belt's answer to Detroit for farm machinery. The company brass also contrasts sharply with the leaders of some other American corporations. Deere became one of the first employers in the nation to strike out on its own in managed care, forming two community-based HMOs that contracted with a group of area physicians to provide care for its employees and those of other self-insured companies. In 1985, Deere set the stage for an even bolder venture into managed care by forming John Deere Health Care, a wholly owned subsidiary of Deere & Co. and the company whose rising costs sent Deere CEO Hans Becherer to BCG's doors.

Matheson didn't expect to find such a willing forum for disease management when he first set foot in Moline. It's the kind of a place where the Grand National Dirt Track motorcycle race is front-page news, and people compare Pat Buchanan to Thomas Jefferson and Abe Lincoln. But Matheson was pleasantly surprised by Deere's employees and its executives. "The word 'straight' comes to mind when I think of them," he said. "They were easy to deal with because you could just go to them and deal with them up front. You could cut to the quick." Matheson was impressed with the company's plans for a staff model HMO, or one where Deere owned the health care facility and where doctors were Deere employees. But he was even more impressed with the partner under consideration for the Deere HMO venture—the famed Mayo Clinic in Rochester, Minnesota. Deere and Mayo had a long-term relationship; the company's former chairman had been on the board of the Mayo Clinic's parent foundation. When Deere decided to set up its staff HMO, it contacted Mayo officials to see if they would be interested in helping out. Deere discussed its plans with BCG and promptly formed a strategic alliance in which Mayo supplied consulting services for the HMO clinic in Moline and two others planned for Waterloo and Des Moines, Iowa.

David Matheson and a team of BCG consultants viewed the contract with Deere as ideal. "It was a chance to help design a health care program from scratch along disease management lines," he said. Moreover, it gave BCG a chance to work directly with an employer sophisticated in its approach to health care and a clinic that had one of the best reputations in medicine. "We collaborated very deeply with the Mayo Clinic," Matheson said. "It was a matter of putting together the right infrastructure to manage diseases. . . . For us, that was the pinnacle."

Deere's medical director was Richard Bartsh, a young M.D. who was a North Carolina family practice physician when he got a call in 1990 asking if he would be interested in a job at Deere's health care subsidiary. A Minnesota native, Bartsh had done his training for his M.D. at the Mayo Clinic. Satisfied with his practice in North Carolina, Bartsh nonetheless was frustrated with certain elements of being a general practitioner. "I had been in family practice for about twelve years. It was your typical practice. At the end of a year, I wouldn't know if I had served my patients well. I had no measures. You know, you get your medical education, serve your residency, set up a practice, and start seeing patients. You are just keeping up and hoping that you are doing well. There is a great deal of deference to what the patients tell you. . . . [John Deere Health Care was] looking for someone with Mayo ties and they started talking about disease management and establishing a system of electronic medical records." The innovative nature of Deere's plan appealed to Bartsh and he joined Deere as medical director and senior vice president in 1991.

A tall, bespectacled young doctor, Bartsh is both competitive and understated. A visitor walking into his office might find him standing near a window gazing out at a long train loaded with huge green and red tractors and combines crawling down tracks adjacent to the Mississippi River. "Excuse me, I'm counting," he says. "I do this every day. There is a J. I. Case [a Deere competitor] plant just up the river. When the train comes along, I count the green [Deere] and the red [J. I. Case] to see who is winning. We're winning today," he says as he returns to his desk with a wry smile on his face. At a nearby Deere clinic in Moline, Mayo's fingerprints are everywhere. But Bartsh's file cabinets also are crammed with reams of data that suggest BCG has been around.

"Early on, the BCG consultants served as a catalyst for a lot of the ideas we use here," said Bartsh. "For two years, they studied John Deere Health Care. They did all of the data manipulation. They used to call it slicing and dicing the data. They were analyzing it to come up with the right clinical questions. They looked at how many patients we had, the number of tests, the number of X rays, the number of C-scans, MRIs."

BCG had a big advantage from the start: Deere's history with medical insurance and HMOs gave BCG a homegrown database. Its consultants could tap the data to investigate cost-effective treatments that were also judged "best practices" by Mayo and people like Bartsh. Capitalizing on the existing knowledge base, BCG began analyzing the economic structure of diseases and classifying Deere's patients to help develop a protocol the HMO and its doctors could use. They looked for expensive procedures and examined the treatment flows, trying to identify "critical junctures" where change could save money and improve care, just as they had done at Boehringer Mannheim and other places. "We looked at lower back pain," Bartsh said, "and found that a stepcare approach had developed." Patients usually were given an X ray. If nothing showed up, they would be given a milogram, in which a physician injects dyes into the body. No one would do surgery until they got a CT scan and finally an MRI. The chain of tests proved to be one of BCG's "critical junctures," an expensive step in the process where big savings could be achieved with active intervention. The MRI was the most expensive but also the best test. If doctors would simply order it instead of demanding the other three steps first, the overall procedure would be cheaper and the decision whether surgery was needed would be made faster. As a result, the HMO decided to implement new care guidelines, authorizing payment for the most expensive step and eliminating the X ray, the milogram, and the CT scan.

Doctors don't always take kindly to such direction. Indeed, physicians criticize disease management as "cookbook medicine" prepared by people who have cost and not health care on their minds. But Bartsh and Richard Van Bell, president of John Deere Health Care, said overcoming such resistance is where BCG's role takes on added importance. Patients often experience frustration at the lack of information or contradictory advice they get at the doctor's office—a reflection of the fragmented, chaotic nature of the medical industry. One element of the industry often doesn't know what the other is doing. In its own operations, for instance, Deere found wide discrepancies in physician practices. When the company reorganized its HMOs in 1985, it created Heritage National Healthplan to service Deere units outside of Moline and its other self-insured customers in Illinois, Iowa, Wisconsin, and Tennessee. "In Tennessee, we found out that 40 percent of the mothers delivered babies by C-section," said Van Bell. "In Waterloo, Iowa, only 15 percent delivered them by C-section. We went to Tennessee and asked why. Their response? They were appalled. The doctors there didn't even know they were doing that. They started looking into it. We found that was just the way things were done in Tennessee."

Bartsh said the way to overcome physician resistance is to analyze the data and create matrices of care for each disease, much in the same way BCG created a portfolio matrix. "If you can figure out the key matrices for these diseases, then the doctors will be measured on what they are doing, not in any punitive sense but in a sense of how they are doing against the data. If you tell a physician that he is doing 40 percent C-sections and everyone else is doing 15 percent, he will try to get closer to the 15 percent because he will want to be like everyone else. The easy part is developing the management strategy. The hard part is, how do you put that strategy into practice? Once you decide what you are going to do, how do you get the data? That's where BCG helped a lot. The people I worked with at BCG were pretty innovative and driven."

No More E.R. Runs for Jody Wellman

Lower-back pain was one of several disease management protocols BCG helped develop at Deere. Within a few years Deere also started developing them for many others, including asthma and diabetes. On paper, the finished products might look easy, says Bartsh: "Most physicians would look at the strategy to manage diabetes and say, 'Hell, anybody knows that. You didn't have to go pay BCG and Mayo all that money. You could have taken me out and bought a pizza and a beer and I could have told you that.' But they are looking at the finished product. It's like looking at the *Mona Lisa* after it was done and saying, I could paint that. Well, maybe you could. But would you have thought of it?"

Van Bell agreed. He said BCG's analysis of the data for asthma helped people like Mrs. Wellman and her daughter Jody. "We found people that didn't know a lot about their diseases. The doctors started looking at the data and we found out a lot. There was a wide range of treatment." Of the money spent on patients like young Jody Wellman, most went for hospitalizations and improper drugs, those early-morning dashes that Mrs. Wellman would make to the emergency room where her daughter was continually misdiagnosed. BCG estimated that Deere could save up to 25 percent on the cost of treating asthma if patients like Jody or her mother could be taught about asthma, how to use peak flow meters to measure the rate of airflow into their lungs, and if diagnostics could be improved to ensure she got the right kind of drugs. As a result, Deere started asthma classes in which physicians, nurses, and pharmacists taught members about asthma, instructed them in monitoring techniques, and told them how to prevent a crisis. Indeed, Kim Wellman walked into one of them and never regretted it: "Before the asthma classes, I was ignorant about the disease and I didn't know what to do. It scared me to death, all that hacking and coughing like she couldn't catch her breath. So I would just run to the emergency room. The classes made a big difference. They taught me the warning signs of when she was about to have an attack, how to use the peak flow meter, what to do if she got real bad, and when to go to the doctor. I haven't had to take her to the emergency room since she's been on the nebulizer."

The John Deere classes had other benefits for Jody. Once she started proper treatment, she grew faster. "They tell you that asthmatic kids don't grow as fast," said Mrs. Wellman. "Over the last year, Jody's grown nearly two inches, from forty-seven and three-fourths inches to forty-nine and one-quarter inches. Had she not been on that medication, it would have been like before, maybe a half-inch of growth." Before she had been properly diagnosed for asthma, Jody had also missed school a lot. School officials actually had forced her to repeat a year, mistaking the complications flowing from her asthma as a learning disability. Now Jody is doing much better in school. "She's been absent only two times the whole year, and she's doing better with her grades, too."

Mrs. Wellman's experience shows the positive impact that consultants can make when the goal of profit maximization coincides with a social good. BCG is doing excellent pioneering work in disease management. It deserves a lot of credit for the accomplishments and innovative thinking it has brought to the world of health care. But a word of caution is in order, too.

Skepticism about the benefits of disease management isn't all that much greater than the reaction in the business world to BCG's portfolio matrix 20 years ago. Deere has one of the best HMOs in the nation. It continually scores top marks in surveys of employees and patients, who like its prompt service. Deere CEO Hans Becherer even dropped his doctor and became a patient at the HMO, as did the United Auto Workers union official who heads Deere's bargaining unit. By applying its disease management strategies wisely, the HMO balances the needs of patients against cost savings and profits. Not all HMOs are as good as Deere's, though. Movements already are afoot in several states for government-mandated HMO guidelines because of consumer complaints about penny-pinching HMOs that bolster their bottom lines at the expense of patients.

Also, the cost reductions achieved at Deere fall short of actually cutting the company's medical costs. At the time the disease management strategies were being implemented at Deere, Van Bell estimated that disease management would save the company 15 percent. But the savings involved money that Deere would have paid had its HMO members chosen traditional fee-for-service medicine. Overall medical costs have continued to rise at Deere's health care subsidiary from $240 million in 1991 to $293 million in 1995, the latest audited figures available. Disease management simply slowed the rate of increase. That is not an insignificant feat in an economy where health care costs continue to soar. But such savings are not the panacea they might initially appear to be.

Lastly, as BCG continues to spread the gospel of disease management, there is no guarantee that any converts will apply the strategy as wisely as Deere. There is little doubt that BCG has helped spread word of disease management beyond the corporate suite. Patients can expect to see more disease management at their HMOs, hospitals, and doctors' offices in the near future. Stories on it already appear in the *Journal of the American Medical Association* and its newspaper. "If disease management sounds a lot like managed care, that's because, fundamentally, it's an advanced, sophisticated form of managed care," said a June 1996 article in the *American Medical News*. "Managed care companies are scrambling to develop their own disease management programs." Meanwhile, as the HMOs expand their disease management programs, they are forming alliances with another BCG client—the drug industry.

"Although most managed care companies don't want it known," said the *American Medical News*, "they are contracting [with drugmakers] for disease management services. Dozens of insurers, employers, integrated delivery systems, hospital networks, physician-hospital organizations, and practices use disease management services, too. No one is keeping count, but drugmakers say they're running scores of disease management programs and that demand is booming. . . . 'Disease management is not coming; it's already here,' said Robert A. Luginbill, executive director of North American Business Development at Eli Lilly. 'It is absolutely certain that we are going to approach health care with the concept.' "

This could have a beneficial impact. Managed care companies have huge incentives to pursue disease management strategies. But they can't implement the strategies alone. Most have the data, access to patients, and the network of physicians and providers who have the experience in patient care. But they lack the additional skills needed, such as experience in clinical and economic research, which are the forte of the drug companies. Already drugmakers aggressively marketing disease management have formed consulting subsidiaries to help managed care clients set up disease management programs. If the drugmakers can share with managed care companies the enormous stores of information on diseases that they compile in their research on new drugs, disease management will expand even faster. But this alliance could have a downside, too.

The drugmakers aren't exactly the Florence Nightingales of the medical industry. They are known for their historically high profit margins. If they use disease management as a marketing tool designed to promote widespread use of their drugs, it could seriously damage the credibility of disease management and undermine the good work that

BCG has done for its clients' customers. Potential troubles already are surfacing. At Eli Lilly & Co. in Indiana, there's a disease management program for depression called ProPartners. It involves individual patient education on the phases of depression and the recovery process and stresses "continuing antidepressant therapy for 4 to 9 months after remission of symptoms." But patients must be prescribed Lilly's controversial drug Prozac to participate, a factor that was criticized by managed care pharmacy directors in a recent survey. They viewed ProPartners as a marketing tool designed to push the use of Prozac.

The danger is that history will repeat itself and BCG's ideas on disease management will receive a lack of scrutiny equal to the dearth of skepticism about the portfolio matrix. BCG, after all, developed its ideas for clients that want to maximize profits, a goal that is not necessarily compatible with the broader public interests involved in a field like health care. Some observers, for example, wonder whether the savings possible in diabetes and asthma treatments can be replicated in other more complex diseases with vastly different economic profiles. But questions like that are not raised in BCG studies extolling the role of drug companies in the health care system.

One thing to keep in mind is that BCG, like any consulting firm, is not infallible. There's no question that the firm's financial success is staggering. Deere wouldn't—or didn't want to—say how much it paid BCG for its engagement, which lasted a couple of years. It is a good bet that the advice wasn't cheap. BCG's billing to Figgie, which occurred during the same time frame as the Deere engagement, ranged from $400 an hour to a whopping $1,300 an hour, according to Figgie officials. Engagements such as the one at Deere have propelled BCG into the stratosphere of the American consulting industry. The company is not the largest in revenues or numbers of consultants. *Consultants News* estimates its 1994 worldwide revenues at $430 million, which was 26 percent above the year before. The company had revenues of $140 million in 1989. A lot of its growth in recent years has come from abroad. Less than half of its estimated 1994 business is in the United States. In terms of revenues, it is larger than Bain & Co. but smaller than its other major competitor, McKinsey & Co., whose 1994 revenues were estimated at $1.5 billion. Nevertheless, BCG is right up there in terms of influence on global corporations, and its consultants fetch high rates. *Consultants News* estimates BCG pulls in

$382,000 for each of its consultants while McKinsey pulls in $475,000. In contrast, Andersen Consulting, the largest consulting firm in the world, pulls in only $125,000 per consultant. But financial success doesn't mean the firm's advice will automatically create better results. Figgie is just one example of an engagement that went awry. The Cleveland-based manufacturer nearly went bankrupt despite BCG's advice. The firm's $1-million-a-month reengineering engagement at NYNEX had an underside, too: BCG helped create a strategy to slash NYNEX's operation expenses by 35 to 40 percent through huge lay-offs, consolidation of operations, and simplifying procedures ratified by years of regulatory comfort. Once the plan was implemented and thousands of NYNEX employees were sent packing, consumer complaints about service at the company soared. Eventually NYNEX had to rehire about a third of the employees it had sacked.

If similar problems with disease management surface, chances are you won't hear much about them from BCG or the consulting industry. The industry's culture demands that it focus on the positive. Consultants like Matheson are proud of the job they have done and feel good about the accomplishments of disease management. He is now the leader of the health care practice at BCG. He made vice president in six years, which is far faster than most. Critics suggest consultants have good reason to feel good: They are making lots of money selling their advice to health care providers. Stories proliferate about the huge starting salaries and the $1 million plus annual compensation packages that veteran consultants pull down. But Matheson says the stories are only partially true at BCG. A relatively new consultant at BCG can earn a six-figure salary fairly quickly, which is probably one reason that BCG and McKinsey were the top choices for European and many U.S. business students in 1995. But he says there are "very, very few" senior-level people who earn the cherished seven figures. Equally important to consultants like Matheson is that they are pushing at the frontiers of strategic thinking with reports like the lengthy essay called "The Promise of Disease Management." It was sent out as a BCG Perspective to senior managers on the firm's mailing list, which has expanded considerably since Henderson's day. "You know, when you write about this business, there is something you should emphasize," Matheson said. "This is a privileged business. Most people get jobs and work their entire lives and never have an impact. Young people who come to work here right out of school go to work and have an impact on their first assignment. They are privileged. This is a privileged business."

Matheson is right. By devising and packaging ideas that go beyond the bottom line, today's consultants have a far larger impact on society than they did in Henderson's heyday. Jody Wellman's story is just one example of their rising influence. There are many others. Consultants now help companies come up with policies on health care, pensions, fringe benefits, and retirement. Outside the workplace, they have an impact on what one reads and on basic social policies, such as how society communicates. As they expand their web of influence, though, they will have to adjust to different measures of the value they create.

At BCG, Matheson proudly suggests that the company's insights, skills transfer, and change management programs create economic value for its clients. At Deere, for instance, BCG's insights about disease management cut the rate of increase in the company's medical expenses and created value for shareholders through increased profits. The program also helped employees by providing better health care services. But measuring the impact of disease management on society and the nation's economy overall require different yardsticks, ones that BCG and other consultants rarely encounter.

The value that consultants create for their private clients resembles a zero-sum game. Instead of creating economic value like a manufacturer, which converts raw materials and labor into finished products that can be sold for a profit, consultants often shift value around in an economy, robbing Peter to pay Paul. At Deere's health care subsidiary, BCG's disease management strategy created improved quality and outcomes at a cost lower than what would have been possible using current treatment approaches. In other words, any savings came at the expense of some existing practice, like referrals to specialist physicians, who would probably get fewer patients sent to them by Deere's generalists using a disease management strategy. That is not bad. In fact, it is good. Deere saves money, and patients benefit. But before anyone can measure whether the strategy benefited society as a whole, he has to know who gained, who lost, and at what cost the savings were achieved. If cost-conscious disease managers like those at Deere thin the ranks of specialists by lowering their incomes, that may be good news for Deere. But measuring whether such a situation benefits society as a whole is a different question and one that management consultants rarely answer.

Chances are, the consultants at BCG will continue to develop and package ideas like disease management and will have both positive and negative effects on society. It will probably fall to some government agency to measure whether the positive exceeds or offsets the negative. Absent such a measure, the only way to judge the value that Matheson and his colleagues bring to society is to look at what they have done for the Jody Wellmans of the world, and that is a lot.

Trying to Make Gold from Lead

GEMINI AND THE TRANSFORMATION FAD

Boston Consulting Group moved into the living room with its health care efforts. Gemini Consulting has tried to move into the boardroom with a process it calls transformation, perhaps the most elegant of the extant consulting fads. It is the one consulting company that seems intent on banishing the industry's troubling arrogance.

There may be no more ominous indoor space on a rainy, cold, fall afternoon than the small conference room at the top of Two Liberty Place in Philadelphia, executive offices of Cigna Property & Casualty Co. The low clouds are so thick that the glass expanses, designed to frame a stunning view of the City of Brotherly Love, reveal only an almost impenetrable, cold whiteness. Peer hard enough into the gloom and a shape emerges. From the conference room, it looks like a set design from a horror movie, a looming, unavoidable presence that, on a sunny day, would be stunning. But bad weather transforms all of that. The view takes in the top of the building that houses Cigna's parent company, a vision so modern, harsh, and angular on a dismal day that it cannot be ignored. If the Prince of Darkness had a penthouse, this is what it would look like. It is too powerful to ignore.

A troubled property and casualty company that has stumbled for years in a thick haze of bad returns, huge losses connected to high-risk insurance, awful morale, and collapsing profits sits right in the shadow of a parent company that demands a leap into the sunshine of high quality and financial returns that exceed 15 percent. The corporate equivalent of alchemy, this turning of lead into gold is a great challenge, made all the more immediate by the ominous presence of the Cigna headquarters, which looms on a gloomy day with all the power of a very successful, but deeply disappointed father. Forces are at work here, 55 stories above the streets of Philadelphia, that will determine whether Cigna Property & Casualty Co. eventually reaches its goal, indeed, whether it survives.

The company is the product of decades of trouble in an era in which it seemed hell-bent to take on as much risk as it could. But that is only the way the problem looks at first glance. Closer to the truth is the fact that Cigna probably didn't know what it was getting into. Long after it sold policies targeting corporations, Cigna learned it would be responsible for a blizzard of claims in complicated environmental cases. Asbestos, toxic waste, natural disasters, civil disorders, these huge claims all seemed to find a home inside Cigna Property & Casualty. When the bills came due, they brought the crushing obligation of billions of dollars in charges to a company that was ill prepared to absorb the cost. Money flowed from corporate headquarters to the property and casualty subsidiary in the hundreds of millions of dollars. Complicating that, Cigna Property & Casualty walked the path of the traditional American corporation, complacent and comfortable in the old culture of the insurance industry, layered with expensive middle management, checkers to check the people who checked the checkers, rusting, unproductive ties to thousands of agents who produced no business, and of course, a Matterhorn of paperwork that gobbled up expensive collections of scriveners and secretaries and adjusters. It also faced blistering competition from dozens of challengers in the insurance marketplace. This was a fat-times formula operating under famine conditions.

Now Cigna is wrestling with a reversal of course, a move that is aimed at taking a loser and turning it into a winner in one of the most complicated businesses of them all. It must be done quickly enough to keep the board of directors at bay and Wall Street pacified despite a dismal track record in an industry that eats its own without much hesitation. It must be accomplished recognizing that there is no way it can accurately assess its long-term liabilities because of the environmental cases, hundreds of which are tied up in court. And all of this must be done in the shadow of that huge building that looms just across the way. A decent interval will be provided for the transition, but the clocks and the computers that measure time and profits are running, and the one thing that seems to surround the corporate headquarters even more than the halo of clouds around the tower is the sense of urgency.

Cigna had tried reengineering, but without much success. Tom Valerio, the former army officer, IBM executive, and ex-consultant who is in charge of Cigna's transformation, says everyone had grown "fairly cynical" about these efforts at change because they had worked on them for years and saw few practical benefits. Valerio, who joined Cigna Corp. as its reengineering officer in 1993, is an engaging, enthusiastic man who seems to have held on to the part of his military training that works the best, the sense of focus on a goal, while abandoning the command and control part that makes some ex-officers seem as though they had been stamped from the same sheet of metal. He was only on the job for three days when Gerry Isom, who had been brought in from Transamerica to reconstruct Cigna Property & Casualty, approached him. Isom was growing frustrated with the pace of change. He wanted Valerio to take on an important assignment helping redesign the property and casualty company. Isom had a plan and knew exactly where he wanted to take Cigna, right up to the top of the list in speciality insurance, but the company was dragging along, the victim of its own history and a persistent inertia that seemed to gobble up and digest any attempt at reformation. Isom wanted something as big as the company itself. And, particularly in light of the other challenges the company faces, that is not the kind of change anyone can make without help.

A couple of hundred miles away, in one of Washington's distant Maryland suburbs, a small community hospital wrestled with challenges that were almost as daunting as those faced by the people who run Cigna Property & Casualty. The geography is friendlier, and the architecture is dated enough to look as though it would fit on an old *Marcus Welby* TV show set, a building full of shiny hallways and the familiar collection of the antiseptic smells, beeping monitors, and low-level intensity common to all hospitals. The numbers are a lot smaller, too. Cigna lives in the confusing world of finance, where risks are measured in terms of billions upon billions of dollars. It has thousands of employees and faces forces as vast as nature. Montgomery County General

Hospital is nothing compared to that, a mere 200 beds, perhaps 750 employees, and a patient pool of about 300,000 people in northern Montgomery County.

But if the scale seems somehow miniature, the people who run the hospital see big problems here, too. The most pressing is the rallying cry that dominates the health care industry of the 1990s: managed care. It is changing everything about the way people receive medical treatment and is touching on all the financial components of medicine. There was a time when a hospital could simply log its customers in at the front door, provide an acceptable range of services without too many embarassing mistakes, send everyone home, and then wait for the insurance checks to arrive. It was a formula for wealth. Doctors could charge what they wanted. Beds, the traditional measure of a hospital's success, could be filled all of the time with everyone from little boys having their tonsils yanked to the very old awaiting high-tech life extension at hundreds of dollars an hour. Whole armies of health care professionals, from licensed practical nurses and aides emptying bedpans to X-ray technicians taking pictures to surgeons performing valiant and expensive procedures could feast on this process, to either lesser or greater degree depending on their status in the stratified world of medical care. It was a profit center before anyone started defining the components of corporations as profit centers.

If revenues looked a little weak, the hospital could increase its per diem charges. Perhaps some expensive new procedures and equipment could be added. A busy, clanking CT scanner could become quite a cash register in a small hospital. New services could be invented. As long as the building was full and humming, the money would come in, usually in great, guaranteed gobs.

Pete Monge is the president of Montgomery County General. Over coffee, he describes what he found when he came to the hospital just over six years ago. Montgomery County General had lost money for three years in a row under a chief executive officer who had been in place for 14 years. "Things kind of came together. They were losing some money and no one was paying attention. When they finally decided there had to be a change, they had had three straight years of losing money at a time when you probably shouldn't have been losing money at all," Monge said. It was quite surprising, given the traditional hospital formula. His friends envied him when he announced he was going to Montgomery General, he recalled. They said it was a plum of a job in a growth area. They assumed that expanding population would keep the beds full and the money coming. But what he found was a hospital that potential patients could easily ignore, either because their insurance wouldn't buy them entry, or because their doctors were doing business elsewhere. He boiled the process down into a simple sentence: "We saw people just going right past us," he said. Along with that, the comfortable old cash cow of a world was disappearing as managed care phased in.

The price tag for medical care became a national scandal. The insurance industry, smelling opportunity, got very tough. Hard questions were asked at every level. And as this process developed, the idea of a community general hospital, the small facility that offers full service, began to mutate. Being all things to all people isn't so easy when Johns Hopkins, with its stunning collection of specialists and vast resources, is just down the road, or when a primary care physician decides she would rather be affiliated with an insurance company that doesn't offer its services at Montgomery County General.

On the insurance end of the picture, in the quest to control costs and maximize their own profits, insurance companies set down regulations and coverage options that slashed the number of hospital days that would be funded for routine admissions and procedures. Unless there are undeniable complications, no one spends much time in a maternity ward anymore. It is a two-day event at most. Even heart patients are shown the door after a brief stay. And when people have mental health crises, their hospitalizations are measured in weeks instead of months. Then there is competition.

Television advertising has arrived on the hospital scene. It is all done very tastefully, generally depicting vast buildings full of the best surgeons and specialists, no matter how obscure the speciality. It's a subtle scare tactic, but one that works: If you are going to get one of the Big Illnesses, it takes a Big Hospital to handle it. We can be all things to all people. You don't want to haul your newly discovered tumor or condition to some 200-bed facility out in the suburbs when you can come to the university hospital downtown. The outcome may be the very same no matter where you take the problem, but somehow the idea of being handled by a big complicated place connected to a university is more comforting to the afflicted than the thought of being way out in the suburbs attended to by doctors who are distant from medical science, generally the star in modern hospital advertising. At least that is the marketing message.

All of these changes have had a huge impact on the revenues of community hospitals. At Montgomery County General, they cut so deeply that Monge and his managers were questioning only a few years ago whether the hospital could survive. It was losing millions of dollars and watching its patient base shrink. Monge and his team were also acutely aware of the projections for health care needs of the future. The nation has half again as many hospital beds as it needs, and the pruning is likely to come with stunning rapidity as government and insurance companies step up the push to squeeze costs out of the system. The old formula that had worked so well for hospitals for so long was failing, and with a rapidity that rocked health care to its very foundation. Monge and his team were able to improve revenues to the point at which the budget actually showed a $700,000 surplus. But he thought those numbers were deceptive, a message he carried to the board of directors.

"I called it being in the river and hearing the waterfalls and not knowing how far down the river it was. That was really the way it felt. We knew something was coming. We had heard about it from everybody else in health care. But it just hadn't hit here yet. We said we have got to do something to dramatically change the way we do business here because it is just not going to work this way," Monge said.

"Somehow we needed to look different," said Marcia Cohen, the hospital's senior vice president for finance. "We needed to be a different organization."

It was time for a complete change of course, and that kind of a change takes some help. Both of these institutions suffered from their own versions of the same problem. Everything had changed around them, and they concluded that the old formula for success, selling more insurance, which meant taking on more risk at Cigna, filling those hospital beds, and increasing the billing at Montgomery General, wouldn't work anymore.

Turning to Gemini

It was not coincidental that they turned to the same place for help, a New Jersey–based consulting company that was marketing "business transformation" as the solution to the challenge of change. It was a formula aimed at identifying a company's problems from the bottom up, crafting a plan, and then implementing it. The argument was that piecemeal fixes simply wouldn't work and that a well-bound strategy plan delivered to the board of directors had little value if no one could figure out how to carry it out. This is such a common problem in the world of consulting that the scene has become a cliché: fat report. Nice binding. Put it on the shelf and forget about it.

That was not the Gemini Consulting formula for transformation. Whether it was a giant insurance company or a tiny hospital, the framework was the same: Change had to be created across every component of a company if the transformation was to work. It was a way of thinking that went far beyond the simplistic and much cherished downsizing nostrums of the 1980s. If the slogan of the consultant-as-Attila-the-Hun in that era was to slash, chop, and burn, this consulting company was suggesting dismantle, carefully examine, and rebuild, with the long-term goal being expansion of the business, not the quick fix of slashing of overhead.

For a brief time, Gemini was the hottest name in management consulting and reflected both the upside and downside of a reality that has followed the consulting industry for years, its propensity for presenting fads as solutions to problems. From management by objective to quality circles to just-in-time manufacturing and on to the most recent of the big trends, reengineering, the industry never seems to run out of marketable philosophies, some of which have led to sweeping changes in businesses all over the world.

It is all part of a time-tested formula that evolved after Tom Peters, a McKinsey & Co. consultant, gathered wealth and fame in the wake of *In Search of Excellence*, published some 15 years ago and the most successful business book of modern times. The recipe: Get an article in the *Harvard Business Review*, pump it up into a book, pray for a best-seller, then market the idea for all it is worth through a consulting company. There have been many variations on the theme, but most fad consulting efforts fit the same pattern.

The books are all like one another in the sense that they present fat collections of case studies that shore up whatever philosophy is advocated. Some of the fads work for a time, only to be replaced by the next thing that comes along. Some of them don't work at all. They are the business world's equivalent of what happens in computer hardware. No one ever lets well enough alone. Ideas, it would seem, are as perishable as laptops. And all the powerhouses of management consulting are fertile places for the development, growth, and marketing of these plans. Offering something different separates the consulting house from the rest of the field, all of which offer a range of services that are very similar.

As a result of the schemes, consultants spend a lot of time trying to explain just what it is they are selling. Sometimes, as in the case of reengineering, the idea seems somehow brilliant at birth, but then backfires. Presented first in a *Harvard Business Review* article by Michael Hammer in 1990, the idea soon became Hammer and James Champy's book *Reengineering the Corporation*, a best-seller that sparked reengineering projects all across the Fortune 500 companies.

But reengineering mutated to such a degree in the process that both authors found themselves writing books and giving lectures aimed at severing the reengineering philosophy from its bastard child, downsizing. To many minds, the words became almost interchangeable. Reengineering took on a cast that seemed to fit almost every situation as managers hastened to find ways to improve the bottom line, generally through cutting costs. This has helped to add an interesting "Ancient Mariner" component to the most recent pitches of its inventors as they struggle to keep alive interest in their initial idea. It is the equivalent of trying to grab the business world by its arm, get it to pause, and then tell the whole, true story. Gemini's variant on reengineering was to come up with a philosophy that included a strong reengineering component, but coated it with a much calmer and more intellectual glaze that made it seem somehow more user-friendly. That was a marketing tactic, not an accident.

Reengineering projects were faltering all over the place because of their size, complexity, and misdirection. Gemini's proposal went a step beyond. It would actually be there to help carry the projects out.

Gemini Consulting was born in 1991 in a merger of the MAC Group, with its emphasis on high-level strategy and academic connections to the best schools in America and Europe, and United Research, a visionary firm that built its reputation on implementation of complicated plans. At its inception, Gemini, with its huge French sister company, Cap Gemini Sogéti, seemed to represent the best of both worlds of consulting, just the right mixture of academia and practicality, along with a high-tech, world-class connection in Paris. It fairly exploded early on as businesses flocked to its sophisticated, complicated, and priccy consulting offerings. Gemini's growth was phenomenal and it added staff by the hundreds. By the time Cigna and Montgomery County General were looking for some big-ticket consulting advice, world revenues of Gemini Consulting had increased to $516 million, a 19 percent improvement over 1992. It was in the top ten of world consulting.

Selling the Product

Brilliant marketing is the hallmark of American business, and Gemini was one of the best marketers of them all. It quickly grabbed the attention of the business press, as eager as CEOs to tap into the latest business school management fad. Amid the backlash against the "drop the report, send the bill, run" mentality, Gemini joined the growing collection of consulting companies that crafted a message based on implementation. It recognized that the most difficult part of any business plan was putting the pieces into place and making it work. The McKinsey and BCG consultants could cozy up to the board of directors or CEO and dazzle with sheer brilliance, the Andersen consultants could talk the language of technology and its many uses, the people from A. T. Kearney could analyze operations. The downsizers could cut and chop.

But Gemini came along at the right time with a philosophy that proposed doing it all, from schmoozing with the CEO to lunching with the maintenance supervisors to assessing the information technology capacities and needs to looking at compensation issues. And, of course, it could help with downsizing, reengineering, and the whole collection of other business school clichés and prescriptions that have come to define the industry of consulting.

What it could not do, it would outsource to other consultants that were more specialized in their work. It had a track record of these partnerships that was so strong, the connection had became a component of Gemini's marketing strategy. And all along, the consultant's credo proclaimed, the emphasis would be on client satisfaction, no small matter in a world that seems to view consultants more as the business equivalent of Hessian troops. If business consulting had come to take on the tarnish of arrogance, an "I-know-better-than-anybody" attitude, then Gemini would emphasize cooperation in its proposals and its practices and craft its consulting to be as user-friendly as it could be.

What Gemini had to offer would be big, a top-to-bottom plan for its clients that would examine all the twists and turns inside a corporation. It would be complicated, digging as deeply into group psychology and motivation as it did into corporate flowcharts and business plans. And, like most consulting experiences at most companies, it would be very expensive. It also had the sheen of success and newness about it, two important components in the fad-conscious world of business.

The pieces of Gemini's plan had been welded into place by the time the bad news became apparent at Cigna and at Montgomery County General Hospital. When it was asked to bid on the two contracts, Gemini was riding high. Later, Gemini would run into its own problems. Amid declines in revenue said to approach $100 million, it would falter to the point at which it was forced to initiate its own round of layoffs and wrestle to cope with something that was all but foreign to its staff of executives and consultants—bad publicity.

By 1994, its American revenues were basically flat, a disturbing prospect for CGS, which had seen Gemini's annual revenues grow to the half-billion-dollar range after only a few years of operation. And CGS was having its own problems in Europe with lagging revenues and stiff competition. Tensions grew between Morristown and Paris. Some important heads rolled after this downturn, which might have been more a reflection of rapid growth and the stiff competition in the American consulting marketplace than any measure of Gemini's philosophy or performance. There were reports of defections as headhunters, salivating at the first sign of bad news, came looking for its most experienced consultants and as some of Gemini's own team searched for jobs elsewhere. Gemini's leaders seemed genuinely confused about how to handle this experience after so many years of success. The rationalization inside the company was that all big consulting firms hit bumps over time, and that this one would smooth out once the company tailored its message a bit and pushed a little harder on the marketing levers.

The assessment in the marketplace was a little more harsh. The business press tarred Gemini with what might be the harshest criticism anyone can apply in the image-conscious world of consulting: It had failed to offer anything that distinguished it from its competitors. This is enough to send everyone at a consulting company racing into deep-strategy sessions. Within a few weeks of this criticism, it was hard to scratch a Gemini consultant or executive without getting a friendly lecture, in great detail, on how the Gemini process was different from anything anyone else brought to the table. Its competitors responded to the trouble, too. Copies of critical articles happened to make their way into media mailings. No doubt, eyes were rolled at appropriate moments during drinks with potential clients whenever the Gemini name came up. Kindness doesn't play much of a role in such a competitive industry. But those problems were years away.

Gemini was secure in its position and firm in its philosophy when the contracts were signed with Cigna and Montgomery General. The cases provide a close look at exactly how consulting works, a state-of-the-art casebook on two very different companies that had essentially the same goal, leapfrogging into the modern era. But it also provides case studies on how consultants sell the fads they create, which in this case is transformation.

The Gemini contact left both institutions changed. They don't do business anymore the way they did business before Gemini came on the scene. It will take years to determine whether the investments were an unqualified success, and there are so many forces at work in both areas, it might well be impossible to apply a relevant measure to the process. To be sure, it also left some bitterness in its path that is a reminder that no one tinkers with the status quo without paying a price.

One measure of the Gemini contact at Cigna and at Montgomery County General is in the accolades the partisans offer in its wake. Both companies said they would not hesitate to invite Gemini, with its armies of eager consultants, its flip charts to die for, its complicated explanations, and its big price tags, back again. Neither would they hesitate to recommend Gemini to other companies looking for transformation.

It is apparent that in addition to accomplishing some big goals, the clients bonded with the consultants, which is a very important part of the Gemini plan. Gemini is proud of both cases, to the point at which the Cigna experience plays a central role in its business book, *Transforming the Organization*. Whatever trouble transformation left in its wake was outweighed by the upside.

All told, the small hospital spent nearly three quarters of a million dollars, and Cigna insiders estimate its Gemini consulting price tag at about $9 million to $10 million. What they got for that was a process that turned both places upside down and examined everything from the plumbing and mechanics of the businesses to their philosophies. It took some deep experience to get the contracts and carry them out, along with a consistency among the Gemini team that was crucial, particularly at Cigna.

A Golden Résumé

Consulting companies generally represent the sum total of the experience they hire. Gemini casts a wide net and collects everyone from the classic MBA grad to the field veteran whose background may be in psychology instead of business. At Gemini, Bob Frisch, instrumental in the Cigna contract, represented a golden consulting acquisition.

He has an advanced business degree from Yale and a few years at Boston Consulting Group, was head of strategy at a consumer products company, served a stint at Gemini, was head of strategy for Sears, Roebuck & Co., and then returned to Gemini, where he was a partner as the firm headed into the Cigna and hospital engagements. He is an expert on Gemini strategy and culture.

The company goes to some lengths to make certain all of its new consultants are advocating the transformation process and, more important, are working from the same page. "I don't know if it is just like religion," Frisch said, "but if I am the commandant of the Marine Corps and I have one platoon here and another platoon thirty miles away, I want to have some confidence that those units are functioning in a certain way, even though I don't have direct command and control. . . . A lot of it is personal relationships and personal coaching behind closed doors and the firm needs to have some sense that there is some consistency to what is being delivered. The way they do that is through culture."

There is a confidence about Frisch that is constructed on deep experience. This is why the best of the consultants are so interesting. He is not arrogant. When he tells a story about advising South African businesspeople on what they should do to enter the world marketplace, or about telling businesspeople in Scotland how they might cope with the declining taste for hard liquor, it makes one sit up and listen.

There is a sense that what he has to say has merit because he has been there, small company and big, strategy and operations. He has lived much of his professional life on the road or in the corridors of power of huge institutions. In the game of business, he is equipped to be the perfect coach, the role Gemini likes its strongest consultants to play the best. This is expertise well worth buying, the kind of background a corporation just doesn't find in-house. It is not surprising that when Cigna came to Gemini looking for big-dollar advice, Frisch was there with his quiet confidence, impressive stage presence, and comfortable brilliance to help ease the way. He is 44 years old, a man with one of the most sterling assets in management consulting: a high résumé value.

Most consultants at Gemini—indeed, most consultants anywhere—don't have that kind of depth. So the hiring process becomes critical. It is not unusual for a Gemini candidate to face six interviews before a hiring decision is made. The impression that is left along the way is very important. Gemini wants consultants who can form long-term relationships, inside the company and, perhaps more important, with clients. It is critical to be at the top of the list of people who get called when corporations run into problems.

Explaining the product is important, too. Consultants are never really far from the overwhelming need to find a simple way to show what they do. At Gemini, that means lots of very complicated graphics and charts. The thought is that, because these kinds of things are favored in business school, they make things more clear. But in the process of depicting all of this, unfortunately, everything sometimes becomes wildly complicated and confusing. It is not unusual for a pro to turn to a guest and say "Understand?" with all of the passion and excitement of one of those college professors one feels compelled to escape as soon as possible. Answer "No, not at all," and a further blizzard of colored lines and charts will emerge, along with high-speed explanations.

This behavior has its roots in business school education, where quantifying and measuring have become obsessions. To be sure, some of these renderings have a clarity and elegance that is stunning. They actually do explain everything quite understandably. And some of them evoke a less flattering assessment: This is what P. T. Barnum would have done had he graduated with a MBA from Harvard. From the smallest consulting house to the biggest, it is typical. At Gemini, it sometimes seems, there is a conclusion that warmer colors on the graphs, and maybe some scents, will help. It is all very New Age California, and quite strange given its New Jersey address.

The heart of what is happening at Gemini is contained in the 314 pages of *Transforming the Organization*, by Francis J. Gouillart, Gemini's senior vice president, and cochairman James Kelly.

Gemini's business philosophy has four components: reframing corporate direction, restructuring, revitalizing, and renewing people, referred to in Gemini shorthand as "the four R's." There is a simple way to describe all of this. It's a process. Gouillart and Kelly make up a high-energy team, with Gouillart's speed-of-light talk the perfect balance to Kelly's quietly intellectual presence.

The framework of the book is a comparison that examines the corporation the way a medical student would examine a body. Companies are living organisms, Gouillart and Kelly posit, and hence require holistic treatment. The holistic doctor looks for the inner powers he can marshal in battling illness and keeping the body in good health. Companies have these reserves of power, too, and reframing, restructuring, revitalizing, and renewing can tap them. It is a dazzlingly complicated metaphor from the very start. Human genomes have 23 sets of chromosomes. Corporations, the authors argue, have 12 corporate chromosomes that "represent the integrated software that governs bio-corporate life." It lists them: achieve mobilization, create the vision, build a measurement system, construct an economic model, align the physical infrastructure, redesign the work architecture, achieve market focus, invent new businesses, change the rules through information technology, create a reward structure, build individual learning, and develop the organization.

Just as with a human body, nothing seems to hold still in this metaphor. It creates the impression of a business as a wiggling, shuffling, flexing, growing, and shrinking thing, with all of its components at play all of the time. The Gemini argument is that evolution into the right thing at the right place at the right time might take millions of years, but that having identified the 12 central elements in business, a corporation can do a lot of changing with some creative gene splicing and transforming across the spectrum. It is a formula for getting from way over here to way over to there, through dozens and dozens of steps taking place all across the company. In the business, this philosophy is viewed as complex and overly elaborate. But readers of business books, which include the captains of industry and their many subordinates, love this kind of presentation precisely because of its complexity. There is nothing more empowering than believing you know a complicated secret. In the case of the Gemini text, the complexity adds a heavy layer of mystique to the process, a sense that anything can be achieved given the right formula. It also sends the message that this transformation business is too complicated to approach without help—preferably help from Gemini. To be sure, it might take 100 pages in the average consulting book to say "Cut costs; find more revenue." But the Gemini effort makes this an elegant journey full of economics, anecdotes about corporate leaders, and pages of devilishly complicated charts.

Individual Gemini pros (and their peers at other consulting houses) concede that life doesn't actually always work this way, that it still comes down to a consultant and the trust he or she has with a particular businessperson. But there are undeniable religious components to the philosophies of consulting houses, belief structures all the young consultants must buy into in their first weeks on the job. All religions need their bibles, and this book was the bible for both the Gemini consultant and the Gemini client.

It is a great piece of salesmanship, particularly when it is aimed at business school–trained executives eager to launch massive campaigns targeting growth and enhanced revenues. This is, after all, how businesspeople talk to one another, through complicated matrices and flip charts and MBA buzzwords. And in Philadelphia and in Montgomery County, Maryland, Gemini found two troubled institutions that were ready to talk and listen.

Something for Gemini, Too

More important for the fortunes of Gemini Consulting, these institutions were ready to buy, unleashing the Gemini process across two playing fields, one full of promise for a consulting company that wanted to find some way to crack the expanding world of change in health care, and the other the perfect testing platform for the elegant theory of business transformation in the face of a huge challenge.

What it created wasn't always pretty and certainly wasn't always comfortable, which may be the hidden message inside of the transformation process. Both of these efforts involved sweeping change and left their share of victims in their wakes, the displaced middle managers at Cigna, the nurses and staff and middle managers at Montgomery General who saw their jobs disappear. This comes as no surprise to anyone who has followed the business of consulting over the years. It is a goal-oriented process, and sometimes the goal is an immediate change aimed at making a client feel the investment was worthwhile.

Cutting costs is the quickest way to do that, however short-lived the benefits. And that usually translates into cutting employees. It created a good deal of confusion at Cigna. One whole army of employees was marching out the door even as a new army of different kinds of employees was marching in.

It is undeniable that transformation changed the faces of two institutions that felt they could no longer live with the old ways of doing business. The efforts at Cigna and Montgomery General remain works in progress, which handily fit into the Gemini philosophy that nothing is ever really over, that change has become a constant.

It is tempting to assess this as a formula that avoids any formal measure of what was actually accomplished. To counter that, Gemini has constructed elaborate systems of measurement against goals so that its consultants and its clients always have a concrete benchmark to apply against the swirling abstraction of change. It gives the client something to look at as the process is under way and the consultants a yardstick to assess their own performance.

In both the hospital and insurance company experiences, Gemini started out with something that is critical to all consultants, and probably even more critical to the companies that hire them: Both clients had a clear idea of what they wanted to achieve along with very high motivation to reach their goals. Neither of them felt they had much of an alternative, given the realities they faced. Change was coming whether they liked it or not, with all the force and speed of an Amtrak express. And both institutions felt they were much in danger of ending up under the very train they should have been riding.

When Marcia Cohen got her first close look at the situation at Montgomery General Hospital, she realized that the solution would have to involve a mixture of cost cutting and more revenue. "When we first started looking at it, it was probably the cost side that got more attention because that was the easiest to grasp. We started talking about reengineering and concluded we needed to do that, but we weren't quite sure what we were talking about. That is when we started talking to the firms."

Three consultants were called in during a full-day retreat for hospital managers: Andersen Consulting, Booz Allen, and Gemini. From the start, Monge recalled, no one seemed to like the Booz Allen offer. "We rejected it because they didn't make a very good proposal," Monge said. "Then we had Andersen and Gemini come in and we decided basically to throw it up to our managers. We told them, 'You guys are going to have to do a lot of this. Who are you more comfortable with?' We thought it was interesting that they picked Gemini overwhelmingly and we didn't think that they would. I didn't think they would be comfortable with the idea that it was going to be a much more open-ended process."

Cohen and Monge recalled the conversations. The other two consultants were offering variations on themes the hospital had already tried. The hospital didn't want to buy something off the shelf. "We had already been here three years and we had some managers who had been in work redesign workshops," Monge said. "I had set them up in groups of maybe eight to ten managers apiece and gave them specific overall ideas to look at. I met with them individually and we did some brainstorming. We put a few things together. Out of a hundred ideas, we came up with ten or twelve about how things could be done differently. But what we found was that nobody in a voluntary-type group felt very comfortable crossing over the boundaries of other people. That is why the earlier process was a success and a failure at the same time. And that was why we decided we needed to get a consultant to help us really push this process."

His managers told him they wanted something that was radically different. "Gemini made it clear that they didn't have a lot of health care experience, but what we were looking for is how to act more like a business. Health care has been great and we have been living in our isolated world, but we needed to act more like a business, and Gemini brought that perspective to the table," he said. The fact that Gemini didn't come in with a well-developed plan played to the consulting company's advantage. Monge and his team didn't want to buy into anything that had the feel of a "health care formula" to it, and the other two consultants basically presented plans that said: "This is the way we do it." Gemini, on the other hand, promised to come to the hospital, involve the entire staff, and then work to implement the changes everyone agreed upon.

All of the consulting companies bid roughly the same price, $750,000 for the project. That doesn't sound like much in the world of consulting, where $1,500-an-hour fees are not unheard of and where revenues have been climbing by the tens of millions of dollars for years. But for a little hospital in a distant Washington suburb, particularly for a little hospital that had worked hard for five years to finally show a profit of $700,000, it was a fortune. It wasn't a huge contract for Gemini, but it was very important because of its plans for entering the health care market. Monge had done his groundwork with the medical staff, but when the package went to the board of directors, there was support for the idea, but resistance to the cost.

"Here we are sitting at $700,000 over our operational profit budget and looking pretty good and we go in and say we think we have to tear this whole place apart. We need to spend all this money and we think we can save, maybe three million to seven million dollars, this huge range of numbers. The board was real nice about it but said they were really not ready for this yet. There was one board member who thought it was stupid and basically felt I needed to change my management team if we couldn't do this ourselves. In that month's period of time between the first presentation and the final presentation, I really agonized over the price tag. It was just a tremendous amount of money for this place, considering too that they had lost two million dollars in those three years before I came," said Monge.

The board didn't actually say it would fire everyone if the project failed. But the message was there nonetheless. "We talked about it. We said we were putting everything we had done for five years on the line. If it doesn't work, it is not just the loss of $750,000, but it would be the loss of credibility and the loss of all the chips we had built up over the years. To me, you might not get canned on day one," Monge said. "But we would have lost so much credibility that you might as well start looking for something else, because you just can't build it up again."

But all the risk wasn't on the hospital side.

Gemini wasn't kidding when it told the hospital it didn't have much experience in health care. True, it had worked with the big pharmaceuticals, but hospitals were different. Working out production schedules and market placement for drug companies was a completely different proposition. There were whole armies of consultants already at work in health care as hospitals wrestled with the changes in the marketplace, but Gemini, still relatively new to the world of U.S. consulting, had little presence. If you want to know what consulting companies are doing, follow the money. They latch themselves onto fat parts of the economy, because that is where the long-term revenues are. Gemini needed to get on board that health care express train, a sentiment Monge and his managers picked up early on in the transformation effort. It gave the client some leverage in the relationship and gave Gemini an added interest in making the plan work. This became clear when Gemini sent some raw consultants into the fray and found out Monge and his team had teeth.

"The . . . college kids didn't last. We had a couple of those and we said, 'Hey, they are not doing their work and they are not pulling their load and they have embarrassed us.' I'll tell you one thing they did after that," Monge said. "They brought in some really good people. I think they tried to start out with people who didn't have much experience in here. There were a couple of times when I went back to them and said, 'You guys die when I die. Because this is your first hospital and you will never work in this industry again. I am on the platform we always talk about, and you have got to realize this is not as easy a thing as you think it is.' "

Monge's description of what happened when he complained, though, seems characteristic of Gemini's consulting philosophy. It always moves as quickly as it can when a client is upset and will not tolerate personnel problems on-site. This is so important that Gemini has fleets of troubleshooters, generally strong consultants with heavy experience, who can sweep in and retake control of a project should trouble arise.

The problems at Montgomery General were solved early on, leaving the hospital, its staff, and its management to the larger task of determining just what the hospital would become, and just how it would get to that point. Because Gemini had worked well before in industrial and business settings on questions just like those, it unleashed its business process on a hospital that wanted to view itself more as a money-making enterprise than as a charity. There is a formula for that at Gemini, and William Wallace, chief operating officer at Gemini at the time, knows it as well as he knows the fields that surround Gemini's American headquarters in Morristown, New Jersey.

It boils down to this, according to Wallace: Gemini crams three months of design and analysis work into one month, with a set of clearly defined goals in mind, say a $100 million target that involves half in increased revenues and half in reduced expenses. The client is wrapped right into this process, adding its own team members to the groups set up to investigate ways of pulling in more money or cutting costs. What comes out of this is a collection of hypotheses that will be used to draft a plan to carry to management. At huge companies, this level of effort might involve 1,000 employees and ultimately reach out to thousands upon thousands more as the consultants and clients search for the information they need to construct their plans.

The scale was much smaller at Montgomery General, but the theme was the same.

Costly and Complex

It is a complicated business, Wallace conceded. "We got the rap in the popular press that we are expensive and complex, and our answer is, well, yes. Change is not simple and to enable a big organization . . . to change is not cheap. You don't do it all at once. You do a piece of it at a time," he said. Scaled way down, that was an important message at Montgomery County General. But even taking matters a step at a time caused problems. If there are no secrets in big companies, there are really no secrets in small institutions. Despite Gemini's efforts to include as many people as possible in the process, Monge found himself spending more and more time in meetings as the transformation process developed, explaining why the hospital had to change. The anxiety level seemed to climb, particularly around the issue of cutting staff.

"We were perpetually calling additional meetings to try to go over this stuff and to try to get the medical staff to understand what we were doing. And even when we did that kind of thing, this kind of stuff still happened," he said, fresh from a meeting in which he had just heard two of his strongest physicians tell him he was crazy for cutting back operating room staff. "It was probably the first time I ever yelled at a physician," Monge said.

After months of team study and consulting days on which Gemini's small staff stayed at the hospital sometimes until 2 A.M., the plan emerged. Montgomery General would no longer be all things to all people. But it would be a lot of things to a very important group of people, those who are in what the hospital manager called "the fifty-plus market." More than half of the hospital's business was focused on that group, anyway, and because it is a well-insured group, both privately and, once Medicare age is reached, federally, it seemed the natural market to tap. There were some assumptions at work, Cohen said. The Gemini process helped identify the fact that all hospitals look pretty much alike and, just as with businesses looking to expand into new markets, Montgomery General had to find a new source of income to tap.

"We figured out that if we did a pretty good job with the over-fifty group, not only would we increase the amount of business we got from that segment, but if we took good care of Mom and Dad for the kids who live in Texas, the word would get around that we are good at everything that we do. You can't do a good job with the grandparents and not do a good job for the children. But to do that we really needed to look at how we could serve that fifty-plus segment across the whole continuum of care instead of just the inpatient part of care. It would be more than medical care. It would be taking them to the movies. It would be social services. It would be everything. And that is where we are right now," said Cohen.

In the process of "shaking the building" and redesigning jobs, Monge said, five of the hospital's 40 managers lost their positions and a few more may go before it is completed. "I am guessing probably 45 people will be gone out of a complement of 750. It is not enough based on what needs to happen here, but we are moving on and doing other things without Gemini's help. There will be other people who fall out of it as time passes." The process has left some hard feelings, both managers agreed. But it also changed the way the remaining staff members view their work.

By the time the Gemini teams were ready to leave, Monge said, Montgomery General was "in sort of a quiet uproar. Because everyone has recognized what will be coming in health care, they know why we have to do this. So the board is okay. But if the doctors get real upset about this and think we are doing this really stupidly, then I will find out how supportive the board really is. We aren't stupid. We know that some of this has to be taken slowly and we need to work around some things. We are not dumb enough to just walk in there and just start chopping when it isn't going to work."

What Monge and his staff ended up with was a new mission, a slimmed-down staff, and a method learned at the hands of the Gemini consultants for taking an organization apart and putting it back together again: transformation. Gemini got something, too: an object lesson in exactly how a small hospital works and where the buttons can be pushed to make it more profitable and more efficient. This is one of the unrecognized processes that is always under way in consulting engagements. The smart companies walk away not only with fat checks, but with something that is much more valuable over the long run, experience in a particular industry, something to carry to the next tier of clients in making the argument for pricey transformation efforts. Sometimes, they create patented processes they sell to other clients, sharing a bit of the take over time with the initial contractor. Generally, industries like health care tend to accumulate the same kinds of managers who will respond to the same kinds of messages. If the Montgomery County General Hospital experience continues to play out well, Gemini will have an important casebook to review with its future clients. It will most certainly become a video presentation for potential health care clients.

And there is no doubt that Gemini does, indeed, plan to have future health care clients. There is simply too much money afloat in health care and too many opportunities to let this industry pass to the Andersens and A. T. Kearneys and Booz Allens. Beyond that, health care could be one of the gems that helps Gemini wrestle with its revenue problems. The company has recognized that it must do something to expand its service offerings because everyone doesn't want to go the whole high-priced business transformation route. That might mean more $50,000 product assembly line reconstructions, more specific problem solving, and a lot more $750,000 hospital transformations. It has taken some important steps to make that happen.

Even as Monge and his staff were discussing their Gemini experience, Kee-Hian Tan, Gemini's senior vice president and global health care practice leader, was having breakfast in a Morristown hotel with Gennaro J. Vasile, at that moment the executive vice president and chief operating officer of Johns Hopkins in Baltimore. Kee-Hian Tan is a brilliant talker and thinker who decided a few years ago, after consulting with some pharmaceutical companies, that health care would be his specialty. He views this area as a bonanza for wise consulting companies because of the pace of change and its potential for growth. Ultimately, that is why the Montgomery County experience is important. There are thousands upon thousands of small not-for-profit hospitals all over the nation, and they all face the same problems that confronted Monge and his staff. In a way, the more confusing the national picture becomes in the business of health care, the better the situation becomes for consultants. All of those small institutions will be desperate for some guidance in the face of changes that could well drive them out of business. Kee-Hian Tan and Gemini are eager to tap that marketplace.

It is a good morning for Gemini and its senior vice president, because he will be announcing later in the day that Vasile has decided to leave Johns Hopkins and join Gemini as its North American leader for the global health care practice. For a consulting company that puts such a heavy value on experience, he is another prime acquisition. Vasile is the health care equivalent of strategy-master Frisch. He has some 25 years of experience in hospital management. He cut costs at Johns Hopkins by $30 million in two years and increased its revenues by $35 million. Before Johns Hopkins, he ran United Health Services, a regional health care system in New York State, and saw its revenues grow from $70 million to $250 million over nine years. And he ran a small hospital before that. He has a doctorate in health services management and an MBA in hospital administration.

Gemini is hoping health care responds to its sophisticated offerings as eagerly as the general business world did a few years ago when Gemini was brand new and all the numbers were heading for the sky. The probable argument will be that health care institutions that don't change quickly and completely will be crushed as the industry mutates under strong economic and political forces. This is a common theme in the world of consulting, where the change argument, driven by business school books that urge a virtual rejection of all that has come before, has been an important tool in getting contracts.

It is easy to get lost in the brave new world rhetoric that surrounds this theme of change, but it is important before leaving the site of Gemini's engagement at Montgomery General to ponder a few questions about what actually happened there and what it might mean. Undoubtedly, the small hospital will become more profitable as it squeezes costs out of its systems and pulls in new business. But is profitability really the most legitimate measure of a hospital's performance? It is easy to spout the shareholder value argument as a measure of success when the client is a publicly held corporation. But, to twist an old Chicago cliché, medicine ain't retailing.

What about intangibles like community support or the loyalty of a long-standing staff of doctors and nurses? No matter how much doctors resist the imposition of outside decision making, accepted financial wisdom seems to dictate that insurance companies know best when it comes to determining what a procedure should cost or how much time it should take. But what if managed care turns out to be this decade's passing fancy? What happens if, in the process of slashing costs, it also slashes expertise? What if targeting the senior citizen market turns out to be a strategic mistake because of political changes that cut the amount of funding available for elderly Americans? How many nurses can a small hospital afford to lose without damaging its reputation for quality care? It is clear that Montgomery General wants to trade its comfortable old status as traditional hospital for the glitter it will take on as a profitable business. But what happens if it becomes an unprofitable business? What if the anxiety over staff cutbacks fuels a drive for unionization among the remaining nursing staff, now stripped of the illusion of paternalism? What if the hospital's big, successful competitors decide they, too, want to be the point of service for an aging population? Then how will this business compete? Can a hospital hold a going-out-of-business sale?

These kinds of questions stretch far beyond the capacity of a Gemini, or of any other consulting company for that matter, to interpret and analyze. It is clear at this point that the hospital, with Gemini's help, is on the way to becoming what it thinks it wants to become. Over the longer term it will become clear whether transformation was a good decision, or just the implementation of a fad that was hot at the moment. All of the decision makers on both sides of the contract seem to be happy with the process.

A Giant Transformation Project

Travel a few hundred miles away and look at transformation on a huge scale. The message in Philadelphia is that life and business are full of uncertainty, which is a central component in the other Gemini story, the one playing out up in the clouds that surround the Cigna buildings.

This is the kind of situation that Gemini's figures and projections seem to fit. Assume you are a consulting company moving into Cigna Property & Casualty and aiming at cutting $50 million in costs and increasing revenues by the same amount, for a $100 million target. Where do you go in these 55 shiny stories to do that? For Gemini, the path led straight to Tom Valerio's office on the fifty-third floor. More than anyone else, he was instrumental in bringing Gemini into Cigna. It was a decision he made, he said, because he knew its product and its people very well. He had one worry early on, that Gerry Isom should know that Valerio himself was a product of the Gemini experience. Would that be a conflict of interest?

This is not a small question. Consultants are moving into and out of corporate positions all of the time. Would it be a conflict of interest, or would it just be a smart business decision because it involved built-in trust up front and deep knowledge of the process? Isom had no problem with Valerio's Gemini connection. And Valerio knew exactly why he wanted Gemini on board.

Isom didn't want to bring in one of the classic strategy teams—McKinsey, for example—because he didn't think it would be a good fit. He didn't want an accounting-type firm because he thought they were mostly focused on technology. The small boutique consultants didn't have the capacity or the capabilities for the size effort Isom wanted. Valerio whittled down the list of possibilities. Symmetrix had been on board at Cigna for a long time, he said, but the company wasn't very happy with its work. Gemini seemed to have the scope and the staff to handle Cigna Property & Casualty's call for a full-scale change.

"In the initial conversations I had with Gerry, he said what I needed to do was get the home office support functions translated. I needed to get human resources, systems, finance, and claims in better line," Valerio said. ". . . The analogy I remember using is this: It is the bottom of the ninth, there are two outs and two strikes and they give you the bat. You get one swing at this. So as opposed to saying, 'Let's scale it down,' we say, let's take the first phase of this and try to turn every stone and look in every closet so in January 1994, when you start implementation, you are really clear. It will confirm things you know and tell you things you don't know, but at least this way we won't have a false start."

In the last quarter of 1993, Gemini sent in its analysis and design teams and the process was under way. "The joke is that I probably killed a few consultants on that analysis there," Valerio said. "We did everything, from shareholder value, high-level executive-type things from a financial perspective down to looking at processes in the collection facility out in Indiana. It was as extensive as we could make it." It amounted to the dismantling of a company that had deep, deep roots in the American insurance industry.

Cigna was born when Connecticut General and INA merged in 1982, and both of those companies brought impressive histories to the partnership. INA had been selling insurance since 1794. It was not only the first insurance company to sell fire coverage outside of city limits, but the first to insure the contents of homes against fire. It was the first company to appoint independent agents (1808) and started its international expansion late in the nineteenth century. It provided accident and health insurance for the U.S. Army contingent of 30 men working on the Manhattan Project in 1942. It introduced the first broad-coverage homeowners policy in 1950 and bought the largest prepaid health care provider in the nation, HMO International, in 1978. Connecticut General was a company of firsts, too, initiating health insurance in 1912, group insurance in 1913, and writing the first accident coverage for airline passengers in 1926. It was the industry leader in developing group medical and surgical insurance and offered the first general group medical insurance in 1952.

How the Property & Casualty subsidiary got into such trouble could be a business school study in itself, but the very short version would involve that mix of money and unforeseen events that is so important to insurance company fortunes. Consider two developments that showed up on the balance sheets at the beginning of 1994. The Los Angeles earthquake led to a catastrophe loss of $97 million. Severe winter weather cost the company another $35 million. Undoubtedly, when it was aggressively pursuing commercial insurance contracts many years ago, no one anticipated the role that asbestos and environmental problems would be playing on the insurance scene. Asbestos has become a nightmare. Although health officials have been warning about its dangers since the beginning of the century, the insurance industry did not realize it would land as a liability on its doorstep until the arrival of the environmental era that began in the 1960s. Before the problem ends, there could be as many as 200,000 claims all over the world representing billions upon billions of dollars in costs for insurance companies. At the end of March 1995, 1,175 Cigna policyholders had outstanding asbestos-related claims with the company, and Cigna was in court on 31 of them. On the same date, it had some 15,500 environmental pollution files outstanding and was disputing all of them. It was also in court battling 454 pollution coverage lawsuits. No one knows where all of this might lead.

"Standard actuarial methods" that are used to measure liabilities don't work in environmental and asbestos matters because there isn't enough case law or enough experience to apply a proper measure. And the court battles are of such a nature that their outcome could determine whether insurance companies carry any liability in these matters at all. If the courts rule against the insurers, the liability price tag could be huge. In the interim, Cigna, which suffers more exposure in these cases because of its role in selling commercial insurance, can't say much at all about its liabilities for the long term. That put an even greater emphasis on the parts of the company that it could control, its structure, and the business targets it wanted to achieve as it was rebuilding itself. While Isom and his team tackled the issue of long-term liabilities (and ultimately decided to isolate the risks in another Cigna subsidiary), Valerio and the Gemini consultants struggled to clear the way toward Isom's goal, which was to put Cigna Property & Casualty in the upper quadrant of speciality insurance companies, a great distance from where it was. To get the process under way, they turned to a consulting tool that is central to Gemini's transformation process, something called a balanced scorecard. The scorecard concept was invented by Renaissance Strategy Group in Lincoln, Massachusetts, and Robert Kaplan of Harvard Business School. The assumption behind the idea is that a company's health can be accurately assessed and problems can be traced to their sources if the scorecard is carefully constructed. It is not so much a strategy tool as a tool aimed at carrying out a strategy that has already been decided.

Isom knew what he wanted to do and he also knew Cigna Property & Casualty was already riddled with many different types of ineffective measurement tools. But the scorecard approach was appealing because of its simplicity. It boils everything down into a couple of handy phrases that describe where a company is and what problems it must attack. Isom assigned his executive council and Gemini advisors and their Renaissance Strategy subcontractors to draft the scorecard. It was a fairly involved process at Cigna that took three months to complete. Some of the issues didn't boil down so easily. There were battles. It probably came as a great surprise to many Cigna insiders that there was confusion about who the actual customer was: the person or interest actually buying insurance, or the independent insurance agent offering the Cigna product.

Isom's council concluded that four main areas needed to be addressed: Finance. Customers. Process. Learning and Innovation. The financial component was obviously first on the list because Cigna Property & Casualty was hemorrhaging so much money, it was upsetting the balance sheet of its parent company. "The combined ratio" was in second place. The combined ratio is an important number in insurance. It adds up all of a company's insurance costs, including underwriting losses and expenses, then divides them by the amount of premiums that come in. Cigna wanted to lower that number. Reducing losses and reducing expenses were then attached as part of the combined ratio effort.

That made up one layer of the scorecard. The executive council decided that improving policyholder satisfaction and improving producer satisfaction were two important components of customer service, with reduction of policyholder losses being a third. In operations, the executive council decided it wanted to reduce loss frequency, reduce the severity of loss, reduce the amount of time it took to handle claims, and improve the "quote-to-sell" ratio, which means doing more business. Learning and innovation, the vaguest of the categories, turned out to be very important because that was the area in which new business could be created.

Exactly how much of the $10 million consulting price tag covered this process is impossible to determine. In the abstract and from the outside, it looks like a huge highlight on a lot of subjects that should have been quite obvious inside of Cigna Property & Casualty. But then, that was one of the company's problems, its inability to accomplish the obvious. The scorecard might seem like little more than another one of those academic exercises applied to the business world, but in this case it became a crucial component of Gemini's transformation effort. Isom decided to build the whole campaign around it. It was important to Gemini, too. Valerio explained from his perspective as a former Gemini consultant and Cigna's transformation officer that the contract represented one-stop shopping, a very important asset in a consulting company's sales pitch. Isom had the strategy in his head already. He didn't need to lunch with a McKinsey consultant to figure it out. Gemini came in and, with Renaissance, constructed the scorecard that would be used to carry it out.

"What I was looking to gain was how do we clarify what it means to be a specialist insurance company and then what do we do to get from here to there," Valerio said. "The way I looked at it, we are here, with a generalist company, poor financial results, bad relations with customers, bad relations with producers whose morale is low, and a lot of money being spent on maintenance of technology. What we now have is a goal that says I want to be a specialist, top quartile, top 25 percent, 15 percent return on equity, great relations with producers and customers. It is exactly the opposite of where we were. You have to figure out what to do first, and the scorecard helped us figure that out."

Merging Ideas

But there was another component of the Gemini process. From the analysis and design period at the beginning through the drafting of the scorecard, Valerio said, what really happened was that the views of the hierarchy of the company and the views of the people who actually do the day-to-day work were merging. It was reconciling those two views, Valerio said, that led to the conclusion there were six initiatives on which Cigna Property & Casualty should focus. From January until December 1994, that was what Cigna did attack, the issues in these six areas, which included producer management, underwriting, claims, two support alignment processes, and information technology.

Did it work? That depends on how the effort is measured. Because of its decision to shift the heavy liabilities in asbestos and environmental cases to Brandywine Insurance, a new subsidiary, Cigna Property & Casualty looks healthier. It shifted enough of its reserves into this new company to cover virtually all potential liabilities. This was accomplished to the chagrin of Cigna's many competitors, a few of which charged the company was setting up a subsidiary that ultimately will end up in the hands of the Pennsylvania Insurance Department, a claim Cigna strongly contests.

What the process clearly managed was a cut in the operating costs of the Property & Casualty division, along with a whole collection of economic and technological changes that should ultimately make the selling of insurance at Cigna a sleeker and more profitable enterprise. Midway through 1995, for example, Isom was able to report that he had turned red ink into black to the tune of about $25 million. That all-important combined ratio number dropped from the mid-130s before transformation to 114. There is a computer program now that walks Cigna's employees through the underwriting process and helps them make better decisions about who they will insure. There is a whole spectrum of services aimed at those independent producers, which could eventually convince them that Cigna Property & Casualty's products are more valuable than the products of its many competitors.

"We're not done yet. We have made a lot of progress, but there is no one answer. I know everyone talks about the problem of changing culture. I think that we have tried to do more than that. It takes years to establish a culture," says Valerio. "What I have always talked about is just changing the way people behave. If you can change the behavior, I think you then start to change the way people view certain things, and you do that gradually. . . . Eventually, I hope there are enough people on the top over on the other side [at the parent company] that say, you know, this is really the place to be."

Pat Jodry's behavior was certainly changed by the experience. Her role in Gemini's engagement at Cigna shines a bright light on the up-side and downside of consulting experiences. She recalls a point at the beginning of the Gemini engagement where, because of confusion about schedules, it was just Jodry and 40 consultants in a room, all eager to start running. It was the beginning of the analysis and design process, with all that work crammed into a short period of time. She rose to it and remains enthused about the feeling. "I called them The Gemini," she said, explaining that the process felt like something straight from *Star Trek*. "I hadn't worked with consultants before and here were a whole bunch of people. A lot of them were just recently out of school so they had all of these ideas and totally different ways of approaching things. It was a technique I had never heard of before, full of tremendous, tremendous energy. They think nothing of getting in at six A.M. and working until ten P.M. I thought, 'Well, this is really great.' "

She was well aware of Cigna's stodginess and old-fashioned way of doing things. She had been branch manager at Cigna's Atlanta special-risk office for five and a half years and was one of ten Cigna members of the analysis and design team. She kept her job in Atlanta and commuted to Philadelphia, going home on the weekends to keep tabs on the local office. Because she had been with Cigna since 1977, she had an encyclopedic knowledge of the place that the young consultants were eager to tap. They wanted to conduct hundreds of interviews with Cigna producers and employees and they didn't want to send Cigna officials to ask the questions, fearing the workers would clam up.

"The Gemini came in and all those things that we had been talking about forever, issues that every one of us knew about, they were hearing and elevating to the senior managers," she said. The fact that the word was being carried by consultants added a layer of credibility that Cigna's own employees couldn't have. Managers who had long since labeled suggestions as "complaints" and had written them off as office griping were forced to listen as the Gemini teams delivered the results of their surveys.

The other crucial component the Gemini teams brought to the process, she said, was experience. There was a tendency inside Cigna to view all problems as unique to the company. But the consultants were able to show the Cigna team members that virtually everything they were concerned about had happened elsewhere, and that tested solutions had already been applied to the problems. "Then the shock set in [as well as] the real disappointment."

It is not a difficult problem to understand. Here is a manager invited to take part in one of the most intellectually stimulating experiences of her life. She bonds with dozens of The Gemini and becomes a part of the *Star Trek* crew. She works hard on the process and becomes invested in its outcome. She concludes that about the most important element of the plan the analysis and design team presents will involve vision, called "leadership and governance."

Gemini takes the package to Cigna management and the one part it doesn't want to buy is "leadership and governance," which touches on everything the A&D team constructed. "Because of that, every one of the streams was missing a critical component and the disappointment was that we had hoped, when we saw this, that [The Gemini] would go back to them and say . . . let us put the components back in there. But of course, that is not what happened. The leadership and governance piece went by the wayside. To be honest with you, that is the difference in a successful transformation, the leadership piece. And so, the transformation has been hampered ever since. It was a disappointment for all of us for a couple of reasons, one because of the confidence built up, the rapport, with The Gemini. . . . You start talking like them. You start approaching the world the way they do. You start looking at things the way they do. Instead of being Cigna people bonding with each other, the Cigna people bonded with The Gemini, so it was a tremendous disappointment."

She described this as a feeling of "betrayal," fully recognizing that no matter how the process felt, any consulting company owes its loyalty to the people writing the checks, not to employees who sweat blood trying to achieve a goal. "I know that Gemini is capable of pulling off transformation. I know they can mobilize an organization. But I know that is a collaborative effort and I know there are some things that need to happen that are very, very painful, and the pain isn't always at the bottom of the organization."

None of that has soured her on Gemini or its process. "I think all consultants are probably the same," she said. "If somebody asked me for a reference . . . some of the people from the Massachusetts Institute of Technology I would recommend. And Gemini is one of the ones I think highly of. To me, it was a failing of both sides. It is just that in our case, the ten people on the team, we all have some of the same issues now.

That was part of what happened . . . it was the bonding. We all felt let down."

There were similar problems at other levels. Despite the many bumps, Cigna's Gemini partners said the transformation process was crucial. Even given those problems, said Paul Harvey, Cigna P&C's vice president for marketing, the company would be "dead in the water" without Gemini's help. "We still have a long way to go and a lot more probably could have been accomplished in a tighter time frame if we would have acted with more urgency and immediacy in making decisions and sticking to them, and just going for it. There is a lot of building consensus in this environment. There is nothing wrong with that. It just takes a hell of a lot of time and energy. And as you are doing that, every quarter the stock analysts are saying, 'Why is your expense ratio still at 38 percent?' Do you tell them it's because you are having a meeting of the minds here? The boys on the street don't care about that. These guys are sharp, astute people. They know that is the same answer you gave last year," Harvey said.

Which is why there is so much tension and fog up on top of the Cigna complex high above the streets of Philadelphia. Gemini obviously views its effort there as a great success because it helped accomplish the initial change in direction Cigna Property & Casualty had to make. But the people at Cigna are using a different measure, one that will play out over the next few years.

Measuring Success

This is a quandary that sits at the heart of many a consulting engagement. How does anyone measure success when there are so many variables at work? Return on investment might seem an adequate measure, but using that kind of short-term assessment might lead to the wrong conclusion. It is entirely possible that a company can be successfully transformed and still fail because of larger pressures in the marketplace that even the sharpest of consultants simply cannot anticipate.

From Gemini's perspective, the Cigna challenge was huge, but it walked away satisfied that Cigna's bosses recognized that a process that might have taken five or six years had been thought out, constructed, greased, and put into place in a much shorter period of time. That is basically what Gemini and its transformation program are all about. To be sure, it was not pretty, but those kinds of aesthetic descriptions are discarded early in the game when a company is focusing on survival. Isom cut the experience to its essence in a conversation with Gemini's Peter Migliorato: "Today we can write business profitably. Our producers are beginning to see the change and have confidence in Cigna again," he said.

As for the trouble along the way, Gemini sees all of that as part of the process. When a consultant tries to engage everyone from the generals to the soldiers in the field in any kind of an effort, let alone a huge transformation, all kinds of problems and political difficulties emerge. In that sense, Jodry's feeling of betrayal is all just part of the pain of change. She was clearly transformed by the experience, too, and is a different kind of Cigna employee today than she was when she was running the Atlanta office. Harvey's sense that everything moved too slowly was another of the realities of trying to transform such a huge institution. He was one of the people Isom brought in to help restructure the place, and it is no surprise that he is eager to do his job. Had the process been simple or painless, there is doubt that Cigna would have needed $10 million in consulting services to help manage it.

But the Gemini experience at the two institutions must carry a cautionary note, one expressed by managers who worked closely with consultants in both cases. The most important element of a consulting engagement is knowing the reason why consultants are being brought into the formula.

Gemini's leaders say the company is selective in accepting contracts and shies away from engagements in which muddled managers are searching wildly for anything that will improve the balance sheet. That may be so, but another truth is that consulting companies will go wherever they are paid to go and attack whatever problem they are assigned to attack. There may be a nobility of purpose to their complicated philosophies, but there is a practicality at work that sometimes offsets that: Consulting, after all, is a business, not a philosophy.

Valerio has his own set of measures of success. "How will we know if we are there? A couple of easy ways," he said. "Of the eighteen to twenty business units, how many are in the top quartile? And of those in the top quartile, how many have financial returns of about 15 percent? . . . In terms of the project, what we were looking for was some-body to help us accelerate getting the foundation in place. What we were looking for was someone to come in here and figure out what the right solutions were and implement them as fast as possible."

He offered an important caveat about hiring consultants. "To the extent that you are not clear about the outcomes you are looking for, you could end up buying services you don't need, solving problems that are major problems, but that don't necessarily advance you to where you want to go. That is the critical part, and the most critical fault people have in spending money on consultants now. I know there are problems to be fixed, but I don't know if the companies that are spending the dollars on consulting are really clear about the outcomes they are looking for," he said.

Gemini was coming out of the Cigna and Montgomery Hospital engagements just as bad news was starting to spread through the company. By the end of 1995, it was facing its own significant challenges. Its chief executive, Daniel J. Valentino, stepped down and was replaced by Pierre Hessler, a vice president at the French parent company and a world veteran of management consulting. It was continuing an aggressive collection of purchases and partnerships aimed at expanding its offerings around the world.

Hessler believes Gemini's collection of skills and transformation efforts separate it from its many competitors. His challenge, he said, would be to mix the cultures of the French parent company, strong in information technology, with the business strategies and implementation strengths of Gemini. It won't be easy. Think of two rooms, one full of technicians who know all about technology and what it can accomplish, and another full of business strategists who are given to blue-sky thinking and close personal relationships. If figuring out how to mix consultants and accountants was the great mystery of the last genera-tion of consulting experience (some of the big companies concluded it just couldn't happen), then mixing information technology and strategy is the great task of the future. CJS and Gemini will do that, Hessler said, not by melding everything together into a tension-filled mess, but by keeping the companies separate until their specific skills are called into play for specific clients. He said he has already seen this process work on a limited basis and believes it can be carefully expanded, as long as it is well orchestrated at the top.

For a consulting company, Gemini has a high learning curve. Its own experience in the marketplace over the past two years has led it to adapt its business transformation proposals, said North American vice president Harry Moser. Potential clients found the prospects of huge transformations intimidating. There was an all-or-nothing component to it that scared some of them away, he said.

Gemini still believes that its holistic approach toward consulting is the only way to go. But these days, it tells its potential clients that they don't have to unleash the entire process at once. It wants them to view transformation as a faucet that can be turned on a little or turned on a lot, depending on the need and depending on how well it works for the client. Moser said it is an adaptation that has worked well in Europe, where Gemini is strong. How well the adaptation works in America could determine whether Gemini finds itself just another huge consulting company struggling to win contracts in a marketplace full of competitors, or on the cutting edge of consulting, where the amalgam of strategy and information technology revives the growth that made it such a strong candidate in its early years.

Too Close for Comfort

INSIDE THE SECRET, INFLUENTIAL
WORLD OF BAIN & CO.

Gemini is an open-door consulting company. But it is hard to get into the front door of Bain, the consulting industry's most secretive firm. One reason is Bain's inclination to develop cozy ties to clients and guard their secrets zealously. But a whiff of scandal also lingers in the Boston halls of Bain, the small but influential company run by the industry's only female chairperson. It shuns publicity as aggressively as a spymeister.

It was late, just before the dinner hour. London was cool and damp as only it can be on a late winter day. Olivier Roux slipped almost unnoticed into the lobby of Heron House, home to Heron Corporation on Marylebone Road just south of Queen Mary's Gardens and Regents Park. A slender, young Frenchman with dark, piercing eyes, Roux moved easily through London's business circles, where a man's suit and tie speak to more than the quality of his tailor. An elevator whisked Roux to the top floor of the building, and he soon stood in the wood-paneled offices of Gerald Ronson, Heron's chairman and one of Britain's most influential and wealthy industrialists. Roux didn't have to tell Ronson why he was there. Anthony Parnes, a maverick broker known around the Stock Exchange as "the animal," already had taken care of that. Parnes was there, too. Roux got right down to business.

Guinness P.L.C., the brewery company famous for its black Irish stout, had launched the largest hostile takeover in British history—a bruising struggle with a supermarket chain over who would get to pay more than $3.8 billion to acquire Distillers, Scotland's leading industrial group and a spirits company that made whiskeys like Johnnie Walker scotch; Gordon's and Booth gin; and sixty other brands with household names. The power struggle reeked with political implications: A British company with strong ties to Ireland wanted to outbid a company headed by a Scotsman for control of the United Kingdom's leading distiller. Guinness's stock price was crucial to its offer, and Ronson had played a key role in support of the bid. Guinness had recruited the industrialist and other well-heeled investors to buy huge chunks of its stock on the open market so the price wouldn't slip and jeopardize its chance to win. Midway through the battle, though, Ronson suddenly stopped buying Guinness shares. He'd already told Parnes to acquire about $15 million worth of the brewer's stock. Now he wanted to know why he should continue. In other words, he wanted to know what was in it for him. Guinness responded quickly and promised Ronson a win-win deal. Roux went to Heron's office to go over the details.

In less genteel circles, the proposition that Roux made to Ronson on that frosty evening might be called something more plebeian, like a "payoff." Guinness, the Frenchman said, would pay Ronson up to 5 million pounds (or $7 to $8 million depending on the exchange rate) plus cover any losses if he would continue to buy up to 25 million pounds (or about $40 million) worth of Guinness stock. Roux didn't describe his proposition in such crude terms. This was no ward office in Chicago or the New York wharf It was London, where gentlemen really act like gentlemen, and Ronson was no Camden market hawker. A self-made millionaire and Margaret Thatcher's favorite industrialist, Ronson cut an imposing figure in "the City," the shorthand for London's financial district. London's power structure flocked to the Savoy for Ronson lunches; he rubbed shoulders with the rich and powerful, owned the largest private company in Britain, and bore the scars of corporate warfare. One simply didn't talk of "payoffs" in such proper company. Instead, Roux called the 5 million pounds "a success fee" that the square-jawed tycoon would get when the fight was over. In other words, Ronson would get a 5-million-pound reward for buying the stock if Guinness won the fight for Distillers. Ronson listened to the details in silence. The whole meeting lasted about an hour. Ronson then instructed Parnes to resume acquiring Guinness stock, and Roux walked out the door, another job well done for Guinness.

It's easy to see how almost anyone on the London stock market in those heady days of the 1980s would assume that the young Frenchman who visited Heron's offices on that wintry day in 1986 worked for Guinness. The giant brewer not only trusted Roux with sensitive assignments, it used him to brief the press on Guinness and its resources. Roux eventually served as director of financial strategy and development at Guinness, sat on the brewer's board of directors, and possessed the only other office on the fourth floor of Guinness's headquarters besides Ernest Saunders, the company's chairman. His word was as good as Guinness, too. Guinness won the fight for Distillers, and Ronson eventually got his 5-million-pound reward. But Roux never really worked for the giant brewer. Olivier Raymond Guy Roux was a management consultant, and he worked for the consulting firm that was advising Guinness, Bain & Co. of Boston, one of the most influential and respected management consulting companies in the world.

Roux would go on to become a notorious figure in Guinness's history. He would help launder illegal payments to respected British wheeler-dealers such as Ronson. After receiving assurances that government prosecutors had no plans to nail him, Roux became the government's key witness against his former colleagues in a scandal that would rock London's financial markets. Years later, Ronson, Parnes, Ernest Saunders, the onetime chairman of Guinness, and a few others would end up in jail largely because of Roux's testimony. But the story of his role in the Guinness scandal is a lot more than a tale about behind-the-scenes chicanery on London's financial markets. It also represents a crucial strain in the story of Bain & Co., the secretive consulting firm whose name is synonymous with cozy ties to clients.

Today Bain & Co. executives oversee a force of more than 1,000 consultants from their pricey offices in Boston's Copley Plaza. In many respects, Bain is not the same company as the one that employed Roux. Most of the people in power during the Guinness scandal are long gone, including William Bain, the founder of the firm. Olivier Roux resigned in 1987, a month after he quit working on the Guinness account, a couple of years before he testified against his former colleagues, and after Bain paid him more than $900,000 on his way out of the door. Orit Gadiesh, a flamboyant Israeli woman whose flashy jewelry cuts quite a figure in the button-down world of management consultants, took William Bain's place. Her elevation to the chairman's job makes Bain one of the few big management consulting firms headed by a woman. The company currently has more than 500 clients in 60 nations, generating an estimated $300 million in revenue, which is about double the firm's billings in Roux's day. And although Bain is overshadowed by bigger strategy consultants such as McKinsey & Co., it ranks right up there in terms of influence in corporate boardrooms. Current or past clients include Chrysler Corp., Baxter International, Monsanto, Dun & Bradstreet, Microsoft, Digital Equipment Corp., and many others.

But for all of its differences with days past, Bain & Co., in many respects, still resembles the company that got ensnarled in the Guinness controversy. It is less secretive than it was in Roux's day, but it remains the most secretive major American consultant. It also continues to covet the close relationships with its clients that led to trouble at Guinness. Even today Bain boasts that it is a practical "hands-on" management consulting company that goes beyond making recommendations; it stays around to implement them. It remains privy to insider knowledge and company secrets. Bain gets financially involved with its clients through its venture capital arm, Bain Capital, which has offices right across the hall from the consulting company. And it can get so intricately involved with clients that some suggest slapping limits on its consultants. "I probably have more cumulative experience in dealing with Bain than 98 percent of the people they deal with," says James Tobin, who worked with Bain consultants on 19 separate projects when he was an executive vice president and chief operating officer at Baxter International, Inc., in the 1980s. "I rate the Bain folks very highly to the point where I use them in my current role as well [as president of Biogen, a biotechnology firm in Cambridge, Massachusetts]. Bain consultants are good people with personality as well as brains, which doesn't always happen in consulting. [But] they'll also overstep their bounds, no question about that. I have always kind of thought of myself as a lion tamer. I had to keep them in line." Indeed, the full details of Bain's role in the Guinness scandal have never been explored publicly. A look at how it became ensnarled in the controversy and how the company changed provides a rare glimpse at the best and the worst of this secretive, influential company. It also shines a long overdue light on the no-man's-land of professional ethics for management consultants.

The Palace Coup

It is no accident that Bain & Co. encountered troubles because of cozy ties to a client. From the day that William Bain founded the firm in 1973, he and his company deliberately took a different approach. The son of a Tennessee food wholesaler, Bain, by all accounts, exuded southern gentility. In his heyday at Bain & Co., he came across as aloof, a gentleman as refined as the Oriental ceramics that were carefully arranged in his elegant dark blue office, which one writer described as a "sanctum sanctorum." He was fit, a jogger and tennis buff who always seemed in top form. Meticulously well groomed, he sipped relentlessly from a bottle of Dr Pepper on his desk and appeared calm and controlled. But a basketball autographed by Red Auerbach, the famous Boston Celtics coach, on a nearby pedestal hinted of a more turbulent side to Bill Bain. He had a competitive streak as intense as that of Larry Bird, the Celtic great. Bain was extremely secretive, too. His code of ethics may have been wanting, but his strict code of confidentiality earned Bain & Co. the nickname "the KGB of management consulting."

The roots of Bain & Co. actually date back to the 1960s, when Bain went to work for his crosstown rival, the Boston Consulting Group. At the time, Bain was making $19,000 a year raising money for his alma mater, Vanderbilt University in Nashville. When Vanderbilt officials decided to set up a business school, Bain sought the advice of Bruce Henderson, the legendary BCG founder and Vanderbilt graduate. Bain impressed Henderson immensely, and the two soon were talking about a spot for Bill Bain at BCG. In 1967 Henderson hired him, even though Bain had no real business experience, and his career took off. Within two years, Bain was pulling down a six-figure salary. Within six years, he'd launched a coup against his mentor. He left BCG to strike out on his own when he failed to wrest control of BCG from Henderson. "Bain didn't leave BCG because of disenchantment, it was quite the opposite," Henderson later said in some correspondence. "He [Bain] tried to talk me into making him president and chief executive in 1972, long before I had any intention of retiring. He was given all that he asked for and more. . . . His departure was a pure power play."

On his way out of the door at BCG, though, Bain took a few other consultants with him and set up shop across town under the name of Bain and Co., setting in motion a Boston rivalry that would span more than two decades. From the outset, Bain cloaked his new venture in the kind of secrecy usually reserved for Central American airlines under contract to you-know-who. Bain consultants didn't carry business cards. They used code names when discussing clients on airplanes. Bain didn't allow documents on desktops, which were usually as immaculate as Bill Bain's. The company adopted stringent codes of secrecy. One journalist who visited a Bain office said a Bain employee accompanied her everywhere; one even waited for her outside the lavatory. Bain prized secrecy for good reasons: Clients value confidential relationships to keep the wrong information from slipping into competitors' hands. But Bain also used secrecy to create a mystique of the consultant as the high priest of high finance.

From the day he opened the doors, Bain infused the company with his values. Bain consultants tended to look like Bill Bain—trim, athletic, and well groomed. Rumors swirled that the company had a dress code, because so many Bain consultants wore dark suits, handmade shirts, and red ties. One former Bain consultant said communal shock registered at Bain when the computer department hired a fat person. Soon BCG had competition in hiring the best and the brightest graduates at Harvard and Stanford. Bain recruited so aggressively that the dean of the Harvard Business School once temporarily banned him from recruiting on campus because of his ruthless tactics.

A control freak by most accounts, Bain demanded uncompromising loyalty from his staff. Other consultants referred to his staff as "Bainies" because their single-minded devotion to the firm invited comparison with "the Moonies," the equally devoted followers of the Reverend Sun Myung Moon and his Unification Church. Bain established and enforced a noncompete clause that barred any consultant who worked for him from competing against him after they left the firm. When two European partners notified Bain in 1983 that they intended to leave the firm and strike out on their own, Bain stalled them in his office long enough for a Suffolk County deputy sheriff to arrive with a notice that he had sued them. His ironclad control extended to his partners, too. Indeed, partners were partners courtesy of Bill Bain. They had no right to specific percentages of the firm's earnings, for Bain simply parceled out profits at year-end as he saw fit. It was hard for his partners to argue because most of them never knew what the firm earned. Bain controlled this information, too.

The most radical thing that Bain did, though, was to change the way his consultants dealt with clients. When Bain opened his doors for business, American consultants were project oriented. Company A would hire a consultant for a specific project, say to improve its accounts receivable. The consultants would move in, study the problem, figure out what to do, write up the recommendations, hand the client a pricey report, and be on their way. Bain didn't think much of that approach. He thought a consultant should get deeply involved in the company's affairs. Bain advocated that his consultants become like insiders, digging into the company and figuring out what it should do to become a leader in its chosen field. To do the job right, Bain told clients, he needed detailed, sensitive information that most companies were reluctant to provide, fearing that a consultant could learn things that might fall into hands of competitors. So Bain hit upon his unique approach.

To ease their fears, Bain promised potential clients that he would work for them alone, only one company in an industry and not for any competitors. In return, Bain asked the client to establish a long-term relationship in which Bain consultants would help implement the strategy he would advocate. He called his approach "relationship consulting," and he demanded that Bain work directly with the CEO, giving the firm access to the pinnacle of the corporation.

Bain's approach might sound pretty tame to the layman, but it was hot stuff in an industry full of consultants who thought nothing of working for two or more competitors simultaneously. At the time, most consultants fashioned themselves as objective professional advisors who didn't get their hands dirty mucking around in their clients' business. Bain's approach prompted criticism that his consultants were substitute managers. "They've gone as far as getting in bed with the client," said James Kennedy, publisher of *Consultants News*, a feisty industry newsletter. "They're using their great name as a Trojan horse to get into a company. Once they get in they open the doors and they're all over the place. . . . What they are doing flies in the face of everything we know about ethics in management consulting." Competitors said Bain's approach appealed to insecure CEOs who couldn't provide their corporations with the vision their salaries demand. But one former Bain partner disagreed, saying "We wanted a paranoid CEO" who could be converted into a powerful executive with Bain's brainpower. By sticking around to implement its recommendations, Bain could sell more than a fat, pricey report; it also peddled tangible results, which are mother's milk for CEOs.

Competitors and critics argued about Bain's techniques, but they couldn't argue with his results. By cozying up to CEOs, Bain soon developed a powerful word-of-mouth constituency at the top levels of corporate America, which hired his company to produce results. Chrysler Motors became a client; so did Baxter, Dun & Bradstreet, Owens Illinois, and Sterling Drug. Bain developed the Bain Index, which charted the performance of Bain client stocks against various indexes once they had hired the consulting firm. He experimented with ways that his fees could be tied more directly to the stock appreciation of his clients, and he set up Bain Capital, a limited partnership designed to expand Bain's direct investment in his clients and give his consultants a stake in the companies they were advising.

Many clients praised Bain's approach. National Steel hired the company in 1981 when it was the highest-cost producer of flat-rolled steel in the country. A task force of Bain consultants soon descended on the company and did a six-month study of the steel market. It told the company to downsize, modernize, cut costs, and adopt a new continuous casting technology for its operations. By 1984, the company, which had been renamed National Intergroup, was the lowest-cost steel producer in the country. Bain's consultants had added an estimated $200 million in annual value to the company, far in excess of its fees. At Chrysler, Bain consultants figured out the cheapest ways to produce the Omni and the Horizon and still retain 99 percent of the options customers wanted. It was a classic Bain approach. Its consultants were everywhere. They invaded one division plant and studied the operations of 1,500 workstations. Consultants talked to salesmen, dealers, marketing executives, and customers. They visited six Japanese carmaker plants, asking how many people worked in the plants, how cars were pulled off the line, the breakdown between direct and indirect labor. Eventually they came up with a plan that allowed Chrysler to cut the price of the Omni by $1,400. The company became well known for its intense analysis. "Bain consultants have a peculiar tenacity about them," said Gerald Greenwald, the chairman of Chrysler Motors in 1987. "They'll dig up fifty-year-old city planning commission records just to understand a competitor's building costs." By sticking around to implement its recommendations, Bain generated continuous billings and its revenues soared. From 1973 into the early and mid-1980s, the firm grew by 40 to 50 percent a year. By 1986, it had revenues of more than $150 million, and the size of its staff had tripled within six years to around 800. "They anchor themselves in the stomach of the business," one former client said. "They forge a dependent relationship. 'If you have a problem, call us.' "

But Bain's approach presented some problems, too. For the client, Bain's close ties to the CEO often didn't sit as well with managers down the line, whose support was needed to accomplish the consultant's goals. "Once Bain gets into a company," a former Dun & Bradstreet executive said, "there is nobody left who is credited with being able to make the decisions and do the analysis that are part of his job." Consultants met resistance as managers complained that the consultants antagonized people, particularly middle managers who, quite properly, viewed them as a threat. "Their product is brilliant," noted the chairman of another management consulting firm. "It's the package that has been a problem. Five million Bainies saying, 'Stand aside, asshole. Here we come.' " The pledge not to work with a client's competitors had a downside, too. Although Bain grew rapidly, it had a narrow client base. Most of the company's billings came from a few big clients who could present problems if they acquired a company that competed with another Bain client. Bain, for instance, had to drop Monsanto, a big client, when it acquired Searle, bringing Monsanto into competition with Baxter, another Bain client. By the early 1980s, Bill Bain decided the best way to expand his client base was to set up an office in Europe, where it would find a huge client in a giant brewery that had fallen on hard times.

Bain and the Beer Barons

Ernest Saunders first walked into Bain's offices in late 1981. Just months earlier, he'd been the world products group manager at Nestlé in Switzerland when a headhunter called to see if he was interested in a big job in London. An ambitious executive who had worked in the upper levels of several global corporations, Saunders soon learned that the job was managing director of Guinness, a position that could lead to a coveted job as a CEO one day. A series of meetings ensued with members of the Guinness family, and in late 1981 the tall and patrician Saunders signed on as the managing director at Guinness. Saunders knew that Guinness faced problems from the outset. Over the prior decade, the company had gone on an acquisition binge, diversifying into a variety of unrelated fields, ranging from yacht rentals and a drug made from snake venom to baby potties and Callard & Bowser sweets. In all, Guinness owned some 250 companies, but no one seemed to have any idea of how they were supposed to fit together. From the way the Guinness family ran the company, you would have thought the barons were in charge of a garage sale rather than a huge corporation with public shareholders. "It was an extraordinary situation," Saunders said. "The management of the company was in the hands of a series of barons. Mr. Purssell [his predecessor as managing director] seemed to have the task of [ringing up] all these barons once every so often to find out how things were going. He would get back some sort of message to the effect that things were not going very well and maybe the budget for the year should be reduced. . . . There was no cohesive management at all."

Saunders' initial meetings with the staff gave him a sinking feeling that things were worse than he originally thought. "Other than this sort of odd telephone call that would ring around the companies, nobody really seemed to have a clue [as to how the parent company was doing financially]. I took off and did a whistle stop of as many companies as I could just to get some personal feel as to what they were doing, how they were doing, and whether they had any management. The results were terrifying. . . . The thing I lacked was tangible figures as to how the companies were doing. It is all very well sitting around a board table having a chat and having a moan. But if you don't have the numbers on a monthly basis, which is what I had become used to at Nestlé, I mean, this was a big gap."

Saunders discovered that the company knew how to make its flagship product—Guinness stout. Unfortunately, no one knew how to sell the hearty brew. Sales of Guinness stout had been declining steadily, shoving the company's stock price down to 50 pence per share, or about 81 cents at the going exchange rate. "We had nobody in the company that could get me the figures I needed," Saunders said. "We had 200 or so companies. I had no idea of how they were doing. I did not know which companies should be kept or which companies should be sold.

But I didn't want to build up a huge overhead of a new accounting department, either. So I thought what I would do is plug in an external resource that would get me facts." Saunder's "external resource" turned out to be a Boston consulting company that was just getting a toehold in Europe.

John Brett Theroux had opened Bain & Co.'s doors on Fitzhardinge Street in London. His first real "find" was the company's landlord—Sir Jack Lyons, a patron of the arts, investor, and socialite who could drop a note to Prime Minister Margaret Thatcher and get a quick response. Theroux leased some space from Sir Jack and soon discovered the old squire was just what he needed—a person of stature who could spread Bain's name around London's insular business world. "After a fairly long set of discussions both in America and here with Sir Jack, we agreed to him . . . being an advisor to our company," Theroux recalled. "We were new in the U.K. as a company and we thought it would be helpful to have someone . . . a door opener and also someone who could help new company get familiar with the way the business and people worked." Sir Jack proved to be a godsend. He hosted lunches at Bain's offices; arranged parties where Theroux and a small band of Bain consultants could meet top businesspeople and Lyons' peers. Meanwhile, Theroux started building a staff, hiring bright young people like Olivier Roux, who worked for one of Bain's American clients, a label maker named Dymo Industries that also had an office in London. By late 1981, Bain's office was up and running when word of the consulting firm reached the ear of Saunders, who was looking for a smart, savvy outside voice to give him some accurate numbers. He called Theroux and set up a meeting.

In many respects, Guinness and Bain were an ideal fit. Saunders didn't set out to develop a long-term, dependent relationship with the consultant. He simply needed an objective outside source to tell him exactly where he stood. He figured he could hire Bain, get his results, and be done with it. There weren't many American firms in London at the time. Big corporations were just starting to understand the significance of global operations. Bain had just what Saunders wanted: the objectivity of an outsider and the required expertise. It didn't have any history with Guinness or personal ties to the old staff to worry about, either. Indeed, within months, Bain's hierarchy would be huddled around a speakerphone during an annual meeting at a Hyatt Hotel in Palo Alto,

California, advising Theroux how to help Saunders depose one of the old guard, Anthony Purssell, Guinness's deputy chairman who was in Saunders' way.

Guinness was an ideal target for Bain, too. It was a consulting firm new to London and eager to make a name for itself by snatching a big, well-known client led by a man determined to turn it around. Bain could do the job Saunders wanted and more. "The main thing Bain offers to its clients," Roux would later testify, "is an understanding of what is happening outside the firm. [It provides] help for the firm to be able to decide how it should develop itself in the future, like telling it about its competitors, telling it about its clients. It also helps build consensus within the company as to what the company should be doing, something that cannot always be achieved without help from the outside. It helps analyze very complicated business situations." There was no doubt that Saunders faced a complicated business situation, and by early 1982 Bain was in Guinness's offices on a fact-finding mission that would lead to what Bain really wanted—a long-time relationship and a lot of billable hours.

Initially, Theroux and another consultant, David Hoare, worked on the Guinness account. They wasted no time drumming up additional business. Hoare told Saunders how Bain could do much more for him: "Bain would get involved in a wider range of topics that would include not just making recommendations but also helping implement those recommendations and, therefore, we would go to greater lengths and spend more time and energy and be more dedicated to the results than most of the competitors of Bain & Co." As soon as they dug into Guinness's records, they showed Saunders what they meant. "The first weakness that Theroux and Hoare pointed out to me," Saunders said, "which I, of course, had already arrived at, was the fact that we had no management accounting. We had no figures. It was their recommendation that we hire somebody that was to be called a controller, a term used on the Continent but not in general use in this country." Unfortunately, Guinness's poor credibility made it hard to recruit a good candidate for the job. "People," Saunders said, "don't like to jump on sinking ships." So Theroux and Hoare did something quite unusual, even for Bain: They suggested that Saunders fill the job with a Bain consultant, Olivier Roux. The young Frenchman had a good head for numbers and could help Saunders straighten things out. Once Guinness's credibility was restored, Saunders could replace Roux with his own person. The logic appealed to Saunders. Indeed, once Theroux cleared the proposal with the Boston office, Roux, in effect, went to work as Guinness's full-time controller, helping Saunders assess the performance of the operating companies, the budgets they submitted, and helping him form an opinion of what to do with them. It was "hands-on" consulting à la Bain.

It is hard to overstate the value of having one of your own consultants in a key corporate position. Roux knew what a consultant could do for a company that needed things done quickly, and he had a firsthand view of what needed to be done. Over the next 6 to 12 months, Roux became a key source of management and financial information for Saunders, whose expertise was sales, marketing, and public relations. Roux formed a team composed of Bain consultants and Guinness employees to start going over the 250 subsidiaries, separating them into brewing and nonbrewing groups. The teams produced reams of data analyzing whether the subsidiaries should be kept or sold. Roux also helped develop a cost-cutting strategy to save as much money as possible at the operating companies. Saunders soon had a three-phase plan for Guinness. Phase one: Stop the hemorrhaging and rationalize the business. Phase two: Rebuild the core brewing business. Phase three: Look outward again with acquisitions. Roux and Bain played key roles in all three phases, helping develop the plans and implement the recommendations. By early 1982, Theroux and Hoare outlined to the board of directors the steps the company should take. Within six months, the hemorrhaging had stopped; within two years from the date on which he had hired Bain & Co., Saunders had disposed of 150 subsidiaries, imposed one of the tightest financial control systems in Britain, and revitalized the sales of Guinness stout. As Guinness's sales soared, so did Bain & Co.'s billings and the size of its Guinness consulting team.

No person was more important to the effort than Olivier Roux, who also symbolized how quickly a young, smart person could rise through the ranks and make a lot of money at Bain & Co. He had joined Bain's staff at age 30. Roux didn't carry the educational pedigree of most Bain consultants. He graduated from a local French business school and went right to work in France during 1973 for Dymo, where he was a salesman and held a couple of low-level management jobs until the company sent him to England in 1979. He joined Bain's staff in May of 1980 and after only 18 months on the job, he became a manager. He reached vice president by 1983, just three years after he joined the company. His rapid ascension was not unusual for a smart and ambitious man in the industry. Even by today's standards, Roux was paid handsomely. Compensation for officers at Bain included a base salary plus two forms of bonus—one based upon the company's staff turnover (the lower the better since turnover is a major cost for consultants), and the other based on Bain's worldwide profitability (the higher the better). By 1984, Roux, at age 34, made $190,000. The next year he jumped to $350,000, and by 1986, he was making $650,000, more than Saunders, who, by then, had become Guinness's chairman and CEO. The salary didn't count all of Roux's perks, either. Each officer and vice president had been given an opportunity to invest in Bain Capital, a multimillion-dollar fund that invested money on behalf of Bain officers and other investors. Roux put $30,000 into the fund, which invests in some of Bain's consulting clients, and stood to get up to five times his money back once the fund sold off the initial investments.

Roux's progress at Guinness was equally rapid, even though he remained on Bain's payroll. And his experience there provides a unique inside view of how Bain works for a client. By mid-1983, Saunders asked him to run Guinness's finance department. Soon he was briefing stockbrokers and the financial press in the City on the company and its progress. By mid-1984, Saunders asked Roux to take a seat on the board of directors, heady stuff for a young man in his mid-30s. Roux cleared the assignment with the Boston office and soon was on the board. This way the kind of high-level access that would make any consulting firm drool, particularly Bain & Co., which commanded the ear of the boss. Meanwhile, Roux continued monitoring the company's expenses and searching the financial landscape in the United Kingdom for suitable acquisitions.

Bain applied its policy of secrecy particularly aggressively to acquisitions. The company treated a client's acquisition policy like the Pentagon treats secret missions. Target firms were given code names; information was compartmentalized; talk was on a need-to-know basis only; and Bain's offices were replete with document shredders and security keys. Roux would disappear behind closed doors in Bain's office and pore over intelligence the consultants had gathered on suitable companies to bring into the Guinness fold. The policies didn't always work. At one point, Guinness launched Operation Sailboat, an effort to acquire the wine and spirits business of a company named Booker McConnell. But the price of the target stock soared soon after a Guinness board meeting, and Saunders aborted the bid, fearing there had been a leak.

More often than not, though, the consulting firm's passion for secrecy kept the information under the tightest of wraps. By mid-1984 opportunity struck just after Roux and Bain had developed a long list of potential acquisitions. A company named W. H. Smith launched a bid for Martins, a chain of newsagent/tobacconist shops. When Martins fought the bid, Bain recommended that Guinness step in as a "white knight," a firm that would rescue the targeted firm from its unwanted suitor. Roux not only pitched the Martins acquisition to the Guinness board, he also negotiated the bid and dealt with the merchant banks and the lawyers. Saunders was titularly in charge of the bid as Guinness's top officer, but Roux and Bain played a crucial role in the process. "I didn't want to be bouncing up and down doing everything," Saunders later said, "and, therefore, the financial matters and a number of other matters were dealt with by Mr. Roux, partly in his capacity as the chief financial officer and partly as a member of the board who was also a vice president of Bain."

Scotch on the Rocks

The acquisition of Martins was merely the start of something big. Saunders was under pressure to expand Guinness's business. Part of the pressure came from bankers and stockbrokers energized by the deal-making frenzy of the 1980s, where nothing seemed too big or outrageous. "[They] basically made it clear to me that Guinness must make a major acquisition very soon because we were entering a phase where the size of the company in terms of its market value was really only that of a regional brewer. We were nowhere near the big boys like Allied Lyons, Bass, and so on. And we had to make up our minds. Either we had to become one of the large players in the drinks field . . . or we had to risk the fact that we were so small we would possibly be taken over ourselves."

The Guinness family wanted to grow, too, for different reasons. "I had a discussion with Lord Iveagh [the family head on the board] and he said, you know, if Guinness had done in its second hundred years what it had done in its first hundred years, then the Guinness business would have been up there with the Rothschilds and people like that. And . . . he said to me . . . anything that will really put Guinness on the world map would have my complete support." Lastly Bain & Co. pressed Saunders to grow and had compiled a list of firms in the beverage business that included Arthur Bell & Sons, which made scotch whiskey. Acquiring it would not only give Guinness a second brand in the drinks business, it would also give the company some profits in England, where its stock was traded. "There was complete enthusiasm with one exception," said Saunders. "There were certain members of the Guinness family that had some personal feelings against—well, it obviously wasn't alcohol because they drank Guinness all the time—but against spirits." Lord Iveagh overcame those feelings, and Bain went to work analyzing the feasibility of a takeover.

The lengths to which Bain would go in assessing a potential target were impressive, even to its critics. Roux led the Bain team that did the acquisition analysis on Arthur Bell & Sons, known locally as Bells. Saunders would later marvel at the thoroughness of Bain's consultants. "Bain had done an extremely detailed analysis on the scotch whiskey business as a whole and on Bells in particular. I would say that having subsequently looked at what information Bells had when [we] acquired it that, through the work done by Bain, we had far more information and knew far more about Bells than it did itself." But Bain's analysis was expensive, too. It charged by the hour, and Bain consultants wracked up lots of hours and expenses working for Guinness. It examined the shipping registry and did a thorough analysis of the economics of exporting scotch whiskey. At one point it spent 680 hours evaluating Guinness's acquisition and strategic options. On another proposed acquisition, Bain spent 386 hours identifying the potential purchasers of the New Piccadilly Hotel, a property that had drawn Guinness's interest. In one month, Bain consultants spent 1,810 hours in meetings with bankers and brokers and doing bid documentation work during an acquisition. The rate per hour that Bain charged varied, depending on the consultant. But there was little doubt that Bain's bottom line benefited immensely from the work. By 1986, Guinness was Bain's third largest client worldwide and it was the biggest in Europe, generating monthly revenues in excess of $1.5 million. But Guinness benefited from the relationship, too. By 1986, profits at Guinness had risen sixfold to nearly $400 million, and the stock price had jumped to $5.75 a share, far above the 81 cents a share had fetched on the open market before Saunders and Bain arrived on the scene. Not all of the increase could be attributed to Bain, but the depth of its involvement with Guinness made it clear that the consultants had a big hand in the brewer's good fortunes.

No one played a bigger role in Guinness's success than Olivier Roux. By all accounts, the bid for Bells was a smashing success, primarily due to Bain's organizational and analytical work led by the young Frenchman. Roux traveled the country with Saunders, making the financial presentations to brokers, bankers, the financial press, and the City. The bid lasted 60 days and had its rough, tense moments. But Guinness succeeded. Once it took over Bells, the brewer put one of its executives inside Bell at a top level to help integrate the company into the Guinness organization. But Saunders kept Bain on the job, too. In fact, he put a member of the Roux analysis team at Bain inside Bells right beside the Guinness executive. "He [the consultant] knew Bells better than they did," Saunders said. The warm relations between the consultants and Guinness were not to last, though, and soon Bain and Saunders would discover that close ties between a consultant and a client can have a downside.

The news that Argyll, a supermarket chain led by James Gulliver, a corporate chief with strong ties to Scotland's financial and political power structures, wanted to launch a bid for Distillers, a huge company that competed with Bells, broke in August 1985. The story in the local business press alarmed Saunders: "We had just got hold of Bells. We had a lot of work to do, and I was concerned about the destabilizing effect any new owner for Distillers [could have] because of what somebody might do to pricing strategies [for Distillers scotches] and so on." The close relationship between Guinness and Bain had evolved into a dependency. Saunders consulted Roux on almost everything, and Roux (and Bain) obliged. As top officers in Guinness, neither Saunders nor Roux wanted to go through another bruising takeover fight, having just emerged from a bitter fight marked by hard feelings. But both men agreed they had to protect their newly acquired markets. They bought a little time when British financial market regulators stepped in and ordered a three-month freeze on the proposed Distillers bid, telling Argyll to clarify its intentions. Saunders told Roux he'd better update the information Bain had compiled on the scotch whiskey industry during the Bells takeover and take a hard look at Distillers.

Even today Bain disputes the accuracy of its reputation for coming in and taking over. But Roux's actions show the domineering influence Bain and other consultants can have by controlling the flow of the information within a client corporation. Roux and his Bain team didn't have the time to do the thorough analysis they had done on Bells. Nevertheless, they soon determined that Argyll had the financial wherewithal to stage an offer for Distillers, and Bain also came up with a conservative estimate of Distillers' market value. A bid for the company had some compelling economic logic for Saunders, a man who was trying to build a worldwide drinks business: "Here was a company with this glorious portfolio of brands," he would later recall. "Okay, we now had Bells, but that still meant we actually had only two brands. I mean, they had Gordons gin, Booths gin, Johnnie Walker whiskey; Black and White, Haig, Pimm's, sixty other whiskeys at least, a vodka. I mean, that is quite a portfolio." Economics wasn't the only thing driving Saunders. He'd gone to Scotland on a goodwill mission to ease some of the lingering hard feelings over Guinness's acquisition of Bells, and all anyone was talking about was the possible takeover of Distillers by Argyll, which was headed by Gulliver, who was born in a small Scottish distillery town. To Saunders's surprise, a number of Scots told him Argyll wasn't the ideal owner of Distillers and suggested that Guinness get involved.

When the three-month freeze ended and Argyll announced it would try to take over Distillers, two elements of Argyll's statement really caught Roux's eye. One was the initial offering price. At just under 2 billion British pounds, it was far below the conservative value that Roux's team attached to the company. "I think it is fair to say that it was a steal at that price," said Roux. The other was Argyll's logic. Roux recalled: "They announced that the way they would make that acquisition worthwhile for Argyll would be in attacking Guinness's business in the U.K. and regaining market share from Bells."

Saunders assembled a team of more than 100 bankers, brokers, advisors, consultants, and company officials at Bain's London offices just before Christmas in a meeting that showed just how influential the Bain consultants had become. "The room was extremely large," Saunders recalled, "there was a huge table and it was packed. We were in the era of megabid mania. The City was awash with money. One was getting approaches from banks all over the world offering all sorts of propositions for any sort of deal that one could think of. Now here was potentially the largest takeover bid that had ever taken place in the United Kingdom and you can imagine that the merchant bank, the stockbrokers, and Bain's, their mouths [were] watering at the fees that they would obviously get if they got involved." The deal had its risks for Guinness; the company was far smaller than Distillers. The minnow would be swallowing the whale. Powerful constituencies existed to go ahead. Tom Ward, a Washington lawyer, board member, and Guinness's man in America, was enthusiastic. He once convinced the U.S. government to exempt Guinness from some draconian import restrictions the Americans had slapped on Nigeria, a prime source of profit for Guinness. The exemption allowed the company to maintain the flow of Guinness into Nigeria, even though all of its competitors had to close their breweries. His political feat gave Ward tremendous influence with the Guinness board. But Roux, still smarting from the rancorous fight for Bells, advised caution. "I was very eager that if Guinness got involved in acquiring Distillers, it did so with the recommendation of Distillers," said Roux. In other words, he said, Guinness should not get involved unless it was as a "white knight." Saunders took the Bain consultant's advice. The board did, too. Those assembled at the meeting soon learned that bankers for Guinness and Distillers were working together on another deal, a relationship that would allow the subject of Guinness as a "white knight" to be raised informally with officials of Distillers. They took to the proposal as if it were a single malt. Indeed, when British securities regulators removed any official barriers to the Argyll offer in the second week of January, Distillers made it clear that the board was more interested in a deal with Guinness. Saunders dispatched two people to negotiate the sensitive details: Ward and Olivier Roux.

Sir Jack, Mrs. Thatcher, and Success Fees

Except for the nearby hotels, the lights usually weren't burning in the stately old buildings surrounding Portman Square on a Sunday night. They were aglow on the night of January 19, though. Saunders had summoned the Guinness board to the company's headquarters at 9 P.M. He had been holed up all day at Bain's offices with Tom Ward, who was on the phone negotiating details of a possible deal with representatives of Distillers, whose board was meeting to consider a friendly takeover by Guinness. Roux was there, too, in a constant discussion with brokers and lawyers, keeping them posted on the progress of negotiations. "We had [the] Distillers board deliberating what they are going to do in Distillers' House; the Guinness board installed at Portman Square from about nine at night and I think progressively getting tucked into the Guinness waiting for us. Around eleven at night, Ward, Roux and myself . . . left the Bain offices and went across to Guinness and, indeed, when we got there . . . Ward made one of his calls to [Distillers] and received conformation that the deal was on." Saunders and Ward flushed out the overall terms of the deal for the Guinness board members, and Roux briefed them on the crucial financial details. By 1 A.M., the board approved a bid of about 2.3 billion British pounds for Distillers, which was higher than Argyll's bid but below the 2.6-billion-pound conservative estimate that Bain had attached to the company.

It didn't take long for problems to surface. The first one was political. The U.K. Monopolies and Mergers Commission can stop any merger or proposed takeover on antitrust grounds. Securities regulators from the government's Office of Fair Trading can refer the bid to the commission for a review if they think the combination might be anticompetitive. "If you're referred," Saunders said, "you are in limbo for six months," or the amount of time it takes the commission to review the bid. "[Argyll] was in the position of having a real bid on the table that had passed the Monopolies Commission hurdle and, therefore, was in the business of persuading shareholders to assent to [its bid of just under 2 billion pounds]. But everybody in the City knew that until Guinness had cleared that commission's hurdle, it did not have a credible bid on the table." On February 13, 1986, the Office of Fair Trading referred Guinness's bid to the commission. The acquisition of Distillers would place Guinness in control of more than 25 percent of production and sales of scotch in the United Kingdom, an almost automatic trigger for a referral. Saunders was stunned, not only at the decision but also at the way the brokers, bankers, and PR people who already had been paid millions of pounds "sort of came along and said: 'Well, cheerio. Bad luck. Better luck next time.' And off they went. I never felt so lonely in my life, you know, sitting there in my office, everybody else having basically given up the ghost."

Bain didn't abandon him, though. Saunders soon started making the rounds of government offices armed with Bain's analysis and its studies on why the bid should not be referred. Eventually he convinced the regulators to let him make a second bid by promising that Guinness would trim its share of the market below the 25 percent threshold by selling off five of the brands it would acquire with Distillers. The trouble was, Argyll had raised its bid above Guinness's price by then, and before long Saunders was back before his board proposing a second bid that would up the stakes for the company. After some soul-searching, the Guinness board increased its bid above Argyll's by offering up to 2.6 billion British pounds in Guinness stock, cash, or a mix of cash and Guinness stock. Government regulators then started scrutinizing the second Guinness bid to determine if it should be referred to the commission, and everyone held their breath—everyone, that is, except for Bain's landlord and door opener, Sir Jack Lyons.

As Bain's regal presence in London, Isadore Jack Lyons had made the consulting firm an emerging presence in financial and social circles. He had an office at Bain & Co., pulled down a $100,000 annual retainer for his services, and earned sizable additional fees for consulting work through his affiliation with Bain & Co. Knighted in 1973, Sir Jack wasn't the kind of fellow you would find hanging around the stock exchanges. In fact, he said he'd never even been to the exchange. "I have seen pictures of it," he said, "and it looks like a ghastly place to me, full of phones and so on." Instead, the retired textile merchant enjoyed the fruits of a successful career at theater benefits or other social events where the rich and powerful gathered. He was a major benefactor of the Royal Opera House at Covent Garden, chairman of the London Symphony Trust, a Commander of the Order of the British Empire, a recipient of the kind of honors that put him on a Christian name basis with prime ministers, including then–Prime Minister Margaret Thatcher. When Saunders called asking his help with this referral business, Sir Jack happily lent a hand. Saunders desperately needed a public government guarantee that Guinness's second bid would not be referred so the City would take his bid seriously. The letter to No. 10 Downing Street arrived shortly after Saunders called Sir Jack. Addressed to the prime minister in Sir Jack's hand, it made the case that

Guinness should not be referred in highly persuasive terms to his friend Mrs. Thatcher. Eventually she personally forwarded it to the minister in charge of the inquiry, and the bid was cleared less than 10 days later.

Saunders nearly threw his arms around Sir Jack. Thanks to the Bain advisor, Guinness's political problem had evaporated. But its financial problems had just started and, as Saunders wrestled with them, even he was surprised to discover how influential Bain and its consultants had become within Guinness. Shortly after the bid was cleared, Argyll again increased its bid for Distillers. The action set off a furious round of meetings in which tensions soared between Saunders and Roux. The Guinness CEO desperately wanted to win the bidding war and challenged Bain to come up with an offer that would guarantee victory. But Roux was opposed to increasing the offer beyond 2.6 billion pounds, Bain's conservative estimate of what Distillers was worth, and he had support from Guinness's bankers. At one point, Saunders called Theroux, Roux's boss at Bain, and complained about the young Frenchman, urging Theroux to "tell him to calm down." Once again, though, the board sided with Roux, and Saunders accepted the decision, although it increased his already tense feelings about the young French consultant. Because of the terms of the offer already on the table, the decision not to increase the bid made the price of Guinness's stock a key feature of its final bid. If the price of a share of Guinness rose, the company's final bid looked better to Distiller's shareholders. If it fell, the offer was not so attractive.

Argyll launched an attack on Guinness's share price through short sales, a stock market technique designed to drive down the price of Guinness stock. Guinness retaliated by scouring the financial landscape for friends who would buy massive quantities of Guinness stock to prop up the price and maintain the attractiveness of its offer. The trouble was, the Guinness offer included illegal, secret guarantees against losses and promises of rewards if Guinness won. In other words, if Guinness won the fight for Distillers, investors such as Gerald Ronson of the Heron Corporation would not only get a "success fee" for buying Guinness stock, the brewer would also cover any losses Ronson incurred buying the shares. Roux played a key role in arranging and processing the payments to Ronson, Tony Parnes, the stockbroker, Sir Jack, and a variety of banks or other well-heeled investors willing to step up and support the brewer's bid. He reviewed the deal with Ron-

son in his offices on that early winter night. He signed off on phony invoices drafted to cover the fees. The money flowed as freely as Guinness with multimillion-dollar fees funneled to offshore companies;
some were routed through Bain as consulting fees paid to advisors by
the consulting firm. Bain then billed Guinness for the fees.

Although the share support operation would later be declared illegal, Roux said he didn't know he was doing anything wrong. The management consulting industry has no code of ethics or official standards
of conduct, so Roux had no guidelines to follow. He said he cleared
everything with his office at Bain, too, and no one there complained
about his conduct. No wonder. The secret program proved immensely
successful to the client, Guinness, the investors, and Bain & Co. By
mid-April Guinness won the fight, taking control of Distillers in a huge
transaction that generated more than $250 million in fees to brokers,
consultants, bankers, and others. About 25 million British pounds (or
$37.5 million) of that money went to Guinness supporters who earned
"success fees" and reimbursement for losses. Saunders, Roux, and Sir
Jack were the men of the hour. From his offices in Boston, none other
than Bill Bain wrote Sir Jack, congratulating the team. "Congratula-
tions on the result of your efforts with Ernest and the team," Bain
wrote. "We are all delighted and looking forward to hearing the story
of how you managed to pull it off." Bain had reason to be delighted. In
1984 and 1985 alone, Guinness had paid Bain $21.5 million in consult-
ing fees, and that didn't include the peak year of 1986, when Bain's
billing ran up to $2 million a month. Unfortunately, though, Bill Bain
was not the only one interested in hearing how Sir Jack had "managed
to pull it off." By December 1986, investigators from the British Department of Trade and Industry wanted to know more about the transactions, too. The inquiry set off a mad scramble within Guinness to
pore over every detail of the effort. Soon Roux told Saunders that he
had heard the inquiry centered on the 25 million pounds in support
payments to Ronson and others, and the stage soon was set for a dramatic display of how much damage a consultant can do.

Saunders had had enough of the young Frenchman by December
1986. Roux seemed increasingly disposed to oppose him at every turn.
As lawyers for Guinness started questioning those who participated in
the struggle for Distillers, Roux balked at cooperating with the attorneys Saunders had selected. Fearing that Saunders would try to make

him a scapegoat, Roux wanted lawyers who would be more disposed to his version of events. The Guinness CEO was furious. He hired the lawyers he wanted and hinted to Bain officials that the company's future relationship depended on Roux's cooperation. As the relationship between the two men deteriorated, Roux met with attorneys for Bain & Co. in mid-December, just as the scandal started to erupt publicly. Bain officials decided that its lawyers would also represent Roux.

Just over two weeks later, Roux crafted a long letter over an even longer weekend in the offices of the lawyers representing him and Bain. It was sent to Guinness's board of directors less than a month after Roux first met with Bain's lawyers, and, by all accounts, it was a bombshell. "Saunders's reactions on opening it were shock and disbelief," said the judge summarizing the Guinness case for the jury. "He noticed his name incorporated in every third line and he felt livid. Mr. Roux had been involved in a classic buck-passing exercise. He [Saunders] regarded the letter as pure poison." The letter, which detailed the payments to support the price of Guinness stock, triggered an inquiry by the full board, and Saunders soon found himself on the hot seat. Roux claimed the whole operation had been Saunders's idea. He said he hadn't known the practice was illegal. Meanwhile, Bain summoned Sir Jack to its London offices and started grilling him about the consulting fees he had earned. Bain's John Theroux recalled returning to London after an overnight flight to confront the situation at his home in Kensington.

He'd been at a Bain & Co. meeting in Boston where the firm's directors had some "significant discussions" about terminating Sir Jack's relationship with Bain. Finally they decided to send Sir Jack a letter giving him the bad news. "Within ten minutes of arriving in my home after an overnight flight, Sir Jack [arrived] and was really quite upset. He was quite agitated, probably understandably. When I arrived at Heathrow, there was a press report about the dismissal of Sir Jack by Bain & Co., which had happened the day before, when I was in Boston, and he was quite upset with Bain & Co. and with me and with everything connected with the situation. He said that he acted perfectly reasonably during the bid and that he had nothing to be concerned about and, in that context, how could Bain & Co. have handled him so roughly. I believe I asked Sir Jack to leave my house. My family was all around. We knew Sir Jack quite well. My children knew Sir Jack. It was a messy situation."

Once Roux's letter arrived at Guinness, the board voted to dump Saunders from the company, and the young Frenchman soon left, too. Just over two months later, he parted company with Bain & Co., but not before he got his final payment from the consulting firm—$925,127. Within a few months he was given limited immunity from prosecution by the British government in return for his testimony in a case against his old client, Saunders, who was charged with 49 criminal charges, and Ronson, Sir Jack, and Tony Parnes. A jury eventually found all guilty, and most of them spent a little time in jail. Saunders served 10 months of a five-year sentence for theft, false accounting, and conspiracy. He got out of jail and went to work as a consultant. Ronson served six months of a one-year jail term. Parnes spent 11 months of a two-and-one-half-year term, and Lyons escaped prison, although he lost his knighthood and paid a huge three-million-pound fine. Bain & Co. emerged from the scandal relatively unscathed, though. Neither Roux nor the consulting firm was charged with any crimes, thanks in no small part to Roux's decision to testify. Roux, in fact, left Bain and became a partner in another London-based consulting firm, Talisman Management Ltd. Bain & Co. didn't get that much bad publicity as the trial played out in the early 1990s, either. Indeed, the British press focused almost exclusively on Saunders, Sir Jack, Parnes, and Ronson, the Guinness part of the story. There was no trial coverage by American newspapers or media.

Jim Kennedy of *Consultants News* marvels at how Bain & Co. survived after one of its consultants turned state's evidence against a former client based on knowledge he'd gained during a consulting engagement. David Bechhofer, a Bain vice president, said the scandal hurt Bain in London's business community for a while. "It hurt us because we are not a very public company," he said. "The London business community doesn't really like scandal, and so that was a challenge for our London office for a while. We worked before, during, and after [the scandal] with Guinness and there was a little bit of separation between Guinness and Ernest Saunders. So it wasn't as if Olivier was testifying against a sitting CEO of a client of ours. That would have been a problem. But the publicity wasn't particularly pleasant and it has been a challenge. [Since then] we've done a lot of work to create a better public image for ourselves or to soften the edges, but a lot of that ended up being on a one-to-one basis in the business community."

The situation also carried a larger message to consulting clients around the world about allowing a consultant to get too close to a company's operations. Eventually, Saunders, Sir Jack, Parnes, and Ronson either landed in jail, paid huge fines, or both, based upon the testimony of a man hired to advise Guinness. Indeed, Roux showed how much damage a consultant can do if the sensitive inside information he needs to do his job falls into the wrong hands once a relationship sours. Anyone pondering a lawsuit against a consultant need only look at Roux's actions to see the danger of confronting your consultant in a courtroom. Consulting firms brag that there's never been a malpractice judgment against a consultant. There are more disputes and complaints than the public record would suggest, though. They're usually settled out of court before they get to a jury or in court. The Roux testimony suggests why.

From Guinness to Gadiesh

The Guinness case prompted soul-searching at Bain's offices back in Boston. Before anyone could take many concrete steps, though, other forces would hurt Bain far more than Roux's testimony damaged its largest European client. The initial Guinness billings had bolstered Bain & Co.'s reputation as the hottest firm in the business. Growth had been meteoric. Bill Bain and Bain's founding partners had stuffed lots of money back into the firm. By the time they were hauling in more than $20 million a year from Guinness, though, they decided it was time to get a little of it back. During 1985 and 1986, they sold 30 percent of the company for $200 million in cash and notes to an Employee Stock Ownership Plan, or ESOP, set up for the purchasers—some 35 junior partners of Bain & Co. It was a complex deal in which Bain & Co. borrowed most of the money to buy the 30 percent stake, saddling the consulting firm with annual interest payments of about $25 million to be paid from future revenues. The deal seemed sound as long as Bain & Co. continued to grow rapidly. But growth had slowed by the time the Guinness scandal broke, partially because the economy started to slow and partially because Guinness and other big clients started cutting back or terminating their use of Bain's services. To this day, the value that Bain and the original founders attached to the firm for the sale remains controversial. Bain valued the consulting firm at about $600 million, about 12 to 15 times its pretax profits and about five times its revenue. At the time, consulting businesses usually sold at multiples of less than two times their revenue. Many Bain officials agree that the price Bain charged the ESOP was inflated, although some say it wouldn't have been unreasonable had the firm continued its rate of growth. But there is no debate about whether the move backfired.

By early 1988 Bain & Co., the "too hot to handle" firm of the 1980s, stunned the consulting world by slashing its own workforce by 10 percent. Bain's revenues were about to decline for the first time in its history. Morale plunged, too. By 1990 things just got worse. The company announced further cuts: Another 17 percent of its workforce, or 213 employees, got pink slips, bringing its payroll down to 1,000 from a peak of 1,400. Big clients like Guinness, Baxter, Chrysler, Dun & Bradstreet, and Canadian Pacific had sharply curbed or terminated their relationships with Bain. Most did not comment on the reasons, although some clients said they couldn't afford Bain's lofty fees. "We're having to look at every expense," a spokesman at Bridgestone/Firestone, Inc., told *Business Week* in explaining why it dramatically cut back on Bain's services when its profits fell two years in a row.

As it turned out, Bain's problems weren't limited to London. Key executives at other clients began to question Bain's pricey advice as the sluggish economy put pressure on budgets. Baxter International had been a huge account for Bain in the 1980s. The company had literally flooded Baxter's halls with consulting teams advising the company on numerous ventures. "At one point in 1988, Baxter had twenty-six different Bain teams operating simultaneously," said James Tobin, the former chief operating officer at Baxter. "A team usually consisted of ten to twelve consultants. Projects would typically last six months or so and result in a recommendation or plan." Tobin, who thinks highly of Bain consultants, said Baxter simply got carried away because Vernon R. Loucks, Jr., Baxter's CEO, thought the consultants were indispensable: "Because earlier things had worked out so well, Vern started to believe everything Bain did would be right. So he put it on autopilot and started believing some things were true that weren't. They did some stupid things. It didn't work out toward the end because he [Loucks] didn't challenge them [Bain consultants] enough. One clear example was [Bain's idea to create] an account executive for approaching the marketplace where one account executive would be in charge of Mass General [Hospital] for all Baxter products and services. Sounds good in principle, but it backfired. It gave the hospital one person to beat up so you start to lose. They'll say, 'Look, if you don't cut your price on this over here, I'm not going to buy that over there.' Pretty soon, the company is making concessions it can't afford. You are slitting your own throat. I told them it would fail and it failed. Vern listened to the consultants. It was one reason I decided I'd better take my act elsewhere." When some of Bain's ideas didn't pan out, Baxter cut back.

The erosion of revenue soon turned into a talent drain. Some 90 consultants left Bain's London office within two years. Internal turmoil rattled the ranks as the former Bainies started rival firms or pursued other interests. Rumors suddenly surfaced that Bain was trying to sell the firm but couldn't find any takers. Worst of all, the growing interest costs associated with the sale of the 30 percent stake to the ESOP ravaged profits and bonuses. The problems tarnished Bill Bain's reputation. A *Boston Globe* piece headlined "Did Greed Cripple Bain & Co.?" led off with a description of "The House," Bain's lavish $4.3 million spread built on three acres of land adjoining the Weston Golf Club just outside of Boston: " 'The House,' Bain's detractors say, 'is the most ostentatious sign of Bill Bain's excesses, the kind of excesses that nearly bankrupted the company he built.' "

Over the next couple of years, Bain would experience its darkest hours. Its ranks rife with dissent and anger and its partners divided over finances, Bain and Co. struggled from one crisis to another. The younger vice presidents clashed with the original partners over the crushing burden of debt the ESOP had assumed when it acquired Bain stock from the founders. Some consultants walked, others stayed, but all were bitter at the tide of events, particularly when the company struggled to come up with a $19 million interest payment in 1991 and nearly went bankrupt. The crisis culminated when Bill Bain resigned in 1991, and Mitt Romney, the son of the former Michigan governor, took over at Bain. A financial wizard from Bain Capital, Romney soon developed a rescue plan. He renegotiated the company's bank debt and, more significantly, extracted $100 million in concessions from Bain and the other founders. By 1993 Bain's fortunes not only started to improve, it also pulled off a first in the consulting industry: Bain and Co. appointed a woman as its chairman and CEO, Orit Gadiesh, the Israeli woman whose flashy dress and vivid personality would cut quite a figure in the staid and proper world of management consulting.

The New Bain

Over the next three years under Gadiesh, Bain & Co. resumed the meteoric growth of its glory days. As of this writing, it has 23 offices around the world and 115 vice presidents; employs 1,400 persons, including about 1,000 consultants; and *Consultants News* estimates its latest revenues at $300 million, which would make Bain the eighteenth largest consulting firm in the world. Ken Dawson, who surveys consulting firms at Alpha Publications, says Bain "is totally unlike any other management consultancy" because of its practical, hands-on approach that emphasizes the generation of financial results for its clients.

Bain wants to put behind it those bad old days when its interests became too entwined with those of its clients. The company still strives for long-term relationships, but it has eased its conflict of interest policy, which had prohibited the company from working for a client's competitors. "For probably close to twenty years we had a relatively strict policy. There were some companies that valued that and some [that] did not," said Bechhofer, the Bain vice president. "The way the policy exists now is, we won't work for companies on competing projects but we could work for [one company] on a growth strategy in Asia and [its competitor] on a distribution strategy in Europe. That wouldn't be a problem. The acid test for us is, we first ask the client if this is a problem. Most of the time they say no, but if they say yes, we don't do it."

Bain is not as secretive as it once was, either, although it still shies away from publicity. And it openly admits that it went too far in the Guinness situation. "We made a mistake," Bechhofer said. "We made a mistake. In the process of working with Guinness, it had a short-term need for a chief financial officer and we [supplied] one of our people . . . to fill that need until [Guinness] could fill it. That was a mistake because it is difficult for anyone to be both consultant and to have somebody in management. Neither he nor we were ever [charged] in any of the scandal, [but] when mud gets thrown, it sticks to everything it hits. But it was wrong, so we changed our policy and we don't do that [use employees in executive positions for clients] anymore."

Bain's client base is probably broader than it was in Bill Bain's heydey, when a few big clients accounted for the lion's share of its revenues. Bechhofer says Bain teams now work for a wide variety of clients. "We've worked with start-ups; we've worked with all different sorts of companies. It is not the size of the company but the opportunity they [present]," he says. Alpha Publications' Dawson estimates that 40 percent of Bain's revenues comes from pure strategy work, 20 percent from clients seeking operational improvements, and the remaining 40 percent from other work, including acquisitions, customer loyalty, sales and marketing, and distribution. Bain's revenues come from the telecommunications and high-tech industries, consumer products, financial services, and industrial and defense, in that order, Dawson says.

And it is reaching beyond the traditional word-of-mouth marketing that characterized the company when Bill Bain was in charge. The company has launched a drive to increase awareness of Loyalty-Based Management, a concept developed by Frederick Reichheld, a Bain vice president. Reichheld argues that companies who develop strong employee and customer loyalty programs can dramatically increase profits. An increase of 5 percent in customer retention for MBNA, a credit card company, increased profits by 60 percent over five years with the practices advocated by Reichheld. Like many of its competitors, Bain is using the publishing world to market the concept. The Harvard Business School Press is publishing *The Loyalty Effect*, a book by Reichheld, who touted the book on a nationwide tour.

But, in many other respects, Bain has not changed as much as it would like outsiders to believe. The consulting firm still prefers to work closely with the upper echelons of corporate America. "We prefer to have a close working relationship with the senior management team," Bechhofer says. "Part of what we are trying to do is create results, have an impact, and create change. That doesn't tend to happen unless it has the blessing of the senior management team. That senior management team can be of a division empowered to make change, or it can be the chief executive of a corporation who is empowered to make change within his company. It is making sure that the person you are working for matches the scope of the issue that you are dealing with, so that you don't end up with an answer but the person you are dealing with says, that may be the right answer but I can't do anything about it." The approach empowers Bain's consultants but it also alienates people in the lower echelons, whose support is crucial if the consultant and the client want to make change work.

James Tobin, the former executive from Baxter International who currently has Bain working for him at Biogen, says Bain consultants have many strengths, but finding their own limits is not one of them. "If you need to know market data, they can get it. If you need to know your competitor's capacity, they can get it. If you need sixteen different marketing plans in cardiac business, they can get it. They're very good at taking the data they find and capsulizing it in such a way that you can understand it and figure out what it means. They are very good at finding out things that you don't think you can find out—legally. But the Bain guys have a tendency to want to widen the boundaries [of a project]. You have to watch that. It is up to you as the manager, the executive, to set the guardrails and to manage Bain. I draw the line when they start telling you what it means. What I have found over the years is that they're better at gathering data than making sense of it. I have more confidence in my ability to declare the meaning than their ability to draw conclusions from the data."

Tobin says he employed Bain this year to assess what Biogen should do now that it has successfully developed Avonex, a new drug used to treat multiple sclerosis. "It took us eighteen years to develop the drug. Now we have a gap in our pipeline. We had Bain working on a project to determine how we should fill that gap—acquire something or accelerate something we already have under way. They helped us answer the question of how best we could accelerate one of our existing projects." He said Bain was the best he has ever seen at dredging up such information. "But you had better draw your own conclusions. They're not implementers, they're not even conclusion drawers. You have to draw the conclusions. You have to do the implementation. That's how I operated with Bain. I found that to be the optimal balance. In cases where they were drawing the conclusions and setting the implementation plans, inevitably it failed." He said consultants lack the nuts-and-bolts experience of executives and managers with hands-on experience.

Tobin and others in Chicago said that executives at Baxter relied too heavily on Bain and paid a price. Bain, they said, became a "crutch" for senior management to second-guess or corroborate the staff when they were at Baxter in force during the late 1980s. "Senior management got a script from Bain with what they wanted to do and went with it," one former executive said. Another former company official familiar with Bain's work at the company agreed: "The Bain consultants did a better job at winning the confidence of Vern Loucks than they did of inspiring trust at the group vice president or unit level," he said. "The Bain people, and I think this is both a strength and a weakness, but these are very young people and in terms of getting the grass to grow, I don't think they have a lot of experience."

Bain competitors say that the company still floods clients with aggressive teams of consultants who always seem a step away from taking over. Although Bain routinely refuses to comment upon its relationships with clients, Bechhofer disputes Bain's critics. "We don't run companies as some of the articles kindly implied," he said. "It would be inappropriate for a consultant to try to do that. We spend less time with the client than our competitors do, but we probably spend more time thinking and worrying about how the work we're doing is going to get incorporated into the business than they do, and that's where some of that criticism comes from. Interesting enough, if you read the literature of the same folks that were criticizing [Bain's approach] fifteen years ago, that's what they are talking about now. And if you look at what CEOs are looking for, they are talking now about a track record of results being more important. And so to a certain extent, it feels like the industry has moved toward us. We were probably a little bit [like] pioneers."

Bain continues to track the price of a client's stock to determine if its stock price rises once the consulting contract is signed. In most cases, it does. But Bechhofer acknowledges it is hard to determine the real meaning of the index, which is monitored by Price Waterhouse. "We don't make a pretension that we single-handedly caused that, and it would be wrong if we did. So [I have] two interpretations of that. One is that companies that outperform the Standard and Poor's index like to work with us. I think they are a little more progressive, change-oriented companies. The second is, we care about results and we track them."

Bain also continues to develop ties to clients that are far closer than those of any other firm in the industry. Bain & Co. is the only consulting firm that has a venture capital arm that becomes financially involved with consulting clients. Some eyebrows were raised at Baxter when Bain Capital acquired Baxter's diagnostics manufacturing business in late 1994 for $415 million. In the past, Bain had been involved in evaluating Baxter's place in the diagnostics business, which at one time was valued at $600 million. Such acquisitions fuel questions about possible conflicts of interest. As a consultant, Bain is engaged to advise Baxter on actions that would maximize shareholder value. How can its venture capital arm then acquire a property for a price that serves its client's interests and those with a stake in Bain Capital, a class that includes some Bain vice presidents?

Bechhofer says Bain & Co. consultants were not involved in advising Baxter on the sale of the diagnostics unit. He also notes that both companies have strict codes of confidentiality and that Bain Capital operates completely independently of Bain & Co.

The sale, a Bain statement said, was part of a restructuring at Baxter in which two investment banking firms were hired to conduct an auction, which included Bain Capital and more than 20 other potential buyers: "After a protracted auction process—with no 'synergy buyer' emerging—Bain Capital came out the higher bidder and was able to complete the acquisition of the diagnostics group." Bechhofer says the company also has a strict policy that prohibits its consultants from investing in any company in which it gains insider information from its consulting contacts. It is just one of many policies and practices, he says, that makes Bain stand out from the pack.

"We have an entire culture that is oriented around generating results," he says. "We talk about the 80/100 rule, which is I would rather have an 80 percent solution that is implementable 100 percent of the time than the perfect answer that you can't implement. An academic would not like that because it is not purist; it is a practitioner's approach. We talk about Monday morning at eight o'clock. What is a client going to do with the work we are helping them with at Monday morning at eight o'clock?"

The Gold Boys' Network

POWER AND GLORY AT MCKINSEY

Bain & Co.'s reputation for secrecy and its closeness to clients present one picture of strategy consulting. But there is no consulting firm in the world that carries more weight into corporate boardrooms than McKinsey & Co., the partnership known widely as "The Firm," by large measure the most influential of them all.

The notion that Jesuits make the best missionaries has persisted for several hundred years, which implies there might actually be something to it, or, alternatively, that all the evidence that might tend to suggest the contrary has been carefully swept out of sight. In fact, both of these are correct.

— *The Jesuits*, by Manfred Barthel

Comparing the history and culture of an ancient religious order complete with an abundance of turmoil and tremendous connections and influence over the course of time to a modern management consulting company might seem a leap of logic, if not of faith. But it doesn't take much looking at either the Society of Jesus or McKinsey & Co. to be struck by the strength of the comparison. Strip away the religious part and what is left is the conclusion that the ancient popes had their shock troops, spies, and influence peddlers, many of them brilliant almost beyond description. At the very least, they were the best-educated collection of priests across history. They seem to have popped up almost everywhere. But the most revealing Jesuit anecdotes are the ones that connect them to a truth that many a McKinsey consultant has recognized over the past six decades of The Firm's existence: The most important body part of a person in power, be it a king or a king's mistress or a chief executive officer or his strongest assistant, is the ear. Win access to the ear and whisper the right message, and your influence will find its true measure.

That is where the Jesuits have always done their best work, be it in the courts of power or in the classroom. And that is where the classic McKinsey consultant has always done some of his most important work, too. From James O. McKinsey and the consulting industry he helped create from his accounting career early in the century, on to Marvin Bower, the man who saved McKinsey & Co. from the pits of failure after McKinsey's death in the 1930s and who led the company with an iron hand into the world of modern business, and on again to its collection of managing directors, it has been a dominant truth.

Whether it was counseling depression-era businesses on survival, postwar executives on how to manage the coming boom, or the modern CEO on the uncertainties and opportunities of the world marketplace, the people who work for McKinsey have always been adept at whispering into the proper ear. For many years, the ability to think and talk fast was one of the most important assets anyone could bring to the company. They are so good at this that McKinsey's own mythology and culture in the world of business are every bit as powerful as the mythology of the Jesuits, although not yet as enduring. If the order is a stunning example of the application of values, discipline, reputation, and access over time, so is the partnership that has come to be known, inside and out, as The Firm.

This comparison of McKinsey to the religious order has come up so many times over the years that it has almost reached the status of cliché. McKinsey's own insiders frequently describe themselves as combinations of Jesuits and U.S. Marines. But that is usually delivered as little more than a throwaway line. The parallels between the order and the consulting company are so strong that it seems the Jesuits of old, given some appropriate Brooks Brothers outfitting, would fit handily into modern McKinsey. And many of the modern McKinsey people, if they traded their Savile Row suits for some old wool cassocks, would probably have fit quite handily into the global role the Jesuits played across history.

McKinsey & Co. might well have created the best business missionaries of all time. But it might also be the beneficiary of the fact that it is able to dispose of its mistakes, hide its embarrassments, and display to the outside a facade that seems almost golden, and at the very least free of obvious dents and tarnish.

To borrow again from Barthel, both of these are correct.

Look at some of the most powerful entities in American business, for example, and the McKinsey influence is apparent. From finance to retail sales, manufacturing to transportation, and on into high technology, McKinsey business missionaries not only whisper and advise at the highest levels, they have a propensity for moving from the consulting world into the executive suite. IBM, Sears, AT&T, American Express, the list could stretch for pages, all huge companies that first bought McKinsey's top-dollar advice, and then saw McKinsey veterans shift loyalties and join executive ranks, frequently turning back to their old employer to buy consulting services. It is one of the world's great old-boy networks. Job placement is only part of the point. When a Fred Gluck moves from directing McKinsey to running Bechtel Corp., in San Francisco, he takes along McKinsey values, experience, and, most important, contacts. There are signs of these connections almost everywhere now, the legacy of decades of consulting and executive contacts.

McKinsey's Golden Connection

McKinsey's name and reputation travel everywhere, perhaps because so many of its veterans shifted into positions of power in key corporations. An examination of their backgrounds makes it apparent that one reason they moved into the highest echelons of corporate America was because their jobs at McKinsey opened important doors. To deconstruct the backgrounds of a few of the more prominent McKinsey graduates is to get a look at what those McKinsey power connections mean and how far they can reach.

Harvey Golub, chairman and chief executive officer of American Express Co., represents one version of the consulting career track. Golub, 56, joined American Express as president and chief of IDS Financial Services in 1984, straight from a senior partnership at McKinsey. His primary job in his last years at McKinsey & Co. was to consult with American Express on strategy and management operations issues, a position that obviously gave him a deep understanding of how the company worked. He had been a junior partner at McKinsey from 1967 to 1974, when he left for a time to become president of Shulman Air Freight.

Golub sits at the top of a $14-billion-a-year corporation that has connections in 160 countries. Its banking arm alone has offices in 37 countries. But his influence isn't limited by his job title at American Express. Senior partners at McKinsey are expected to reach out to their communities by serving on boards and doing the kind of pro bono work that enhances The Firm's reputation. That is a practice Golub has carried with him from his McKinsey days. He serves on the boards of the American Enterprise Institute, Columbia Presbyterian Hospital, Carnegie Hall, the New York City Partnership, the New York City Chamber of Commerce and Industry, the United Way of New York City, the Business Roundtable, and the Bretton Woods Committee. He also sits on the President's Committee for the Arts and Humanities and the President's Advisory Council for Trade Policy Negotiations.

Louis V. Gerstner, Jr., now the driving force behind IBM's revival, is another McKinsey consultant who followed the path from advising American Express directly into its corporate offices. He has been in charge at IBM since 1994, but he arrived at that position after stints at American Express and RJR Nabisco. Gerstner joined American Express in 1978 after 12 years at McKinsey, the last five of them working on the American Express account. He was president at American Express from 1978 to 1989 and chairman and CEO at RJR Nabisco from 1989 to 1992. His influence, too, reaches far beyond IBM. He serves on the board of the New York Times Co., Bristol-Myers Squibb Co., The Japan Society, RJR Nabisco, Inc., and the New American Schools Development Corp., along with his former board position with McKinsey and a board seat with AT&T.

Another McKinsey standout, Michael H. Jordan, was a consultant from 1964 to 1974, then shifted to one of The Firm's big clients, PepsiCo Inc., where he was chairman of international foods and beverages from 1974 to 1992. He left Pepsi to take a partnership at the investment firm of Clayton, Dubilier & Rice from 1992 to 1993, and then jumped into the job he holds today, chairman and chief executive officer of Westinghouse Electric.

Jordan, 60, a chemical engineer who was on Admiral Hyman Rickover's staff during four years in the Navy, has fostered a complete restructuring of Westinghouse, one of the most complicated ventures in modern business history. He is an internationalist and has been active in promoting U.S. trade abroad, even as he has expanded Westinghouse's portfolio to include CBS Broadcasting. Jordan serves on the President's Export Council, which advises the White House on expanding foreign trade.

As with Golub and Gerstner, Jordan's influence reaches far beyond the confines of the company he has been so aggressively reconstructing. He is chairman of the board of the College Fund/UNCF, and on the boards at University of Pittsburgh Medical Center and the Allegheny Conference on Community Development. He also sits on the boards of Rhône-Poulenc Rorer, Inc., Melville Corp., Dell Computer Corp., and the Aetna Life and Casualty Co.

These three McKinsey veterans now control corporations with annual sales that run into the hundreds of billions of dollars, companies so big and so aggressive that, just by changing course, they can change the face of American business culture and send reactions ranging from ripples to tidal waves around the world. Gerstner, Golub, and Jordan have been the people to watch in American business for many years, and not a business magazine profile or a newspaper account of a major announcement passes without giving due notice to their backgrounds at McKinsey & Co.

But they are united in more than just the line "McKinsey & Co., consultant" in their vitae. All of these men have been aggressive and, their supporters would claim, visionary in what they have done within their companies. Boldness is one of the earmarks of a McKinsey background. And there are signs aplenty of boldness at American Express, Westinghouse, and IBM. What didn't work at Westinghouse, for example, had a tendency to disappear. And IBM was not shy in aggressively shedding personnel, despite its legendary "job for life" reputation. Gerstner was also credited with rebuilding much of American Express during his years there. All three of these companies were stumbling through difficult times or had lost their competitive edge before Jordan, Gerstner, and Golub came on the scene. It was no coincidence that by the time they made their jumps into the corporate hierarchy, they had collected decades of hands-on experience with The Firm.

Just as the Jesuits have earned their reputation for intelligence, cunning, and impact over time, there is simply no denying the brilliance of McKinsey's consultants and their influence in modern business history. The reasons are the same in both cases. Intellectual vigor is one of the key components in joining and surviving at either institution. A predictable religious zeal has always wedded the priests to the Jesuit tradition and values. McKinsey, too, commands zeal and loyalty from its consultants, along with a strict adherence to a set of clearly defined values.

Gluck is a case in point. Not at all the typical business consultant, he actually was a rocket scientist at Bell Labs before he joined McKinsey and is credited inside the company for instilling an intellectual liveliness that separates McKinsey from almost all its peers in consulting. Jordan, too, who is certified as a nuclear engineer in addition to his background in chemistry, brought a Navy and technical background to his consulting tasks at McKinsey, something that set him aside from the business school grads like Gerstner who have been so frequently favored inside The Firm.

When McKinsey goes searching for new consultants, it always starts at the top of the field of candidates, whether it be at the Harvard Business School, where it has long had a reputation for reeling in Baker Scholars—the top 5 percent of each class—by the bundle, or lately at a collection of other universities around the world. It allows The Firm's clients to make important assumptions about the teams McKinsey sends in to do the actual work. Over the past few decades, business culture has become so tightly bonded to the idea of graduate school academic performance that when a McKinsey consultant arrives, there is no doubt he or she will be on the same page as the brightest executive the company can present. They will be speaking the same language and sharing the same values as they attack specific problems. The Firm's true power may rest somewhere behind that crucial assumption. The only real measures of success for consulting companies are the weight given to their advice and the implementation of their recommendations. By exercising its intellectual vigor at the top of companies, then, McKinsey has always been able to exert influence where it matters most, in the corporate office.

It can whisper at the very best time into the most important ear.

The process does not always work. McKinsey has shared in its own collection of flops over time. Business philosophy is as changeable as the weather, and what might have seemed a brilliant suggestion in one era could yield disaster in another.

On a much larger scale, as the artificial borders that separate businesses from one another around the world began to bend, break, and then disappear, as once disconnected nation-state governments began to swim in a global ocean, McKinsey, too, moved into a global mode. It has abandoned the American cultural and business attitudes that dominated The Firm from its inception. Deliberately and with a single-mindedness of purpose that seems remarkable in such a confusing world, it is no longer directly connected to its own roots. It is not now an American company and probably hasn't been for 20 years. Its nerve center sits in New York. Its managing partner works in downtown Chicago. Its Global Institute is on Pennsylvania Avenue in Washington, D.C., a short walk from the White House. But its truest address is in the capitals and industrial centers of the world. It is a United Nations of business consulting, with one crucial difference: It works.

This is a company that has, in effect, its own Department of State and its own United Nations in the form of a board of directors that is genuinely global. It has its own Central Intelligence Agency in the tiers of well-educated specialists in an endless variety of disciplines. Partners in Germany assess the work of partners in the Chicago office. Ambitious young men shift their lives and their expertise to Moscow, where they make their contacts, build the local staff, and wait for the day the Russians finally break through the muck of transition and emerge into a capitalistic sunlight—or at least into dependable currency and stable economic growth. Consultants from New Delhi show up in Houston, consultants from San Francisco in Tokyo. A man whose field of expertise might have been physics finds himself studying the economy in Scandinavia. A veteran McKinsey consultant sits within a hop, skip, and a jump of the White House and discusses what it means that banking in New York is 20 times as efficient as banking in India. In a way, McKinsey & Co. is its own world government, but a lot more fleet of foot and mind than the bureaucracies that infest the older model.

As for McKinsey's reputation with its clients, its own stature in the roller-coaster world of business consulting is one measure of its value.

Consulting companies blow hot and cold, depending on the economy and depending on their own ability to market their products. The Firm has tried to avoid the fads that are such meat and potatoes for newcomers to the consulting field. It offers the whole array of business services, but seems wedded to none of them in particular. Stability over time seems to be the goal. McKinsey has had its ups and downs, too, but many more ups than downs.

For many years, the chieftains have paid dearly for its services. There are CEOs who will never again turn to a McKinsey consultant for advice, just as there are challenges and stubborn cases McKinsey can choose to ignore. But The Firm's corporate enemies do not form a large group and are vastly outweighed by the legions that pay for objective, high-quality analysis and advice. It comes down to a question of value: McKinsey will send very smart people to work hard to produce whatever a client wants. If that is a blue-covered report intended to sit on a shelf somewhere forever, then the client can rest assured it will be the best blue-covered report he ever ignored. If it is an action plan or a specific goal, the same vigor will be applied.

The big names and major partners are the magnets, but the grunt work of preparing in-depth reports and working on project implementation happens at a different, much lower level. Anyone with any sense, for example, would delight in spending a few days with the kind of people who head The Firm—Rajat Gupta, the internationalist; his predecessor, Fred Gluck; or Marvin Bower himself, who could talk all about McKinsey right back to its beginning (but won't, of course). They are inherently interesting, great teachers, and wonderful talkers. But those are not the people who show up from Monday through Friday to do the actual consulting.

Because of that reality, The Firm has played its part in the birth of the criticisms that plague the darker side of management consulting. If there is one theme that pops up all over the industry, it is that consulting companies have a tendency to send a lot of green talent into the field.

One former American Express insider, for example, complained that in his experience, McKinsey's people were primarily interested in telling management exactly what it wanted to hear and kept sending in new consulting teams that never had much of a chance to learn the business. To be sure, in the strange world of management consulting, that might have been exactly what American Express wanted at the time. McKinsey has, indeed, provided the cover many an executive needed to carry out distasteful dismissals, restructurings, downsizings, and changes in course, all elements at play over American Express's recent history.

It is not the biggest consulting company in the world. That medal goes to Andersen Consulting, which had revenues in the $4 billion to $5 billion range and employed some 40,000 consultants at the end of 1995. But Andersen's interests are tightly tied to technology, an expensive reality that inflates its numbers. With a little over 3,000 consultants all over the world and no technology component to speak of, McKinsey still collected an estimated $1.5 billion in revenues in 1994. By another measure, it is certainly the most successful of the generalist strategy firms, well ahead of Boston Consulting Group.

McKinsey & Co. has one of the most sophisticated public relations efforts in the industry, but it shuns the kind of publicity other consulting companies thrive on. It is reluctant to present its consultants for interviews, but garners tremendous acclaim in business circles by emitting a constant stream of articles for the *Harvard Business Review*, in-depth studies of the world economy from its Global Institute, and book after book about the obtuse complexities of productivity management, international finance, and state-of-the-art management philosophy.

McKinsey has little trouble arranging high-level discussion seminars for corporate chiefs all over the world, and it can throw in a healthy collection of Nobel Prize laureates and government officials almost at will. People who know McKinsey say every key office has one person whose primary goal is buffing image. Lesser consulting companies might deliver nuts-and-bolts presentations, but McKinsey always seems to arrive with the equivalent of a new Mercedes-Benz. More important, it knows exactly where to park it.

The Firm's Image

The image is so carefully presented that the new McKinsey consultant is trained in how to behave with his or her clients. Where to keep the hands during a presentation is crucial (not in the pockets and always above the table when seated). Eyes being the mirror of the soul, the

McKinsey consultant always keeps that crucial visual contact, but never to the point at which it makes the target uncomfortable. Overhead charts and graphs are okay, but only rarely and not at all if they draw attention away from the individual. Objectivity is so important that McKinsey consultants are lectured on the potential conflicts of interest involved in using what they have collected to make investment decisions. If all of this seems petty, it is important to remember that McKinsey's people are always being watched, first by the client, who will be solicited for comments that can make or break a new consultant's career, and then by superiors, who participate in what must amount to the most excruciating, intensive performance reviews anywhere.

Senior McKinsey partners might spend a third of their time serving on committees to review the work of their peers and subordinates. This is considered one of the most important tasks of all, measured by the fact that the chance of "making it" to a senior level at The Firm is stacked against everyone the first day they walk in the door. The odds against rising to a senior partnership are 11 to 1.

McKinsey & Co. is a magnet for money. There is apparently so much of it that those who succeed at rising to partnership can anticipate salaries of over $1 million a year. McKinsey may even be one of the best places of all to fail, or at least to leave, partially because it goes to some lengths to make certain that the departing consultant lands well.

But The Firm, as many a former McKinseyite can testify, may not be the most comfortable place to work because it is so obsessive about ongoing performance reviews and driving out those who just can't make it. This isn't hyperbole. Performance reviews obtained in a court case reveal page after page of written commentary and criticism on how well the candidate stacks up against McKinsey's standards. It is not a question of whether a person is a team player, for example; it is how much of a team player he is and how he handles relationships with his peers and with clients. The reviews are meticulous in detailing faults and setting recommendations for improvement. They reflect an intensity that has built up over a long time. Undoubtedly, the reviewer's own experiences over the years of McKinsey vetting inform the process. There is clearly no time for coasting for the young associate who wants to make a career of McKinsey.

Four of every five hires will disappear in the first five years. The winnowing will continue even for those who make it through this tough "up or out" period. The Firm is so comfortable with this process that, should concerns about revenue arise, it can simply cut the number of people it allows in the front door, knowing full well that the attrition that occurs across the company will quickly take care of the problem. Those who leave generally leave peacefully, knowing that they are part of an army of former McKinseyites that shifts handily into the upper echelons of the most powerful companies in the world. Gupta said he spends much of his time, for example, counseling partners on their careers and on whether they should stay at McKinsey. He will often recommend a departure, particularly for those partners who have attractive offers. It is never a situation in which McKinsey will improve salary or offer other enticements, Gupta said. Instead, the conversation always amounts to a discussion of whether it is in an individual's best interest to stay on at McKinsey or go for a better opportunity.

But as progressive and warming as Gupta's explanation might seem, for the new arrivals there is another formula at work. From the first day they walk into whatever office McKinsey has chosen for them, the pressure is on. It is abundantly clear to everyone that what McKinsey wants to do is get rid of most of them and keep only those who best fit the McKinsey mold.

Those who make it successfully through the toughest vetting process in management consulting continue to play their roles in one of the most valuable alumni associations in business history. They meet in New York at least once a year, as hearty and successful a collection of happy capitalists as one is likely to find anywhere in the western hemisphere. They renew old ties and undoubtedly make mental notes and contacts that will lead to enticing opportunities all over the world.

A World-Class Leader

As The Firm's current chief, Calcutta-born Gupta should not be viewed in standard chief executive officer terms. McKinsey & Co. does not operate like a typical corporation. Instead, it is a high-caliber partnership where consensus of the partners dictates the course of events. His election three years ago was the culmination of a process of internationalization that began deep inside McKinsey decades ago. Sipping hot tea in a comfortable office he keeps in his home in Winnetka, 20 miles or so from McKinsey's Chicago office, he speaks with gentle authority about The Firm and its reputation.

Most of those who pass through McKinsey, he says, value it the way they would value a continuing connection to a beloved old school. A calm departure from McKinsey is an important part of the firm's strategy, he says, because The Firm recognizes that it is frequently involved in growing the executives who will run corporations all over the world. It also knows that it has been so selective in allowing young consultants to come in that it is already dealing with an elite that will have a long life in the world of business.

"We hire outstanding people in their own right, whether they are continuing at McKinsey and are very successful at McKinsey or not," said Gupta. "Our point of view is simply that some people will continue here, some will be leaders elsewhere . . . the nature of the development process here is absolutely outstanding. And then the nature of the process about their leaving is a very dignified one, and something that is befitting a person who has a very high set of intrinsic leadership qualities and somebody who will be successful someplace else. So we try to make sure that is the case." That is important, because much of McKinsey's success flows from the fact that it has long-running and deep connections. One of its most dependable assumptions is that those who have left McKinsey to succeed elsewhere are likely to turn again to McKinsey when it comes time to spend consulting budgets. The theory is that if the client recognizes that the money was well spent, the relationship will continue over the long term. The Firm has another goal, too, that goes along with its globalization. Gupta says McKinsey's mission is to play an influential role in every important economy in the world.

The Firm is willing to wait for years and years for these relationships to develop. It can afford to do that because its revenues from around the world all shift into one vast budget. The individual performance of one new office will not determine salary and compensation there, but McKinsey's performance around the world will. Because its revenue picture is so healthy it can wait for years for its missionary outposts to start delivering the profits.

In China, in Russia, in Indonesia, its consultants open offices, develop the local talent, build connections, and wait for them to start producing. But The Firm doesn't plop people down just anywhere.

Generally, Gupta says, a partner will express an interest in opening an office and gather a few consultants who are willing to go with him. Once they are on the ground, the search will begin for appropriate locals. They are invited to apply and go through the same McKinsey process as consultants hired in the United States. But the target is eventually to develop local offices everywhere that thrive on their connections in the local economy. All of this flows from an early recognition within McKinsey that the world of business was changing, that academic credentials from the best American schools would not necessarily translate into success overseas. Gupta's experience is a template for how it can work.

After a stint in New York, Gupta led McKinsey's Scandinavian practice for five years before the office was turned over to the locals. "It was a very missionary kind of effort," he said, because it was aimed at creating both a staff and a demand for McKinsey's consulting services. "When I felt it was time for the Scandinavians to run it, it really became an insider to that economy and to that practice, frankly, in a way that I could never become an insider, because I am not a Scandinavian. At the same time, it was very much a McKinsey office, with the same values and the same process."

Before any McKinsey consultant is a native of another land, he is first, a McKinsey consultant, connected to his partners and to his institution. The goal is to reach across all artificial boundaries and create a network that embraces a unity of purpose. McKinsey has shunned the more common practice in consulting of gobbling up competition or smaller companies that offer special expertise. Instead, it chooses to grow its own. Up front revenue is not the point. Influence is what seems most important to McKinsey's fortunes. It has already gathered that level of connection in the United States. One reason The Firm doesn't have to beg for work is that its presence is assumed everywhere from AT&T to IBM to Hewlett-Packard to Sears and a hundred other top-tier businesses. Traditionally and deliberately, it deals first with the top echelon of business leadership.

Other consulting companies create vast case studies, complete with testimonials from their clients, endorsements, and media tours of headquarters. Or they are brought in by vice presidents or CEO underlings who are interested in achieving some narrow goal. But McKinsey is simply there, sometimes invisibly, generally at the CEO and board level and, always before anything else, discreetly. The one rule most McKinsey consultants and former consultants seem to value above all others is the rule of confidentiality. Under no condition will the people at McKinsey speak on the record in any detail about the problems of their clients, although their clients sometimes speak about them. "You would not expect a doctor to be talking about his other patients, or an attorney about his clients," Gupta says. It was Marvin Bower's lifelong goal of shaping McKinsey in the image of a classic law firm that led to this particular approach toward client relationships. It is an almost confessional relationship, and one of the certainties that separates McKinsey from the rest of the consulting pack.

These people are remarkably good at keeping quiet at the right time. They will gab and ramble and reminisce for hours about The Firm and its history and its values, about their theories of the world marketplace, about the exact point at which the world sits on the path to a global economy. But ask them what specific role they played when Sears seemed hell-bent on frittering away its reputation, or what they were doing when CBS moved from top to bottom in the world of broadcast news, and it is as though they were struck by a plague of silence. Insiders may agonize about Texaco's decision to dump McKinsey during the consulting firm's own troubled years in the 1970s, when it seemed to be facing the prospect of long-term decline. But whatever secrets they picked up along the way remain just that.

Former McKinsey consultants will chat at length about problems inside The Firm, generically about difficult clients, about cases in which McKinsey's treasured values were bent or broken. But not on the record and not by name and not in any way that could be handily traced. The long-term ties to the place are too valuable to put at such risk. No matter where a former McKinsey consultant might land, there is always a chance he or she will run into The Firm at some other point or in some other context. Having McKinsey as an ally in some nasty internal corporate struggle could be a priceless asset, the equivalent of having your own business Jesuit to call upon.

If some strange virus were to cause a sudden loosening of tongues among the McKinseyites, the results would most likely put them alongside the rest of the industry, a place they do not want to be. They do what a lot of other people in a very competitive business do: They collect money for selling advice, albeit at a much higher level than most and at a much heftier price tag. In the process, they sacrifice the glories of public acclaim. That also frees them from the embarrassment of public failure. It is a formula that has worked well for a long time.

One former McKinsey pro, armed with a brilliant collection of academic credentials, says it was and is a terrific place full of great people. But not perfect. Dante's circles of hell come to mind. The anointed new consultant admitted to the first circle gets the best cases, the best mentoring, and the best avenues to partnership. The second circle, challenging cases and a good chance at advancement. Circle three, some cases but not much attention and not much prospect of partnership. Circle four, the worst place of all. Wretched clients, minimal chance for advancement, little attention from partners.

It was, this former consultant recalled, a very uncomfortable place to be. There was heavy emphasis on truth telling, on cooperation, on the idea of a nonhierarchical existence. There were people at the place who actually walked the talk. The problem was that everyone didn't always play by the rules. There was a hierarchy, and being on the wrong side of it was like being doomed. Sucking up and being the right kind of character, then, is as important at McKinsey as it is anywhere. Telling the truth at the wrong point might not be so well received, although there were those who trotted out unpleasantries, survived the heat, and went on to thrive. Being at McKinsey was so insulating that those who left had to spend their first year in the real world "just getting the shit kicked out of them so they know what the world is like."

It is not the kind of description McKinsey & Co. would advance about itself, but it has a "fly on the wall" sense to it that helps cut through McKinsey's platinum exterior. "You knew that once you became a partner, you would probably be making in the area of a million dollars a year. Investment bankers were making more, but that is the only group. Say you are on a plane and you meet somebody. It doesn't matter what kind of a jerk you are, the minute you say McKinsey, people take notice. It was a very seductive lifestyle," the former consultant said.

But it was not always comfortable. Reports were sometimes written in such a way that their flawed conclusions and data kept a client happy. On the other hand, sometimes solid recommendations were presented even though the consultants knew full well the client would not follow them. There were internal politics to deal with, too. None of that is exclusive to McKinsey & Co. in the world of consulting. The problems may be a function of the pressure to perform, or a product of the overwhelming need to win a client's short-term approval regardless of the long-term costs. There is a mercenary component to management consulting that tends to lead some consultants into doing exactly what the ratepayer wants in a bid to seem brilliant and keep everyone happy.

Even Gluck, who worked for the military part of Bell Labs and who was among the first technology experts brought into the MBA-studded world of McKinsey, recalls that his first few months on the job were not happy. A lot of people thought there was no place for an engineer inside a management consulting company. No one would invite him out on jobs. No one had any idea about what to do with a man who had spent much of his professional life working on antiballistic missile systems. A senior partner, during one of those crucial performance reviews, said he thought it was a big mistake for McKinsey to hire anyone who was dumb enough to spend 10 years inside a research lab. Here he was, 32 years old, very old for a new consultant, far away from Bell Labs, and facing an uncertain career at the most rigorous place in consulting. It all changed for Gluck when he stood up and told the truth about a crucial engagement that was going way wrong and presented his ideas on how to fix it. He said he told his McKinsey friend Michael Jordan that he assumed he was doomed, that it was all over. But Jordan told him not to worry, that he had told the truth. Overnight, Gluck was welcomed as a hero in the New York office for reflecting what McKinsey & Co. believed was the most important of its values, the truth-telling part.

Again, it is part of the mystery and wonder of the place that conflicting accounts of life at McKinsey can be accurate. There are mixes of consulting heaven and consulting hell there. Gluck was obviously a few steps outside of the fourth circle when he began, but advanced to the first circle quite handily, just by being Gluck. Playing by the McKinsey rules, which are aimed at encouraging an outspoken aggressiveness on client issues, obviously works. Or, at the very least, it worked for him.

One Woman's Claim

It didn't seem to work so well for a young woman in Texas who came to McKinsey with good academic credentials, a professional demeanor, and bundles of ambition to advance through the McKinsey ranks to partnership level. In fact, it all went so wrong at some point that the whole matter ended up in federal court—after an initial complaint was filed with the Equal Employment Opportunity Commission—where Suzanne Porter charged she had been a victim of discrimination because she was a woman.

McKinsey disagrees on all points and won summary judgments dismissing a number of the claims, among them sexual harassment based on Porter's charge that she was the target of a whole collection of inappropriate comments from men over time and the argument that McKinsey blackballed Porter in her attempts to get a job at Bain & Co. But other issues are still on the table, among them the argument that the deck is stacked against women at McKinsey, and whether there is merit to her claim that The Firm hurt her chances at two other consulting companies.

Suzanne Porter v. McKinsey & Co., Inc., is not a simple story for The Firm, whose lawyers have sealed much of their side of the court record. What you get in this case is something like a picture of the Loch Ness monster, some bumps on the water and what looks like a head, but not enough data at all to say exactly what the entire animal looks like. Porter and her attorney are reluctant to discuss the details. They simply referred all inquiries to the clerk's office of the U.S. District Court in Dallas, where *Porter v. McKinsey* created a fat, if spotty, account of one person's life inside one McKinsey office. It is clear that Suzanne Porter did not get what she wanted from McKinsey. Aside from that, the court record reveals a lot about the way McKinsey works, how its consultants are paid, and how it decides which hopefuls are tapped for partnerships and beyond. The big question that remains is why advancement didn't happen for Suzanne Porter, with McKinsey saying she just didn't measure up, and Porter charging discrimination.

The idea of working for a consulting company was planted in Porter's head just before she went on leave from her job in the treasury department of Amoco in the mid-1980s to go to business school at the University of Texas. She said she knew she wanted to enter some kind of service business, and consulting seemed ideal because it involved working for a client and meeting high standards. She was on the front end of what was to become a rush to consulting for business school graduates, not only because it promised high income for those who succeeded, but because it was a good avenue into the upper echelons of corporate America. On top of all that, for Porter, it was challenging. "There would be a rigor about the work that would be substantial. . . . I just kind of liked that pace of activity," she recalled. "I focused on investment banking and consulting, which wasn't atypical for someone in business school. . . . I was at the University of Texas and we didn't have recruiting at that time from Boston Consulting Group or Bain. Basically it amounted to McKinsey and Booz Allen and some of the Big Eight firms. McKinsey just stood out as a firm that had a lot of diversity in terms of the industries that it served, yet my feeling at the time was that they did a lot of strategy work, which I found particularly interesting."

She knew McKinsey was high on the list of consulting companies she was interested in, but she didn't know much about the place. She attended one of McKinsey's public forums at U.T., submitted her résumé, and waited. First there was a general chat with the McKinsey representatives. After that the interview process moved on to the next level, where she was given some casework to see how she responded. "There is usually some anxiety as to whether or not you managed to touch on all of the things the person is looking for," she said. But she performed well. She got a phone offer first, then an offer in the mail. McKinsey was interested enough to ask her to push up her starting date. It already had assignments for her. She began working at McKinsey on March 3, 1986.

The assignments she got made it seem as though she had arrived at that first circle level of success at McKinsey in Dallas. McKinsey said she worked with EDS, Republic Financial Services, Enron, American General, Tenneco, Zale, and Children's Hospital accounts. The clock was running. Expectations at McKinsey are very high, and the time frame for achieving them is relatively short compared to the life span of a career. The track to junior partnership is a five-to-seven-year run, with many stopping points along the way for rigorous assessment and feedback from superiors and fellow workers. Because everyone involved in the suit is constrained from commenting, and because McKinsey rarely talks about these matters, what exists of Suzanne Porter's experience at McKinsey is a court record. It is *Rashomon*-like in the sense that each side seems to be describing different characters.

"In addition, through her work in McKinsey's health care practice, she had exposure to partners in McKinsey's Los Angeles and Cleveland offices, whose evaluations and impressions of her performance were considered, both in the periodic performance review process and in the decision of the Texas office not to nominate her for possible election to principal," said McKinsey manager Tom C. Tinsley in an affidavit. Tinsley had been a partner at McKinsey since 1984 and worked in the Texas office since 1986. He has been the manager there since September of 1994. His testimony presents a detailed look at how McKinsey works and provides an echo of what the former McKinsey consultant meant when the comparison to Dante's *Inferno* was offered.

McKinsey consultants start out as associates, Tinsley said, and are assigned to one or more engagement teams supervised by senior consultants. After two or three years at The Firm, the consultant who does well becomes an "engagement manager" supervising a team. Two or three more years at that and the title "senior engagement manager" is conferred. But that isn't just a title. The superiors at McKinsey raise the bar for their senior engagement managers and watch them closely. At any time during the course of this experiential leap, The Firm can decide the character just isn't going to make it. "At that point he or she begins transitioning out of the firm," Tinsley said. At about the five-year point, the people who run McKinsey's local offices start to consider whether an individual is going to make it to the next stage, that of election to principal—the equivalent of a junior partner's position in a law firm. Only one in five make it to principal. And of those who make it to principal, only one in two are elected to a director's position, which is similar to the senior partner's job in a law firm.

But it's not a simple matter. A candidate must complete three steps to be elected a principal. The first, Tinsley said, requires nomination by the local office based on the decision of the partners in the office that "the consultant meets the standards applied worldwide to all principal candidates." The locals can nominate as many people as they wish at this point. Step two requires approval by a "Principal Candidate Evaluation Committee" of 16 or so partners that is responsible for reviewing and making recommendations on all the principal nominees from all the McKinsey offices around the world. Anyone who makes it through that gateway is then at step three: an elect/nonelect decision by a subcommittee of The Firm's board of directors.

A Tough Employer

The complexity of the relationships involved in this process defies description. Suffice it to say that McKinsey & Co. may be the pickiest employer in the world when it comes to the level of scrutiny its employees must face. The Firm says the same standards are applied to everyone; all of them are based on McKinsey's Mission and Guiding Principles statement, which includes demands of "superior quality work, commitment to client service, contribution to the partnership through teamwork and collaboration and assumption of the responsibility of self-governance." The specifics on how these ideals are to be applied are a little more malleable. A candidate has to be willing to seek advice without trying to control situations. A candidate has to display a willingness to develop and care for people, inspire others, be enjoyable to work with, be dedicated to clients, display "partnership behavior" (whatever that is), and show personal integrity, judgment, and maturity. It helps a lot if a candidate has a good mentor or, perhaps as much as a mentor, a protector, to represent the candidate's interests in the circles of power.

This is the point at which the pathways of memory between institutional McKinsey and aspirant Porter start to part. She states and presents some witnesses who say that she was all of that and more. McKinsey, although it advanced her all the way to senior engagement manager status by the beginning of 1991, less than five years after she walked in the door, argues her performance "exhibited both strengths and weaknesses. She was a great talker, was energetic and enthusiastic about her work, and devoted a lot of energy to her engagements," Tinsley testified. But he said she had trouble working in a team environment and "often required a high degree of supervision." Usually it takes about 18 to 24 months to be put on the principal list for senior engagement managers. But by August 1991, Porter was told "her performance on her most recent engagement was not satisfactory." Later in 1991, according to Tinsley, the partners determined she was a year to a year and a half behind "in her development." In June of 1992, the McKinsey Texas partners decided not to recommend her for election to principal. She was told a month later and, typical of McKinsey's gentle departure policies, was given a "transition period" of six to nine months at full pay. She stayed at McKinsey until April 30, 1993.

Porter tells a different story, beginning with the notice from Tinsley that she was not going to be nominated for principal. He gave her the news, she said, "then followed that statement with, given that the need . . . there is a need for additional core client experience and your husband is moving to Boston, we don't think it makes sense to proceed," according to an affidavit in the case. Her plan had been to travel to Boston on weekends to visit her husband while he attended Harvard. Part of her claim is based on the argument that McKinsey was using the status of her husband to determine her employment future. In addition, experience with important McKinsey core clients is critical to advancing, and Porter claims that at several points during her years there, she raised questions about not being assigned to more core client cases. The response from her superiors, she said, was that the cases she handled were very important and that she was headed for a partnership nonetheless.

Porter also said that she was well reviewed and advanced along the McKinsey path and received fat bonuses every year for job performance. She said she was told many times over the years that she was on the pathway toward partnership, a first in the Texas office for a woman. She and her witnesses alleged that women at McKinsey were not as well brought along as men, that their review meetings tended to be somewhat superficial, that favored men were given specific critiques that explained in great detail what needed to be done to advance.

Porter's case also forced open a couple of the most firmly closed doors inside McKinsey. Her professional witnesses got access to some of the information they needed to assemble documents measuring how much money she had missed out on making as a McKinsey partner and The Firm's overall track record on women. Her attorneys turned to Dr. Lucia Albino Gilbert, who has spent a decade on research and teaching about women's career development issues, as their expert witness to review the status of women inside McKinsey. She applied a long list of standards to the consulting company and concluded that Porter was, indeed, the subject of sex discrimination. Women, she noted, make up less than 5 percent of The Firm's 465 principals and directors. There were no women in that position in the Dallas office during Porter's time there, although one was elected a principal in 1995. Between 1978 and 1993, 22 women and 127 men were hired by the McKinsey Texas office. By January of 1993, she noted, 12 of the men but none of the women were employed either as principals or as a director in the local office. Beyond that, 41 percent of the women over that time frame left as associates compared to 27 percent of the men. There was a similar pattern at the engagement manager level. Attrition for women at the senior engagement manager's level was 100 percent for women and 30 percent for men. "These figures are consistent with reports of what has come to be known as the glass ceiling—the existence of invisible, artificial barriers blocking women and minorities from advancing up the corporate ladder to management and executive level positions," she wrote in her report.

Looking more closely, Gilbert cited two cases in which Porter had challenged male McKinsey partners on studies they had completed. This constituted "out-of-role" behavior: Essentially in the view of critics of male reactions to that kind of challenge, Porter was not playing the woman's role. There was something called a "null environment" problem, too. In such cases, Gilbert said, women are given false impressions of their status in organizations or get vague, nonspecific feedback on their performance.

She reviewed the performance papers of two McKinsey men who were up for principal election and compared them to Porter's. She found different patterns. Both men were provided clear steps that were necessary to "promote their development." Both men were said to need strong mentoring. "Feedback to Ms. Porter was more global in nature and took the form of such general suggestions as 'step away from the analytical work to get a more complete picture,' and 'become more relaxed with the inevitable change/uncertainty and ambiguity inherent in our work,' or 'continue to work on team dynamics.' "

One piece of information in the case covers the "evaluation of economic damages of Suzanne Porter," a report from Dr. Everett G. Dillman. McKinsey produced figures that led him to conclude that by 1995, people who had been elected as principal, the junior partner level, at McKinsey were making $417,730 a year in salary, bonuses, and benefits. By 1995, for example, the base salary of a principal was $175,000 a year, with a bonus of $155,117, $18,000 in retirement benefits, and an $8,883 increase in value in treasured McKinsey stock. Additional "awards," medical benefits, and life insurance coverage pushed the package in one case to $447,830 a year. The long-term projections of the difference between being a McKinsey consultant and a self-employed consultant over the lifetime of a healthy career moved into the $30 million range. It is just one small glimpse of the profits available in the McKinsey world of blue-blood consulting. And that is one big way McKinsey and the Jesuits are different.

What becomes of Suzanne Porter's case is a matter for the U.S. District Court to decide. Short term, the Texas office got some sensitivity training it didn't anticipate, and another woman was finally elected to the principal level. How much of the case reflects a reality the whole male-dominated consulting business has yet to come to grips with—that women are playing a bigger and bigger role in the life of American business—is another question. A long-term guess would be that more and more women will succeed, not only at McKinsey, but at its competitors, because consulting companies are supersensitive to their images and aware of the fact that it is important to keep clients comfortable. McKinsey has been good at that for a long time, and it is no accident.

A Company with Deep Roots

History follows institutions everywhere, sometimes like a nagging relative and sometimes like a welcomed old friend. It can be a warning of unhappy events that must be avoided, or it can be a template upon which an organization is constructed. In the case of McKinsey & Co., it is both. What exists today is a partnership that has its roots in the depths of the depression, in what amounted to a big consulting engagement that made a lot of important enemies, and in the turmoil and battles that ensued. What remains of James O. McKinsey's company, the firm he founded and then left to head Marshall Field & Co. in Chicago, is simply the name and a chunk of McKinsey's early consulting philosophy.

But what a business archaeologist would find at the bottom if he dug down through the decades of McKinsey's history is an uncommonly determined man who wanted to cleanse the business of management consulting of its questionable reputation and replace it with status that would equal that of medicine or the law.

Marvin Bower is retired now and living in Florida and well into his tenth decade. He still sends an occasional memo to Rajat Gupta and his old friends and partners at McKinsey. A lawyer first by training but always more fascinated by the problem solving inherent in high-level consulting, Bower has won patron saint status within McKinsey, and within the world of consulting in general. He remains a man of high standards who insisted almost from the beginning that McKinsey & Co. would be a partnership that lived or died on the basis of its reputation. His working assumption was that The Firm's contributions to its clients would be so apparent that there would be no question about its standing in the field.

He has been, at different points, both McKinsey's nagging relative and its welcomed old friend. His own oral history of the company was presented as a case study at the Harvard Business School in 1956. It remains the most complete public document on McKinsey's early history and it is full of revelations that help explain why McKinsey is the way it is today. The issues have changed and the revenues have exploded since that time, when The Firm was primarily concerned with business in the United States. But if one wants to know what it was like at the creation, this study has the feel of Genesis about it, with Marvin Bower playing the role of a persistent supreme being.

Unlike God, Bower had no idea what he wanted to do in the beginning. A fresh graduate of Brown University in 1925, he took his father's advice and went to Harvard Law School. To help pay the way, he got a job collecting debts for a Cleveland law firm. He was so good at it that he was collector of debts in the summers of 1926, 1927, and 1928. He wanted to work at the prestigious Jones, Day firm in Cleveland after graduation, but his grades weren't good enough. So he went to Harvard Business School, amassed a fantastic academic record, including election as editor of the *Harvard Business Review*, and finally got his Jones, Day, job upon graduation. It was important experience. At Jones, Day Bower found himself deeply engaged in the problems of companies wrestling with the depression. He loved analyzing the structural business problems, but hated writing up legal documents, which he found boring.

From all of that, he recalled, came a valuable idea. He felt his studies of business were amateurish and superficial. But it would be good to apply the same professional standards involved in law practice to a business practice. In 1932, he met James McKinsey and realized that McKinsey, who was using his background as an accountant to develop business strategy, was on the right track. He joined McKinsey's consulting company and, in a comment a little more revealing than he probably realized, said: "I took the train to New York with a definite program in mind and a determination to do as much as I could to help James O. McKinsey and Company develop into the kind of firm that I had envisioned."

McKinsey was not an easy man. While he had great esprit with clients, he was tough on his own colleagues. He believed all achievers thrived on criticism, so he heaped it on them in great measure. Praise was rare. Bower liked that, he said, because when praise and criticism are handed out in equal measure, the target recalls only the praise. What he didn't like was McKinsey's attachment to the world of accounting. He felt there was an implied conflict of interest in arrangements in which accounting companies sought income from clients for consulting. This was prescient on Bower's part, almost an augury of the problems that would come much later for consulting companies that were attached to big accounting firms. By 1934, Bower was the manager of McKinsey's small New York office. He convinced McKinsey there should be no accounting function there, that it should only consult.

But, as detailed in Chapter 1, things were not going well at James McKinsey's consulting company. After his death the enemies he made in slashing away at Marshall Field & Co. had nothing good to say about him. By 1938, McKinsey was losing money, its reputation was under attack, and its partners were complaining. And so the old merger was dissolved, and a new company, which might have been called "Not Yet McKinsey," was formed under an unusual agreement that saw the New York office operate as McKinsey & Co. and the Chicago office operate as McKinsey, Kearney & Co. It had to happen that way because the partners were obligated to pay 21 percent of all earnings to the McKinsey estate over several years. This amalgam operated until 1946, when the McKinsey partners in New York decided to sever all ties to A. T. Kearney in Chicago. But that was a struggle, too. Bower said it was resolved when he recommended to Kearney that he call his new firm "A. T. Kearney & Co." and sell the McKinsey name to the New York McKinsey partners.

A nominal relationship remained, but from that point onward, McKinsey & Co. and A. T. Kearney & Co. would become competitors. The Firm had finally been born, and Bower, with his New York train ride plan still in mind, knew exactly what he wanted to do with it. By the mid-1950s, McKinsey was pursuing a strategy that saw it follow a "top management approach" to consulting, which meant it would enter a contract only with the approval and cooperation of a client's chief executive officer. McKinsey's competitors thought that was foolish and would limit the amount of business available to The Firm, but Bower and his partners knew that starting at the top and winning important friends was the best path toward having McKinsey's recommendations carried out.

There was one of McKinsey's attributes that Bower seized upon and nurtured throughout his years at McKinsey: the need for consulting to develop its own sense of profession. There were very practical reasons for this.

Forging Professional Values

"Unlike the legal and accounting professions, our profession performs services that client executives often believe they can and should perform for themselves. Even after they have been invited in, the consultants cannot produce value for the client unless they secure real cooperation and support from the managers . . . we must bring the client something extra, be it problem solving competence, experience, technical know-how, independence or standing. Clients must also believe that we will not disrupt the organization more than is necessary and that we can be trusted," Bower said.

Doctors and attorneys had recognized for years that the only way to gain the status they sought was to apply some standards of competence, ethics, responsibility, and independence. Bower reasoned that this was a good set of target ideals, not only because they would give McKinsey the icing of professionalism, but because they would pay off over the long term.

From the beginning, that was Bower's goal. He pursued it relentlessly, applying the standard to everything from the kind of clients McKinsey would accept—"large and prestigious companies"—to the kind of consultants he would hire. Early on, it abandoned department stores and the work that had led to the "management engineer" label Bower so detested. Time management and job evaluation studies could be someone else's specialty, not McKinsey's. It abandoned executive recruiting in 1951, feeling it just didn't send the right message about objectivity. And it decided that if there were signs a client would drag his feet on McKinsey recommendations, or wasn't being forthcoming, McKinsey would decline the contract.

There would be no advertising.

"We cannot solicit without making express or implied promises of results. In an organization that becomes a client under such circumstances, the people can take a 'show me' attitude because the consultant has implied valuable results. . . . Leading law and accounting firms do not solicit clients, nor do we," Bower said. This was another touch of prescience. Promising what is not delivered has become the casus belli in a string of lawsuits against modern consulting companies. To this day, there is so much of an emphasis at McKinsey on connecting at the top of an organization that it is difficult to tell from the outside where the management ends and the consulting begins. The goal is to have the client conclude "That was valuable" rather than to have McKinsey consultants trying to prove a visit was worth the price.

Besides, Bower recognized that McKinsey had found a better way to spread the word. Its first book was *Supplementing Successful Management,* an effort that flowed from the debates and sessions that led to the reorganization of The Firm. It amounted to a handbook of McKinsey philosophy, something no other consulting firm had at the time. Within a year, McKinsey had sent 2,600 copies of the hardcover book to clients and prospects. It didn't seem like advertising, even though it was. The Firm also started holding "clinic dinners" for clients and prospects in 1940. Twenty-five or thirty executives would be invited to a dinner lecture with firm members and a guest speaker who would address business topics.

Inside The Firm, consultants were developing special industry expertise. Even though the partners didn't believe there was much of a future in consulting for insurance companies, one of The Firm's principals, Dick Neuschel, asked Bower for the chance to try to build an insurance practice. He did that by writing articles for business journals and making contacts. Before long, he had one major client. It worked out well and led to more business for McKinsey.

It might all sound like ancient history, but from the book through the dinners and on to publishing business review articles, the formula Bower and his partner invented in the 1940s works well for McKinsey to this very day. It still doesn't advertise much, but it is difficult to turn anywhere in the world of management consulting without running into some McKinsey influence. The sincerest flattery is at work, too. Getting published somewhere important is a central goal of almost all executives at consulting companies everywhere. There is nothing like waving around a *Harvard Business Review* article to impress prospective clients.

But Bower's influence didn't end there. Perhaps the most important change at McKinsey in the early years was a shift away from James McKinsey's idea that the best consultants would be men who had gathered a lot of experience in the field. The new McKinsey & Co. was aiming its guns at top management, and it would not do to send in wizened old field veterans to make suggestions to CEOs. After all, companies had whole armies of wizened old field veterans to turn to, and the track record indicated the bosses weren't in much of a mood to take advice from the subordinates. Once again, Bower had a plan in mind. His passion for turning consulting into a profession led McKinsey to borrow from the fields of law and accounting.

Law and accounting firms did not generally turn to the industry for their candidates. Instead, they harvested them from the best schools. Then they turned them into the professionals they wanted them to become. World War II, which gobbled up the best and brightest for years, got in the way of the new McKinsey hiring plan. But by the time the conflict had quieted and streams of the best started moving through business schools again, McKinsey was ready. In 1953, its partners decided to start tapping graduate business schools for the consultants of the future. There were concerns that the level of management McKinsey wanted to reach would not react well to collections of well-dressed know-it-alls poring over all the private details of their corporations. But

McKinsey's reputation was growing, and the assumption, eventually accepted by the partners, was that it would be able to attract the best of the best.

On top of that, turning to business schools solved a big problem for McKinsey (although it may have created another one no one thought about at the time). It was not easy to get into graduate business school. And it was not easy to graduate near the top of the class. That meant higher education had already set two high standards McKinsey would not have to worry about if it selected its candidates from only the strongest schools. The unanticipated downside of this philosophy is that McKinsey has ended up with a very narrow potential pool of candidates. They might be brilliant. They might be as sharp as the edge on a straight razor. They might have fire in their guts. And they might also look as though they were carbon copies of one another.

Tapping Harvard

Marvin Bower took all of this very seriously, to the point at which the Harvard Business School became the primary recruiting pool for new McKinsey consultants. It was a comfortable fit for Bower, who maintained his long-standing connections with Harvard Law and the Harvard Business School and who was one of Harvard's biggest and most dependable contributors.

McKinsey wasn't looking for just any HBS graduate. Bower wanted the best of the best, and at Harvard that meant the Baker Scholars. Over time, McKinsey gathered them up in huge clumps. By one estimate, The Firm recruited 1,000 Baker Scholars over the years. It almost seemed to some as though there was a direct connection between the number of Baker Scholars McKinsey collected and the amount of money Bower gave to Harvard. The assumption was there for all the Baker Scholars: McKinsey would be waiting for them.

There were good reasons why McKinsey wanted the best of the Harvard men. Harvard Business School was the chief advocate of the case study method of graduate education. The professors would present the case studies and problems, and the students would have a day to learn what they could, recommend fixes, and defend their positions. More than half of a student's grade was constructed on the basis of these classroom performances. Books and lectures were fine, of course, but Harvard produced a different kind of character, a graduate who had been trained to think almost instantaneously and always on his feet. Business schools all over the world might be able to churn out brilliant graduates, but not brilliant graduates who were so facile at defending themselves and their ideas. In a business that lives on impressions, dazzling the client is important. Marvin Bower didn't want any McKinsey consultants stumbling over their notes and shuffling their feet and guessing at weak solutions. Dazzling professionalism was the goal. And Baker Scholars were dazzling, as wonderfully well equipped to whisper into the ear of the receptive CEO as any Jesuit had been prepared to counsel a head of state. "Baker Scholars tended to be intelligent generalists who could expound on any issue, and whose natural inclination to remain silent on topics they had no background in had been systematically broken down. In effect, McKinsey paid a premium for students who were good at 'winging it,'" wrote J. Paul Mark in *The Empire Builders: Power, Money and Ethics Inside the Harvard Business School.*

Bower's influence extended to the point at which he not only helped dictate how business would be taught at Harvard, he was instrumental in derailing any attempt to change a process that had been so beneficial to McKinsey over the years. Harvard was going through a transition in the late 1970s after Derek Bok took over its presidency. Bok thought the case study method of education had outlived its usefulness and that it was time for a change. Bower disagreed. Strongly. Mark notes that it was Bower who drafted a 52-page report to Bok late in 1979 that argued there was no justifiable reason to change the curriculum or the method of instruction at Harvard Business School. The report was released a month after Bower's favorite for dean of the business school, John H. McArthur, got the job.

"The secret of success is constancy to purpose," Bower's report said, quoting British Prime Minister Benjamin Disraeli. It was a phrase that applied as well to Bower as it did to Bower's review of the situation at the Business School. But Bower's influence didn't stop there. Shortly after he moved into the post, McArthur met with Bower and Bower asked him whether the Business School would like to have a new endowment, a new chair. That would cost between $1 million and $2 million, McArthur said. No problem, Bower replied. He would use his connections with Japanese businessmen, one in particular who was indebted to

McKinsey because The Firm had saved his bank from a disaster. In November 1981, McArthur went to Japan to pick up the check that would be used to fund the Matsushita Chair of Leadership at HBS.

Bower obviously assumed this level of patronage would ensure McKinsey's continued access to the Baker Scholars, but the consulting business was headed into a period of strong growth and a collection of relative newcomers to the field, Boston Consulting Group, Bain, and the brilliant and engaging business school professor Michael Porter's Monitor consulting company, were starting to lure the best and brightest away from the McKinsey path. BCG and Bain were considered the bright new places to land for those who wanted to consult. McKinsey was in danger of becoming passé. Besides, there was the question of salaries and sign-up bonuses. McKinsey was paying $55,000 a year to its new consultants, $10,000 short of the BCG and Bain offers. And Bain had developed a bonus program that saw new Baker Scholar grads collecting fat checks if they signed up the first day the job offer was made. The amount would shrink on the second day if the offer wasn't taken, and again on the third day, and so on. Because money speaks so clearly to business types, Bain was able to get all 18 of the Baker Scholars it approached on the first offer in 1980. By 1982 and 1983, McKinsey was forced to reach down to the next level of students for its recruits.

Bower was livid. In a true measure of his own strategic skill, he found a way to up the ante, to the point at which his competitors were driven from the game. If Bain was offering fat bonuses, and Monitor and BCG were benefiting from the Michael Porter connection, he would shift the benefit focus to the school itself. The Marvin Bower Fellowship Program started with an endowment of $2 million, which would grow by $500,000 a year if McKinsey was able to fill its quotas for Baker Scholars. McKinsey then turned up the heat under the recruitment process. First-year school experiences generally provided an early glimpse at the Baker Scholars of the future, and by 1985 McKinsey & Co. had found a way to tap that pool before the honors were even awarded. The best and brightest of the class of 1986 found themselves mightily wooed by McKinsey, with 100 of the strongest students receiving invitations from McKinsey to come and talk about summer job opportunities.

By the time they graduated, many of them as Baker Scholars, the following year, they were already at McKinsey's front door. Most of the interns were offered full-time jobs on graduation and started with McKinsey in 1986. The details of how all of this happened remain closely held. The message, however, was clearly written: Don't mess with Marvin Bower.

Bower had been retired from McKinsey for almost two decades by the time all of this played out. But his commitment to The Firm and his influence at Harvard Business School remained so strong that he was still able to play the master consultant's role. It is little wonder, then, that he is such a legend in the world of consulting. It is very rare to run into a character who actually lives up to what is said about him, but even in a McKinsey & Co. that has moved quickly to meet the demands of consulting on the world scale, Bower's dictates and the tone he set over his decades with The Firm continue to serve as McKinsey & Co.'s mission statement and bible wrapped into one.

Casting a Wider Net

The Firm continues to follow his philosophy in hiring the best graduates available, although it has been reaching far beyond Harvard and its MBAs to do that over the past few years. There are 48 Baker Scholars working for McKinsey now. The Firm has hired a total of 79 Baker Scholars since 1986. The Marvin Bower Fellowship is still in operation at HBS. But the framework that Bower created has been changing since Gluck's years as managing partner. Perhaps because he came from the world of engineering, a world of vastly different connections and values than the world of business schools, McKinsey has broken away from business school hiring of late.

In 1995, 43 percent of its 756 fresh new consultants were not business school graduates. One reason is that McKinsey has been growing so rapidly that the pool of business school types simply isn't big enough. While it still collects its business school standouts, it searches these days for people with broader experience and education. Another reason is that it is coming to depend on a different set of skills. Because the game board of management consulting for McKinsey is now world scale, diplomatic acumen could well play as important a part in McKinsey's long-term future as business acumen did in the past. It doesn't hesitate to collect candidates from the Fletcher School. Economic analysis and the measurement of the economies of entire nations is part of McKinsey's modern agenda, so it looks for candidates steeped in that most dreary of sciences.

The "up and out" policy Bower instituted and defended in the face of demands from inside for change remains a keystone in the partnership. It makes McKinsey a pressure cooker for the young consultants who go to work there, but it also sets a high and closely measured set of standards that guarantees those who survive the process will be on the same page in the planning book. It continues to shun the fads that seem to define some of the other consulting companies. McKinsey will reach deep into the grab bag of consulting practices to find the methods that seem to work best, but it has been scrupulous in avoiding an attachment to any single philosophy, probably realizing that these strategies change too quickly to be dependable. This year's shiny new idea becomes next year's albatross or gets bumped off the consulting menu by some new business review whizbang.

And maybe more important than any of that, McKinsey & Co. spends a great deal of time checking on its own health, protecting its reputation, and ensuring that its platinum exterior remains just that. It is clear in conversations with Gupta that before he is a citizen of the world and a reflection of the cultures and values of a place far away from the United States, he is a McKinsey man through and through, just as Bower was. "One of the great values of The Firm," says Gupta, "which is another legacy of Marvin, is to leave The Firm stronger for the next generation, and Marvin indeed practiced it." When he retired, he could have collected a fortune by cashing in his McKinsey private stock. Instead, Gupta said, he returned his equity to McKinsey. "He also made sure this firm would never go public the way it is governed. So there is a very strong position toward McKinsey's objective of becoming the preeminent consulting firm."

Gupta's own descriptions of McKinsey and how it operates are measures of how complicated the task has become. While he conceded, for example, that connecting with chief executive officers is crucial, he rejects the argument that that is McKinsey's primary target. "It is true, we have a relationship with more CEOs than anyone else, and we have an agenda-shaping kind of relationship. But it has always been true that our relationships are multilevel and carry across organizations. One of our great values is in our ability to penetrate deep into an organization and see what is really happening and synthesize that and bring that to CEOs. It is not like McKinsey is always brought in by the CEO. If a CEO doesn't want to change, it is a difficult thing to bring about change in that organization. But sometimes the CEO is driving it and we are partners with that person bringing about change. And sometimes the CEO lets things happen and we are partners with a lot of people involved."

If The Firm seems at points as though it is primarily an exclusive club that pumps out its own version of IBM's organization man, Gupta rejects some of that description and insists it only looks that way because it is such a tight partnership. "It is a meritocracy and there is a big difference between that and a club. It is a club in the sense that it is a partnership. We care about each other. Once you prove yourself as a partner you get a lot of room and leeway . . . we take a long-term view of people's contributions, but fundamentally, it is a meritocracy . . . if the contribution is there, it is there, in the end."

Gupta knows McKinsey doesn't very much reflect any of the cultures in which it does business. Elite organizations rarely do. The world doesn't move in lockstep on a whole collection of social issues. The question arises as to why McKinsey doesn't have more women or minorities in positions of power. Despite the Porter lawsuit and criticism from outside, Gupta argues that the way McKinsey looks today is more a question of history than of its own attitude.

"I am absolutely not happy about where we are, although we are making progress. Over time it has shifted. A lot of people who were hired at McKinsey were Americans, entrepreneurs, but now that is no longer that sort of case. Now we have Germans who open offices in Brazil or who have gone to Taiwan. We have people from the United Kingdom going to South Africa. You have a lot of mixing now, a melting pot, and that has changed a lot more in the last ten to fifteen years, but it was the expected result of an organic growth."

It has been centuries now since the Jesuits lost their political influence on the world stage, one of the inevitable consequences of change. And this is where the comparison with McKinsey must end, save for the final note that if a consulting company can have the equivalent of an Ignatius of Loyola, the Jesuit founder, that mantle would fit Marvin Bower quite comfortably. There is another difference, too, probably best illustrated in McKinsey's decision a few years ago to open its

Global Institute. It is an object lesson on the importance of testing the winds of change and adapting to take the best advantage.

In his bright, uncluttered office in McKinsey's suite on Pennsylvania Avenue in Washington, D.C., Bill Lewis runs the Global Institute and ponders questions that reach far beyond whether any company will buy into a McKinsey proposal for this transition or that change in strategy. He and the McKinsey people who serve one-year fellowships at the institute—generally among McKinsey's best thinkers—are measuring world economics from the broadest perspective they can create. If one thinks of McKinsey as its own kind of nation, then this is its intelligence agency, a well-funded think tank that studies world economies in depth, then issues reports available to anyone who wants them. They are free of charge, but worth their weight in whatever currency you want to spend. They buy goodwill and page after page of publicity for McKinsey and help create the consulting relationships that will carry The Firm well into the twenty-first century.

That it is here is no surprise. All the big consulting companies have think tanks that grind out reports. Why it is here is another matter, and one that touches on how McKinsey has been able to stay so far up the mountain of management consulting. In the middle of the turmoil of the 1980s, with the Soviet Union in collapse and America's productivity lagging to such a degree that there were questions about what role it would play in the world, McKinsey started talking to the CEOs of Europe about the future. The Germans had questions about what was likely to happen.

And McKinsey did not have the answers. In fact, it found itself in a very weak position. Its MBAs might well have been glib and quick on their feet, but macroeconomics was another matter. "We did conferences in Europe with some of the leading CEOs there for three or four years, and then we had one in New York and one in Tokyo," Lewis said. "What we realized as a firm is that we were either going to have to invest to get better informed and to understand better what was happening in the world's economy and the global economy and really help our CEOs, or we were going to have to get out. We were going to embarrass ourselves because in the end, we were draining what little we had to stay."

The Firm had two options: It had to buy into the study of economics in a big way, or it had to leave the field to the collection of academics and macroeconomists who were already talking to the business leaders of Europe. Ultimately what that meant is that it would have to abandon the potentially profitable path of consulting on economics and just stick to business.

Some of the partners were confused. Why should McKinsey spend to create something new when it was already doing very well? The answer, Lewis says, rests partly in The Firm's inherent sense of curiosity about how the world operates, since it now operates on the same level. The unspoken answer, speculation invites, is that The Firm did not at all like the feel of being bested by a collection of economists and academics.

"I mean, we are so successful, why change? Why do anything different? That is always a challenge for successful organizations. Of course, what we tell our clients is that that is just the time when you invest and do something different to maintain that success. In a narrow sense, we were taking some of our own medicine," Lewis said.

And so the institute was born and now runs on one tenth of 1 percent of McKinsey's revenues. It is, Lewis says, deeper than the CIA in the sense that it can call on McKinsey partners everywhere in the world for their special expertise. It is aimed at making certain McKinsey never again faces questions about the global economy from savvy CEOs for which it has no answers. On the surface, it might seem like an academic exercise. But if it follows the course that Bower and his successors helped set over the past six decades, undoubtedly it will become a magnet, not only for clients eager to take advantage of McKinsey's special expertise, but also for the consultants of the twenty-first century who will want to make their start, and perhaps their careers, at a company that presents truly global opportunities.

"If we are going to do it, we need to do it right and well and pay attention to what is important and what differentiates McKinsey from what other organizations can do," said Lewis. "If we do all of that, our clients will be served. The ultimate driving force needs to be what do our clients need and how do we serve them best. If we do that well and have the right kind of talent, everything else will take care of itself."

Keeping Dangerous Company

CAVEAT EMPTOR

With a corner on the market for arrogance, McKinsey & Co. may question why it should change its ways given its successful track record. But one of its former consultants suggests that big firms like McKinsey had better watch out. Consultants now face more threats to their future, and McKinsey isn't immune to them. Unhappy clients and employees seem more prone to file lawsuits; customers demand breaks on fees. But the biggest threat looms within the secretive fraternity: It challenges consultants to practice what they preach.

In 1991 EG&G, Inc., a Wellesley, Massachusetts, scientific and technical products company, staged a major shift in strategy. It walked away from a huge chunk of business with its biggest and oldest customer—the U.S. Department of Energy, which accounted for about half of the company's $2.7 billion in revenues and more than a quarter of its profits. The stunning shift involved issues as fundamental as the company's roots. EG&G had worked with the federal energy establishment and the old Atomic Energy Commission for years. It had had a hand in every nuclear explosion the government had orchestrated since the one that leveled Nagasaki in World War II. When Hazel O'Leary took over the department, though, the Clinton administration's energy secretary adopted an adversarial approach to the department's contractors, and the company's relationship with the government soon frayed. EG&G came under fire for its management of the Rocky Flats nuclear weapons plant in Colorado, and it balked at new Energy Department rules that seemed unreasonable: Mrs. O'Leary wanted EG&G to assume additional liabilities and come up with another $250 million in working capital. So the company announced it would quit bidding for most of its Department of Energy contracts when they expired, prompting analysts to project that EG&G's revenues would fall by nearly 50 percent, and that employment would plunge to 12,000 by 1996, far below its 1991 peak of 34,000. So dire were the forecasts that CEO John M. Kucharski's daughter, then a graduate student in business at Marquette University, phoned her father and asked: "Dad, are you really sure you know what you're doing?" At that point, Don Peters, EG&G's vice president and director of planning, called in the consultants.

"We had decided that we wanted to develop the commercial side of our business," he said, a reference to a group of EG&G products that ranged from medical instruments and airport security systems to micromachined sensing and control components for industrial and consumer markets. Peters said he called 15 to 20 consulting firms into EG&G because "we needed to develop a new planning diagnostic. Most of them wanted to engage four to five people per task. They said they would send their people in, work with our people, and then come up with some solutions that would allegedly solve the problem. But they were expensive; I figured it at about $500,000 a man-year."

Peters said he never really asked the firms to submit formal bids, though, because one of them, the Planning Technologies Group, of Lexington, Massachusetts, so impressed him that he hired the company right after the initial talks. "I looked at the PTG approach, which is different from most consultants', and picked them because they brought the background and capabilities of the other firms but, in my opinion, were much more cost-effective." PTG eventually designed a planning diagnostic, and EG&G injected new life into its commercial business. By the time PTG's consultants were done, they had won a powerful endorsement from EG&G and Peters: "They brought their McKinsey backgrounds with them plus the technological knowledge," he said. "They saved us a lot of money. . . . I would say the savings from other firms were on the order of 50 percent."

Peters' experience with PTG is a graphic example of the threat that a new generation of nimble, agile competitors represents to the major consulting firms profiled in *Dangerous Company*. For decades the big consulting houses like McKinsey, Bain, BCG, Anderson, Deloitte & Touche, CSC Index, and Gemini have told clients that they should adopt ruthless efficiencies to survive in an increasingly competitive world. Now, though, in an ironic twist, consultants like those at PTG pose the same kind of threat to the big consulting houses.

By no means are firms like PTG the only challenge that consultants face in the future. Competitors have long been a fact of life in the industry. Individual consultants who break with the major firms and strike out on their own are as common as flowcharts. Examples are plentiful. Just one shows what a skilled alumnus can do to the most prestigious houses. After working for McKinsey & Co. for 12 years, Chadrika Tandon set up her own firm advising banks, a McKinsey specialty, on how to cut costs and improve service. Over the past decade, she has thrived, and Tandon Capital Associates, Inc., has hired six other McKinsey consultants to help her pick up clients like Riggs National Bank and Mid Atlantic Corp., customers that might have otherwise flocked to the doors of Tandon's former employer.

Consultants at the big houses face a range of other challenges, too. Customers now seem more willing to file lawsuits against them, as several disgruntled clients have done in recent years. Even if the consultants don't end up in court, malpractice claims are rising. "I can guarantee you that there are more claims than what you will find in a court record," says Mark Hutchkins of Media Professional, Inc., a Kansas City firm that writes insurance on consulting firms. "I don't know that consultants are being singled out in our increasingly litigious society, but there were more lawsuits filed against them this year than last year and there were more last year than the year before." Hutchins says the court filings pale in comparison to the claims filed against underwriters who insure them.

In the upper stratosphere of the industry, an ominous labor shortage also looms on the horizon for the blue-chip firms. In the lower reaches, firms like Ernst & Young offer relatively cheap consulting services like Ernie, an accessible on-line service where small companies can get consulting through desktop computers for an annual flat fee as low as $6,000. How consultants deal with these threats and how they respond to new challenges will determine if they will be as successful during the next century as they were in the one that is about to end. But consultants like those at PTG represent a threat of a different order. In its drive to win more customers, the company and its principals are raising a sensitive subject that once was taboo among consultants—the soaring cost of their fees, particularly the huge incomes racked up by major partners of the firms.

Mouseketeers Gone Yupple

From the moment a visitor walks in the door of PTG's headquarters in a small brick building nestled in the Massachusetts countryside, it is evident that PTG is a consulting firm of a different ilk. In the Boston skyscrapers about an hour's drive to the east, harried young MBAs struggle to make it big in the button-down world of management consulting. They scurry down the halls of firms with blue-chip names like BCG or Bain. They all seem extraordinarily clean cut and well scrubbed; it's like the Mouseketeers turned Yuppie. At PTG, the consultants are just as well groomed, but the principals wear Dockers, jeans, and open-collared shirts. One sees few white shirts and ties; the atmosphere is more casual, less stuffy. "See that," says Douglas Ferguson, a PTG principal, pointing toward a television set playing the tape of a CNBC newscast involving PTG, "that's the only day in the history of this place that everyone wore a suit and tie."

The dress code is not the only thing that is different. Mason Tanaglia, a former McKinsey consultant, founded the firm in 1990 and lured former McKinseyites like Ferguson to PTG with an irreverent view of the blue-chip consulting firms that probably makes their former colleagues wince. Tanaglia and Ferguson view the industry as a collection of anachronistic professional service firms that cling to the status quo to protect the ability of the major partners to pull down their seven-figure incomes. "Let's say you are a senior partner at McKinsey, BCG or Bain. How much do you make?" asks Ferguson, who answers his own question. "They charge a lot for their time." Seven-figure incomes are not unusual. Indeed, some consultants probably make as much as or more than the CEOs who hire them.

"Let's say they are charging five thousand dollars a day," he continues, "and they are working two hundred days a year, which is virtually impossible. That's only a million dollars, and they have to pay help and expenses. They are making those fees because they have a lot of other people [or employees] whom they don't pay as much." The trick, of course, is to bill out the employees' time at lofty partnerlike rates and pay them as juniors, who earn far less. The difference goes to the bottom line and eventually finds its way into the big partners' pockets. "The more people you have working for you, the more you are going to make," says Ferguson. "So the system is set up so you are always looking for leverage. Don't get me wrong, this is all with the best interests of the client in mind. But the economics of it are that you have a senior partner, who might have a junior partner, who would have a senior consultant, who would have a junior consultant, who then has a business analyst working for him. You've got a lot of people. There are three implications of this. Clients end up paying for a lot of people, so [the engagement] is expensive. The second thing is, there must be some communications law, but the more people you have involved in the process, generally the longer it takes to get something done because of the communication pathways that exist. And you end up leaning toward a model [in which] the end product is 'Let me tell you what to do.' The value added is in a recommendation that this is the right way to go." The advice usually comes in a big, fat, expensive report.

The status quo has worked well for consultants for many years, Ferguson says, but alternatives are emerging with the growing sophistication of information technology, and they could dramatically affect the future: "I was at McKinsey from 1984 to 1990. One of my frustrations . . . was that there was heavy emphasis on the end or the goal—the answer to a problem. And at McKinsey, they are truly the world's best problem solvers, they are great at analysis. But I realized that people change their behavior and organize their businesses for reasons that are far more complicated than rational analysis. And if you really want to affect behavior, you have to understand all of the elements of how decisions are made and how the organization operates. Otherwise you run the risk of writing a report that is elegant and analytically correct but doesn't have any impact because . . . the organization might not accept it. . . . So one of the challenges when you are in the consulting profession is how do you make sure you are involved in things other than strictly telling people what to do, and information technology is part of the answer to that."

Traditionally, Ferguson says, clients hire McKinsey, BCG, or Bain because of the techniques they use, or because the experience and data they have gained over the years give them expertise in resolving specific kinds of problems. Consultants usually come into a client's office to assess the situation, and the meter starts running right away, mainly because it takes time and extensive face-to-face meetings to gain understanding and consensus on problems. Thanks to information technology, though, a lot of these expenses can be cut by firms like PTG. Some of the information and experience traditionally hoarded by the big firms is now available through the Internet or other electronic information systems, Ferguson says. More significantly, he adds, PTG capitalizes on interactive groupware information systems like Lotus Notes to interact with the client from the outset to share information, gain knowledge about the problem, and allow the client to work directly with the consultant.

"In the approach we take," Ferguson says, "the insight is that clients don't want reports. They want to be able to do the problem solving themselves but they need to be given an environment in which that can happen. So what we do oftentimes is develop models that look at their businesses in different ways." The problems posed on the models can be made available to clients through Lotus Notes and "they [the clients] can change the assumptions and see how [different solutions to a problem] play out. When the members of the management team are using the model themselves, they can put in their own biases, they can deal with their colleagues in a room, they can see the interplay on what is important to various people in a room and [watch] the organizational dynamics play out." It's "virtual consulting." PTG uses E-mail, the Internet, and groupware information systems like Lotus Notes to involve the client's employees in the engagement rather than show up with a huge contingent of consultants and assistants. "We'll have a group of ten people collaborating with each other, some from PTG, some from the client. That allows our consulting process to be much more efficient. . . . If the content is on a path that the client no longer thinks is productive, he can tell me on the spot . . . rather than wait six weeks for me to present our findings. . . . We don't tell people what systems to put in, we don't put in systems. We understand how to apply technology to high-level problem solving. . . . Our costs are not as high, because we do it faster and we don't have as many people involved. The cost savings are on the order of 30 to 50 percent of other [firms] like McKinsey. . . . Our value is much more in delivering the model and running the sessions that look at the model and figuring out what changes need to be made than in handing them a hundred-page report . . . that tells them what to do."

Lotus Notes allows extensive and instantaneous computer communications between the consultant and the client, including linkage of the client to the consultant's database. "They saved us a lot of money early on," Peters says. "Instead of all those meetings and travel, we used Lotus Notes to communicate. I knew exactly what was going on every minute." PTG founder Tenaglia elaborates: "You [the client] can bring the outside consultant right up to speed on any project, no travel, no meetings. That cuts down cycle time, drives down costs, and makes the process incredibly efficient. Clients expect that kind of efficiency now; even more, they want to be part of the problem-solving team. Notes is not a 'software solution' that consultants sell to clients, it's a tool that enables consultants to collect, store, and share knowledge."

Ferguson says the big houses such as McKinsey, BCG, and Bain could adopt similar models. In fact, some of them—McKinsey, Andersen Consulting, and Gemini—claim they have. But such models are just glorified E-mail if there's not a 100 percent commitment to directly linking the client to the consultant's database. And Ferguson doubts that will happen anytime soon because of the culture at major houses like McKinsey. "The challenge for the large consulting firm is not that they couldn't understand [our] model. I mean, it makes rational sense to them. The challenge is you have an existing infrastructure, an existing culture and an existing way of doing business that is truly violated by this model, and somebody doesn't make money by having thirty people work for them. The skills you need to manage [the McKinsey model of doing business] are different than the skills you need to manage [the PTG] model. You [also] need to have a pretty good understanding of how technology can be applied to problem solving . . . in addition to having some substantial knowledge of the problem. So imagine that you are a senior partner at McKinsey. I think it is hard for you, even if you see the vision, I think it is hard for you to make the changes within your own organization and still keep up your income."

The folks at McKinsey, BCG, and Bain, of course, would never agree with Ferguson's assessments. Others, like David Maister, a former

Harvard professor, author, and expert on professional service firms, partially agree. Partners earn those huge salaries and bonuses by tacking premiums on the rates charged for underlings, he says, but he doesn't agree that the big firms can't stay competitive. "There is a countervailing force to this with the emergence of worldwide, best-practices databases," says Maister. "It is easier for the big firms to tap into them and share data." If the professional service firm model is, indeed, an anachronism, it is not evident yet, either. Last year McKinsey, Bain, and BCG all said their revenues were up by double-digit percentages, including a lot of repeat business from satisfied clients. *Consultants News* editor Tom Rodenhauser also suggests caution at PTG's claims about its lower fees: "They probably do come in around 50 percent below McKinsey," he says, "but that is 50 percent below some really high rates. These guys [Tanaglia and Ferguson] both came out of McKinsey. They know what the market will bear. It is 50 percent lower, but 50 percent lower than what?" Nevertheless, PTG, which includes 11 other consultants who once worked for BCG, Bain, and McKinsey, is raising provocative questions, and it is doing something right. Since its founding only six years ago, it has been growing at an annual rate of 30 percent and now is listed in *Consultants News'* "100 Leading Management Consulting Firms in North America."

"I think PTG is a very interesting firm, and it's doing a great job," said Rodenhauser.

Fire the Consultants

Technological breakthroughs aren't the only threats the industry faces. Some challenges emanate from clients themselves, who are becoming increasingly critical as the cost of consulting soars. Executives like Al Dunlap, the current Sunbeam Corp. and former Scott Paper CEO—nicknamed "Chainsaw Al" for his budget-slashing devotion to higher shareholder value—slams most consultants as people who deserve a pink slip. "Scott [Paper] spent thirty million dollars on consultants before I arrived. Thirty million! And look at the mess they were in," he says. "All consultants do is tell you what you want to hear. Scott had stacks of consultants' handsomely bound ten-year strategic reports. If you're surrounded by similar reports, do what I did: Get a firm grip on the stack with both hands, and throw them out. Then fire the consultant who wrote them. . . . Consultants generate ten-year plans for CEOs to take to their boards. That way, the CEOs and the consultants buy themselves a credibility policy for ten years, a kind of cover-your-ass pension plan. When none of the plans or predictions has worked out ten years later, 'unanticipated developments' can be blamed, and some of those can get pretty creative." Dunlap uses consultants, but he thinks they should be kept on a tight leash. "Hiring consultants works only when they're given a specific timetable and a targeted outcome. The process should not be too fluffy or open-ended." Other CEOs less animated than Dunlap agree. Arthur Martinez of Sears says companies should curtail their use of consultants for carte blanche engagements and focus their efforts on tightly drawn assignments where results can be easily measured.

Part of the problem, of course, is that consultants earn a lot of money. The 1980s featured the investment bankers as the Masters of the Universe, the well-heeled wise men who earned huge fees in multi-billion-dollar deals. Consultants are the 1990s version of the story. Tales abound about partners with huge incomes, MBAs with six-figure starting salaries, and business school gurus who charge space-age speaking fees. But the downside to this, at least from the consultants' perspective, is that they are under increasing pressure to link high fees to results. Consultants across the spectrum are experimenting with contingency fees. In some cases, such as at Andersen Consulting, the arrangements involve sinister incentives, such as the case in which Andersen linked the size of the fee to the number of jobs that its consultants could eliminate. In other cases, the consultants' fees are tied to the amount of money a client can save or the additional business generated by the engagement. "They all say that their clients are insisting on risk-sharing," says James Kennedy of *Consultants News,* who is a critic of the trend. "That's just a euphemism for contingency billing or contingency payments." Kennedy says the idea of consultants being held accountable for their fee sounds good on paper but there is a downside. He says contingency billing puts pressure on the consultant to make decisions for a client: "It sounds as American as apple pie. [But] a professional doesn't do that. The decision making should rest with the client. . . . What about the doctor that performs the operation and the patient dies. Is he supposed to say, 'Well, I won't charge you anything because it didn't work out?' The professional is paid for his time and his experience. Long-term, I think, it is still best to separate it [the fee and the service], even though it seems to be going very much in the opposite direction. Maybe the answer is some sort of compromise."

Where Have All the Baby Boomers Gone?

That may be a lot easier than it sounds, though. As technology and clients increase the pressure to lower consulting fees, labor market developments are putting an upward pressure on the industry's prime expense—the amount of money consulting firms must pay to lure new, young talent. This is a crucial challenge for the industry. "People are the most important asset of a professional service firm [like consulting]," says Maister, the respected author of two books on managing professional service firms. He says the economics of these firms require that they have a constant flow of raw talent coming in the front door so they can sustain growth and charge clients premium rates for the junior consultants. The persistent demand for fresh young bodies creates a vicious cycle, though. As the young consultants move up the experience chain and earn more money, one of two things has to happen. In the best houses, most of the young consultants are denied the fruits of partnership and go elsewhere, opening up slots for new, young, junior consultants that the firm can bill out at premium rates to keep the money rolling in. This is the primary reason the industry has a legendary "up or out" promotion policy, particularly in blue-chip firms like McKinsey. But the continuous recruiting simply intensifies the already strong demand for new talent. Of course, the most talented juniors become partners, which makes the situation worse. Additional partners put even more pressure on the company to hire more juniors to support them. "In the next decade and beyond," Maister says, "the ability to attract, develop, retain, and deploy staff will be the single biggest determinant of a professional service firm's competitive success."

Unfortunately for the industry, consultants will have to compete with other service firms for that raw talent, and labor market demographics are working against them, a fact that carries implications for anyone who has to hire a consultant. "Each year since the mid-1960s,"

Maister says, "the number of new entrants into the workforce, in every developed country, expanded dramatically as the 'baby boom' generation reached their twenties. In the United States, the number of people in the 25-to-34 age group rose between 1965 and 1985 from approximately 17 percent of the total population to nearly 23 percent," including a record high percentage of university graduates. The increase helped companies scouring the marketplace for professional labor. "In this environment, the relative neglect of strategic thinking about the people marketplace by professional firms may have been appropriate," says Maister. "You don't worry too much about something that is in plentiful supply. However, this environment has begun to change."

The percentage of the population aged 25 to 34 started to decline in 1985 and will drop continuously over the next twenty years. In America this group will fall from 23 to 17 percent. Meanwhile, there is a surge in demand for professional workers, particularly as the information economy takes root. "Educated people with a few years of business experience are in increasing demand by businesses of all types, and will have many more options in building their careers than their baby-boom elders," Maister says. "To place the potential impact of this in perspective, consider the following statistic: The 'oil shock' of the early 1970s was caused by only a 5 percent shrinkage in worldwide supply. Professional firms are facing a 25 percent shrinkage in their nonpartner labor force. There is going to be a *huge* people shortage and its effects will be major."

Maister first made his projection when his book, *Managing the Professional Service Firm*, was published in 1993. More recently, he said his projection remains on target, although he says the labor shortage hasn't proved as dire as he suspected. Consulting companies, he says, have compensated for the problem by expanding the range of people they hire. There was a time when the McKinseys, Bains, and BCGs of the world coveted the business school graduates with MBAs. That's still true. But a greater proportion of their junior consultants are people who got liberal arts or other degrees. Half of the people hired by McKinsey last year were not business school graduates. The same trend is true at the other firms, says Maister.

It's not as if the consultants are going out to Silly Putty University and hiring journalism majors. They hire smart young people from the best schools. They are paying them well and training them in internal programs that are probably better than what the students would get in business school. Nevertheless, watch out. The new consultant who shows up on your doorstep ready to tell you how to run your business may be someone fresh out of Psychology 202.

So, with that in mind, there are a few things to remember if you end up in Dangerous Company. If the experience at Sears is any indication, a good consultant is no substitute for a good leader. Likewise, if there are any lessons to be drawn from the disaster at Figgie International, it is that bad management leads to bad consulting. Beware of carte blanche engagements, too, and philosophical gurus who say they have all the answers. Be particularly wary of the latest fads, which tend to spread through the industry and business like an epidemic. As Eileen Shapiro, a McKinsey veteran who now has her own company, says in *Fad Surfing in the Boardroom*, her book about fads in consulting, "The hard truth is there are no panaceas. What is new is the sheer number of techniques, some new and some newly repackaged versions of older methods, that are now positioned as panaceas."

Shapiro sees fads as a flight away from responsibility on the part of corporate managers, who want the perks of being at the top and the fat salaries but not the hard decisions. Such managers want to outsource decision making, she says, but looking for "the answer" in someone else's formula may be a huge mistake.

"The truth is that you can do it [make hard decisions] a whole bunch of different ways if you think. Thinking must be the hardest job in the world. What people want to do is . . . outsource it to a mantra or a methodology like reengineering. People want the perks and salary of management, but they don't want to do the job. It is not a nice way of putting it, but I think that is what is happening. The fad meisters encourage it."

Dangerous Company's Checklist

And so here are some specific guidelines, gleaned from people who have used consultants poorly and used them well over the years, along with a lot of interviews with consultants and former consultants and the reading of too many books that seemed to have all of the answers.

1. Why are you doing this? Before you sit down to talk to a consulting firm, it would help to have some idea of what it is you want to achieve. The more clearly the goal is defined, the greater the chance of reaching it. If you don't know what you want to do, don't make the call.

2. That being achieved, ask yourself, Do I need outsiders to help reach this goal? That depends on the goal. Don't forget to assess the brilliance within your own company before you go trying to buy some from outside. Maybe you don't need an army of consultants. Maybe you just need your very own MBA, whom you can easily steal from a consulting company.

3. If I hire a consulting company, which characters will they send? Be ruthless in this part of the process. If you know the reputations of the partners, or if they display a special, tested expertise, demand that they pay good and frequent attention to your needs. Make it a part of the contract. If they are promising the best, make certain that is what shows up. Do not be meek about sending away people who make you uncomfortable.

4. What will it cost? (And how long will it take?) Avoid open-ended arrangements and vague promises. Demand specificity in contracts, including the dark parts about what happens if the consulting engagement doesn't work. Be tight with your money. Base payments on performance and on your satisfaction. If the task involves high risk, make certain the consulting company is sharing in the risk, not just in the rewards, of the relationship.

5. Never give up control. The best consulting engagements do not take over operation, they complement them. Make certain your own managers retain control over everything, share in decision making, and understand that for the duration of the contract, they are responsible and in charge.

6. Don't be unhappy for even a day. Ignored consultants can shower down all kinds of havoc on a company. If you sense something is going wrong, confront it immediately and demand repairs. Consultants do not answer to boards of directors, but you do. At these prices, happiness should be assumed.

7. Beware of glib talkers with books. The fact that someone can stack up case after case in which a practice seemed to work is no guarantee it will work for you. Insist on tailor-made consulting engagements that recognize the unique nature of your business. If you are buying

into the book pitch, ask how much time the actual author will be on-site working through his philosophies, then listen closely to the response. Don't be afraid to trim elegant proposals right down to their essence.

8. Value your employees. One of the most common complaints about consultants is that they talk down to the locals or ignore their ideas. Long after the consultants leave, your staff will be on board. How they feel about the outsiders has a lot to do with whether the engagement will work. The best consulting companies know this and will go to great lengths to avoid morale problems. You are buying intelligence, not arrogance.

9. Measure the process. Make certain you have your own internal measure of how a procedure is progressing. Consulting companies do, and they generally try to make this a part of the process. But there is a big conflict of interest in this area and their inclination is to make you happy and stay fully engaged. Find someone you trust who knows what a devil's advocate is and let him or her monitor the consulting process. Listen frequently to the advocate's report.

10. If it's not broke, don't try to fix it. This is a great cliché, but more than an afterthought. It is in the consulting company's interest to find trouble where you see calm waters. The consultant's goal will be to sell much broader involvement than you might want or need. They can't help it. It is part of their nature. But it doesn't have to be part of yours.

Perhaps the best advice is the oldest. Almost five centuries ago, Niccolò Machiavelli, the man who wrote *The Prince* and whose name became synonymous with sinister plots, had this to say about seeking advice: "Here is an infallible rule: a prince who is not himself wise cannot be wisely advised. . . . Good advice depends on the shrewdness of the prince who seeks it, and not the shrewdness of the prince on good advice."

ACKNOWLEDGMENTS

This book would not have happened without the help of Douglas Frantz of *The New York Times*, and his wife, Cathy. Many thanks for your kind deeds and encouragement. We still owe you a first-class meal in a New York restaurant.

Because research is nagging and unforgiving in its demand for detail, it was most rewarding to have the loyal, patient, and, most of all, professional help of Marja Mills in preparing this book. We send to her best wishes in everything and note that an archaeologist digging through the mountains of paper in our tiny, film noir office would observe that up to a point, everything was tremendously well organized, then fell quite mysteriously into chaos. We would like to note that we did that ourselves, without her help.

Dominic Abel remains our favorite literary agent. We salute his tremendous collection of vintage cookie jars and applaud his sage advice in handling the small print in this effort much to our advantage. There is nothing like having a good advocate in the process of book writing, and we register not a single complaint.

We walked into John Mahaney's office at Times Books full of data and quotes and ideas and walked out eventually with the outline of a book in our heads. We thank him for his patience in dealing with the cantankerous, newspaper side of our personalities. The measure of the man as editor is that, even as page after page dropped from the manuscript under his pencil, we did not rush to New York to throttle him.

Instead, we listened closely and heard the voice of wisdom and experience. He is always welcome to visit our office. Given its condition, we understand why he would not want to.

A lot of people who cannot be named talked to us about the business of consulting. Among those who can be named is James Kennedy, of *Consultants News*, in Fitzwilliam, New Hampshire, an engaging host and, best of all, a man with great stories to tell. We would also like to thank Tom Rodenhauser, of *Consultants News*. Jill Totenberg, formerly of Gemini Consulting, and Stu Flack, at McKinsey & Co., proved invaluable in providing very straight answers and access to the right characters. Lois Therrien, at Andersen Consulting, is the complete public affairs professional. To all three, thank you for being responsive when you could, and absolutely straight in saying when you could not. Ann Mara, formerly with Boston Consulting Group, was a consummate professional. Special thanks to David Matheson and Sandra Moose for their time and patience. Ron Culp and Sam Falcona, at Sears, were invaluable, as were many anonymous officials at courthouses around the country, particularly in the Cuyahoga County Court in Cleveland, Ohio. A special thanks, too, is in order for the folks at Newgate Reporters in London for their hospitality and patience.

We could not have researched and written the book without the support of our superiors at the *Chicago Tribune*, in particular, editor Howard Tyner and managing editor Ann Marie Lipinski. They were willing to be flexible during two difficult years that included a presidential campaign, the Democratic National Convention, the death of a cardinal, and too many other big stories to mention. It remains very good to have a day job.

Thank you to the helpful people at the Evanston Public Library, which opened its new building even as we were cranking up our research efforts.

We were not around much in our typical lives during the research and writing of this book. To those loved ones and friends who missed us, we send apologies. To those who didn't even notice, we suggest following John Mahaney's advice of *amping up* the attention level a little. To those who were happy we were gone, we announce at a high decibel level that we are most definitely back.

NOTES

Chapter 1. The Price of Advice

Page 3 . . . **almost half a billion dollars by conservative** . . . Estimates of consulting fees are collected from five documents on file with the Federal Communications Commission as "Annual Report of AT&T Communications, Inc." covering the years 1989 to 1994. The tabulations are conservative because they include only fees paid for what appeared to be traditional consulting services, with the exception of fees for Andersen Consulting, which mixes its technology and strategy services.

Page 4 **It has lurched and shifted** . . . For an exhaustive examination of AT&T's troubles, see: "AT&T: Will the Bad News Ever End?," *Business Week*, October 7, 1996. Although the article notes that AT&T remains profitable, its percentages of growth in earnings and revenue, along with stock appreciation, have been far outpaced by competitors'.

Page 4 **It has turned** . . . Judith Dobrzynski's excellent news analysis "AT&T Choice Under Fire: Did Search Go Wrong?" discusses stock market reaction to John R. Walter's selection. The article notes that one-day bumps are not unusual when a company turns to a relative unknown in succession decisions, but it also points out that the second and third looks at the decision were unfavorable, too.

Page 5 **"I don't know . . ."** Private interview, October 21, 1996, with former AT&T executive. Interestingly, he insisted that his comments be reviewed in the context of his best wishes for his former employer. He insisted his own small-scale experiences with consultants he had hired proved fruitful, but involved small, clearly defined projects.

Page 6 **Hundreds of smaller companies** . . . This is one of those cases in which there were literally too many small consultants to list. In the process of tabulation, the authors avoided counting payments to companies that were clearly on board to straighten out computer hot spots or conduct seminars, not classic consulting assignments.

Page 6 **AT&T states generally that** . . . Repeated attempts were made to get breakdowns of actual services provided by the consultants. At best, the company would discuss its consulting contracts only in very general terms as one of the results of the government breakup of AT&T.

Page 6 **Each of them has a** . . . These descriptions come either from consulting company offerings of their services or from discussions of the consulting industry in *Management Consultancy Services in the USA*, Alpha Publications' 1995 survey of consulting companies.

Page 7 **It costs about** . . . Although McKinsey & Co. never discusses its fees, various court records, articles, and interviews frequently cite the cost of $250,000 per team.

Page 8 **"My guess is that** . . ." Interview with A. Michael Noll, October 14, 1996. Noll is one of a legion of AT&T followers who obsessively track the course of the company. He has written frequently about AT&T and its management problems over the years.

Page 10 **Management consulting has become** . . . This is a figure that has some controversy attached. People who follow the industry and industry insiders are forever debating what a management consulting company actually is. The purists always sever anything that smells too strongly of technology from the mix. The authors took a different tack. If it called itself a duck, then it was awarded full duck status in their measurement of the industry.

Page 15 **Put a plastic card** . . . All of these examples are collected from the annals of various consulting companies, with Andersen entering the field early on in advising credit card companies. Andersen has also been in the forefront of the computer intelligence business, used by car rental companies among other business interests.

Page 17 **In one way, it is James O. McKinsey's legacy** . . . *Management and Consulting: An Introduction to James O. McKinsey* (Utica, N.Y.: Cornell University Press, 1978) is the best and only exhaustive examination of McKinsey and his career. It traces his beginning as "a barefoot hillbilly" born in Mexico, Missouri, and the poverty of his early life, his amazing academic career, and the founding of his consulting company. The details on McKinsey's life come from this fascinating little book. Details of the larger story of McKinsey's disaster at Marshall Field & Co. come from *Give the Lady What She Wants!*, by Lloyd Wendt and Herman Kogan, published by the company in 1952. For more details, see the chapter "McKinsey's Purge."

Page 24 **In death, McKinsey was hailed by *American* . . .** From an editorial in *American Business* magazine, December 1937.

Chapter 2. The Few, the Proud, the Totally Insane

Page 26 **To thousands of his employees . . .** "America's Toughest Bosses," *Fortune*, February 27, 1989, and Cleveland *Plain Dealer*, January 30, 1994. Some details about Mr. Figgie's brash style were first reported in *Fortune* and in several excellent articles by Diane Solov and Sandra Livingston in *The Plain Dealer* during the early months of 1994 when Figgie's problems first surfaced publicly.

Page 28 **Some of the problems were acute . . .** "There He Goes Again," *Forbes*, October 31, 1988; speech by Harry Figgie, Jr., to insurance agents in Cleveland, Ohio, 1988; Figgie International annual reports for 1989 to 1993; authors' interviews with several former Figgie executives. Harry Figgie never tired of outlining his business philosophy. The authors distilled much of his philosophy and strategy from his comments in these sources and from interviews with former executives.

Page 29 **Between 1989 and 1994 . . .** *Deloitte & Touche LLP v. Figgie International, Inc.*, Case No. 278359, Common Pleas Court, Cuyahoga County Court, Ohio, and *Figgie International v. Boston Consulting Group*, Case No. 1:94 CV 1763, U.S. District Court, Eastern Division, Northern District of Ohio. The totals for the spending were taken from documents filed in these lawsuits. Figgie officials accused Boston Consulting Group of providing erroneous market studies and business reports and of overbilling the company for its consulting services. The company leveled many of the same allegations at Deloitte & Touche. The charges that Deloitte & Touche padded its bills and passed on entertainment costs in stripper bars came in depositions of Deloitte & Touche officials. Thomas Lawson of Deloitte & Touche admitted entertaining Figgie officials in the stripper bars, but said he didn't submit the expenses as reimbursable items to be billed to Figgie. Both Boston Consulting Group and Deloitte & Touche denied the charges in the lawsuits, which were settled out of court.

Page 29 **The controversy involving . . .** Authors' interviews with John Fox and Keith Ferrazzi of Deloitte & Touche and David Matheson, Boston Consulting Group. The lawsuits were settled out of court. As part of the settlement, the parties to the litigation are prohibited from disclosing the terms.

Page 30 **Harry Figgie grew up** . . . "A Dream Comes True," speech by Harry Figgie, Jr., to the Newcommon Society of the U.S., Richmond, Virginia, November 6, 1985; "Moving to the Future," Cleveland *Plain Dealer* magazine, March 23, 1985; and "A Heavy Hitter Comes Home," *Cleveland* magazine, March 1990. The details of Harry Figgie, Jr.'s youth and early business career came from the above sources. In his speech at the Newcommon Society of the U.S., Figgie spelled out his early business philosophy and the development of his "nucleus theory," some details of which also were mentioned in various company annual reports.

Page 31 **In 1965, he took the company public** . . . "A Dream Comes True," speech by Harry Figgie to the Newcommon Society of the U.S., Richmond, Virginia, November 6, 1985; various company annual reports; and *Charles Miner and Anne Howells v. Harry Figgie, Jr., et al.*, Case No. 93CV001575, Common Pleas Court, Lake County, Ohio, October 18, 1993. In its early years, Figgie International was named ATO Corp. Figgie had the name changed to Figgie International in the 1980s after he hired a public relations firm that recommended he attach his family name to the company. The details on the stock prices and Figgie's holdings came from company annual reports, interviews, and its proxy statements. The plaintiffs in *Charles Miner and Anne Howells v. Harry Figgie, Jr., et al.* alleged that Figgie enjoyed the extensive perks. The suit was eventually settled with an agreement in which the Figgie family agreed to pay plaintiffs about $3.3 million. Harry Figgie, Jr., also gave up millions of dollars in salary, bonus, consulting fees and rights to purchase Figgie stock as part of the settlement.

Page 32 **"He had these amazing instincts,"** . . . Authors' interviews with Richard DeLisle at various times during 1994 and 1995. DeLisle and several other former officers or executives at Figgie confirmed the details of how Harry Figgie, Jr., ran the company. "Hard Core" documents filed in the litigation also support DeLisle's recollections of Figgie.

Page 34 **Figgie's board gave Harry** . . . *Charles Miner and Anne Howell v. Harry Figgie, Jr., et al.*, Case No. 93CV001575, Common Pleas Court, Lake County, Ohio. October 10, 1993. The details of Harry Figgie's relationship with his board were part of the allegations in this litigation, but also were part of proxy statements the company issued detailing the financial ties between Figgie and his board members and in depositions filed in connection with the litigation involving Deloitte & Touche. The "you have a rocket up your ass" quote came from the deposition of Larry Schwartz filed in the Cuyahoga County Court, October 5, 1995.

Page 35 **Figgie's concerns about the future** . . . "There He Goes Again," *Forbes*, October 31, 1988. Some investors were not happy with Figgie's stock buyback scheme because he paid for the purchase by issuing a new class of stock that had only 5 percent of the voting power of the old shares. One analyst attacked him in *Forbes* for his selfish ways and said he showed a "complete disregard for the shareholder." The details of jobs that Figgie gave to family members were part of the Miner litigation and also were confirmed in stores in the Cleveland *Plain Dealer* and in *Business Week*. Figgie defended the hiring of family members.

Page 36 **The main problem on the staff's mind . . .** Authors' interviews with various former Figgie executives; *Charles Miner and Anne Howells v. Harry Figgie, Jr., et al.*, Case No. 93CV001575, Common Pleas Court, Lake County, Ohio, October 10, 1993; and *Moskovitz Executor et al. v. Mount Sinai Medical Center*, Supreme Court of Ohio, January term, 1994. Several former Figgie executives confirmed the staff's concern about Dr. Figgie's lack of actual manufacturing experience, which was a matter of record. Details about Dr. Figgie's medical career were included in the medical malpractice suit in which the family of Margaret Moskovitz was awarded $6.2 million in damages from Dr. Figgie. The award was affirmed by the Ohio Supreme Court in a ruling that also noted that Figgie had altered medical records to conceal his failure to recommend a biopsy that could have detected that Ms. Moskovitz had a rare form of malignant soft-tissue cancer. An arbitration panel in the case concluded that Moskovitz could have survived had the biopsy been performed. Harry Figgie's hiring of his son at a salary that would exceed $1 million a year was confirmed in the company's proxy statement. Dr. Figgie's statement that he ran Clark Reliance on slow afternoons was first reported in the Cleveland *Plain Dealer.*

Page 37 **But Harry III differed from his father . . .** Authors' interviews with several former Figgie executives and deposition of Larry G. Schwartz, vol. 1, *Deloitte & Touche LLP v. Figgie International, Inc.*, Case No. 278359, Common Pleas Court, Cuyahoga County, Ohio, October 5, 1995. Most details of Figgie's demeanor in the office came from interviews with former Figgie executives. Some details were confirmed in newspaper reports, too. The authors didn't use any details unless they were confirmed by at least three sources. In his deposition, Larry Schwartz confirmed that he and Dr. Figgie placed the massive machine tool order.

Page 38 **It didn't take long . . .** Authors' interview with Paul Kearney, winter 1994. Kearney and several other former Figgie executives confirmed the details of this meeting. Some details also were confirmed in the depositions of Craig Giffi and Thomas Lawson filed in connection with the Deloitte & Touche litigation. All executives vividly recalled the "Valdez is coming" theme struck by Dr. Figgie. The plot of the movie was confirmed

by a March 1971 review of the movie by Gene Siskel published in the
Chicago Tribune.

Page 40 **As the key man in charge** . . . Deposition of Thomas Lawson, vol. 1,
Deloitte & Touche LLP v. Figgie International, Inc., Case No. 278359, Common Pleas Court, Cuyahoga County, Ohio, July 1995. All details of Lawson's background and his initial encounters with Dr. Figgie came from his
deposition.

Page 41 **As Lawson and Giffi would soon** . . . Authors' interviews with various
former Figgie executives; company annual reports; internal Figgie records;
Figgie International letter supporting credit for Research and Development tax credit on the company's 1991 tax return prepared by James P.
McCormick, partner, Deloitte & Touche, September 1, 1992; and deposition of Larry G. Schwartz, vol. 1, *Deloitte & Touche LLP v. Figgie International, Inc.*, Case No. 278359, Common Pleas Court, Cuyahoga County,
Ohio, October 5, 1995. The relationship between Clark Reliance and Figgie International was described in general terms by several former Figgie
executives. It was also mentioned in the lawsuit filed against Figgie by
Charles Miner, and details of the relationship were disclosed in the application for the R&D tax credit. Schwartz's recollection of his problems implementing world class and his and the doctor's views of consultants were
detailed in his deposition.

Page 42 **The two consultants had a** . . . Authors' interviews with Craig Giffi,
John Fox, and Keith Ferrazzi, Deloitte & Touche, fall 1996; *Deloitte &
Touche, 1990, The First Year*; and *The Big Six*, by Mark Stevens (New York:
Touchstone, 1991).

Page 44 **By mid-1990, a proposed** . . . Deposition of Gerald J. DeBrunner,
managing partner and vice chairman of Deloitte & Touche Consulting,
September 21, 1995, *Deloitte & Touche LLP v. Figgie International, Inc.*,
Common Pleas Court, Cuyahoga County, Ohio; a Deloitte & Touche interoffice memo from Bill Bottger to J. Michael Cook, Deloitte & Touche
chairman, December 5, 1990; and an October 25, 1990, letter to Larry C.
Schwartz from Thomas Lawson. The existence of the cost-sharing
arrangement between Clark Reliance and Figgie International mentioned
on page 44 came from the Figgie International letter supporting R&D
credit on the company's 1991 tax return prepared by James P. McCormick,
partner, Deloitte & Touche, September 1, 1992.

Page 45 **The consultants had their work** . . . Figgie International letter supporting R&D tax credit on 1991 tax return prepared by James P.
McCormick, partner, Deloitte & Touche, September 1, 1992; depositions
of Larry G. Schwartz, Craig Giffi, and Thomas Lawson, *Deloitte & Touche
LLP v. Figgie International, Inc.*, Common Pleas Court, Cuyahoga County,

Ohio, 1995; letter to Harry Figgie III, M.D., from Thomas Lawson, October 17, 1991, and Figgie International proxy statements. The true condition of Clark Reliance was disclosed in the tax letter. The details of how Showpiece operated came from the Schwartz, Giffi, and Lawson depositions. The financial details of the ties between board members and the company came from various Figgie International proxy statements.

Page 48 **The directors showed up** . . . Deposition of Larry G. Schwartz, *Deloitte & Touche LLP v. Figgie International, Inc.,* Common Pleas Court, Cuyahoga County, Ohio, 1995. The details of the board meeting were fully disclosed in the deposition of Schwartz, who was at the meeting. Some details were also disclosed in the depositions of Craig Giffi and Thomas Lawson, both of whom also attended the meeting.

Page 49 **Lawson liked the Valdez business** . . . Depositions of Thomas Lawson, Craig Giffi, and Larry G. Schwartz, *Deloitte & Touche LLP v. Figgie International, Inc.,* Common Pleas Court, Cuyahoga County, Ohio, 1995, and interview with Harold Wallace, an attorney with the National Center for Manufacturing Science, Ann Arbor, Michigan, August 1995. The details about Lawson's experiences at Figgie and the projections of revenues all came from his deposition. The details about fee increases were disclosed in the deposition of Craig Giffi, which was also the source of his experience at Figgie. The authors also interviewed Giffi in 1996 after the litigation was settled. Although he disputed the conclusions that Figgie's lawyers drew from his testimony, the interview confirmed the facts in his deposition.

Page 52 **As things got more complex** . . . Interoffice memo by Glen Lindemann, president, Scott Aviation, April 1991, filed in *Deloitte & Touche LLP v. Figgie International, Inc.,* Common Pleas Court, Cuyahoga County, Ohio, 1995; Figgie International, Inc., annual reports, and deposition of Larry G. Schwartz, *Deloitte & Touche LLP v. Figgie International, Inc.,* Common Pleas Court, Cuyahoga County, Ohio, 1995. Details of the division presidents' skepticism came from Lindemann's lengthy memo. The statistical data on page 53 came from Lindemann's memo and were confirmed in annual reports.

Page 53 **The strategy might have sounded** . . . Authors' interviews with Richard DeLisle, 1994 and 1995; internal records of Scott Aviation and deposition of Larry G. Schwartz, *Deloitte & Touche LLP v. Figgie International, Inc.,* Common Pleas Court, Cuyahoga County, Ohio, 1995. The details of DeLisle's experience at Scott Aviation came from several author interviews and from internal Scott Aviation documents that confirmed DeLisle's account of his tenure there. The disclosure of consulting fees that ranged up to $1,300 per hour came from Schwartz's deposition.

Page 57 **DeLisle was not alone** . . . Depositions of Thomas Lawson, Craig Giffi, and Larry G. Schwartz, *Deloitte & Touche LLP v. Figgie International, Inc.*, Common Pleas Court, Cuyahoga County, Ohio, 1995; Figgie International, Inc., letter supporting claims for R&D tax credit on 1991 tax return prepared by James P. McCormick, partner, Deloitte & Touche, September 1992. The details of the problems encountered at Clark Reliance and later at Figgie came from the R&D tax credit letter, which spelled out the problems in excruciating technical detail. Details concerning the number of Deloitte & Touche consultants at work, their compensation, and the unpaid invoices came from the Lawson, Giffi, and Schwartz depositions.

Page 58 **Other troubles quickly overshadowed** . . . Depositions of Larry G. Schwartz and Richard Barkley, *Deloitte & Touche LLP v. Figgie International, Inc.*, Common Pleas Court, Cuyahoga County, Ohio, 1995. Schwartz's deposition detailed the problems at Scott and in Georgia. Barkley's deposition discussed the other problems.

Page 60 **Others in Figgie shared** . . . Depositions of Thomas Lawson and Larry G. Schwartz, *Deloitte & Touche LLP v. Figgie International, Inc.*, Common Pleas Court, Cuyahoga County, Ohio, 1995; *Bankruptcy 1995*, Harry Figgie, Jr., Little, Brown and Company, 1992. The details of the unraveling of affairs at Figgie were described by both Lawson and Schwartz in their depositions. Many of the details were confirmed in Giffi's deposition, too. There were a couple of occasions on which Schwartz and Lawson confirmed entertaining Figgie executives in stripper bars, but Lawson said he didn't include the outlays in expense accounts that were later charged to Figgie.

Page 62 **The decision worried Lawson** . . . Depositions of Thomas Lawson, Craig Giffi, and Larry G. Schwartz, *Deloitte & Touche LLP v. Figgie International, Inc.*, Common Pleas Court, Cuyahoga County, Ohio, 1995, and testimony of Charles Miner, *National Labor Relations Board v. Automatic Sprinkler Corp.*, NLRB, Cleveland, Ohio, 1991. Details regarding Figgie's rising tab with Deloitte & Touche and the disputes involving padded bills came from the depositions of Lawson and Giffi. Although lawyers for Figgie confronted Giffi with contradictions between the hours billed to the company and the Deloitte & Touche time sheets for the engagement, Giffi denied any bills were padded. He said there was no legitimate connection between billable hours and time sheets. Details on the firing of Miner came from his testimony in the NLRB case. The reporting on the meeting between Skadra and Giffi and the suspension of payments came from the depositions of Giffi and Schwartz.

Page 65 **"They come in and they tell you** . . . Authors' interview with Charles Miner, summer 1995.

Page 66 **A month later, Figgie's** . . . Transcript of Lehman Brothers Eleventh Annual Diversified Companies Seminar, Park Lane Hotel, New York, November 3, 1993.

Page 68 **By springtime 1994** . . . Deposition of Larry G. Schwartz, *Deloitte & Touche LLP v. Figgie International, Inc.*, Common Pleas Court, Cuyahoga County, Ohio, 1995; letter to Dr. H. E. Figgie III from G. Guy Sorrell, partner, Deloitte & Touche, May 1994; authors' interview with Ira Gamm, public relations department, Figgie International, August 1995; Cleveland *Plain Dealer*; and authors' interview with John Fox, summer 1996. Most details about the final meetings and the unraveling of the Figgie's involvement with the company came from Schwartz's deposition.

Chapter 3. The Jobs Elimination Festival

Page 73 **Buried in a court file** . . . Details about the O'Neal Steel Co. case can be found in the Circuit Court of Jefferson County, Alabama, in *O'Neal Steel, Inc., a corporation, and O'Neal Metals, Inc., a corporation, plaintiffs, v. Arthur Andersen & Co., S.C., a partnership, defendant,* Civil Action No. CV9406403, filed September 12, 1994.

Page 74 **But down in Count "I** . . . Exhibit A in the lawsuit is a 15-page letter from Andersen Consulting to Emmet O'Neal III, vice chairman of O'Neal Steel Co. The letter explains various terms of the contract. On page 7, it details "operating efficiencies" and outlines the "risks and rewards" of the project, including the sliding schedule of penalties and bonuses depending on "reduction in need for employees."

Page 76 **Only a few decades ago** . . . Andersen's own company history details the fascinating birth and development of computing and consulting, along with some of the bumps the company hit along the way. It notes that inside of Andersen there was strong resistence to entering the computing field back in the 1950s, but details how wiser heads prevailed in the struggle.

Page 76 **Today, Andersen is the strongest** . . . *The Big Six*, by Mark Stevens (New York: Touchstone, 1991). Stevens' book offers an excellent discussion of Andersen's leap into the world of management consulting and the attendant infighting that ensued.

Page 77 **In fiscal 1994, in the United States** . . . These figures from Andersen Consulting only hint at the company's phenomenal pace of growth and, to be sure, are already dated and probably on the low side.

Page 79 **Terry Neill has been with** . . . In a wide-ranging interview on July 12, 1995, Neill talked not only about his decision to join Andersen, but many of his experiences over the years, some of which are included at the end of this chapter.

Page 79 **An attrition rate that has** . . . There is some debate over this figure, which has been frequently cited in various business press articles. Andersen provided the 16 percent figure. Part of the problem, Dataquest Inc. reported in its 1994 study of Andersen Consulting, is the work demand placed on young consultants.

Page 80 **Carol Meyer is in charge** . . . Interview, July 10, 1995.

Page 81 **If Neill with his science** . . . Profiles of individual Andersen standouts were provided by Andersen Consulting.

Page 82 **With the addition of** . . . Andersen's public affairs staff was most insistent in stating that the company did not want to be defined solely in terms of its connection to technology. This is apparently part of a marketing strategy aimed at moving beyond the company's old image.

Page 84 **Andersen is one of the** . . . There is no overstating this company's passion for accommodation. After a long day of note taking and observation at one of the company's media seminars, the author's computer and notes were stolen from his home. Within a week, Andersen had reproduced and presented the entire seminar on videotape.

Page 85 **Despite all this sophistication** . . . Andersen has so many product lines and services that the mind boggles at the presentation. This, again, is a likely function of the marketing push to move beyond its old image as computer guru.

Page 85 **Ask Rudy Puryear** . . . Interview, July 18, 1995.

Page 88 **Welcome to Harley-Davidson** . . . True to its nature as a totally focused New Age company, Harley-Davidson resisted all attempts at interviews on consulting on the grounds that it simply would not add value to Harley's products. However, Andersen's Tom Arenberg enthusiastically outlined the company's efforts. For a solid discussion of Harley's history and amazing resurgence, see "Full Throttle," by Charles Leroux, *Chicago Tribune Sunday Magazine*, June 6, 1993.

Page 94 **It is a very old building** . . . The Retail Place in Chicago is a must-see place for anyone interested in how modern consulting companies market their products. The visit was part of one of Andersen's media tours.

Page 97 **In Stamford, Connecticut, in Superior Court** . . . The details of this complicated case are contained in *UOP, plaintiff, v. Andersen Consulting, defendant*, Superior Court, Judicial District of Stamford/Norwalk at Stamford, CD950144480s. Originally filed March 14, 1995, then refiled May 30, 1995.

Page 99 **All of those things seem to be** . . . This case has been closely followed in *Consultants News* and a number of other publications, with the main theme being that consulting companies should be careful about what they promise their clients, and clients should be careful about what they accept.

Page 105 **Andersen's Keith Burgess** . . . An engaging world traveler, Burgess discussed the Russian case with one of the authors during an Andersen media seminar and expanded on the theme in a later telephone interview.

Chapter 4. Taming "The Monster of the Midway"

Page 110 **In days past, Sears** . . . Interviews with Arthur Martinez in September 1996. The authors conducted extensive interviews with Martinez in which he spelled out his theories about the use of consultants and their value to his efforts to turn around the nation's second largest retailer. Martinez confirmed that Sears had used McKinsey & Co. and Monitor extensively as consultants in the past. Monitor's engagement at Sears was first reported by *Business Week* magazine in its February 11, 1991, issue.

Page 111 **In many respects, the story** . . . *The Big Store: Inside the Crisis and Revolution at Sears,* by Donald R. Katz (New York: Viking, 1987). The details about Sears' history were originally reported in Katz's excellent book on Sears. The earnings information and sales figures were confirmed in other public reports on Sears' financial results.

Page 112 **Edward Riggs Telling learned** . . . The details of Telling's history at Sears on pages 112 to 122 are well told in Katz's book *The Big Store.* The authors relied heavily on Katz's reporting, which Sears officials acknowledge to be an accurate account of those years, although some former officials quibble with some details. In many instances, the authors supplemented Katz's narrative with details, observations, or statistics from other sources such as *Business Week,* the *Chicago Tribune,* and *Fortune,* all of which covered the turmoil at Sears extensively, and with independent interviews with former Sears officials or analysts of the company.

Page 119 **Ed Brennan, the homegrown** . . . "The Big Store's Big Trauma," *Business Week,* July 10, 1989; "Can Ed Brennan Salvage the Sears He Designed?," *Business Week,* August 27, 1990; and *The Big Store: Inside the Crisis and Revolution at Sears,* by Donald R. Katz (New York: Viking, 1987). Brennan's years at Sears on pages 119 to 126 were drawn from these three sources plus independent interviews with former Sears officials. Again, the authors supplemented the *Business Week* and Katz accounts with statistics, observations, and information from independent sources.

Page 121 **What was wrong was** . . . Authors' interview with Arthur C. Martinez at Sears headquarters, September 1996.

Page 122 **But Sears' most devastating** . . . "Are the Lights Dimming for Ed Brennan?," *Business Week*, February 11, 1991, and authors' interview with Liam Fahey, October 1996.

Page 123 **Monitor talked a good game** . . . Monitor Company's brochure provided to authors in 1995 by officials of the consulting firm. The material provided by Monitor described in its own words the company's mission and characteristics.

Page 124 **A by-product of Monitor's** . . . Authors' interview with Edward Brennan, October 1996; "Don't Write Sears Off," *Forbes*, November 28, 1988; and "Why Bigger Is Badder at Sears," *Fortune*, December 5, 1988. Some details about "everyday low pricing" were taken from all three of the above sources. A controversy still rages over exactly who originally advocated "everyday low pricing" at Sears. Brennan said the concept was a by-product of Monitor's work at Sears. Officially Monitor refused to comment, but one source at the consulting firm said it was opposed to Brennan's application of "everyday low pricing" at the time he decided to implement it. In the end, Michael Bozic, the head of the retail group at the time, got blamed for the policy. He was demoted by Brennan and eventually left the company, although he was widely viewed as a "fall guy" for the disaster. One point that almost everyone interviewed agreed upon was that Monitor's overall work at Sears left a lot to be desired.

Page 125 **As the 1990s approached** . . . "Sears Faces a Tall Task," *Business Week*, November 14, 1988; "Why Bigger Is Badder," *Fortune*, December 5, 1988; "Are the Lights Dimming for Ed Brennan?," *Business Week*, February 11, 1991; and "Smaller But Wiser," *Business Week*, October 12, 1992. Details on Brennan's stewardship of Sears during the late 1980s and early 1990s came from the above sources and from Sears' annual reports covering the period.

Page 126 **Arthur Martinez had been vice chairman** . . . Authors' interview with Arthur C. Martinez, Sears headquarters, September 1996. Martinez himself provided most details of his recruitment by Sears, although his account was supplemented by some published reports in the *Chicago Tribune* and *Financial World*.

Page 128 **Martinez's wife, Liz, was** . . . "Arthur Martinez, CEO of the Year," *Financial World*, March 26, 1996; "Trying to Turn Around the Giants," *Chicago Tribune*, January 14, 1996; "Deft Quickstep, Fast Turnaround Propel Martinez," *Chicago Tribune*, August 6, 1995; "Architect of Change," *Chain Store Age*, April 1993; authors' interview with Martinez; and *P. A. Bergner & Co. v. Arthur C. Martinez and Sears Roebuck & Co.*, Case No. 92CV6501, U.S. District Court, Southern District of New York, November 1992. Many details of Martinez's background originally were reported in the sources above. Martinez confirmed all of them in interviews with the authors. The details about Martinez's employment agreement came from the Bergner litigation and Sears' 1996 proxy.

Page 129 **"My first set of actions . . .** Authors' interviews with Arthur C. Martinez at Sears headquarters and on tour of company stores, September 1996. The quotes and detailed accounts of Martinez's actions at Sears on pages 129 to 138 came from extensive interviews with Mr. Martinez in September 1996. The authors interviewed Martinez both at the company's headquarters in Hoffman Estates and during a daylong tour of a new store on Long Island, New York, and a return trip from New York in the Sears plane.

Page 137 **A Chicago-based consulting firm . . .** *A. T. Kearney*, publication of A. T. Kearney, Inc., and *Solid, Stable and Successful*, Management Consultants International (Dublin: Lafferty Publications, 1996).

Page 137 **Martinez had already heard . . .** Authors' interviews with Anthony J. Rucci, executive vice president, Sears, August 1996, and with Arthur C. Martinez, Sears, September 1996. All details of the Kearney engagement came from these two interviews. The authors supplemented their interviews with details from Sears' financial reports and published accounts in the *Chicago Tribune* and the *Milwaukee Journal*.

Page 140 **Battery sales accounted for only . . .** "180 Jobs Cut with Loss of DieHard," *Milwaukee Journal*, May 19, 1994. The account of the contract dispute given by Johnson CEO James Keyes was reported by the *Milwaukee Journal*.

Page 142 **Rucci's "isolated exception" is . . .** Authors' interview with Anthony J. Rucci, executive vice president, Sears, August 1996, and phone interview with David Ulrich of the University of Michigan, October 1996.

Page 144 **Sears has made other sweeping . . .** "Yes, He's Revived Sears. But Can He Reinvent It?" *The New York Times*, January 7, 1996, and authors' interview with Arthur C. Martinez, Sears headquarters, September 1996.

Chapter 5. "A Medicine Man in a Room Full of Funeral Directors"

Page 146 **Kim Wellman remembers . . .** Authors' phone interviews with Kim Wellman, July 1996. Mrs. Wellman provided all the details of her daughter's treatments and difficulties.

Page 147 **In coming years, patients . . .** Disease management has been the subject of several articles in the health care trade press. The *Journal of the American Medical Association* (*JAMA*) called it a "rapidly burgeoning concept." Other publications, such as *Medical Economics*, have gone further. There is also some dispute over who actually coined the term "disease management"—a consulting firm or another source. The authors traced the first public mention of the term to an article in the *Best Review*, an insurance industry publication, written by two Boston Consulting Group consultants.

Page 148 **On another level, though** . . . *Consultants News*, July–August 1996; "The Pain of Downsizing," *Business Week*, May 9, 1994; "Strategies for Public Television in a Multi-channel Environment," Boston Consulting Group Study, March 1991; "Big Challenge: Reform Russia's Oil Industry," *Oil & Gas Journal*, August 1994; and authors' interview with David Matheson, senior vice president and head of health care practice area at Boston Consulting Group. The revenue estimates used are from *Consultants News*, which has been estimating the industry's revenues for more than a decade. Details on the NYNEX engagement came from John Byrne's excellent article on NYNEX in *Business Week*.

Page 149 **The son of a Tennessee Bible** . . . Videotaped interview of Bruce Henderson by George Stalk of Boston Consulting Group. The interview and biographical material on Henderson were provided by Boston Consulting Group.

Page 149 **Henderson had a big problem** . . . Authors' interviews with James Kennedy of *Consultants News*, September 1995 and July 1996; and videotaped interview with Henderson. The background information on Henderson on pages 149 and 150 came mainly from his videotaped interview and from some sample Perspective columns provided to the authors by BCG. Kennedy's quotes were taken from two interviews.

Page 151 **When Henderson founded BCG** . . . "The Henderson Revolution," by Michael Rothschild, *Upside* magazine, December 1992; and authors' interview with Sandra Moose, vice president, Boston Consulting Group, July 1996. The background on the state of the industry when Henderson founded BCG came from Rothschild's story in *Upside*. Many details on Henderson's background came from materials provided to the authors by BCG and from the interview with Moose.

Page 152 **Under Henderson's logic** . . . *Competing Against Time*, by George Stalk, Jr., and Thomas M. Hout (New York: The Free Press, 1990); and "The Henderson Revolution," *Upside* magazine, December 1992. For a detailed discussion of the experience curve and other tools developed in the industry, see "Competing Against Time," by Stalk and Hout, both of whom work as BCG consultants.

Page 154 **Henderson had egalitarian** . . . *Fortune*, August 31, 1987. For an excellent account of Ira Magaziner's tenure at BCG, see Peter Petre's piece in *Fortune*. Magaziner declined to return several phone calls to go over the details, but other BCG sources confirmed the account used here.

Page 155 **But Henderson found fault** . . . *Competing Against Time*, by George

Stalk, Jr., and Thomas M. Hout (New York: The Free Press, 1990), pages 10–11; *The Product Portfolio: A Boston Consulting Group Perspective*, undated, by Bruce Henderson; and interview with Sandra Moose, vice president, Boston Consulting Group, September 1995, Boston, Massachusetts. The details on the development of the product portfolio matrix and the theory behind it on pages 155 to 158 came from the above sources and interviews.

Page 158 **Despite its notoriety . . .** "Effects of Portfolio Planning Methods on Decision Making: Experimental Results" by J. Scott Armstrong and Roderick J. Brodie, *International Journal of Research in Marketing*, January 1994. The study by Armstrong, a professor at the Wharton School at the University of Pennsylvania and Brodie, a professor of the University of Auckland, is one of the few empirical studies done on the matrix. In an interview, Armstrong said his criticism of the matrix got a hostile reception from his colleagues in academia. In a subsequent study, he found most articles that criticize the status quo or management "folklore" that often emanates from consultants gets a similar reception. No authoritative source has knocked down the Armstrong and Brodie study, though.

Page 159 **One executive who has . . .** Authors' interview with Stuart Early, Human Relations Department, Amoco Oil Co. A practice leader in Amoco's organization capabilities group, Early supervises some 130 people and had experience using the BCG matrix.

Page 160 **David Matheson was . . .** Authors' interview with David Matheson, senior vice president, Boston Consulting Group, July 1996.

Page 161 **"The mean at BCG is really . . .** Authors' interview with Robert Frisch, vice president, Gemini Consulting, September 1995.

Page 161 **Matheson fit right in. . . .** Authors' interview with David Matheson, senior vice president, Boston Consulting Group, July 1996; and *Stipulation, J. Anthony Aldrich v. The Boston Consulting Group*, CA 91-10756-N, U.S. District Court, District of Massachusetts. Details about Matheson's background and early assignments came from the interview with him. As a privately held company, BCG does not publicly disclose its finances. The revenue figures and the ESOP data came from Aldrich's suit, which included audited financial statements for 1982 through 1989 for BCG and excerpts from worldwide officers meetings. The authors supplemented the material in the Stipulation with an undated Bruce Henderson Perspective that disclosed details of the ESOP.

Page 162 **Boehringer Mannheim Group had . . .** Authors' interview with Jerry Moller, president and CEO of Boehringer Mannheim Group, June 1996. All details of the Boehringer Mannheim history and relationship with BCG came from the interview with Moller. Matheson also disclosed many of these details. There were few contradictions in the accounts given by the two executives.

Page 164 **The BCG consultants found** . . . "Diabetes: New Findings, Better Outcomes," *Patient Care* magazine, February 15, 1995; "Diabetes Care: A Systems Approach to Diabetes Care," by Roger S. Mazze, Ph.D., *Diabetes Care*, June 1994; and "A Modern Scourge: A Three-Part Series on Diabetes," *Chicago Tribune*, February 5–7, 1995. Details about the cost of coverage and the characteristics of diabetes came from the above sources.

Page 165 **Matheson and his consultants** . . . Authors' interviews with David Matheson, senior vice president, Boston Consulting Group; and "The Promises of Disease Management: A Senior Management Perspective," The Boston Consulting Group, 1995. The authors interviewed Matheson on four different occasions, twice in his Boston offices and twice via phone. Details of how BCG consultants applied disease management strategies to Boehringer Mannheim and other businesses came from the Matheson interviews. The senior management perspective provided additional details about how the technique was developed at BCG.

Page 165 **Boehringer Mannheim obviously** . . . Authors' interview with Jerry Moller, president and CEO of Boehringer Mannheim.

Page 166 **One of the nice things** . . . Authors' interview with a former BCG official who once set up the company's CEO conferences; interviews with Sandra Moose, BCG vice president, July 1996.

Page 169 **Matheson and his team** . . . Authors' interviews with David Matheson, senior vice president, Boston Consulting Group, 1995 and 1996.

Page 171 **BCG argued that a** . . . "Bringing a Systems Orientation into the World of Managed Care," by David Matheson and Craig Wheeler, *Best Review*, February 1987; and interviews with Matheson in 1995 and 1996. The arguments of Matheson and Wheeler, another BCG consultant, came from the *Best Review* articles. Matheson disclosed details about BCG's contacts with the pharmaceutical industry and its initial contacts with Deere & Co. in interviews.

Page 173 **Deere's medical director was** . . . Authors' interview with Richard Bartsh, senior vice president and chief medical officer, John Deere Health Care, and Richard Van Bell, president, John Deere Health Care, June 1996; "John Deere and Mayo Establish Strategic Alliances Between Payers and Providers," *Health Care Strategic Management*, May 1994; and "Deere Offers Glimpse of Health Care Future," *Chicago Tribune*, January 25, 1992. Bartsh and Van Bell provided most details about BCG's involvement with Deere. Many details were supplemented by the articles in the *Health Care Strategic Management* newsletter and the *Chicago Tribune*.

Page 176 **"Before the asthma classes . . .** Authors' interview with Mrs. Kim Wellman, July 1996.

Page 178 **The drugmakers aren't exactly . . .** "Disease Management Fact and Fiction: Survey and Analysis," Scott Levin Health Care Publications, 1996. For an excellent survey and description of disease management practices around the nation, see the Scott Levin survey. Details on specific programs being promoted by drug companies came from this exhaustive survey.

Page 179 **One thing to keep in mind . . .** Depositions of Craig Giffi and Larry G. Schwartz, *Deloitte & Touche v. Figgie International, Inc.,* Common Pleas Court, Cuyahoga County, Ohio, 1995, and interviews with David Matheson, senior vice president, Boston Consulting Group, 1995 and 1996. The Giffi and Schwartz depositions reveal the details about BCG's rates at Figgie International, including a statement by Walter Vannoy that BCG's rates were the highest he'd ever seen. In an interview, Matheson denied that any BCG consultants draw pay of $1,300 an hour. The other quotes in the final pages of the chapter are from the interviews with Matheson.

Chapter 6. Trying to Make Gold from Lead

Page 183 **There may be no more . . .** Comments on Cigna Property & Casualty came during a visit with Cigna executives and workers in Philadelphia on October 30, 1995.

Page 183 **A troubled property and casualty . . .** Descriptions of the company are gleaned from its annual and quarterly reports to the Securities and Exchange Commission in 1992, 1993, 1994, and 1995 and from *Hoover's Handbook Database* via America Online.

Page 185 **Tom Valerio, the former . . .** Interview with Valerio at Cigna Property & Casualty, October 29, 1995.

Page 185 **A couple of hundred miles away . . .** Authors' visit to Montgomery County General Hospital, October 30, 1995, included interviews with the executives cited in this chapter.

Page 189 **It was not coincidental . . .** At the time, Gemini was marketing itself as the brain pool for vast business transformation efforts, a sales pitch that has since been whittled down because of market resistance to huge consulting engagements.

Page 189 **It is all part of a time-tested . . .** For a good discussion of the book-writing process and its pitfalls, see *The Witch Doctors: Making Sense of the*

Management Gurus, by John Micklethwait and Adrian Wooldridge (New York: Times Books, 1996).

Page 190 **Reengineering projects were faltering** . . . Even the authors of the original reengineering books were forced to concede that the effort had gone way off track. They argued in subsequent publications, though, that the problem was that managers simply didn't go far enough, and came up with formulas to help with that problem, too.

Page 193 **The assessment in the marketplace** . . . Gemini got cool reviews almost everywhere after its initial hot arrival on the consulting media scene. As of 1996, it was reporting itself to be back on track and viewed the downturn as one of the regular bumps that affect all consulting companies.

Page 194 **At Gemini, Bob Frisch** . . . Frisch talked about consulting in general and his years at Gemini in an interview in Evanston, Illinois, September 18, 1995.

Page 195 **Consultants are never really far** . . . Charts to explain just about everything were much in evidence during the authors' visit to Gemini in Morristown, New Jersey, on August 23 and 24, 1995. The company provided wide access and extensive interviews for this chapter.

Page 199 **Three consultants were called in** . . . Peter Monge interview. These kinds of bake-offs are quite common and have led consulting companies to put such heavy emphasis on the sales pitches that many of their best and most senior consultants spend most of their time in this role.

Page 202 **It is a complicated business, Wallace conceded** . . . As part of its management churning, Wallace left Gemini in 1996.

Page 208 **How the Property & Casualty subsidiary** . . . For a good review of Cigna's difficulties in the world of high-risk insurance, see articles by David I. Turner of the *Philadelphia Inquirer* during 1995.

Page 209 **No one knows where all of this might lead.** This is literally true and lifted from the company's strategic discussions as filed with the Securities and Exchange Commission. Cigna's splitting off of its riskiest business into a subsidiary, although under court challenge, made the picture look better. But the resolution of the long-term court battle over asbestos claims will provide the genuine measure of how deep the trouble might be for Cigna and a handful of other highly exposed insurers.

Page 212 **Pat Jodry's behavior** . . . Interview with Pat Jodry, October 29, 1995. Jodry's remarks should not be taken out of context. While she spoke frankly about the consulting experience and the problems at Cigna, there was never any doubt during the discussion about her loyalties to the company and her interest in its success.

Page 217 **He offered an important caveat** . . . Valerio was strong on one of the most important attitudes uncovered during the research for *Dangerous Company:* It is absolutely critical that managers know exactly what they want from consultants and that they keep a sharp eye on the goals.

Page 218 **Gemini still believes** . . . While the company has not yet returned to its era of exploding revenues, its receipts were up in 1996, and it appeared Gemini would at least come up even with 1995 totals.

Chapter 7. Too Close for Comfort

Page 219 **It was late, just before** . . . Testimony of Olivier Roux, *Regina v. Ernest Saunders et al.*, Central Criminal Court, Southwark, London, England, February–August 1990; "Secret Source of Market Intelligence and Self-made Millionaire Went to Office After Court," *Financial Times*, August 28, 1990. The details of Roux's visit to Ronson's offices and the deal he sealed came from his sworn testimony and from the judge's summation of evidence at the trial. Details on the backgrounds of Parnes and Ronson came from profiles in *Financial Times*. In the trial, Parnes denied that he heard Roux talk of a success fee in the meeting, but Roux said he did.

Page 221 **It's easy to see how** . . . Testimony of Olivier Roux, *Regina v. Ernest Saunders et al.*, Central Criminal Court, Southwark, London, England, February 1990. The 5-million-pound reward paid to Ronson actually went to companies under the control of Heron, which was owned by Ronson.

Page 221 **Today Bain & Co.** . . . . *Consultants News*, July 1995; testimony of John Brett Theroux, *Regina v. Ernest Saunders et al.*, Central Criminal Court, Southwark, London, England, February 1990; *The New York Times*, May 1, 1994; *Business Week*, June 19, 1995; *Business Marketing*, May 1994; and *Crain's Chicago Business*, April 4, 1994. Statistics on Bain's size and revenues came from *Consultants News*. An attorney questioning John Brett Theroux in the Guinness case quoted Bain documents that said Olivier Roux was paid $925,127 when he left Bain & Co. Details about Orit Gadiesh came from *The New York Times* and several other articles on Ms. Gadiesh, and details on Bain clients came from *Business Week*, *Business Marketing*, and *Crain's*.

Page 222 **But for all of its differences** . . . Authors' interviews with James Tobin, president of Biogen, Inc., March and June 1996; *Health Industry Today*, November 1994; and *Phillip Roman & Co. v. Bain Capital*, Superior Court, Suffolk County, Commonwealth of Massachusetts, October 1994. Details about Bain Capital investments and partnership practices came from *Health Industry Today* and the Roman litigation.

Page 223 **It is no accident that** . . . Private correspondence of Bruce Henderson, September 1984; "The Bain Cult," *Business* (London), June 1986; "A Consulting Firm Too Hot to Handle," *Fortune*, April 1987; "Counselor to the King," *The New York Times Magazine*, September 24, 1989; Memorandum on Bain Capital Investments, Bain Capital, Inc., June 1992; and "Orit Gadiesh: Pride at Bain & Co. (A&B)," *Harvard Business School*, January 1995. The details on Bain's origins, personality, and history came from the above sources. In his private correspondence, Henderson gives a particularly arresting account of Bain's departure from BCG, calling it the spark that set off an "eight days' war" within BCG.

Page 225 **To ease their fears, Bain** . . . "Counselor to the King," *The New York Times Magazine*, September 24, 1989; "Shedding the Mystique," *The Boston Globe*, May 2, 1988; and "A Consulting Firm Too Hot to Handle," *Fortune*, April 1987. Details on Bain's "relationship consulting" came from the above sources. The quote from Kennedy came from *The Boston Globe*.

Page 226 **Competitors and critics** . . . "A Consulting Firm Too Hot to Handle," *Fortune*, April 1987. The details of Bain's past relationships with clients all came from *Fortune*.

Page 227 **Ernest Saunders first walked** . . . Testimony of Ernest Saunders, *Regina v. Ernest Saunders et al.*, Central Criminal Court, Southwark, London, England, June 1990. Saunders' background and his initial history with Guinness all came from his testimony.

Page 229 **John Brett Theroux had** . . . Testimony of John Brett Theroux, *Regina v. Ernest Saunders et al.*, Central Criminal Court, Southwark, London, England, April 1990.

Page 229 **In many respects, Guinness** . . . Testimony of John Brett Theroux, *Regina v. Ernest Saunders et al.*, Central Criminal Court, Southwark, London, England, April 1990.

Page 230 **Guinness was an ideal target** . . . Testimony of Olivier Roux, *Regina v. Ernest Saunders et al.*, Central Criminal Court, Southwark, London, England, February 1990.

Page 230 **Initially, Theroux and** . . . Testimony of David Alexander Hoare, *Regina v. Ernest Saunders et al.*, Central Criminal Court, Southwark, London, England, April 1990.

Page 231 **It is hard to overstate** . . . Testimony of Olivier Roux and Ernest Saunders, *Regina v. Ernest Saunders et al.*, Central Criminal Court, Southwark, London, England, February–June 1990. Roux's role in Guinness came from his sworn testimony and from the sworn testimony of Saunders, who also disclosed the details about Guinness's acquisition procedures. Roux's background, compensation information, and Bain's bonus calculations all came from Roux's testimony.

Page 233 **More often than not, though . . .** Testimony of Ernest Saunders and Olivier Roux, *Regina v. Ernest Saunders et al.*, Central Criminal Court, Southwark, London, England, February–June 1990. The testimony about early acquisitions was drawn from both Roux's and Saunders' testimony. The information about the Guinness family came from Saunders' testimony. The developments regarding Argyll on pages 235 to 237 came from the testimony of both men.

Page 237 **Except for the nearby hotels . . .** Testimony of Ernest Saunders, *Regina v. Ernest Saunders et al.*, Central Criminal Court, Southwark, London, England, June 1990. Saunders gave a vivid account of the developments in January and February 1987 in his testimony.

Page 239 **As Bain's regal presence in . . .** Sworn interview of Isadore Jack Lyons with Department of Trade and Industry, Central Criminal Court, Southwark, London, England, January 1987. Sir Jack's lengthy interviews with the department's investigators were read into the court record in *Regina v. Ernest Saunders et al.*, from May 11 through May 15, 1990. All details about his background and position came from his sworn testimony.

Page 240 **Saunders nearly threw his arms . . .** Sworn testimony of John Brett Theroux, Ernest Saunders, and Olivier Roux, *Regina v. Ernest Saunders et al.*, Central Criminal Court, Southwark, London, England, February–June 1990, and sworn interview of Isadore Jack Lyons with British Department of Trade and Industry, Central Criminal Court, Southwark, London, England, May 1990. Details about Roux's deteriorating relationship with Saunders were included in the testimony and statements of Theroux, Saunders, Roux, and Lyons. The details of the share support operation came from the same sources and were repeated in the testimony of several of the defendants. The figures on Bain's income came from the testimony of Theroux, Roux, and a summation of the case delivered to the jury by Mr. Justice Henry, the judge who presided over the trial.

Page 241 **Saunders had had enough of the . . .** Testimony of Ernest Saunders, Olivier Roux, and John Brett Theroux and summation of Mr. Justice Henry, *Regina v. Ernest Saunders et al.*, Central Criminal Court, Southwark, London, England, February–August 1990. Various details of the deterioration of the relationship between Roux and Saunders came from the testimony of the two men and Judge Henry's summation. The details of Sir Jack's dismissal from Bain came from Theroux's testimony.

Page 243 **Once Roux's letter arrived . . .** "From Executive Suites to Cells and Back Again," *The Times* (London), February 16, 1993; "Jury Finds Four Guilty of Guinness Offences," *Financial Times*, August 28, 1990. The jail terms, fines, and sanctions against the defendants were reported in *The*

Times (London) and the *Financial Times*. Although all had pleaded inno-
cent to the charges, the jury found Saunders guilty on 12 counts in the
indictment. The jury returned unanimous verdicts on two charges of
theft from Guinness; two charges of conspiracy to contravene Section 13
of the Prevention of Fraud Act; and seven of false accounting. On one
charge of false accounting, he was found guilty by a 10–1 majority. Although Ronson returned the 5.8 million pounds Heron received from
Guinness, the jury returned unanimous guilty verdicts against him on a
conspiracy charge under the Prevention of Fraud Act, a charge of theft
from Guinness, and two false accounting charges. Parnes, too, agreed to
pay Guinness two million pounds in an out-of-court settlement, and the
jury returned unanimous guilty verdicts against him on three false accounting charges and one of theft from Guinness. All six verdicts against
Sir Jack Lyons were unanimous, including one on conspiracy to contravene the Prevention of Fraud Act, one of conspiracy to contravene section 151 of the 1985 Companies Act, one of theft from Guinness, and
three false accounting charges.

Page 244 **The Guinness case prompted** . . . "Can Bain Consultants Get Bain
& Co. Out of This Jam?," *Business Week*, February 11, 1991; "Did Greed
Cripple Bain and Company?," *The Boston Globe*, February 26, 1991; and
"Bain to Reduce Staff by 10 Percent," *The Boston Globe*, April 13, 1988.
The details of the sale and loss of clients came from *Business Week*, al-
though they were reported in several other media, too. Details on the lay-
offs and troubles at the company also were extensively reported in *The
Boston Globe*.

Page 245 **As it turned out, Bain's problems** . . . Authors' interviews with James
Tobin, president of Biogen, March and June 1996.

Page 246 **The erosion of revenue soon** . . . "Bain & Company International
Expansion," Harvard Business School Case Study, November 1994;
"Physician, Heal Thyself," *Forbes*, February 1991; "Can Bain Consultants
Get Bain & Co. Out of This Jam?," *Business Week*, February 11, 1991; and
"Bain and Company Plans Major Layoffs," *The Boston Globe*, October 30,
1990. The details of Bain's troubles are well documented in the above
sources.

Page 246 **Over the next three years** . . . *Management Consultancy Services in the
USA* (Beaconsfield, Bucks, England: Alpha Publications, May 1995); "Orit
Gadiesh: Pride at Bain & Co. (A) and (B)," Harvard Business School, January 1995; authors' interview with David Bechhofer, vice president, Bain
& Co., Boston, Massachusetts, September 1995; and "Loyalty Based Management," *Harvard Business Review*, March–April 1993. Details on Bain's
recovery from its troubles were drawn from all of the above sources.

Page 249 **James Tobin, the former** . . . Authors' interviews with James Tobin, president of Biogen, Inc., March and June 1996.

Page 250 **Bain also continues to develop** . . . Authors' interview with David Bechhofer, vice president, Bain & Co., Boston, Massachusetts, September 1995.

Chapter 8. The Gold Boys' Network

Page 252 **"The notion that Jesuits** . . . From *The Jesuits*, by Manfred Barthel (New York: William Morrow, 1984), part 10, page 175. *The Jesuits* is a wonderful book for anyone interested in influence peddling and the connection between power and religion. Undoubtedly, the people at McKinsey have not yet read this book, although they should because of the story it tells of the use of advice at the highest level.

Page 253 **From James O. McKinsey** . . . There is a continuing debate about when and where consulting actually began in the United States. But there is no doubt at all about McKinsey & Co.'s dominant role in its development, particularly in the latter half of the twentieth century.

Page 253 **For many years** . . . As also noted later in the chapter, this penchant for wanting consultants who could think on their feet has tied McKinsey & Co. for many years to the Harvard Business School, where thinking on one's feet is one of the central goals. For a detailed discussion of McKinsey's connections and influence at Harvard, see *The Empire Builders: Power, Money and Ethics Inside the Harvard Business School*, by J. Paul Mark (New York: William Morrow, 1987).

Page 254 **Look at some of the most** . . . Biographical information about former McKinsey consultants who moved into executive positions at companies where they had once consulted came from the individual companies.

Page 257 **Gluck is a case in point** . . . Comments in this chapter from Gluck came from a July 1996 telephone interview.

Page 260 **McKinsey has little trouble** . . . This is an important point. McKinsey & Co. most likely invented the social event/seminar method of selling its business many decades ago, when Marvin Bower, James McKinsey's successor at the company, decided it would be a fine way to explain services to the upper level of target companies. The first was in 1940 and was called a "clinic dinner." Generally, the sessions involved 25 or 30 business leaders and a guest of honor, along with McKinsey's heavyweights. Bower was also among the first to recognize the value of publishing books. *Supplementing*

Successful Management was published in 1940. This comes from the Harvard Business School case study 9-393-066, August 24, 1994, recounting an extensive interview on McKinsey's early history and philosophy with Bower in 1956. McKinsey continues to hold very private seminars for captains of industry all over the world.

Page 260 **The image is so carefully . . .** These details come from an admittedly dated but very interesting article about McKinsey & Co. published in *Forbes* on October 19, 1987. The article includes "presentation techniques" aimed at telling McKinsey consultants how they should appear when delivering presentations.

Page 261 **Senior McKinsey partners might . . .** Interview with McKinsey Managing Partner Rajat Gupta, June 5, 1996. Gupta was quite forthcoming on questions of employment at McKinsey and how consultants are let go. He agreed that there may be nowhere else in the business world where employees are so heavily scrutinized as they work their way toward junior partnerships.

Page 261 **Four of every five . . .** This is part of the McKinsey legend that is backed up in various interviews with its chief consultants and spokesmen. The sense in these conversations was that it was almost as much an honor to be asked to find work elsewhere as it was to stay at McKinsey, an assessment with which many departed consultants would most likely disagree.

Page 262 **As The Firm's current chief . . .** The structure of the company is by no means informal. Securities and Exchange Commission documents that were part of a debate over whether McKinsey & Co. should make public disclosures of its stock value and revenues indicate the details of the partnership are specific and quite exacting, even to the method of returning treasured McKinsey & Co. stock upon death. The SEC case was filed May 26, 1994, and ultimately settled in McKinsey's favor.

Page 265 **Former McKinsey consultants . . .** One departee referred to the existence of a McKinsey "mafia" at high levels in corporations all over the world. The chance of running into one of them is so high that it encourages everyone to avoid public comments that might cause trouble later.

Page 266 **One former McKinsey pro . . .** This person was so concerned about creating a flap with comments that an agreement was extracted that nothing would be written about the interview without a prepublication review. The interview was in June 1996.

Page 268 **It didn't seem to work so well for . . .** The allegations and McKinsey & Co.'s denial are contained in *Suzanne Porter, plaintiff, v. McKinsey & Co., defendant*, Civil Action No. 3:94-CV-1456-D, U.S. District Court for the Northern District of Dallas.

Page 268 **The idea of working for** . . . Interview with Suzanne Porter, Dallas, Texas, January 1996.

Page 269 **The assignments she got** . . . Deposition of Suzanne Porter, in *Porter v. McKinsey.*

Page 270 **"In addition, through her work** . . . Deposition of Tom C. Tinsley, *Porter v. McKinsey.* Tinsley managed the McKinsey & Co. Texas office.

Page 272 **Porter's case also forced open** . . . Deposition of Lucia Albino Gilbert, *Porter v. McKinsey.*

Page 273 **One piece of information** . . . Deposition from Dr. Everett G. Dillman, *Porter v. McKinsey.*

Page 274 **History follows institutions everywhere** . . . McKinsey history and Bower's perspective come from the Harvard case study previously cited. Other historical information about Bower and the Harvard Business School come from the book *The Empire Builders*, also previously cited.

Page 283 **The Firm continues** . . . The breakdown on hiring comes from McKinsey spokesman Stuart Flack.

Page 286 **In his bright, uncluttered** . . . From an interview with Bill Lewis.

Chapter 9. Keeping Dangerous Company

Page 288 **In 1994 EG&G, Inc.** . . . . "Saying So Long to Uncle Sam, Veteran Cold War Contractor EG&G Marches into the Commercial Market After Turning Its Back on Energy Department," *The Boston Globe*, September 11, 1994; and authors' interview with Don Peters, vice president and director of planning, EG&G Inc., October 1996.

Page 290 **By no means are firms like** . . . "A No-Pain, No-Gain Regimen Gets Results in Trimming Fat," *American Banker*, November 1993; and authors' interview with Mark Hutchline, Media Professionals, Inc., October 1996.

Page 290 **In the upper stratosphere** . . . "II-E-E-E-RE'S Ernie," Ernst & Young LLP news release, May 1996, and authors' interview with Tom Rodenhauser, managing editor, *Consultants News*, October 1996.

Page 291 **From the moment a visitor** . . . Authors' interview with Douglas M. Ferguson, principal, The Planning Technologies Group, Inc., Lexington, Massachusetts, September 1996.

Page 294 **Lotus Notes allows extensive.** . . Authors' interview with Don Peters, vice president and director of planning, EG&G Inc., October 1996, and "Firm Demonstrates 'Virtual' Consulting," *Consultants News*, October 1995.

Page 294 **The folks at McKinsey, BCG** . . . Authors' interview with David Maister, chairman, Maister Associates, Inc., October 1996, and authors' interview with Tom Rodenhauser, managing editor, *Consultants News.*

Page 295 **Technological breakthroughs aren't** . . . *Mean Business,* by Albert J. Dunlap (New York: Times Business, 1996).

Page 296 **Part of the problem, of course,** . . . Authors' interview with James Kennedy, founder and consulting editor, *Consultants News,* September 1995.

Page 297 **That may be a lot easier** . . . *Managing the Professional Service Firm,* by David Maister (New York: The Free Press, 1993), and authors' interview with Maister, October 1996.

Page 299 **So, with that in mind, there** . . . Authors' interview with Eileen Shapiro.

INDEX

ABOUT THE AUTHORS

JAMES O'SHEA is the deputy managing editor for news at the *Chicago Tribune*. He is also the author of *The Daisy Chain*, a 1991 book about the savings and loan crisis. A veteran journalist who has held a variety of reporting and editing positions at the *Tribune* and *The Des Moines Register*, O'Shea has won numerous journalism awards, including the Sigma Delta Chi Distinguished Service Award, a prestigious national award presented by the professional journalists fraternity that O'Shea has won twice, and the Associated Press Mananging Editors National Public Service Award. He lives in Willmette, Illinois, with his wife, Nancy, and has two children, Brian and Bridget.

CHARLES MARTIN MADIGAN is an award-winning senior writer at the *Chicago Tribune*, where he has been writing and editing national and international news stories since 1979. He has also served as the *Tribune's* national editor and Washington editor. Previously, he spent ten years with United Press International in the United States and the Soviet Union. Madigan has received the Amos Tuck Award for Economics Writing from Dartmouth College and *The Washington Journalism Review* Award for Consumer Reporting. Mr. Madigan lives in Evanston, Illinois, with his wife, Linda, and their three sons Eamon, Brian, and Conor. His hobbies are Irish music, guitars, American history, and messages on his answering machine, which have assumed legendary status.